Nicholas Wells

SAMS Teach Yourself
KDE
in 24 Hours

SAMS

A Division of Macmillan Computer Publishing
201 West 103rd St., Indianapolis, Indiana, 46290 USA

Sams Teach Yourself KDE in 24 Hours

Copyright © 1999 by Sams Publishing

International Standard Book Number: 0-672-31608-0

Library of Congress Catalog Card Number: 98-83128

Printed in the United States of America

First Printing: April 1999

01   00   99   4   3   2   1

Trademarks

Warning and Disclaimer

EXECUTIVE EDITOR
Jeff Koch

AQUISITIONS EDITOR
Gretchen Ganser

DEVELOPMENT EDITOR
Sean Dixon

MANAGING EDITOR
Brice Gosnell

PRODUCTION EDITOR
Gretchen Uphoff

COPY EDITOR
Pamela Woolf

PROOFREADER
Billy Fields

TECHNICAL EDITOR
Kurt Wall

SOFTWARE DEVELOPMENT SPECIALIST
Craig Atkins

INTERIOR DESIGN
Gary Adair

COVER DESIGN
Aren Howell

LAYOUT TECHNICIANS
Brandon Allen
Stacey DeRome
Timothy Osborn
Staci Somers

Contents at a Glance

Introduction   1

PART I INSTALLING AND RUNNING KDE   **5**

1   Understanding the KDE Project   7
2   Installing KDE from Scratch   21
3   Starting and Exiting KDE   33
4   Reviewing the KDE Setup   55

PART II CUSTOMIZING YOUR KDE SETTINGS   **69**

5   Exploring the Desktop   71
6   Managing the KDE Environment   89
7   Configuring KDE Options   109
8   Using KDE Themes   133
9   Managing Files in KDE   153
10   Learning More KDE File Management   175

PART III SYSTEM ADMINISTRATION FOR KDE   **193**

11   Using KDE System Management Utilities   195
12   Using KDE Utilities   221
13   Managing Network Connections in KDE   237
14   Managing Printing in KDE   257
15   Accessing the Internet from KDE   269
16   Using the Command Line in KDE   289

PART IV USING ADDITIONAL KDE APPLICATIONS   **299**

17   Using Graphics Utilities in KDE   301
18   Using KDE Text Utilities   315
19   Using KDE Business Tools   335
20   Using KDE for Entertainment   355

21   Finding and Installing Additional KDE Applications   373

22   Integrating Non-KDE Applications into KDE   385

PART V   DEVELOPING FOR KDE   **405**

23   Getting Started with KDE Development   407

24   Developing for KDE   419

      Index   433

Contents

INTRODUCTION   **1**

PART I INSTALLING AND RUNNING KDE   **5**

HOUR 1 UNDERSTANDING THE KDE PROJECT   **7**

Understanding the Background of KDE..7
    Goals of the KDE Project 9
    Development Model 10
    The Graphical Toolkit of KDE 11
    International Scope of KDE 13
Summarizing the KDE Project 13
    Components of KDE Base 14
Participating in the KDE Project 15
    Learning to Work on KDE Projects 16
Comparing KDE to the GNOME Desktop..16
Summary 18
Questions and Answers...18
Exercise..19

HOUR 2 INSTALLING KDE FROM SCRATCH   **21**

Reviewing Your X Window System 22
Downloading the KDE Files...23
    Deciding Which Files to Download 24
    Reviewing the Downloaded Files 26
Installing KDE 27
Configuring KDE as Your Graphical Environment 28
Reviewing the Installed KDE Files 29
Summary 30
Questions and Answers...30
Exercises 31

HOUR 3 STARTING AND EXITING KDE   **33**

Starting KDE in OpenLinux..33
    Starting Another Window Manager in OpenLinux 1.3 35
    Starting KDE in Previous Versions of OpenLinux 35
Starting KDE in SuSE Linux 36
Starting KDE from a Clean Install 37
    Starting the X Window System in Red Hat Linux 37
    Starting KDE from the `startx` Script 38
    Reviewing the Initial KDE Startup 39

Diagnosing Trouble Starting KDE 39

Logging Out of KDE 40

    Using a Standard KDE Logout 40

    Using the Emergency Exit..42

Setting Up a Graphical Login with kdm 43

    Initializing xdm 43

    Setting KDE as the Graphical System for xdm 45

    Changing from xdm to kdm 45

    Using the kdm Log in Prompt Dialog Box 46

    Changing the Background in xdm or kdm 47

Configuring kdm..47

Summary..52

Questions and Answers..53

Exercises 53

HOUR 4 REVIEWING THE KDE SETUP   **55**

Defining a User of KDE 55

Reviewing the Contents of the .kde Directory 56

    The config Subdirectory..57

    The apps Subdirectory...58

    The applink Subdirectory 59

    The bin and boot Subdirectories...61

    The dev, icons, and mimelnk Subdirectories 61

Reviewing the Desktop Directory...63

    The Autostart Folder 64

    The Templates Folder 65

    The Trash Bin Folder...66

    Placing Other Items on the KDE Desktop 67

Other Notes on KDE Setup 67

Summary..67

Questions and Answers..68

Exercises 68

PART II CUSTOMIZING YOUR KDE SETTINGS   **69**

HOUR 5 EXPLORING THE DESKTOP   **71**

Reviewing the KDE Environment 72

    The Taskbar 72

    The Desktop...74

    The Panel 76

    The Main K Menu 78

Using the KDE Online and Pop-up Help 78

Using KDE Pop-up Help..79
Using Help Buttons 80
Learning to Manipulate KDE Windows 80
Using Standard Window Tools 81
Keyboard Control of Windows 82
Using the Keyboard in KDE...83
Using Multiple Desktops 85
Switching Between Desktops 85
Renaming Desktops..85
Summary..86
Questions and Answers..87
Exercises 87

HOUR 6 MANAGING THE KDE ENVIRONMENT   89

Working with Application Windows..89
Switching Between Windows 90
Moving Applications Between Desktops 92
Introducing the KDE Control Center 92
Setting Panel and Taskbar Options 93
Setting the Location of the Taskbar and Panel 94
Setting the Panel Size 95
Setting Other Panel and Taskbar Options 96
Clearing Your Desktop 98
Adding Desktops 98
Changing How KDE Windows Appear and Operate 99
Changing Which Buttons Are on the Title Bar 100
Defining a New Title Bar 101
Defining Window Policies...103
Summary..106
Questions and Answers..106
Exercises 107

HOUR 7 CONFIGURING KDE OPTIONS   109

Choosing Colors and Wallpaper 109
Setting the Background Color 110
Choosing Wallpaper...113
Using a Color Scheme..115
Setting Up the Screensaver..117
Selecting Screensavers 119
Adding Screensaver Options 120
Enabling Desktop Positioning Features 120
Using Active Desktop Borders 121
Using Magic Borders..122

Choosing a Language 122
Selecting Display Fonts 125
Configuring Desktop Icons...127
Using Style Options 128
Configuring Sounds 129
    Setting the Bell Sound..129
    Defining Sound Events 130
Summary..132
Questions and Answers..132
Exercises 132

HOUR 8 USING KDE THEMES   133

Understanding KDE Themes 133
Finding a KDE Theme 135
    Searching for Themes 135
    Downloading a Theme 137
Installing a KDE Theme...138
    Preparing the Archive 138
    Reviewing the README File 139
    Creating KDE Directories 140
    Copying Graphics Files...140
    Updating the Configuration Files 141
    Choosing the Theme in the Control Center 144
    Restarting KDE 147
    Using Installation Scripts 148
Getting Rid of a Theme 149
Creating Your Own KDE Theme 150
Summary..151
Questions and Answers..151
Exercise..152

HOUR 9 MANAGING FILES IN KDE   153

Understanding the KDE File Manager..153
    Integrating kfm and the Disk Navigator into KDE................................154
    How kfm Is Used...154
    How the Disk Navigator Is Used...155
Browsing Your Local File System 156
    Running Programs from kfm..158
    Defining an Application in kfm..159
    Using Drag and Drop 163
Using kfm Bookmarks 164
Configuring kfm 165

Choosing How to View Objects 165
Selecting Cache Settings 168
Configuring the Browser Options 170
Reviewing the kfm Configuration Files 172
Summary 172
Questions and Answers 172
Exercises 173

HOUR 10 LEARNING MORE KDE FILE MANAGEMENT 175

Creating KDE Links 175
Creating a Program Link 176
Creating a Device Link 178
Using the Autostart Folder 181
Placing Objects on the Desktop 183
Modifying the Main Menu 186
Modifying the Panel Icons 189
Summary 191
Questions and Answers 191
Exercises 192

PART III SYSTEM ADMINISTRATION FOR KDE 193

HOUR 11 USING KDE SYSTEM MANAGEMENT UTILITIES 195

Setting Keyboard and Mouse Options 196
Setting Up International Keyboards 198
Using kfind to Locate Files 200
Working With the Files You Find 201
Performing Advanced Searches 203
Using kpackage for Software Maintenance 205
Managing Initialization Scripts 207
Defining Some Terms 207
Running the SysV Init Editor 209
Managing User Accounts 211
Adding and Modifying Users 212
Managing Groups 214
Viewing System Information 214
Summary 219
Questions and Answers 219
Exercises 220

HOUR 12 USING KDE UTILITIES 221

Using the ark Archival Utility 221
Extracting Files from an Archive 222
Creating a New Archive 225

Using the Scientific Calculator 227
Using KNotes 230
Learning About Other KDE Applications 233
Summary 234
Questions and Answers 234
Exercises 235

HOUR 13 MANAGING NETWORK CONNECTIONS IN KDE   237

Understanding Linux Networking 237
Checking Your Ethernet Connections 238
Establishing a PPP Connection 242
    Understanding PPP 242
    Starting the Kppp Utility 242
    Configuring a Kppp Account 243
    Configuring Kppp Options 248
    Reviewing Other KDE Connectivity Tools 251
Managing Samba Within KDE 252
    Using the KDE Samba Monitor 253
Summary 254
Questions and Answers 254
Exercises 255

HOUR 14 MANAGING PRINTING IN KDE   257

Understanding Linux Printing 257
Reviewing Your Print Configuration 259
    Using Linux Print Utilities 259
    The /etc/printcap File 261
Using K-LJet to Configure Printing 262
    Setting Paper Options 263
    Setting Printer Options 264
    Configuring Operations 265
    Setting Font Options 266
Summary 268
Questions and Answers 268
Exercises 268

HOUR 15 ACCESSING THE INTERNET FROM KDE   269

Checking Your Internet Connection 269
Reading Email with KMail 270
    Configuring KMail 270
    Reading Messages 276
    Creating a New Message 279
Browsing Newsgroups 282

Configuring the KDE News Client 283
Reading Newsgroup Messages 285
Summary 287
Questions and Answers...287
Exercises 288

HOUR 16 USING THE COMMAND LINE IN KDE   **289**

Understanding the Command Line...................................289
Opening Terminal Emulator Windows 290
Starting from Another Terminal Window 291
Using the Single-Command Entry 292
Using the Character-mode Console 293
Configuring kvt...293
Setting Color and Font Options.................................294
Setting Input and Display Options 296
Summary 297
Questions and Answers...297
Exercise..298

PART IV USING ADDITIONAL KDE APPLICATIONS   **299**

HOUR 17 USING GRAPHICS UTILITIES IN KDE   **301**

Using KView to View Graphics Files...............................301
Manipulating an Image 303
Using the Image List and Slide Show Features 305
Using KPaint to Create Bitmapped Images 306
Manipulating an Entire Image....................................307
Drawing a New Image...309
Choosing Object Colors 310
Using Cut and Paste 311
Exploring Other KDE Graphics Utilities 311
Summary 312
Questions and Answers...313
Exercises 313

HOUR 18 USING KDE TEXT UTILITIES   **315**

Using the KDE Text Editor...315
Starting the Text Editor 316
Using Basic KEdit Features 318
Setting Up KEdit Options 322
Viewing Text Documents 324
Viewing Other Document Types.......................................325
Using the PostScript Viewer 325
Using the DVI Viewer 330

Summary 332
Questions and Answers..332
Exercises 333

HOUR 19 USING KDE BUSINESS TOOLS   335

Using the Address Book 335
    Adding and Managing Entries...336
    Using Address Book Entries 338
Using the KOrganizer 340
    Exploring the KOrganizer 340
    Creating a To-do Task List 342
    Saving Information 345
    Managing Appointments 345
    Configuring KOrganizer Options 348
Using the Time Tracker 350
    Defining a Task 350
    Tracking Time for Tasks 351
Using Fax Features 352
Summary 353
Questions and Answers..353
Exercises 354

HOUR 20 USING KDE FOR ENTERTAINMENT   355

Reviewing Your Sound Card and Related Devices.....................356
Using the CD Player 356
    The Display Screen 357
    Adding CDDB Information..357
    Configuring the CD Player 360
    Exploring the Rest of the CD Player......................................363
Using Other Multimedia Tools 364
Playing Arcade Games 365
Playing Other Games 368
Summary 370
Questions and Answers..370
Exercises 371

HOUR 21 FINDING AND INSTALLING ADDITIONAL KDE APPLICATIONS   373

Locating Additional KDE Applications 374
Downloading KDE Applications 375
Preparing New KDE Applications 377
    Checking for Development Libraries 378
    Unpack the Application Archive 379
    Make the Source Tree 380

Installing the New Application 381

Running the Application 381

Summary 382

Questions and Answers..382

Exercises 383

HOUR 22 INTEGRATING NON-KDE APPLICATIONS INTO KDE   **385**

Reviewing a Few Non-KDE Applications 385

Locating Applications to Integrate with KDE 388

Creating Application Links..390

Adding to the Desktop, Panel, and Menus 394

Adding an Application to the Desktop 394

Adding an Application to the Main Menu 395

Adding an Application to the Panel 397

Adding MIME Types 398

Defining a New MIME Type..399

Summary 402

Questions and Answers..402

Exercises 403

PART V DEVELOPING FOR KDE   **405**

HOUR 23 GETTING STARTED WITH KDE DEVELOPMENT   **407**

Reviewing Software Development Concepts 408

Using KAppTemplate 409

Installing KAppTemplate 409

Running KAppTemplate 410

Exploring the Source Code Tree..412

Reviewing the main and widget Files 414

Reviewing the ksmb.cpp File..415

Changing the Source Code 416

Summary 417

Questions and Answers..418

Exercises 418

HOUR 24 DEVELOPING FOR KDE   **419**

Reviewing the Libraries 419

Expanding the Sample Application 420

Learning More About KDE Programming..427

Summary 431

Questions and Answers..431

Exercises 432

Congratulations..432

INDEX   **433**

Dedication

This book is dedicated to the KDE team, whose selfless dedication to creating something useful for the rest of us is leading Linux to new heights.

Acknowledgments

My technical editor, Kurt Wall, provided many helpful review comments during the preparation of this book. After seeing his name all over the Caldera-Users mailing list for some time, I was pleased to hear that he was going to be reviewing my work. His technical background did much to improve my efforts (though any remaining errors are still mine—please send me an email if you find one).

I had the pleasure of working with Gretchen Ganser and Sean Dixon at Macmillan publishing. Despite the pressures of working in the computer book industry, they have always been pleasant and professional (here's hoping I never give them reason to be otherwise).

The KDE team must be congratulated on the release of KDE 1.1 as this book was being finished. Many improvements and fixes, a more refined interface—a lot of good work continues to come from the dedicated members of the team.

And of course, this project would not have been finished without the support and encouragement of my wife Anne.

About the Author

NICHOLAS WELLS (nwells@xmission.com) is the author of several books on Linux-related subjects, including *Sams Teach Yourself StarOffice in 24 Hours*. After leaving Novell to join Linux-based start-up Caldera, Inc., he worked as the director of marketing for several years before realizing that writing about technology was more fun than selling it. He left Caldera to write and consult full-time. When he's between projects, he likes to read, garden, and generally avoid his computer for a few days.

Tell Us What You Think!

As the reader of this book, *you* are our most important critic and commentator. We value your opinion and want to know what we're doing right, what we could do better, what areas you'd like to see us publish in, and any other words of wisdom you're willing to pass our way.

As the Associate Publisher for the Operating Systems team at Sams Publishing, I welcome your comments. You can fax, email, or write me directly to let me know what you did or didn't like about this book—as well as what we can do to make our books stronger.

Please note that I cannot help you with technical problems related to the topic of this book, and that due to the high volume of mail I receive, I might not be able to reply to every message.

When you write, please be sure to include this book's title and author as well as your name and phone or fax number. I will carefully review your comments and share them with the author and editors who worked on the book.

Fax:	(317) 581-4770
Email:	opsys@sams.mcp.com
Mail:	Associate Publisher Operating Systems Sams Publishing 201 W. 103rd Street Indianapolis, IN 46290 US

Introduction

When people talk about Linux becoming a true desktop operating system—something that can replace a Windows or Macintosh system for daily use—they're usually saying it because they've seen KDE.

Linux already has the stability, speed, and appeal needed by many users. It already has thousands of native applications, including personal productivity tools such as WordPerfect, the Wingz spreadsheet, and Oracle tools. What Linux lacked was ease of use—a simple, familiar interface to access the features that Linux provides. KDE gives you that interface.

What Is KDE?

Started just two years ago by Matthias Ettrich and continued now by hundreds of contributors, KDE is a complete desktop environment. New tools are regularly added for additional graphical system administration and networking capability, but KDE already includes features such as

- Multiple virtual desktops, each individually configurable
- Drag and drop between windows
- An Autostart folder
- Pop-up main menu with a personal section
- Taskbar, with Alt+Tab application selection
- Dozens of *applets* for common uses (editor, calculator, calendar, and so forth)

For those more familiar with the technical side of Linux, KDE includes

- Its own window manager, fully configurable from the graphical Control Center
- A graphical login (xdm replacement), also configurable from the Control Center
- An object-oriented programming model that makes new applications easy to create
- A user interface definition and programmatic guidelines to create new KDE-aware applications
- Clear definitions of KDE components and locations so that it can be run on any Linux system

Why Teach Yourself KDE?

This book doesn't assume that you know anything about KDE, although you've probably at least seen the user interface and might have played with the menus or a few applications.

If you're a new Linux user working with a Linux product such as Caldera OpenLinux or Red Hat Linux, this book will guide you through the KDE interface, teaching you how to use its graphical configuration tools, how to set up menus and Autostart options, and how to configure the look and feel of your desktop to meet your needs.

If you're an experienced Linux user, this book can provide insight into how the KDE Project is organized. The directory structure and principles behind KDE are explained as example applications are demonstrated. You will learn how KDE accesses applications, where you can place graphics, and how you can hand-edit or explore configuration files to get the most out of KDE.

If you already use KDE every day, you might be surprised by how much more there is to know about it. It's easy to get into a regular pattern of use with the desktop and applications you use from day to day, but when you start to learn more about them, you find all sorts of new and useful things that you could have used all along. KDE is a complete environment; the more you learn about it, the more you'll find to like. Regular KDE users will discover new applications, configuration options, and usage tricks to make KDE even more productive for them. They will also learn more about the underlying structure of the system and how the KDE Project got started and continues to provide new features at an amazing speed.

If you're hoping to develop KDE applications, this book ends with a gentle introduction to KDE development. It doesn't teach you C++ (which you'll have to know to work much with KDE), but it does describe some tools that are available, and it walks you through a sample application to show how easily you can create a new KDE application and begin to add functionality to it.

A lot is happening for KDE; stories in the press, inclusion in most of the world's Linux distributions, and now a book dedicated to it. I hope that after reading this book you'll end up as enthusiastic about the usefulness of KDE and its prospects for the future as I am.

How to Use This Book

This book is designed to teach you the latest version of KDE in 24 concise one-hour sessions. Each hour starts with an overview of the topic to inform you what to expect. This overview helps you determine the nature of the lesson and whether the lesson is relevant to your needs.

Each lesson has a main section that discusses the lesson topic in a clear, concise manner by breaking the topic down into logical component parts and explaining each component clearly.

Interspersed in each lesson are special elements, called Tips, Cautions, and Notes, which provide additional information.

A tip informs you of a trick or element that is easily missed by most new KDE users. Feel free to skip these hints and additions; however, if you skip reading them, you might miss a shorter or more efficient way to accomplish a task described in the main text.

A caution deserves at least as much attention as the body of the lesson, because these point out problematic elements of the operating system or a *gotchas* that you want to avoid while using the operating system. Ignoring the information contained in a caution could have adverse effects on the stability of your computer. Be careful to read every caution you run across.

A note is designed to clarify the concept being discussed. Notes also contain additional information that might be slightly off-topic but interesting nonetheless. Notes elaborate on the subject, and if you're comfortable with your understanding of the subject, you can read these to add to your knowledge or bypass them with no danger.

Each lesson concludes with a summary of what you have just learned, a Question and Answer section that answers the questions users new to KDE most frequently ask about that particular lesson's subject, and exercises that will advance you in further, hands-on study of that lesson's topic.

PART I
Installing and Running KDE

Hour

1 Understanding the KDE Project

2 Installing KDE from Scratch

3 Starting and Exiting KDE

4 Reviewing the KDE Setup

Hour 1

Understanding the KDE Project

In this hour, you will learn about the origin and organization of the KDE Project. Because the development of KDE isn't like that of other graphical desktops you've used, this hour introduces you to some background that will help you understand better the things you'll learn in later hours.

You also learn how you can participate in the KDE project if you want. In addition, the GNOME desktop is introduced. Because a number of KDE versus GNOME debates continue to take place, this section informs you of the issues at stake.

Understanding the Background of KDE

KDE is a complete graphical desktop environment for UNIX. If you've used other versions of UNIX or Linux, you know that having a graphical interface is not that unusual. But the simple window managers provided by many UNIX systems (and more Linux systems) do not provide the complete, integrated functionality that users of a desktop computer really need to be productive.

As UNIX technology grows in popularity because of the Internet and the growth of Linux, ease-of-use becomes a larger problem. The technology of UNIX and Linux is sound; it has been used for 30 plus years and is well-proven. But as thousands of new users begin to work with UNIX and especially Linux systems, they do so without the professional experience that made UNIX gurus of the past able to make their UNIX systems perform well.

KDE resolves the ease-of-use issue by providing a complete graphical environment, where applications can be launched, system configuration tools are graphically accessible, and new applications can be written to integrate into a well-known environment.

 KDE can be used on other UNIX systems, such as Solaris and Irix. This book uses Linux as the OS platform, but nearly all the information applies to other UNIX variants as well (including most of the installation and file placement details). Differences between KDE running on various versions of Linux are noted throughout the text.

By late 1996, Linux was already well known in computing circles, being used by millions around the world and written about widely in computer magazines. Because Linux includes the source code to the operating system, allowing anyone to update or alter it, this type of project came to be called *Open Source* software.

The success of the Linux phenomenon created an atmosphere in which other very large projects using the Open Source model could also succeed.

 KDE is an acronym for the K Desktop Environment. What does the *K* stand for? Nothing—just like *X* in the X Window System.

The KDE Project was founded in October 1996 by Matthias Ettrich. It wasn't long before hundreds of developers from around the world began to participate.

As of late 1998, the KDE Project encompassed over 800,000 lines of source code. KDE has been developed faster than any comparable software development project in history.

KDE is now organized as a foundation (for legal and liability reasons), with official representatives around the world (see Figure 1.1). You can find the Web page containing a list of these representatives at `http://ettrich.priv.no/kde_official/` `representatives.html`.

FIGURE 1.1

The KDE Project has official representatives around the world.

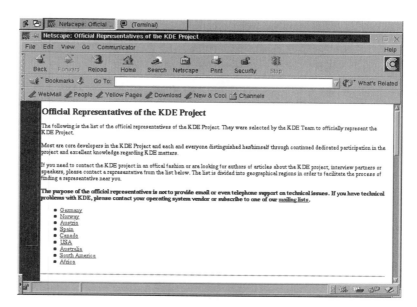

Goals of the KDE Project

The goals of the KDE Project are ambitious. Its participants seek to create a complete desktop environment equal to that of the Macintosh or Microsoft Windows—I might even say better than the Macintosh or Windows.

Users of Macintosh and Windows systems have always enjoyed the ease-of-use of their systems. Users of the X Window System have enjoyed the power and flexibility of their systems. KDE seeks to combine the best features of both worlds.

KDE isn't a clone of any other system; it seeks instead to pull the best features from different systems and craft them into a complete integrated graphical environment.

From a technical standpoint, KDE aims to include the following features, which are missing from the existing crop of graphical environments for X:

- A common drag-and-drop protocol between applications and the core desktop
- Simple, dialog-based desktop configuration for all desktop features and applications
- A unified help system that can be accessed by all applications
- A common application development framework
- A compound document framework similar to CORBA or ActiveX

- Increased network transparency on the application level
- An easy-to-use developer's kit (SDK) to make it easy to create compatible applications

From the user's perspective, the most important goals are these:

- Presenting an attractive, modern-looking desktop
- Avoiding application problems with network connections (making the network transparent to the desktop and its applications)
- Integrated online help providing consistent access points and user interface for all applications
- Providing a consistent look and feel for all applications, including menus, keyboard shortcuts, color schemes, and so forth
- Creating an international product, with keyboard, menu, online help, and application support in many languages (see the section "International Scope of KDE" later in this hour)
- Providing hundreds of integrated applications

Not all these goals have been met in KDE 1.1, but plans are in place for KDE 2.0 to meet these goals and many others that are specific to certain components of KDE.

> One of the largest development projects for KDE is the KOffice suite of applications. KOffice includes a word processor, spreadsheet, graphical tools, and other applications, integrated with each other and KDE. KOffice has been released in beta form, but it isn't covered in this book. For more information, visit `http://koffice.kde.org`.

Development Model

To develop a project as large as KDE in only two years, the KDE Project has organized into groups that lead the development. Each working group includes a committee that receives software components from the developers working on that project. The committee reviews all proposed fixes and features, and then votes on which of these to include in the KDE.

The core tenets of the KDE developers are these:

- Focus on your goal and get the software up and running as soon as possible.
- Start with reasonable functionality and configurability, and then improve it iteratively over time.

- Use available tools rather than reinventing everything. (See the next section on Qt, "The Graphical Toolkit of KDE.")
- When making a suggestion, change "we should" to "I will"; grandiose plans are useless unless you are willing to put in the work.

All developers communicate via email lists. Most of these lists are open to anyone who wants to read the messages as the development progresses, but only those who have shown some skill and background knowledge can post messages to the lists. This keeps the lists from being cluttered with messages from uninformed spectators.

The KDE developers and supporters do meet in person occasionally. The KDE One conference was held in December 1997. Other conferences are announced on the KDE Web site at http://www.kde.org/events.html.

Most of the KDE components that are described in this book are part of a core *distribution* of KDE. This is similar to a Linux distribution, in that it is a complete collection of software, easy to download and install. Anyone can get the latest stable KDE distribution from the KDE FTP site: ftp://ftp.kde.org or a local mirror site.

Many additional KDE applications are available from the KDE FTP site, but are not included with the core distribution of KDE.

This is similar to the Linux model, where the kernel and certain applications are gathered into a distribution. Other Linux applications are available for download. The difference is that the KDE distribution is maintained by the KDE team instead of by commercial vendors such as Caldera and Red Hat.

The Graphical Toolkit of KDE

In order to create a complete desktop environment in record time, the KDE Project chose to use a commercially produced graphical development toolkit called *Qt*, from Troll Tech in Norway.

The Qt toolkit is a C++ class library that includes all the graphical primitives used by KDE to create windows, dialog boxes, and so forth. A great advantage of the free software community in general is the ability to accept the work of others and build on it. According to the KDE Project leadership, KDE could not have been developed nearly as quickly if a toolkit had been developed from scratch. Qt is a high-quality, cross-platform development kit that gave the KDE Project a jumpstart on pursuing its ambitious goals.

The decision to use Qt has been the subject of fierce debate, however, among Open Source purists who opine that the inclusion of Qt poisons KDE because of its license terms, which are not quite as open as those of KDE itself. In particular, the supporters of the GNOME desktop project (described later in this hour) have been vocal in denouncing KDE for using Qt.

Further discussion of these issues can be found on the KDE Web site at `http://www.kde.org/kdeqtfoundation.html`, at `http://www.troll.no/announce/qpl.html`, or at various other KDE- and Linux-related mailing list archives and Linux publications.

While the debate has raged in the free software community, thousands of unsuspecting users have downloaded or purchased an inexpensive copy of KDE (usually with Linux) and used it contentedly without the slightest qualm regarding the license of the Qt toolkit.

For the record, these are the facts:

- Qt is a commercial product from Troll Tech.
- Qt includes source code to the class libraries in the toolkit.
- Anyone can develop software using Qt and give it away as long as the source code to the software is included.
- Anyone can make changes to the Qt source code as long as those changes are submitted back to Troll Tech for inclusion in the main product.

Troll Tech has also recently announced a true Open Source license for their toolkit, removing many of the concerns that some developers had regarding KDE.

If a company wants to sell a product based on Qt without giving away source code, they must purchase a commercial license to Qt. Ah, there's the rub.

Even so, two additional projects are in place to protect the free nature of KDE (information on both of these is available on the KDE Web site).

- The Free Qt Foundation is set up to provide a succession plan for the Qt product should Troll Tech "change its mind" or go bankrupt.
- The Harmony project is creating a clone of the Qt toolkit under a true Open Source license (using the GNU General Public License). This project is proceeding in parallel with KDE development, and could, in theory, provide a new toolkit to be swapped for the Troll Tech product when Harmony is finished.

International Scope of KDE

KDE has been developed by an international cast of programmers, writers, and others. Started by Matthias Ettrich in Germany, KDE rapidly encompassed participants from many countries. This diverse group encouraged the development of a completely localized (internationalized) KDE.

From its beginnings, KDE has included the necessary technical components to easily work in multiple nations. The basis of these is the concept of using message files to hold all the text presented onscreen. Message files can be easily translated by nonprogrammers. The text from the selected language message file is displayed automatically onscreen by KDE.

As you'll see in Hour 7, "Configuring KDE Options," setting the language for KDE is as easy as selecting from a drop-down list and restarting the desktop. Documentation for core applications (and many noncore applications) is already available over 30 languages, including Greek, Russian, Chinese, and Romanian. The translation team currently consists of over 100 people.

Other international settings—such as time zone, currency, preferred date format, keyboard layout, and so forth—are part of all KDE applications, such as the KOffice suite.

KDE is available worldwide, from about 71 mirrored FTP sites in 30 countries. Although most of the communication on KDE mailing lists and discussions takes place in English, KDE participants recognize the international nature of their work and regularly seek advice from others on how to make their work applicable to a worldwide audience.

As you read sections of the KDE Web site or documentation, you'll find strange spellings and sentences. Many writers for KDE are not native English speakers, but they produce a great deal of KDE material in their free time. I try to put away my red pencil and appreciate the work they've done.

Summarizing the KDE Project

The KDE Project uses the concept of a distribution, just as the Linux developers do. The KDE distribution, however, is smaller (typically about 45MB installed) and is complete as downloaded from a KDE mirror site.

Hour 2, "Installing KDE from Scratch" describes the components of KDE in more detail as you download and install the pieces that you need. In general, however, the KDE distribution is composed of the major components shown in Table 1.1.

TABLE 1.1—MAJOR COMPONENTS INCLUDED IN THE KDE DISTRIBUTION

Name of Component	Description
KDE Base	The core of KDE: the window manager, file manager, and so forth (see Table 1.2)
Libraries	Run-time libraries for the graphical objects and other functions used by many KDE applications
Graphics	Viewers for fax, TeX DVI, PostScript, and bitmapped graphics (a simple paint program and fractal generator)
Utilities	Applets: a calculator, text editor, hex editor, file compression tool, PIM, and so forth
Multimedia	Sound utilities for MIDI and WAV, audio CD Player, Sound Mixer
Admin	User administration and initialization script configuration
Network	Client tools for email, dialed and PPP connections, and news reader
Toys	Additional utilities that are not required to run KDE, but are interesting or fun
Games	Many types of great cool games: Minesweeper, Tetris, poker, Asteroids, and so forth

Components of KDE Base

The only parts of KDE that you must have installed are the KDE Base packages. These form the core of KDE that all the other integrated applications referred to in Table 1.1 use to run correctly.

To help you understand more about how KDE is organized, Table 1.2 lists the components of the KDE Base group of applications.

TABLE 1.2—COMPONENTS OF KDE BASE

Component	Description
kaudio	The audioserver, running in the background to process audio files
kbgndwm	A background manager for the main window manager, kwm
kcontrol	The central control panel
kdehelp	The help browser (a basic Web browser), launched by choosing KDE Help, pressing F1, or choosing a Help button in a dialog box
kdm	A graphical login system similar to xdm
kfind	The Find tool, accessible from the default KDE Panel

Component	Description
kfm	The file manager, used to browse the file system when you open a directory from the Panel (can also be used as a basic Web browser)
kfontmanager	A manager for the fonts used in KDE applications
kmenuedit	The utility for editing the menu entries of the Panel and the taskbar (both part of kpanel)
kpanel	The Panel and taskbar (the main methods of accessing applications and utilities in KDE)
krootwm	A module for managing the root window; used by the kwm window manager
kscreensaver	The screensaver utility; configured via an option on the main menu
kvt	A terminal emulation program (a command-line window in KDE)
kwm	The window manager used by KDE; configured by options in the KDE Control Center
kwmcom	The communications tool for the kwm window manager
kwmpager	The pager for the kwm window manager (provides multiple desktops for the window manager)

Not all the components of the KDE base collection are required to run KDE. Some, such as the kaudio server and the kdehelp program are useful but not required. The KDE team has included all these components in KDE Base because they constitute a complete core of functionality onto which other programs specific to networking, administration, and so forth, can build.

Participating in the KDE Project

Everyone working on the KDE Project works as a volunteer. If you have skills you would like to add to the effort, your contribution is welcome. The KDE Web site maintains a list of projects that need help at any moment, located at http://www.kde.org/jobs.html (see Figure 1.2).

Although starting with a small KDE application might be a great way to learn or refine your C++ programming skills, you don't have to be a developer to participate in the growth of KDE:

- Writers prepare documentation for a variety of new KDE applications, including the KOffice suite.

- Translators prepare online help and documentation in many languages.

- Speakers give presentations about KDE (introductory, technical, marketing, programming).
- Webmasters create and maintain Web pages to explain KDE and link to relevant news and technical information.

The KDE Web site includes lists of projects you can work on, with contact information to receive more information.

FIGURE 1.2

The KDE Web site maintains lists of projects that new participants can work on.

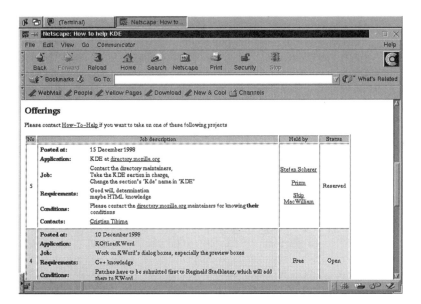

Learning to Work on KDE Projects

If you're interested in programming for KDE, you can start with the information in Hour 23, "Getting Started with KDE Development," and Hour 24, "Developing for KDE." Several development mailing lists are available on the KDE Web site, and a KDE programming tutorial can be downloaded as well.

Some knowledge of C++ or other object-oriented programming languages (such as Smalltalk, Python, or similar languages) is helpful, but you might be able to learn by imitating example code to get started.

Comparing KDE to the GNOME Desktop

Because you might have questions about GNOME as a product related to or competitive with KDE, this section provides a little background information.

GNOME, the GNU Network Object Model Environment, is an effort to provide an object-based desktop environment and related utilities and applications to UNIX and UNIX-like operating systems.

The GNOME Project was started in August 1997, apparently in reaction to the unfavorable opinion that some free software supporters held toward the KDE Project's use of the Qt libraries (because of the license of Qt, as described earlier). Ironically, some components of GNOME were developed by starting with the KDE source code.

GNOME currently has hundreds of developers worldwide working on it. It also has the financial backing of Red Hat Software, a major Linux vendor that has provided employees to work full-time on GNOME.

GNOME is available from `ftp.gnome.org` and many mirror sites. Information on GNOME is available at `http://www.gnome.org` or by searching for GNOME on Linux information sites such as `www.linuxhq.com`, `www.linuxcentral.com`, `www.freshmeat.net`, or `www.lwn.net`.

How are GNOME and KDE similar? The following list points out some basic things that KDE and GNOME have in common:

- Both are attempts to create a standard, easy-to-use desktop for UNIX and Linux.
- Both are available in binary and source code form for many Linux and UNIX variants.
- Both use object-oriented technology to quickly build a robust graphical environment.
- Both rely on a graphical toolkit to speed their development efforts (Qt for KDE, GTK+ for GNOME).
- Both depend on an international volunteer development community.
- Both freely distribute the results of their work.
- Both include many applications for networking, games, system administration, interface configuration, and so forth; both are working hard at completing an office suite.
- Both are receiving a lot of attention in the free software community.
- Both are distributed most widely as part of a Linux operating system product (Red Hat for GNOME, every other Linux distribution for KDE).

There are also major differences between GNOME and KDE, as the following list illustrates:

- As of January 1999, KDE has been released as version 1.1 and is stable enough to use from day to day, with concrete plans for release 2.0; GNOME has not yet reached version 1.0 and might be difficult for nonprogrammers to use.
- KDE uses a commercial graphical class library: Qt from Troll Tech, which now has an Open Source version as well; GNOME uses an Open Source graphical library called GTK+ (used in GIMP and other popular Open Source software).
- KDE includes a window manager as part of its base distribution and installation; GNOME sits on top of your existing window manager (whichever you choose, so long as it is GNOME-compliant; fvwm2 is one example).

Notice that the list of common traits is longer than the list of differences. Arguments will continue to rage on development mailing lists, but both projects are pushing forward the use of UNIX and Linux as powerful and complete desktop operating systems.

In fact, the KDE and GNOME teams are working closely toward cross-compatibility of applications and the ability to share other resources (perhaps using an object system based on Object Request Broker (ORB) technology).

Summary

This hour introduces the KDE Project and describes both what it includes and how you can be involved in its continuing development, if you're interested in that. You learned about the core packages that comprise KDE and how KDE is prepared as a complete distribution, ready to install. You also learned what the GNOME Project is. The next hour walks you through a complete installation of KDE.

Questions and Answers

Q Can I use both KDE and GNOME on my Linux system?

A Yes, sort of, but not at the same time. You should be fairly familiar with both projects so you can reset configurations as needed to work with both. Check the KDE and GNOME Web sites for information about integrating these two systems in the months to come.

Q I want to create a new application for KDE. How do I get started?

A Read this book, especially the last two hours on KDE development. Refer to the KDE Web site often to become familiar with what's already been done and what development tools are available. Subscribe to the KDE mailing lists so you can get to know the other KDE developers.

Q How much commitment is required to help with the non-programming parts of KDE, such as documentation, speaking, or translation?

A A solid commitment to the principles involved (free software and cooperative development) is imperative. Beyond that, you can spend just a couple of hours per month, or work on a single brief project and be done with it. The KDE project is well coordinated to make use of small slices of volunteers' time.

Exercise

1. Review the KDE Web site, including the list of available KDE applications. Which applications would be useful to you? Which are included in the KDE distribution?

Hour 2

Installing KDE from Scratch

In this hour, you will learn how to install KDE on your system. Although several Linux systems (such as Caldera OpenLinux and SuSE Linux) now include KDE as part of the default installation, being able to install KDE from ground zero will teach you a lot about the KDE system.

This hour describes how to get the KDE files, where they end up on your Linux system, and to make it all happen. If you already have KDE installed and want to start using it, you can skip to Hour 3, "Starting and Exiting KDE."

The latest version of Caldera OpenLinux installs KDE by default. We'll use a Red Hat 5.1 installation as the basis for installing KDE from scratch. Tips for using other versions of Red Hat and other Linux systems are provided along the way. This installation also works for Red Hat 5.2.

Reviewing Your X Window System

The steps you follow in this hour assume that you have a working installation of Red Hat Linux version 5.1. In particular, you need to have your graphical X Window System already up and running. (The default X Window System for Red Hat 5.1 is shown in Figure 2.1.)

FIGURE 2.1

Red Hat 5.1 uses the fvwm2 window manager in its default graphical configuration.

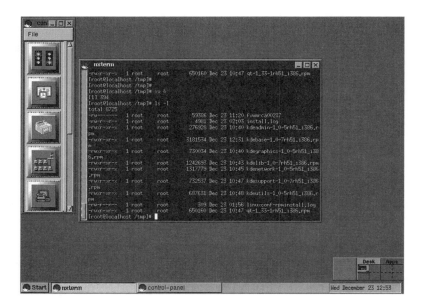

 The KDE files available for download as described here (and thus the installation described here) will not work on a Red Hat 4.x Linux system.

The file that controls the configuration of your X server (Xfree86 by default) is /etc/X11/XF86Config. After you have created this file using a configuration tool (such as XF86Setup), you can start the X Window System by using the following command:

```
$ startx
```

When you enter this command, the xinit program reviews files in the following order, executing the commands found in each applicable file.

- An .xinitrc in the user's home directory (a hidden file).
- The default xinitc file located in /etc/X11/xinit/ (not a hidden file); used only if no .xinitrc file is found in the user's home directory.

- An .Xclients file in the user's home directory (a hidden file).
- The default Xclients file located in /etc/X11/xinit/ (not a hidden file); used only if no .Xclients file is found in the user's home directory.

The process of starting X differs slightly on other Linux systems. The process also differs if you are using the xdm graphical login manager. (A replacement for xdm called kdm (included as part of KDE), is described in Hour 3.)

After you have installed and configured KDE as described later in this hour, using the startx command will start KDE.

Downloading the KDE Files

If you're using Caldera OpenLinux 1.3 or later you can complete a standard OpenLinux installation and begin using KDE immediately by logging in and entering the kde command (see Hour 3).

For any Linux system, you can try the KDE files from the CD included with this book. If the correct files for your version of Linux are not included on this CD, you'll need to download the appropriate files as described here. Although KDE runs on all Linux systems, the configuration of a KDE system varies slightly from one Linux version to the next. For this reason, it causes minor configuration problems if you use the KDE packages for one Linux system (such as Red Hat) to install KDE on another Linux system (such as SuSE or Deblan). If you use the KDE files from the CD, you can also review any README files that are included with them.

The installation described here is for KDE 1.1, which is a stable version. Beta copies of later versions of KDE might also be available, but you won't be working with them here.

All the KDE files are available from ftp://ftp.kde.org or from dozens of mirror sites around the world. Table 2.1 lists some major mirror sites if you find ftp.kde.org to be busy (it often is, although it is hosted by Caldera Systems, Inc. in the U.S. and has a very fast Internet connection).

TABLE 2.1 A SELECTED LIST OF MIRROR SITES FOR ftp.kde.org

Mirror Site	Location
ftp://gd.tuwien.ac.at/hci/kde	Austria
ftp://sunsite.cnlab-switch.ch/mirror/kde	Switzerland
ftp://ftp.fu-berlin.de/pub/unix/X11/gui/kde	Germany
ftp://ftp.tsc.uvigo.es/pub/linux/kde	Spain

continues

TABLE 2.1 CONTINUED

Mirror Site	Location
`ftp://ftp.au.kde.org/pub/kde`	Australia
`ftp://mirror.nucba.ac.jp/mirror/KDE`	Japan
`ftp://ftp.is.co.za/linux/windowmanagers/kde`	South Africa
`ftp://ftp.varesearch.com/pub/mirrors/kde`	U.S.-California
`ftp://canine.resnet.gatech.edu/pub/kde`	U.S.-Georgia
`ftp://ftp.synesis.net/pub/mirrors/kde`	Vancouver, BC
`ftp://ftp.us.kde.org/pub/kde`	U.S.-Utah

Deciding Which Files to Download

As you review the FTP site with the KDE files, you see that the archive is divided into sections based on which archive type you want to use: `rpm`, `tar`, or `deb` (Debian archive). If you're working on a non-Linux UNIX system, you should choose the `tar` subdirectory to download the KDE files.

The `deb` subdirectory is appropriate if you are installing KDE on a Debian Linux system.

Because you're installing on Red Hat 5.1 here, the `rpm` directory is used in this section.

> Many, if not most, of the available Linux distributions support the rpm package format.

The `rpm` subdirectory contains the following subdirectories, reflecting the versions that the KDE rpm files are built and tested for. Choose the subdirectory for the Linux version that you're running:

- `Caldera-OpenLinux-1.2`
- `Caldera-OpenLinux-1.3`
- `DLD-5.4`
- `RedHat-5.1`
- `RedHat-5.2`
- `RedHat-Sparc`
- `SuSE-5.3`
- `generic`

Although the versions of KDE for Linux are very similar, several library and compiler issues are resolved by choosing the subdirectory with files prebuilt for your version of Linux.

In the RedHat-5.1 subdirectory that is used for this installation, you can select the `i386` directory for the Intel version of Red Hat Linux. Next, select the Binary directory for the binary files (you can learn about the source files beginning in Hour 23, "Getting Started with KDE Development," but you won't download or describe them here.)

The contents of the Binary directory is shown here (I've added the full directory path to the top of the listing for reference as you explore the KDE FTP site):

```
ftp://ftp.kde.org/pub/kde/stable/latest/distribution/rpm/RedHat-5.1/i386/
binary/
```

```
Up to higher level directory
kde-rh5x-i386-1.1.lsm               939 bytes Thu Jan 28 05:40:00 1999
kdeadmin-1.1-1rh5x.i386.rpm         376 Kb    Thu Jan 28 04:50:00 1999
kdebase-1.1-1rh5x.i386.rpm         5530 Kb    Thu Jan 28 04:53:00 1999
kdegames-1.1-1rh5x.i386.rpm        2151 Kb    Thu Jan 28 04:56:00 1999
kdegraphics-1.1-1rh5x.i386.rpm     1057 Kb    Thu Jan 28 04:57:00 1999
kdelibs-1.1-1rh5x.i386.rpm         1896 Kb    Thu Jan 28 04:59:00 1999
kdemultimedia-1.1-1rh5x.i386.rpm    927 Kb    Thu Jan 28 05:01:00 1999
kdenetwork-1.1-1rh5x.i386.rpm      2782 Kb    Thu Jan 28 05:04:00 1999
kdesupport-1.1-1rh5x.i386.rpm       760 Kb    Thu Jan 28 05:07:00 1999
kdesupport-1.1-2rh5x.i386.rpm       760 Kb    Fri Jan 29 13:59:00 1999
kdetoys-1.1-1rh5x.i386.rpm          159 Kb    Thu Jan 28 05:07:00 1999
kdeutils-1.1-1rh5x.i386.rpm        1117 Kb    Thu Jan 28 05:08:00 1999
korganizer-1.1-1rh5x.i386.rpm       435 Kb    Thu Jan 28 05:10:00 1999
qt-1.42-3rh51.i386.rpm              817 Kb    Thu Jan 28 05:10:00 1999
qt-devel-1.42-3rh51.i386.rpm       2630 Kb    Thu Jan 28 05:14:00 1999
qt-rh51-i386-1.42-3.lsm             623 bytes Thu Jan 28 05:41:00 1999
readme-redhat-rpms.html              11 Kb    Thu Jan 28 05:14:00 1999
readme-redhat-rpms.txt               12 Kb    Thu Jan 28 05:14:00 1999
```

Now for the good news: You don't have to download all the files in this list! First, notice all the files with `.lsm` extensions. These are descriptive files that you don't need to download.

The files that you need to download to completely install KDE are listed in Table 2.2.

2

TABLE 2.2   FILES TO DOWNLOAD FOR A COMPLETE KDE INSTALLATION

File to Download (First Part of Filename Only)	Description
kdebase	The core packages of KDE (window manager, Panel, taskbar, and so forth)
kdesupport	A collection of non-KDE libraries for graphics, MIME- typing, and similar common operations
qt-1.42	Graphical toolkit libraries used by all KDE applications
qt-devel-1.42	Graphical libraries for developing new KDE applications (optional; download if you're interested in developing KDE applications)
kdelibs	Other libraries used by all KDE applications
kdeadmin	Administrative utilities (optional but highly recommended)
kdenetwork	Networking utilities (optional but highly recommended)
kdeutils	Additional system and user utilities (optional but highly recommended)
kdegraphics	Graphics programs and viewers for various formats (optional but recommended)
ktoys	Additional utilities; not games, but not necessary for a fully-functional KDE system
korganizer	A personal organizer for tasks, events, and so forth. (Similar to Microsoft Outlook)
kdemultimedia	Multimedia programs such as a CD Player and Sound Mixer (optional)
kdegames	Games (optional)

If you have a 28.8KB or higher modem, downloading all the KDE packages in Table 2.2 should take less than two hours. The total size of the items in Table 2.2 is about 20MB.

Reviewing the Downloaded Files

Although the list of packages in Table 2.2 provides a complete KDE installation, some packages listed on the KDE FTP site require comment:

- The eight application packages—kdeutils, kdeadmin, kdenetwork, kdegraphics, kdemultimedia, kdetoys, korganizer, and kdegames—are sets of applications that are part of the default KDE menu and are generally very useful. If you're short on hard disk space, however, you can omit any of them.

- The Qt-develop package is used for developing KDE applications or recompiling the KDE source code. See Hour 23 for more information.
- The gcc to egcs HOWTO document (not an rpm package) is a tutorial on changing packaging compiled with the standard gcc compiler (in C++ mode) to the egcs compiler (the C++ compiler used in Red Hat 5.1). This information is not applicable unless you're compiling or developing KDE components on Red Hat.

Installing KDE

Log in as root to perform the KDE installation. All users on your Linux system will have access to KDE when you have finished.

> If you want to install KDE on a Red Hat 5.0 system (rather than 5.1 or 5.2), you must first install an updated package of C++ libraries. Get the file from a Red Hat FTP site (ftp.redhat.com or a mirror) and install it with this command before using the commands that follow:
>
> ```
> # rpm -Uvh libstdc++-2.8.0-8.i386.rpm
> ```

Change to the directory where the KDE packages are stored and execute these commands in a terminal window. The exact version numbers (thus filenames) might differ depending on the latest stable release available when you download these files:

```
rpm -Uvh qt-1.42-1rh51.i386.rpm
rpm -Uvh kdesupport-1.1-7rh5x.i386.rpm
rpm -Uvh kdelibs-1.1-7rh5x.i386.rpm
rpm -Uvh kdebase-1.1-7rh5x.i386.rpm
```

> The preceding commands must be executed in this order or the installation will fail.

The -Uvh options on the rpm command indicate to install as an upgrade (being mindful of existing KDE packages on the system), print a nice progress bar during the file installation, and display any relevant informational messages (the v option is for Verbose mode).

Next, install the KDE applications using these commands. These can be executed in any order, and you can skip any that you decide not to download:

```
rpm -Uvh kdeadmin-1.1-5rh5x.i386.rpm
rpm -Uvh kdegraphics-1.1-5rh5x.i386.rpm
rpm -Uvh kdenetwork-1.1-5rh5x.i386.rpm
```

```
rpm -Uvh kdeutils-1.1-5rh5x.i386.rpm
rpm -Uvh kdemultimedia-1.1-5rh5x.i386.rpm
rpm -Uvh kdetoys-1.1-5rh5x.i386.rpm
rpm -Uvh korganizer-1.1-5rh5x.i386.rpm
rpm -Uvh kdegames-1.1-5rh5x.i386.rpm
```

KDE is now installed on your Linux system!

Configuring KDE as Your Graphical Environment

As described earlier in this hour, the `startx` command uses several files to determine what programs to start as your graphical environment.

KDE provides a simple script to review these files and set them up to use KDE as the default graphics system when you start the X Window System with the `startx` command. You should review all the instructions in this section to be certain that KDE is correctly configured to run on your Linux system.

While logged in as root, use this command to set up KDE as the default graphical system for any user on your Linux system:

```
# /opt/kde/bin/usekde username
```

This script creates a file named `.Xclients` in the user's home directory. This file is referred to when the X Window System is started.

The usekde script will detect any existing `.Xclients`, `.xinitrc`, or `.xsession` files in the user's home directory and rename them `.Xclients.orig` and so forth as it creates new files.

> Users can execute the `usekde` script at this point to set up KDE as their graphical system.

An alternative method can be used to define KDE as the graphical setting for all users on your Linux system.

KDE provides a new version of the default `Xclients` file located at `/etc/X11/xinit/Xclients.kde`. Executing these commands replaces the default copy of `Xclients` with the KDE-specific copy:

```
$ cp /etc/X11/xinit/Xclients /etc/X11/xinit/Xclients.redhat
$ cp /etc/X11/xinit/Xclients.kde /etc/X11/xinit/Xclients
$ chmod a+x /etc/X11/xinit/Xclients
```

The final step to prepare to run KDE is to include the KDE Binary directory in your PATH environment variable so the KDE programs can be located. Use this command from a command line before executing the `startx` command (this command applies to the default `bash` shell):

```
$ export PATH=$PATH:/opt/kde/bin
```

> Add the previous PATH command to your `~/.bashrc` or other startup file so it is always part of your PATH.

Now you can start KDE with this command:

```
$ startx
```

Additional details about starting and exiting KDE are provided in Hour 3.

Reviewing the Installed KDE Files

Almost all the files installed by the KDE packages described in this hour are placed in the `/opt/kde` directory. Exceptions are small configuration files such as `/etc/X11/xinit/Xclients.kde`, which are not used until you rename them, as described previously.

The subdirectories of `/opt/kde/` are described in Table 2.3.

TABLE 2.3 SUBDIRECTORIES OF `/opt/kde`

Subdirectory	Contents
bin	Program files used throughout KDE, including core features and add-on applications
cgi-bin	Scripts used by the KDE help system to process help requests
include	Header files used to access functions throughout KDE
lib	System libraries used by KDE applications, installed by the kdesupport and kdelibs packages
share	Shared resources (icons, other graphics, application links, and so forth) used by all KDE users

Summary

This hour walks you step by step through a complete installation of KDE. You learned how to download the KDE files and which files were optional. You also learned how to configure your system to make KDE start as your graphical environment. Finally, you began exploring the KDE files. In the next hour you continue learning about the KDE files as you learn how to correctly start and exit KDE.

Questions and Answers

Q I'm using a different version of Linux, not mentioned in this hour. How can I install KDE?

A Try downloading the KDE files from the generic subdirectory on the KDE FTP site. This set of files is not as easy to use (you'll have to read through the instructions carefully), but it doesn't make assumptions about your Linux system, which the Caldera or other specific KDE packages do.

Q I have an older installation of KDE. How can I upgrade?

A The rpm commands shown in this hour should upgrade any existing version of KDE. If you have problems, you can check the KDE site for additional instructions, or try removing the old version of KDE using the rpm -e command. Be careful to backup important files before fiddling too much with your system.

Q I need to know where all these files are being installed. Where can I look?

A The easiest way is to use the kpackage utility to view the KDE packages, the files they each contain, and information about them. The kpackage utility isn't included with the default KDE distribution, but is included with Caldera OpenLinux. See Hour 11, "Using KDE System Management Utilities." As an alternative, use the rpm -q command to query the packages that you installed during this hour. The rpm man page contains complete instructions for querying rpm packages on your system (type **man rpm**).

Q What is the minimum set of files I can download just to try KDE?

A Leave out all the packages of applications. Just download and install the following as described in this hour:

- qt-1.42
- kdesupport
- kdelibs
- kdebase

This will provide a main menu (sparse but functional), and the file manager and Panel. (Table 1.2 provides a list of what the kdebase package includes.) Be sure to follow the steps to make KDE your default graphical environment after installing these packages.

Exercises

1. If you're running Caldera OpenLinux, review the kde script to see how Caldera makes kde your graphical environment.

2. Visit the KDE FTP site and review the README or other informational files for the version of Linux that you're running. What additional information can you find to help you understand how KDE is set up on your system?

2

Hour 3

Starting and Exiting KDE

In this hour, you learn how to start and exit KDE. In particular, you see how KDE functions on the major Linux distributions. Startup options are described and the logout process is also outlined.

Starting KDE is generally a simple process, but reviewing it in this hour will help you troubleshoot if any problems occur. This will also enable you to add a graphical login to KDE. (This graphical login is called kdm; it's similar to xdm on other UNIX computers using the X Window System.)

Starting KDE in OpenLinux

If you are running Caldera Systems OpenLinux, starting KDE is very easy. Each time you log in to your user account on OpenLinux, a message informs you that you can start the graphical system by using the `startx` command or the `kde` command. The next section, "Starting Another window manager in OpenLinux," describes using the `startx` command when you *don't* want to use KDE.

When using Caldera OpenLinux, you don't need to complete the configuration steps outlined in Hour 2, "Installing KDE from Scratch." If you have, both the startx command and the kde command will start KDE. In that case, the following section on using another window manager in OpenLinux won't apply.

You must configure the X Window System by running the XF86Setup program before attempting to start KDE.

The default installation of OpenLinux includes the complete KDE 1.1 distribution. The KDE Binary directory is also added to each user's PATH variable so that KDE programs can be located.

To start KDE, enter the following command after logging in:

$ kde

When you use the kde command, the file /etc/X11R6/xinit/kdeinitrc is used as a parameter to start the xinit program. The kdeinitrc script takes care of many housekeeping tasks relative to starting KDE. Here is an example:

- KDE-specific directories are created in the user's home directory.
- Templates are copied from the /opt/kde/share directories to the user's home directory.
- A *magic number* password is automatically generated for the kfm program (the manual procedure is described in detail later in this hour for non-Caldera installations).

Finally, the kdeinitrc script calls the /opt/kde/bin/startkde script to launch the KDE programs.

Because the kdeinitrc script creates the necessary directories for each user, OpenLinux users won't see messages notifying them about directory creation and so forth, as described later in this hour, for starting from a clean KDE installation.

If you want to personalize your KDE setup by automatically starting additional graphical programs or setting up environment variables when you launch KDE, enter this command:

`$ cp /etc/X11R6/xinit/kdeinitrc ~/.kdeinitrc`

Then edit the .kdeinitrc file in your home directory as needed.

Starting Another Window Manager in OpenLinux 1.3

If you want to try the other windowing system included with OpenLinux (which is unrelated to KDE), use this command:

`$ startx`

to start the fvwm window manager and the Looking Glass desktop (which was the default desktop in previous versions of OpenLinux) (see Figure 3.1). The startx program uses the file /etc/X11R6/xinit/xinitrc rather than kdeinitrc as a parameter to start the xinit program.

3

FIGURE 3.1

The fvwm window manager and Looking Glass can be started in OpenLinux by using the startx *command instead of the* kde *command.*

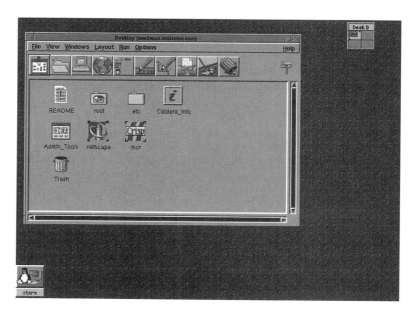

Starting KDE in Previous Versions of OpenLinux

In previous versions of OpenLinux (prior to 1.3), KDE was either not included or included as a beta release. In no case was it installed by the default installation.

If you want to use KDE on a version of OpenLinux prior to 1.3, follow the instructions in Hour 2, except choose the appropriate OpenLinux directory to download the rpm files (rather than the RedHat 5.1 directory).

You will need to review the README files in the OpenLinux FTP directory for special instructions; but in general, you can follow the instructions given for the Red Hat installation, and then the instructions later in this hour to start KDE from a clean installation.

The KDE default directory is always /opt/kde. The /etc/X11 directory referred to for Red Hat is /etc/X11R6 in OpenLinux.

Starting KDE in SuSE Linux

The latest release of SuSE Linux includes KDE 1.1 as the default desktop environment.

After you have the X Window System configured in SuSE Linux, using XF86Setup, xf86config, or another of your choice (see the SuSE installation guide for details), you can use this command to start the graphical system:

```
$ startx
```

By default, this command starts the fvwm2 window manager.

However, KDE is installed as part of the default SuSE installation. To change the SuSE configuration so that KDE will launch when you use the startx command, enter this command while logged in as a user who should use KDE:

```
echo ì/opt/kde/bin/startkdeî>~/.xinitrc
```

This command creates a local .xinitrc file for a single user.

If you want all users on your SuSE Linux system to use KDE by default when they enter the startx command, you need to follow these steps:

1. Start a text editor.
2. Open the file xinitrc located in the directory /usr/X11R6/lib/X11/xinit.
3. Find the line near the end of the file (within 10 lines or so) that reads
   ```
   exec fvwm2
   ```
4. Place a pound sign (#) in front of this line so it is a comment (not executed). This is the line that starts the default fvwm2 window manager.
   ```
   #exec fvwm2
   ```
5. Add a new line below the fvwm2 line:
   ```
   exec /opt/kde/bin/startkde
   ```

6. The two lines now look like this:

```
#exec fvwm2
exec /opt/kde/bin/startkde
```

7. Save the file and close the text editor.

Now when any user executes the `startx` command, KDE will start.

If you have altered your SuSE setup so that fvwm2 is not the default window manager, you have to take that into account and edit the `xinitrc` file differently than the procedure just given.

This procedure should also keep KDE as the desktop if you use xdm or kdm for a graphical login (described later in this hour).

3

If you're using an older version of SuSE Linux, use the installation instructions provided in Hour 2, but use the SuSE subdirectory to download the KDE files rather than the Red Hat subdirectory.

The instructions in the remainder of this hour refer to the Red Hat distribution, but they also apply to using KDE on SuSE Linux, including setting up kdm. Note, however, the different locations of X startup files in the directory structure, as you can see from the procedures in this section.

Starting KDE from a Clean Install

The information in this section builds on the procedures described in Hour 2.

After you have KDE installed, you need to set up the X Window System so that it starts the KDE window manager and associated programs rather than the default window manager on your Linux system (fvwm2 in the case of Red Hat 5.1).

Starting the X Window System in Red Hat Linux

The standard method of starting the X Window System is to execute the `startx` command:

```
$ startx
```

The `startx` command uses the xinit program to start up X on your system and launch the window manager and initial programs defined in your `xinitrc` files and `Xclient` files, as described in Hour 2.

 The xinit program is a binary program file not a script. Don't use an editor or other command to try to review its contents.

To have the xinit program start KDE, you simply include the `startkde` script (part of the KDE installation) in the files that xinit uses to start X. These files can be system-wide (located in the `/etc/X11/xinit` directory), or per-user (located in the `.Xclients` file within a user's home directory).

The next section describes how to easily set this up for your new KDE installation.

Starting KDE from the `startx` Script

When you install KDE, a sample `Xclients` file is placed in the `/etc/X11/xinit` directory. You can make this file the default used by xinit for all users by executing these commands:

```
$ cp /etc/X11/xinit/Xclients /etc/X11/xinit/Xclients.redhat
$ cp /etc/X11/xinit/Xclients.kde /etc/X11/xinit/Xclients
$ chmod a+x /etc/X11/xinit/Xclients
```

Alternatively, you might not want all users to automatically use KDE. In fact, if you're accustomed to using another windowing system on Linux, you can set up one user account to use KDE for testing or review and leave other user accounts with the system's default window manager.

To set up a single user account to use KDE, follow these steps:

1. Log in as the user who should have KDE specified as his or her desktop.

2. Execute this command:

   ```
   $ /opt/kde/bin/usekde
   ```

   The message informs you that a new file was created specifying the startkde program as the X client to run for this user.

   KDE is now your default desktop; to change this, delete `/home/username/.Xclients`.

3. Add this command to your `.bashrc` file or other startup script so that KDE files can be located each time you log in:

   ```
   export PATH=$PATH:/opt/kde/bin
   ```

Don't try to use the `startkde` command directly. The `startkde` script assumes that the X System has been initialized by the xinit program before `startkde` is called.

Now you can start KDE from the character-based console with the command

```
$ startx
```

Reviewing the Initial KDE Startup

The first time you start KDE for any user, several directories are created in the user's home directory. The contents of these directories are the subject of Hour 4, "Reviewing the KDE Setup."

When you start KDE, several dialog boxes inform you of the directories that are being created.

In addition, you see a dialog box asking you to change the password in the file `~/.kde/share/apps/kfm/magic`.

This password is a code used by the file manager program kfm. You won't ever have to remember or enter this password, but it should be unique among users on your Linux system. The password, used as an internal security mechanism, is a number of at least 9 digits.

To update the magic file with a new password number, enter this command, substituting your own number for my less-than-creative example:

```
?$ echo 1234567890123>magic
```

Or, use the following command provided by the KDE installation:

```
$ magic_passwd 1234567890123
```

If you started KDE before using the preceding command to alter the password in the magic file, you might have to restart KDE before the file manager (kfm) will function.

Diagnosing Trouble Starting KDE

If the best-laid plans go awry and KDE doesn't start when you use the `startx` command, check the list of possible causes and answers given in Table 3.1:

TABLE 3.1 PROBLEMS AND FIXES WHEN KDE DOESN'T RUN

Problem	How to Fix It
The X Window System used to work, but now it won't start.	Rename the `.Xclients` file in your home directory. If X works now, see whether you have special modifications in your `/etc/X11/xinit/Xclients` file that need to be added to the `.Xclients` file in your home directory.
The X Window System starts, but it uses a different windowing system, not KDE.	Assuming KDE is installed on your system, check to see whether an `.xinitrc` file in your home directory is directing which window system gets started before the `.Xclients` file created by the `usekde` script is seen. If you find `.xinitrc` in your home directory, rename it to something else (`.xinitrc.save`) and try again.
KDE tries to start, but it fails, returning to the character console.	Are you out of disk space? KDE creates some temporary files during startup. Try the `df` command to review your hard disk space.
	If you see a lot of error messages with Qt...in them, you might not have installed the correct version of the Qt libraries for the binaries that you're running.
	Did you install the KDE packages in the order given in Hour 2: kdesupport, kdelibs, kdebase? You might need to use the `rpm -e` command to uninstall the packages and reinstall the rpm files in the correctorder.
	Does the `/etc/ld.so.conf` file contain a reference to `/opt/kde/lib`? If not, add it and run the program `/sbin/ldconfig` to update the system.

Logging Out of KDE

When you log out of KDE, the X Window System closes and you return to a command line in Character mode (the console).

The following sections describe how to log out of KDE.

Using a Standard KDE Logout

KDE includes a Logout option that can be accessed from several places. Choose Logout from any of these locations:

- The bottom item of the main menu (accessed by clicking the K icon on the Panel)
- The X icon on the Panel (see Figure 3.2)

FIGURE 3.2

*The X icon on the
Panel initiates the
logout process.*

Click here to log out

- The bottom item on the pop-up menu that appears when you right-click the background of the KDE Desktop (see Figure 3.3).

FIGURE 3.3

*The right-click menu
on the desktop includes
a Logout option*

The right-click menu is useful if you've hidden or shut down the Panel and taskbar to free up space on your desktop. See Hour 6, "Managing the KDE Environment," for details on configuring the Panel and taskbar.

Whichever method you choose to log out, the screen is darkened slightly and a confirmation dialog box appears.

If you have only KDE applications open when you choose Logout, the confirmation dialog box includes only two options: Logout and Cancel. Choose the Logout button in the confirmation dialog box to close down KDE and return to the character console.

The applications that you have open in KDE, such as file system browsing windows and configuration screens, will appear as you left them the next time you start KDE.

If you have non-KDE applications running or terminal emulator windows, which could have been used to start any application, KDE presents a different logout confirmation dialog box.

From this dialog box, you can't do anything to the open applications (such as selecting and closing them). But this confirmation enables you to see applications that are open. You might decide to choose the Cancel button, close or save data from these open windows, and then choose the Logout command again (at which time the confirmation dialog box appears again).

> Although the confirmation dialog box warns you otherwise, KDE attempts to restart non-KDE applications the next time you open KDE. The warning is given because KDE might not be successful in locating and starting non-KDE applications that you have running when you log out of KDE.

Using the Emergency Exit

Occasionally, things go wrong. When they go wrong in KDE (or X, or Linux in general), you may not be able to access any of the logout buttons and menus described in the previous section.

When that happens, you can use the emergency exit for the X Window System: press Ctrl+Alt+Backspace.

This key combination shuts down KDE and the X Window System *ungracefully*. That means that if you were in the middle of something, your work will not be saved, your open windows and running programs will not be noted by KDE, and you could conceivably cause other problems.

However, when you can't get the X Window System to respond to any other commands, this last resort is a handy thing to know.

Setting Up a Graphical Login with kdm

When you install Linux, the X Window System is not typically configured automatically. Intel computer hardware is too diverse to guarantee that the graphical configuration will function correctly. Relying on the graphical interface initially, as many other UNIX systems do, is risking having no display at all.

UNIX systems such as HP/UX or IBM AIX, which are preconfigured with their operating systems, use an attractive graphical login screen, without ever displaying the Character mode console that appears after installing Linux on a PC.

After you have Linux installed and the X Window System running, however, it's simple to change to the graphical-only login that never displays a Character mode console. This program is called xdm, the X Display Manager.

The following section describes how to set up xdm on your Linux system.

Initializing xdm

The use of the xdm program relies on the *run level* of your Linux system. A run level is a *mode* within the Linux kernel that indicates which features or programs to start or allow to run. Normally, your Linux system starts in run level 3, indicating a standard, multi-user operation.

If you change your initialization scripts to indicate run level 5, indicating the X Window System, the xdm program will start automatically when you reboot, and you won't see the character console again.

Before altering your initialization scripts to use xdm each time you boot, follow these steps to be certain that the xdm program is working correctly.

1. Log out of the X Window System (KDE).
2. Enter this command at the console to temporarily switch to run level 5 and use xdm:

   ```
   # /sbin/telinit 5
   ```
3. When the log in prompt appears, log in and see that KDE appears.
4. If a problem occurs, press Ctrl+R to exit the graphical log in screen and run this command from the console to return to standard Character mode:

   ```
   # /sbin/telinit 3
   ```

If you encountered problems as you followed these steps, consult the documentation for xdm or your Linux system to correctly configure xdm before proceeding with the steps that follow.

After you're sure that xdm is working, you can alter your initialization scripts to permanently use xdm. To change your initialization scripts to run level 5 at boot time and use the xdm graphical login screen, follow these steps:

1. Log in as root.
2. Use a text editor to open the file /etc/inittab.
3. Find the line in inittab that looks like this:

   id:3:initdefault:

4. Change the 3 to a 5 so that the line looks like this:

   id:5:initdefault:

5. Save the inittab file.
6. Enter this command to switch to run level 5 using xdm:

   # **init 5**

> Each time you restart your computer, the character login prompt will appear for a moment, but then a graphical screen will appear with an area where you can log in to your system.

7. When you log in, the window manager or graphical desktop starts as it previously did when you entered the startx or kde command.
8. When you exit KDE or any other window manager, you return to the graphical login screen.

To shut down your Linux system when using xdm (and thus without access to the Character mode console), open a terminal window, log in as root or use the su command, and then execute this command:

shutdown -t3 -r now

Or, when viewing the graphical xdm login, follow these steps:

1. Press Ctrl+R. A command prompt appears.
2. Enter this command:

   # **init 3**

   The xdm program is stopped.

3. Use this command to shutdown and reboot your system:

```
# shutdown -t3 -r now
```

You can also use your standard Linux shutdown procedure rather than the shutdown command given here.

Setting KDE as the Graphical System for xdm

The xdm program uses a different initial script to start up the X Window System: /etc/X11/xdm/Xsession rather than the script named as a parameter to the xinit program or the xinitrc file.

Nevertheless, the xdm program still reaches the same point as the xinit program, where it looks for an .Xclients file in the current user's home directory, or a system-wide Xclients file in /etc/X11/xinit.

The catch is that the xdm program *first* looks for a file named .Xsession in the user's home directory. Thus, if your home directory contains this file, xdm might never see the Xclients file that you created from Xclients.kde in the previous section in order to start KDE as the default graphical environment.

Remember, the /etc/X11 directory is called /etc/X11R6 on some Linux systems.

The resolution to this problem lies in renaming the .Xsession file in your home directory, using the following command line:

```
$ mv .Xsession .Xsession.saved
```

Then exit the window manager and log in again using xdm to see whether KDE is started by xdm. Then review your saved .Xsession file to see if any special options need to be added to a .Xclients file in your home directory, or if you can add the startkde script at the bottom of your .Xsession file to start KDE from that script instead of from the local or system-wide copy of .Xclients.

Changing from xdm to kdm

When xdm is working and runs KDE, you can easily change to the KDE version of the desktop manager, called kdm.

The advantage of using kdm over xdm is simply its integration with KDE features and the capability of configuring kdm from the KDE Control Center (which you'll see a lot of in the rest of this book).

To make your Linux system use kdm instead of xdm, follow these steps:

1. Log in as root.

2. Open the file /etc/inittab in a text editor.

3. Find the line in the file that looks like this (probably the last line of the file):

   ```
   x:5:respawn:/usr/bin/X11/xdm -nodaemon
   ```

4. Place a pound sign in front of it to make it a comment (saving it for future use if needed).

5. Enter this line after it:

   ```
   x:5:respawn:/opt/kde/bin/kdm -nodaemon
   ```

6. The two lines now look like this:

   ```
   #x:5:respawn:/usr/bin/X11/xdm -nodaemon
   x:5:respawn:/opt/kde/bin/kdm -nodaemon
   ```

7. Save the inittab file and exit the text editor.

> If you're already running xdm, you can use the init 3 command to shut down xdm. Follow the steps given previously in this hour to restart run level 5 with kdm.

Using the kdm Log in Prompt Dialog Box

When you start your system (or log out of KDE) you see the kdm login prompt dialog box. The following steps describe how to use the fields in this dialog box:

1. From this dialog box, you can choose a user from the list of icons shown or enter the username in the Login field.

2. Next, enter a password in the Password field (nothing will appear in the field as you type).

3. Press Enter to log in or choose the Go! button.

4. If you want to shut down your Linux system, choose the Shutdown button. Another dialog box appears where you can choose Shutdown or Shutdown and Restart (ignore the third option, Shutdown kdm).

5. To use the Shutdown dialog box, enter the root password in the empty, unlabeled field provided and press Enter. The OK button becomes active. Choose OK to shut down your system.

Only use the Default session type. Failsafe provides a special debugging mode; it won't start up your KDE Desktop.

Changing the Background in xdm or kdm

When you use the procedure in the previous section to start using kdm, you'll notice that the background image stays the same as it was in xdm. In Red Hat Linux, this background is a giant Red Hat banner with "Tux" the penguin.

When using kdm, you can configure the background to use any wallpaper or graphic image that you choose. Those configuration options are described in the next section. But first you must set one more configuration option to enable the kdm configuration to affect the background.

Both xdm and kdm use the file /etc/X11/xdm/Xsetup_0 to determine the background of the login screen. Follow these steps to make the KDE configuration apply to the kdm login screen:

The background that you configure for kdm will also apply if you switch back to using xdm.

1. Open the file /etc/X11/xdm/Xsetup_0 in a text editor.
2. At the end of the file, after the line containing the xbanner command, add this line:
   /opt/kde/bin/kdmdesktop
3. Save the Xsetup_0 file and close the text editor.

This procedure enables the background configuration described in the next section to operate.

Configuring kdm

To configure kdm, you use the main menu that you access from the K icon after starting KDE. The hours that follow provide extensive detail about the KDE screen and configuration options. This section describes only configuration of the kdm program. You must be logged in as root to configure kdm.

The kdm program runs separately from the rest of KDE. The configuration tool for kdm runs as part of KDE, but you can also use kdm with other window managers.

To configure kdm, open the main menu by choosing the K icon. Then choose Settings, Applications, Desktop Manager. The dialog box shown in Figure 3.4 appears.

FIGURE 3.4

The Appearance tab of the KDM Configuration dialog box determines how the login prompt for kdm appears.

From this dialog box, you can set up the appearance of the login prompt when kdm starts. You can change any of the following options, or leave them all as they are by default:

- Enter new text in the Greeting string field. This text appears at the top of the login prompt.
- Click on the KDM logo graphic to open a selection dialog box where you can choose a new graphic as the icon in the login prompt.
- Choose Motif or Windows as the GUI style from the drop-down list.
- Choose a language if the default language is not correct.

The Fonts tab (shown in Figure 3.5) enables you to select a font for each of three items in the login prompt:

- The greeting
- Failure messages if an incorrect username or password is entered
- Standard descriptive text in the prompt dialog box

FIGURE 3.5

The Fonts tab enables you to select a font for each of three types of text in the login prompt dialog box.

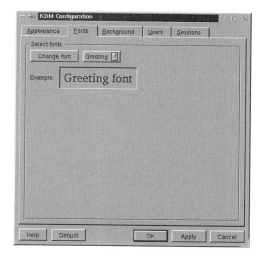

To change a font, select Greeting, Fail, or Standard from the drop-down list. Then choose the Change font button.

The Select Font dialog box appears (see Figure 3.6) where you can define the font to be used for the text type that you selected.

FIGURE 3.6

The Select Font dialog box enables you to define a text style for the kdm login prompt.

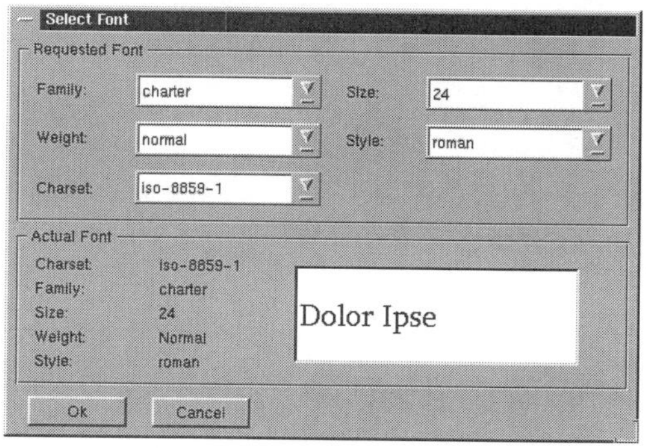

When you choose OK in the Select Font dialog box, you can see what the text will look like in the small Example window of the Fonts tab.

The fun part of the kdm configuration is the Background tab, shown in Figure 3.7.

FIGURE 3.7

The Background tab enables you to select the color and background for the kdm login screen.

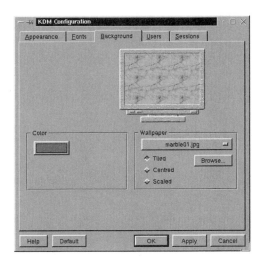

First, select a color for the background by clicking on the color button and choosing a color from the Select Color dialog box that appears (see Figure 3.8).

FIGURE 3.8

The background color for the kdm login screen is selected in the Select Color dialog box.

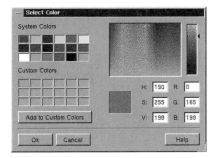

The background color won't be visible if you choose a tiled or scaled wall paper.

Next, choose a wallpaper design by selecting from the drop-down list in the Wallpaper field.

When you select a wallpaper graphic from the list, you have three options for how it will be displayed:

- *Tiled*. Use the graphic as a repeating pattern across the entire screen, starting at the upper-left corner and filling the screen.

- *Centered.* Use the graphic as a picture, centered on the background (with the background color visible around it).

- *Scaled.* Use the graphic as a picture, but scale it to fill the entire screen (with no background color visible around it). This option might not produce optimal results. If you'd like to use a full-screen image, create a graphic that matches the size of your screen and use the Centered option.

The images provided by the KDE distribution are intended as Tiled wallpaper images. You can use any GIF or JPEG image you choose as wallpaper, however. Use the Browse button to locate it in your file system and specify it as a centered or scaled image for your kdm wallpaper.

The Users tab defines which user accounts are shown in the kdm login prompt dialog box. All users can type a username at the Login prompt to log in using kdm. The icon makes it a little easier for nontechnical users to know what to do. The user's password is still required, of course.

In the Users tab (see Figure 3.9), you choose any user from the All Users field and press the >> button to add that user's name to the Selected users list.

FIGURE 3.9

The Users tab enables you to select which users are shown as selectable icons in the kdm login prompt dialog box.

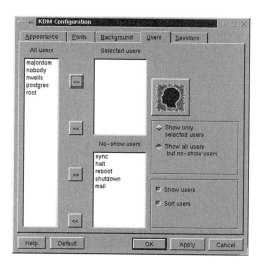

Two radio buttons enable you to select which users to display in the kdm login dialog box: those in the Selected users list or all regular users on the system (excluding system users such as *mail* and *halt*).

The Sessions tab (see Figure 3.10) enables you to configure advanced kdm options. Probably the only option that will concern you at this point is the Allow to Shutdown field, where you can specify which users can click the Shutdown button to shut down the system from the kdm login prompt dialog box.

FIGURE 3.10

The Sessions tab configures advanced kdm options, including who can shut down the system from the kdm login prompt dialog box.

Allowing nonroot users to shut the system down could be a huge security problem if you're working on a network or have multiple persons using your Linux system. It does provide a convenience, however, if you are the only one using your Linux system and you don't want to always log in as root before shutting down Linux.

Other fields in the Sessions tab enable you to define the command used to shut down and restart the system, and define session types that kdm can use.

Summary

In this hour you learned how to set up your graphical system to start KDE, and how to exit KDE. You learned about the xdm and kdm programs, which provide a graphical log in. You also learned how to configure the kdm program using the KDE Control Center options. In the next hour, you will learn more about where KDE stored programs and configuration files, including the information stored in each user's home directory.

Questions and Answers

Q **The xdm program doesn't seem to work. Any suggestions?**

A First, check to see that's it's installed on your Linux system. Second, try starting the X Window System without xdm to see that it's configured correctly. If these check out, review the online manual page for xdm, init, and inittab to learn more about how to get xdm running.

Q **I'm already running a previous version of KDE on a previous version of Caldera OpenLinux (or Red Hat Linux). Do I need to reconfigure the system as described in this hour?**

A If you already have a previous version of KDE running, the upgrade process (using the command `rpm -U`) should update all your KDE files without touching the scripts that start the X Window System. The result is that KDE should start just as it did before upgrading, without any action on your part beyond executing the upgrade for the KDE packages.

Q **Can I continue to use xdm with KDE, rather than switching to kdm?**

A Sure. kdm is a separate program from the rest of KDE. You can choose xdm without any ill effects on KDE. Of course, you won't have the benefit of configuring xdm from a graphical dialog box, as you can do with kdm, but if xdm is already working for you, that might not matter.

Exercises

1. Explore the contents of the `xinitrc` and `Xclients` files on your system, both in the `/etc/X11/xinit` directory and in your home directory. (The copies in your home directory are hidden files, use `ls -a` to see them.) What can you learn from these files about how the graphical environment is started?

2. Experiment with logging out of KDE while different programs are running. Which are restored when you restart KDE, and in what state are they restored? Can you find where information about what applications to restore is located? Try using Ctrl+Alt+Backspace to exit the X Window System. Is anything restored the next time you start KDE?

Hour 4

Reviewing the KDE Setup

In this hour, you will learn how KDE interacts with your Linux file system and your home directory. Hour 2, "Installing KDE from Scratch," describes the files you used to install KDE. This hour describes the files that are in place after KDE is installed.

The KDE files in your home directory are particularly relevant to this hour, because understanding how KDE uses the files that it creates in your home directory will help you see how KDE works at a deeper level. If you don't want to understand KDE at a deeper level, but just want to learn how to run the graphical desktop, you can skip to Hour 5, "Exploring the Desktop," and return to this hour if the need arises as you explore your home directory later.

Defining a User of KDE

Each user on your Linux system has a separate home directory where that user's files are stored. When a person logs in to a Linux user account and starts KDE, KDE creates a set of files (or uses the ones already created by a previous KDE session) to determine how to setup that users KDE environment.

 If you're using Caldera OpenLinux, the KDE directories are created automatically; you won't see any notice of them being created.

As described in preceding hours, your Linux system must have KDE defined as the default graphical environment using the appropriate X Window System initialization files, or a user must have local files in the user's home directory to indicate that KDE should be used for that user.

The home directory of each user who has started KDE contains a set of configuration files, located in the hidden directory .kde (the dot indicates a hidden item), and a Desktop directory where the contents of the KDE Desktop are stored.

You can see the contents of the .kde configuration directory with this command:

```
$ ls -la ~/.kde
```

The only item it contains is the share subdirectory. Not very exciting yet, but in this hour you'll explore the .kde directory in detail.

Using the ls command, you can also see that the Desktop directory contains three subdirectories: Autostart, Templates, and Trash. The Desktop directory contains whatever appears on your KDE Desktop. Again, more about this directory is provided later in this hour.

Reviewing the Contents of the .kde Directory

The .kde directory contains all the shared data and configuration information used by KDE to manage your graphical environment.

The share/ subdirectory of the KDE Installation directory contains shared icons, graphics, program links, and many other items. The subdirectories of /opt/kde/share are shown in this listing:

```
$ ls -l /opt/kde/share/
total 12
drwxr-xr-x  11 root      root           1024 Nov 17 01:04 applnk
drwxr-xr-x  42 root      root           1024 Nov 17 01:10 apps
drwxr-xr-x   2 root      root           1024 Nov 17 16:25 config
```

```
drwxr-xr-x    3 root        root          1024 Nov 17 01:04 doc
drwxr-xr-x    3 root        root          4096 Nov 17 01:10 icons
drwxr-xr-x   27 root        root          1024 Nov 17 01:04 locale
drwxr-xr-x    8 root        root          1024 Nov 17 01:04 mimelnk
drwxr-xr-x    2 root        root          1024 Nov 17 01:05 toolbar
drwxr-xr-x    2 root        root          1024 Nov 17 01:04 wallpapers
```

All the items from this area that require individual copies or user information are reflected in the share subdirectory of the .kde directory, as shown in this listing (note that some items such as wallpaper are only needed in the system-wide share directory):

```
$ ls -l ~/.kde/share/
total 10
drwx------    2 nwells      users         1024 Nov 20 12:17 applnk
drwx------    6 nwells      users         1024 Nov 25 19:09 apps
dr-xr-xr-x    2 nwells      users         1024 Nov 20 12:48 auto
drwxr-xr-x    2 nwells      users         2048 Nov 20 13:45 bin
drwxr-xr-x    2 nwells      users         1024 Nov 20 12:48 boot
drwx------    2 nwells      users         1024 Dec 26 10:14 config
drwxr-xr-x    2 nwells      users         1024 Nov 20 13:50 dev
drwx------    3 nwells      users         1024 Nov 20 12:17 icons
drwx------    4 nwells      users         1024 Nov 20 12:17 mimelnk
```

Depending on the applications that are installed in your KDE environment (such as StarOffice or BRU), you might see additional subdirectories that were created by those programs.

4

The config Subdirectory

The config subdirectory of ~/.kde/share contains configuration files for many KDE applications, including the KDE window manager, Panel, file browser (kfm) and other core applications.

If you're familiar with Microsoft Windows .ini files, the configuration files in this directory use a very similar format.

These configuration files contain sections of information. Each section includes one or more options, each with a value. For example, part of kwmrc, the configuration file for the KDE window manager, kwm, is shown in this listing (you might recognize some of these options as you read Hour 5:

```
...
[Buttons]
ButtonC=Off
ButtonD=Close
ButtonE=Maximize
ButtonF=Iconify
ButtonA=Menu
ButtonB=Sticky
[General]
WindowMoveType=Transparent
AltTabMode=KDE
TitlebarDoubleClickCommand=winMaximize
FocusPolicy=ClickToFocus
ElectricBorderPointerWarp=FullWarp
WindowSnapZone=10
ControlTab=on
RstartProtocol=rstart -v
WindowResizeType=Transparent
Button3Grab=on
AutoRaise=0
TraverseAll=off
BorderSnapZone=10
WindowsPlacement=smart
...
```

The configuration files in the config directory are modified when you use the KDE graphical utilities to select options. Then the corresponding application reads the configuration file and uses the options indicated.

The contents of the configuration files can be edited manually using a text editor if you know what you want to change. Until you're very familiar with KDE, however, I recommend using the graphical utilities described in this book. They don't provide access to every possible option, but they do prevent corrupted configuration files.

Some of the configuration files are empty. They appear in the file listing but have a size of 0. These empty files are included so that the corresponding application can always query the configuration file, even when no additional information is provided by the configuration file. Don't erase them.

The apps Subdirectory

The Configuration directory includes a single file for each of many KDE applications. Some applications, however, require that more detailed information be saved. The apps subdirectory provides a location where KDE applications can create their own subdirectory for storing temporary files, user data, templates, and so forth.

The information in the apps directory is user specific. A system-wide apps directory with a similar function is located at /opt/kde/share/apps.

You can see an example of how the apps directory is used by exploring the kdehelp or kfm subdirectories under the apps/ directory.

 KDE applications will generally create and populate their own subdirectories in apps/ as you use them. For example, if you've never opened the kdehelp application, you won't find much in the apps/kdehelp subdirectory.

The contents of the apps/kfm directory are shown here:

```
$ ls -l kfm/
total 5
drwx------   2 nwells   users       1024 Nov 20 11:51 bookmarks
-rw-r--r--   1 nwells   users        116 Dec 26 10:14 desktop
-rw-r--r--   1 nwells   users         36 Nov 20 11:51 magic
-rw-r--r--   1 nwells   users         26 Dec 26 10:14 pid_0.0
drwx------   2 nwells   users       1024 Nov 20 11:51 tmp
```

From this listing, you can see that the kfm program creates several files, rather than stuffing all the needed information in a single configuration file in the config directory.

The applink Subdirectory

The applnk subdirectory (~/share/applnk) contains links to applications that will appear in the Personal submenu of your main menu. By default, this directory will be empty, and no Personal submenu will appear on your main menu. But as you install KDE-aware applications, they can add links so that an application will appear on the menu for easy launching.

StarOffice 5.0 for Linux is one such application. If you select the KDE integration option when you install StarOffice 5.0 for Linux, it adds files to the applnk directory so that it appears as in this listing:

```
$ ls -l
total 3
-rw-r--r--   1 nwells   users        288 Nov 20 12:17 PSetup.kdelnk
-rw-r--r--   1 nwells   users        229 Nov 20 12:17 Setup.kdelnk
-rw-r--r--   1 nwells   users        498 Nov 20 12:17 StarOffice.kdelnk
```

The corresponding view of the main menu with the Personal submenu open appears in Figure 4.1.

FIGURE 4.1

The Personal menu contains items defined by the `.kde/share/applnk` *subdirectory.*

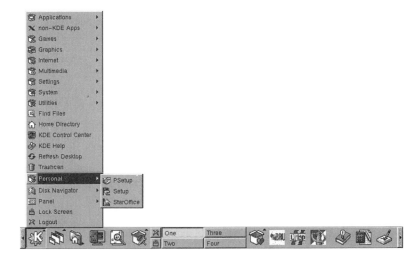

Notice that the files in the `applnk` directory have a file extension of `kdelnk`, and that this is the same as the files in the `~/Desktop/Templates` directory. If you look at one of the files in the `applnk` directory, you see that it is really a pointer to a program that will be executed when that item is selected from the Personal menu. The contents of the `StarOffice.kdelnk` file are shown in the following listing:

```
$ more StarOffice.kdelnk
# KDE Config File
[KDE Desktop Entry]
SwallowTitle=
SwallowExec=
BinaryPattern=soffice;
Name=StarOffice
Protocols=file;ftp;http;
MiniIcon=so.xpm
MimeType=application/x-scalc;application/x-smf;application/
➡x-sdraw;application/x
-sds;application/x-swriter;application/x-sgl;application/x-sda;audio/
➡x-wav;image
/gif;image/jpeg;image/tiff;image/x-xbm;image/x-xpm;text/html;text/plain;
Comment=StarOffice
Exec=/home/nwells/Office50/bin/soffice %f
Icon=so.xpm
Path=/home2/usr/pl
Type=Application
Terminal=0
```

At this point in the discussion, the most important line to review in the preceding listing is the `Exec=` statement (fifth from the bottom). This line indicates the program that will be executed when StarOffice is selected from the `applnk` submenu.

In later hours, you'll learn how to insert applications into the Personal submenu. Your own links will then appear in the `applnk` directory.

The `bin` and `boot` Subdirectories

The `bin` and `boot` subdirectories are copies of other directories on your Linux system. The KDE programs use these subdirectories as local copies of system files.

- The `boot` directory is a copy of the `/boot` directory, and contains items such as the system map and the initial boot message used by LILO when starting your computer.

- The `bin` directory contains several dozen standard utility programs, most of which are located in `/usr/local/bin`. These include utilities such as rpm, gzip, cp, and mount.

These programs can be used by KDE programs without concern for permission restrictions that might interfere with use of the corresponding system files. Unfortunately, these copies might use about 5MB of space in your home directory. The directory size might also grow as you continue to use various KDE programs.

The `dev`, `icons`, and `mimelnk` Subdirectories

4

The `dev` subdirectory contains information about system devices that are used by KDE applications. Initially, it is empty. Applications that need to use it will create device pointers in this subdirectory.

The `icons` subdirectory is an archive of graphics files (in xpm format), which KDE applications can use for desktop icons, the Panel, or for other situations that require an icon. A few basic icons are included. You can add additional icons to this subdirectory if you choose to. Many icons can be downloaded from the KDE themes site (`kde.themes.org`) or other KDE archive sites (see Hour 2).

Many standard icons are included in KDE. You can replace existing system icons (located at `/opt/kde/share/icons`) with user-specific icons by placing an icon of the same name in your local `share/icons` directory. Any new icons for applications that you install can also be placed in this directory.

The `icons` subdirectory also includes a mini-subdirectory where a smaller version of the default icons is stored. You should include a mini version of the icon in the mini-subdirectory whenever you create or add new icons to your `share` directory.

Mini icons are used in the title bar of an application, on the taskbar, and on the Panel when Tiny mode is selected (as described in Hour 6, "Managing the KDE Environment").

 Standard icons are 32 × 32 pixels; icons in the mini subdirectory are 16 × 16 pixels.

The `mimelnk` subdirectory contains subdirectories for text and application links. Each of the files in these subdirectories defines a new *MIME* type for KDE. Information in the `mimelnk` file includes

- The MIME type representation (for example `application/x-swriter`)
- How to identify a file of that type (using a file extension)
- The application used to read that type of file
- The icon used to represent a file of that type onscreen
- Other comments and information

 MIME (Multiformat Internet Mail Exchange) descriptions are an Internet standard used to classify and describe data types so that operating systems, email programs, and other applications will know what to do with files that they work with. A MIME type defines how to recognize a type of file and what to do with files of each type.

 Dozens of standard MIME types are included in KDE. Only new or additional MIME types must be added to your system using the `mimelnk` directory as described here.

For example, if you install StarOffice 5.0 for Linux using the KDE integration features, the installation program places new MIME type information in the `mimelnk/application` subdirectory. The following listing shows the contents of the `mimelnk/application` subdirectory after installing StarOffice 5.0 for Linux:

```
$ ls -l
total 7
-rw-r--r--   1 nwells   users         193 Nov 20 12:17 x-scalc.kdelnk
-rw-r--r--   1 nwells   users         191 Nov 20 12:17 x-sda.kdelnk
```

```
-rw-r--r--   1 nwells    users        193 Nov 20 12:17 x-sdraw.kdelnk
-rw-r--r--   1 nwells    users        191 Nov 20 12:17 x-sds.kdelnk
-rw-r--r--   1 nwells    users        191 Nov 20 12:17 x-sgl.kdelnk
-rw-r--r--   1 nwells    users        191 Nov 20 12:17 x-smf.kdelnk
-rw-r--r--   1 nwells    users        350 Nov 20 12:17 x-swriter.kdelnk
```

These MIME type definitions can be used by KDE applications to work with StarOffice files. For example, the contents of the `x-scalc.kdelnk` file are shown here:

```
$ more x-scalc.kdelnk
# KDE Config File
[KDE Desktop Entry]
MimeType=application/x-scalc
Comment=mime type
DefaultApp=StarOffice
Comment[pl]=Typ mime
Icon=sdc.xpm
Type=MimeType
Patterns=*.sdc;
Comment[de]=Mime Type
```

Any application (including the standard KDE file manager, kfm) that comes across a file with the SCD file extension will use the definitions in this `mimelnk` definition. That is, it will use the StarOffice application to edit the file, the `sdc.xpm` icon to represent the file onscreen, and so forth.

Reviewing the Desktop Directory

The Desktop directory contains directories and files that refer to objects on the KDE Desktop. Although Hour 10, "Learning More KDE File Management," contains detailed information on using the KDE Desktop, a review here will help you understand the directories used by KDE.

The default KDE Desktop includes three icons:

- Autostart folder
- Trash bin
- Templates folder

Each of these three items is represented by a subdirectory in the Desktop directory. This is shown by the `ls` command:

```
$ ls -l ~/Desktop
total 3
drwx------   2 nwells    users       1024 Nov 20 11:51 Autostart
drwx------   2 nwells    users       1024 Nov 20 11:51 Templates
drwx------   2 nwells    users       1024 Nov 20 11:51 Trash
```

These subdirectories are briefly explained in the sections that follow.

The Autostart Folder

The Autostart folder contains programs that are started automatically by KDE when the graphical environment is initialized. This folder is similar to the Startup folder in MS Windows or other operating systems.

By default, nothing is contained in the Autostart folder. You can place links in the Autostart folder, which refer to programs anywhere on your Linux system. You learn the details of doing this in Hour 10.

> If you left an application or KDE window open when you logged out of KDE, KDE attempts to reopen that application or window the next time you start KDE. This doesn't mean that the application is part of the Autostart folder. Programs in the Autostart folder will be started even if they were not running when you last exited KDE.

You can double-click on the Autostart folder on the desktop to open a file-browsing window that shows the files contained in the folder.

The Autostart subdirectory does contain a single hidden file, even when you haven't placed any program links in it. This is the .directory file, which contains a description of the subdirectory used by the Desktop program to set display and behavior characteristics.

You can see this file listed with this command:

```
$ ls -la ~/Desktop/Autostart/
total 3
drwx------    2 nwells    users          1024 Nov 20 11:51 .
drwx------    5 nwells    users          1024 Nov 20 11:51 ..
-rw-r--r--    1 nwells    users           933 Nov 20 11:51 .directory
```

You don't have to ever do anything with this file, but it's instructive to know that it's there. Looking inside the .directory file, you see the name of the item, plus a translation and comment on the item in several languages. The contents of the .directory file for Autostart are shown in the following listing.

```
$ cd ~/Desktop/Autostart
$ more .directory
[KDE Desktop Entry]
Name=Autostart
Name[it]=Avvio
Name[de]=Autostart
```

```
Name[no]=Autostart
Name[pl]=Autostart
Name[es]=Inicio
Name[sk]=Auto'tart
Name[fi]=Käynnistä
Name[fr]=Démarrage
Name[cs]=Autostart
Name[pt]=Arranque
Name[pt_BR]=Arranque
Name[sv]=Autostart
Comment[no]=Programmer som vil bli startet ved oppstart
Comment[pl]=Programy uruchamiane przy starcie KDE
Comment[fi]=Aloitettaessa käynnistettävät ohjelmat
Comment[cs]=Programy spou'tìné pøi startu KDE
Comment[sk]=Programy spú'>>ané pri 'tarte KDE
Comment[es]=Los programas en esta carpeta serán ejecutados al inicio de
cada ses
ión
Comment[fr]=Programmes qui seront lancés à chaque démarrage
Comment[it]=I programmi contenuti in questa cartella vengono eseguiti
all'avvio
del KDE
Comment[pt]=Programas que são executados no início de cada sessão
Comment[pt_BR]=Programas que são executados no início de cada sessão
      Comment[sv]=Program som startas automatiskt vid inloggning
```

> The content and format of the .directory files described here are very simi-
> lar to the KDE link files you'll learn about in later hours, especially Hour 10.

4

The Templates Folder

The Templates folder contains sample files that you use to create new items on your
KDE Desktop. These templates come in six types, matching the types of items you can
place on your desktop. The following listing shows the contents of the Templates directory:

```
$ ls -la
total 9
drwx------   2 nwells    users      1024 Nov 20 11:51 .
drwx------   5 nwells    users      1024 Nov 20 11:51 ..
-rw-r--r--   1 nwells    users       802 Nov 20 11:51 .directory
-rw-r--r--   1 nwells    users       538 Aug 19 12:04 Device.kdelnk
-rw-r--r--   1 nwells    users       275 Aug 19 12:04 Ftpurl.kdelnk
-rw-r--r--   1 nwells    users       320 Aug 19 12:04 MimeType.kdelnk
-rw-r--r--   1 nwells    users       248 Aug 19 12:04 Program.kdelnk
-rw-r--r--   1 nwells    users       298 Aug 19 12:04 URL.kdelnk
-rw-r--r--   1 nwells    users       364 Aug 19 12:04 WWWUrl.kdelnk
```

These templates are actually links similar to a Linux symbolic link. Each contains information to guide KDE in displaying and operating on that desktop item.

Looking at the first part of the content for one of the template links, `Program.kdelnk`, you can see that items such as name, icon, program to execute, and so forth, are specified as properties of this template item.

```
$ more Program.kdelnk
# KDE Config File
[KDE Desktop Entry]
Type=Application
Exec=
Icon=exec.xpm
TerminalOptions=
Path=
Terminal=0
Comment[fr]=Application
Comment[pt]=Aplicacão
Comment[pt_BR]=Aplicacão
...
```

When you create new desktop items, you can edit the properties of these links using graphical dialog boxes provided by KDE using right-click pop-up menus or standard menus in file-browsing windows.

The Trash Bin Folder

As with other advanced graphical environments, KDE provides a Trash bin where you can drag file icons when you don't want the file any longer. Files are stored in the Trash subdirectory until you empty the Trash bin, using a desktop menu. At that time, the items are deleted from your Linux system.

The particular benefit of a Trash bin on a UNIX-based system is that deleting files is permanent. No Undelete feature is included as part of standard Linux or UNIX. The Trash bin lets you move unwanted files out of your way, but save them for a while in case you need to retrieve them.

You can place files in the Trash bin by dragging them from other file browsing windows and dropping them on the Trash icon on the KDE Desktop. Details of this are provided in Hour 9, "Managing Files in KDE."

As with the Autostart folder, you can view the contents of the Trash folder (files that you have dragged and dropped in the Trash) by clicking on the Trash icon. This opens a window from which you can drag files back to your main file system areas if needed.

Also, as with the Templates and Autostart subdirectories, the Trash subdirectory includes a `.directory` file that includes properties and localized (multilingual) messages for this desktop item.

Placing Other Items on the KDE Desktop

When you place other items on the KDE Desktop using the procedures given in Hour 10, most of the items will be links to other files. Thus, each desktop item will take very little space in the Desktop subdirectory of your home directory. The exceptions are when you drag files to the Trash bin. Those files are stored in the Trash subdirectory, and will use space in your home directory until you empty the Trash bin to delete the files permanently.

Other Notes on KDE Setup

The KDE packages described in Hour 2 install all their files in `/opt/kde` and its subdirectories. Installation on specific Linux distributions might place a file or two in other locations. For example, Caldera OpenLinux includes the `kdeinitrc` file in the `/etc/X11/xinit` directory, and Red Hat Linux includes some additional KDE documentation in the `/usr/doc/packages/kde` directory.

Certain environment variables are also set up to help KDE function correctly.

The `KDEDIR` environment variable is used to point to the KDE directories located at `/opt/kde`.

This variable is defined by Caldera OpenLinux in the `/etc/profile` startup script; you should add it to other Linux distributions' startup scripts (probably in the `/etc/profile` script) after installing KDE.

The KDE directory, `/opt/kde`, and the KDE binary directory, `/opt/kde/bin`, should also be added to the `PATH` variable in the `/etc/profile` script, or in a local copy of a user's login scripts. Again, this is part of the OpenLinux default installation, but must be added to other Linux systems when you install KDE.

Summary

In this hour you learned about the subdirectories used by KDE, both for the complete KDE installation, and for each user running KDE. You explored the KDE subdirectories in each user's home directory and learned how KDE uses configuration files—especially `kdelnk` files—to define and manage information. You learned about the Desktop

4

directory and how KDE stores information in subdirectories such as Trash and Autostart. The next hour explores the graphical KDE Desktop in more detail, including the taskbar, Panel, and main menu.

Questions and Answers

Q Do I have to explore all these text configuration files to use KDE?

A Not at all. I'm showing the content of these files to provide a good technical foundation for understanding how KDE operates. If that's not something that interests you, you certainly don't need to know it to use KDE. In fact, even creating new MIME types, adding items to menus, and performing other configuration details can be done from a graphical dialog box. That's part of the power of KDE.

Q Many of the files mentioned here don't show up when I list the files on my system. Why not?

A First, be sure to use the `ls` command with the `-a` option to show all files, including hidden files (many KDE configuration files described here are hidden files). In addition, the KDE installation you're working with might be located in a different directory. Although `/opt/kde` is the standard location, KDE can be installed in a different directory. Ask you system administrator for help or search through your file system for some of the files named in this hour to see where KDE is stored.

Q Can I make the Trash folder really delete files instead of just moving them to the Trash folder to await emptying?

A No, this configuration option isn't provided. The Trash folder provides a safety feature for users who aren't accustomed to the *permanent* nature of removing files in Linux. Files can be sent to the Trash, but then retrieved later if needed. You can empty the Trash regularly, reviewing the files as needed, to see if anything should be retained.

Exercises

1. Starting with a file in the `mimelnk` directory or the `MimeLnk.kdelnk` file in the Templates directory, define a new MIME type for KDE to use with one of the file types that you use on your system (such as a word processor or compression format). How many similar formats does KDE include by default? How can you test this MIME type to see that KDE recognizes it?

2. Later hours describe how to use `kdelnk` files to update the Panel and main menu. See if you can add an item to the Personal submenu of the main menu by creating a `kdelnk` file for an application on your Linux system and adding it to the appropriate KDE subdirectory.

PART II

Customizing Your KDE Settings

Hour

5   Exploring the Desktop

6   Managing the KDE Environment

7   Configuring KDE Options

8   Using KDE Themes

9   Managing Files in KDE

10   Learning More KDE File Management

HOUR 5

Exploring the Desktop

In this hour you begin working onscreen with KDE (finally, I can hear you saying). This hour explains the onscreen components, such as the desktop, the Panel, and the taskbar.

You also learn in this hour how to manipulate the KDE windows using the standard window dressing and commands provided by KDE, and how to move around using the desktop mouse and keyboard commands.

The views of KDE that you see in this hour are taken from Caldera OpenLinux, which installs KDE by default. The icon settings and location of the Panel and taskbar described in this hour might be different if you installed KDE on a different vendor's copy of Linux. However, KDE still contains the same features and you shouldn't have any trouble applying the screens you see here to what you see on your own system.

Reviewing the KDE Environment

When you start KDE, you see a full graphical screen that looks similar to Windows 98, a NeXT, or other full-featured graphical desktops. This initial KDE screen is shown in Figure 5.1.

FIGURE 5.1

The initial KDE screen as it appears after installation.

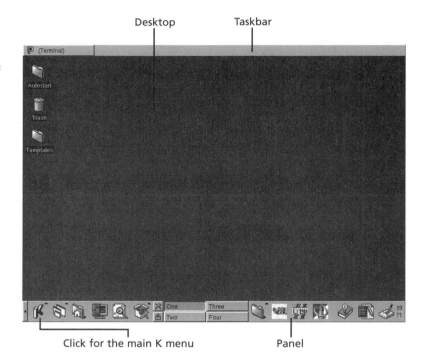

The components of this initial screen are described in the sections that follow.

The Taskbar

The KDE taskbar is located across the top of the screen. The taskbar shows a button for each of the applications that you start in KDE. As you work with multiple applications, you can always click on a button in the taskbar to switch to the application named on that button.

As you start more applications, the buttons get smaller (and harder to decipher because the amount of text on each button diminishes). If you open enough applications, the taskbar expands to two lines of buttons.

If you have used Microsoft Windows 95, the taskbar is like the list of open windows and applications that appears along the bottom of the screen, to the right of the Windows Start menu.

The taskbar is always visible, and it always contains the same applications (that is, the items on the taskbar don't change as you switch to different desktops). As you learn about using multiple desktops in KDE, keep in mind that the taskbar always shows all the open applications, not just the applications on the desktop that you're viewing.

Pause on that thought: The taskbar shows all open applications. Actually, the taskbar shows all the windows that you've opened in KDE. Now, most of those will be applications, such as a game, a utility, a copy of StarOffice or ApplixWare, and so forth.

But when you open a terminal window, the taskbar doesn't keep track of what you do in the terminal window. If you start a graphical program from a command line, that application will appear as another item in the taskbar because it opened a new window in KDE.

If you start a character-based program that opens its own terminal window, that window will be added to the taskbar. But you can also start multiple programs from a single command line without opening additional windows. None of those programs will appear in the taskbar.

The bottom line is this: The taskbar doesn't show everything that's happening for your user account. To see more about what's happening, you can use the ps command in a terminal window. The ps command shows you all the programs that are running with your user ID. It's a little cryptic, but Figure 5.2 shows what the output of the ps command might look like:

FIGURE 5.2

Use the ps *command to show all programs running with your user ID; use the taskbar to move between open windows.*

The important part of the ps command is the far right column, which shows the name of all running programs. The left column, labeled PID, shows the process ID for each program.

If you hide the Panel (as described later in this section), three other options are added to the taskbar. These are a mini-K menu icon, the Disk Navigator, and a window list drop-down menu (similar to the taskbar itself in content). The section on the Panel provides a description of the K main menu and the window list. The Disk Navigator is described in Hour 9, "Managing Files in KDE." The taskbar, with these icons showing, appears in Figure 5.3.

FIGURE 5.3

When you hide the Panel, the K main menu, the Disk Navigator, and the Window list are accessible from icons on the taskbar.

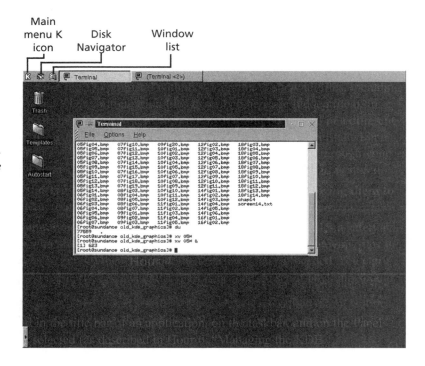

Main menu K icon   Disk Navigator   Window list

The taskbar appears at the bottom of the screen in some Linux installations. You'll learn how to place it wherever you choose in Hour 6, "Managing the KDE Environment."

The Desktop

The desktop is the background on which things happen in KDE. Applications appear, program icons are stored, and your favorite pictures are displayed (more on that later).

Only two things really need to be said about the desktop at this point.

First, you can place items on the desktop so that they are immediately available to you. This is similar to the desktop or background in the Macintosh Finder, in Microsoft Windows 98, or in many other UNIX desktops. The Desktop subdirectory in your home directory (described in Hour 4, "Reviewing the KDE Setup," contains the links that appear on your desktop when you start KDE. You'll learn how to place items on the desktop in Hour 10, "Learning More KDE File Management."

Second, the desktop background, which appears in shaded blue by default (on the first desktop of the OpenLinux installation of KDE), can be changed to whatever you'd like. This is just like the wallpaper on a Windows system, except you can have multiple desktops, each with a different wallpaper and switch between them instantly. Wallpaper is part of a KDE Theme, or graphical look, which is the subject of Hour 8, "Using KDE Themes."

 The concept of multiple desktops is described later in this hour.

The three items on the default KDE Desktop include:

- *Trash.* You can drag unwanted items from the file browser (described in detail in Hour 9) to the Trash icon. If you want to permanently delete them from your Linux file system (freeing the space they occupied), you can right-click the Trash icon and choose Empty Trash bin from the pop-up menu.

  If you click on the Trash icon, a file browser window appears where you see any files that you've dragged to the Trash bin.

- *Templates.* Contains samples of the links that you can put on your KDE Desktop. You'll learn more about the Templates as you create desktop items in Hour 10.

- *Autostart.* Contains programs that KDE starts automatically when you launch KDE. You can place links to programs in this folder to have them launched at start-up. Hour 10 provides more details. Click on the Autostart icon to display the contents of the Autostart folder, showing which files will be auto-started.

These three desktop items are subdirectories in the ~/Desktop directory, as described in Hour 4.

You can right-click your mouse on the background of the desktop to use a pop-up menu that includes limited functionality such as Logout and Arrange icons.

5

The Panel

The Panel is a toolbar of applications, utilities, and tools; you can access any of these immediately by clicking one of the icons on the Panel. The KDE Panel is similar to the Dock in the old NeXT system, or many similar utilities available on other Linux systems.

Using the Panel is also similar to placing icons on your desktop for quick access to a program, but the Panel always sits on top of other windows, so you can always access the icons on it.

Some of the items on the Panel are system management tools rather than applications. Those receive special attention in this section. Several of the Panel icons have a small arrow in the upper-right corner. This indicates that you can click the icon to see multiple options.

A pop-up description appears next to each Panel icon if you place your mouse over the icon for several seconds. (These help tools are described later in this hour.)

Because the applications that appear on the Panel are specific to each Linux distribution, and you can change them yourself if you choose, I'll only describe some key system management tools and special icons as they appear on the Panel from left to right.

> The Panel is the part of the KDE configuration that is most likely to differ between Linux distributions. Each vendor chooses which applications and utilities should be on their installation of the KDE Panel.

- The *Hide/Show button* is a narrow arrow on both the far left and far right edges of the Panel. If the Panel is taking up too much screen real estate, you can choose either button to hide the Panel. When you do so, the K main menu, Disk Navigator, and Window list icons are added to the taskbar as described previously.

  You can't get rid of the Hide/Show arrow unless you kill the kpanel application, which also closes the taskbar. This purist approach leaves you with only the right-click menu to navigate on a practically blank screen.

- The *K icon* brings up the main menu for KDE. The next section describes this menu in more detail.

- The *Window List icon* pops open to show a list of the desktops and open windows on those desktops. You can use this list like the taskbar to switch to any open window (see Figure 5.4). Multiple desktops are described later in this hour.

- The *Home Directory icon* opens a file browser showing the contents of your home directory.

FIGURE 5.4

The Window List icon displays a list of desktops and the open windows on each desktop. Selecting an item switches to that window.

- The *Control Center icon* opens the KDE Control Center, which is used for most of the KDE configuration covered in later hours. You can also open the Control Center from the K menu.

Figure 5.5 shows the Home Directory and Control Center icons.

Control
Center

FIGURE 5.5

The Home Directory icon opens your home directory in a file browser. The KDE Control Center opens when you choose the Control Center icon.

Home
Directory

5

The middle section of the Panel contains several icons that don't match the style of the others on the Panel. These include

- *Logout button.* Choose this button (see Figure 5.6.) to end this KDE session. A confirmation dialog box prepares you for log out.
- *Screen Lock button.* Choose this button (see Figure 5.6.) to start a blank screen saver, which requires that you enter your Linux password to return to KDE.

FIGURE 5.6

The Logout and Screen Lock actions are provided as Panel buttons and also on the K menu.

Switch Desktop buttons

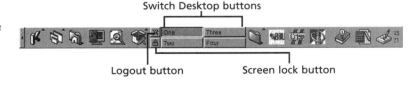

Logout button   Screen lock button

Although the screen lock feature is handy, you can still press the Ctrl+Alt+Backspace keys to completely exit X and return to a Linux command line (still logged in with your user ID).

- *Desktop buttons.* By default, KDE starts with four desktops. These are described later in this hour. You can switch between these different desktops by clicking on one of these buttons (or selecting it from the Window list icon's pop-up menu).

The Main K Menu

All the features and tools of KDE are consolidated into the main menu, which you access by clicking the K icon (see Figure 5.7.) Because the hours that follow explore virtually all the options on the K menu, no further details are given at this point.

FIGURE 5.7

The main menu is accessed by clicking on the K icon in the Panel (or in the taskbar if the Panel is hidden).

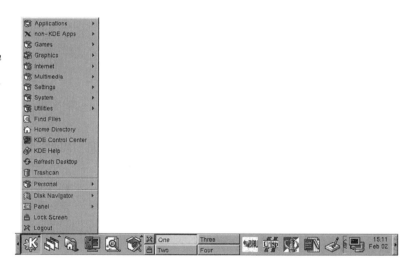

Most of the items on the main menu have submenus of options. These options are actually programs that are started by the kpanel program when you select a menu item.

The items included on the main menu can be configured as you choose. Hour 9 describes how to alter the menu items.

Using the KDE Online and Pop-up Help

KDE includes hundreds of pages of online help that you can quickly access when you have a question about how to do something in KDE. In addition to traditional online help that you can view in a default Help Browser, KDE provides pop-up hints for menu items, icons, and dialog boxes to show you what an item is used for.

You can access the KDE online help by choosing KDE Help from the main menu or by choosing Help on Desktop from the pop-up menu when you right-click on the background of the desktop. The main Help screen is shown in Figure 5.8.

FIGURE 5.8

The KDE online help is displayed in a simple Web browser.

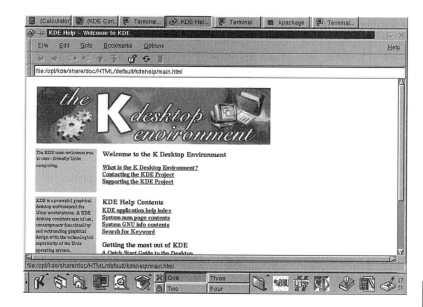

The KDE online help is viewed in a simple Web browser. You can choose any link to jump to another topic in the help. Although the help is extensive, no searching capabilities or index is provided.

Using KDE Pop-up Help

By default, small yellow pop-up messages describe most items on the KDE screen when you leave your mouse pointer sitting on an item for a few seconds (see Figure 5.9).

FIGURE 5.9

Pop-up messages tell you the purpose of an item when you leave your mouse pointer over it.

5

Using Help Buttons

Most of the applications that are part of the default KDE installation include online help that can be accessed via help buttons in dialog boxes. For example, Figure 5.10 shows the Background tab of the Display Settings dialog box, where you can see a Help button in the lower-left corner.

FIGURE 5.10

Most KDE applications include help buttons that provide context-sensitive online help.

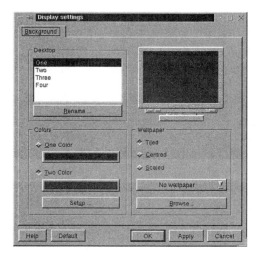

When you choose a help button, the help viewing program kdehelp is launched, and the relevant portion of the help file is displayed.

As in other operating systems, the online help provided in KDE is application-dependent. Although KDE includes the mechanisms to integrate online help with the user interface, you will find different levels of compliance; some KDE applications provide little or no online help, especially applications that are still under development. Also, non-KDE applications (see Hour 22, "Integrating non-KDE Applications into KDE") won't use the KDE help system, though they might have their own online help mechanism.

Learning to Manipulate KDE Windows

The flexibility that Linux provides can also be a challenge at times; every new project can create its own way of doing things. Fortunately, KDE follows some fairly standard conventions in how graphical windows are manipulated.

This section describes how to work with the standard windows as they are configured in Caldera OpenLinux. Most of the operations will be very familiar to you if you've worked with any other graphical system, including Microsoft Windows 98.

That said, you can alter most of the window features that are described in this section. Later hours describe how to move the placement of window dressing items and how to add new items or remove items altogether from the window controls.

Using Standard Window Tools

Figure 5.11 shows the top line of a standard KDE window. Identify these components on the figure so the descriptions that follow make sense:

FIGURE 5.11

The title bar and window controls shown here are standard for all KDE windows. But you can change how and where they appear.

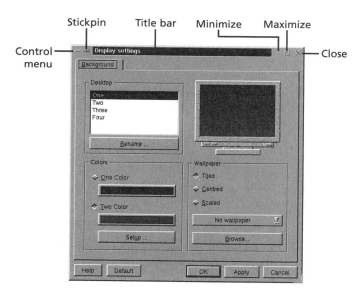

Stickpin   Title bar   Minimize   Maximize

Control — menu

Close

• The *Control menu*, on the far upper-left corner of a window, provides a pull-down menu of window control options (described later in this hour).

• The *Stickpin* button sticks this window to the root background, so that the window appears in all your KDE Desktops, rather than remaining on one desktop.

• The *Title bar* displays the title assigned to this window.

• The *Minimize* and *Maximize* buttons change the size of the window.

• The *Close* button closes the window (and the application, if this is the application's main window).

Table 5.1 describes how to perform common window operations using these controls and the mouse.

5

TABLE 5.1   WINDOW CONTROL OPERATIONS

Operation	How to Do It
Move the window to a new location onscreen	Click on the title bar and drag the window
Activate a window (so keyboard input goes to that window)	Click on the title bar or any border of the window
Show the window Control menu	Right-click on the title bar or press Alt+F3
Resize the window	Move the mouse pointer to the lower-right corner of the window; when the pointer changes to a corner-arrow, click and drag to resize
Maximize the window so it fills the available screen space	Double-click on the title bar or choose the Maximize button
Restore the window to the size it was before being maximized	Double-click on the title bar again or choose the Maximize button again
Minimize the window so it only appears as an item on the taskbar	Choose the Minimize button
Make the window *stick to the glass* of your monitor, always appearing on top of other windows	Choose the Stickpin button
Close a window	Choose the Close button or double-click the Control Menu button

Keyboard Control of Windows

The Control menu (see Figure 5.12) can be used to perform basic window manipulation tasks using the keyboard or mouse.

If you prefer not to use the mouse to click on the Control Menu button (a dash on the far left of the title bar), you can access the control menu from your keyboard by pressing Alt+F3. Use the up and down arrow keys to select an item on the menu. Some notes on these items are provided here:

- When you have maximized a window, the *Maximize* option changes to Restore, which changes the window back to the size it was before being maximized.
- *Iconify* is the same as *Minimize*, hiding the window so it only appears on the taskbar.

- Choosing *Move* or *Resize* activates the window so you can use the arrow keys to move or resize the window. When you have finished using the arrow keys, press Enter to deactivate the Move or Resize mode.
- *Sticky* selects the Stickpin icon, so the window appears on all your KDE Desktops.
- Choosing an item from the *To Desktop* submenu sends the window to that desktop (see Hour 6).

FIGURE 5.12

The Control menu includes the standard window movement options. It can be accessed with mouse or keyboard.

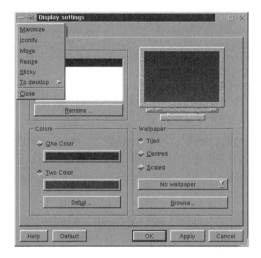

Using the Keyboard in KDE

Although KDE provides a great graphical environment for Linux, many users prefer having keyboard access to functionality. KDE provides many keyboard shortcuts.

- Arrow keys can be used to select menu items from open menus and submenus.
- Alt+Tab and Alt+Shift+Tab switch between open windows listed on the taskbar that are located in the current desktop. (This is similar to using Alt+Tab in Microsoft Windows).
- Pressing F1 calls up online help for the current window.
- Pressing Tab repeatedly scrolls through the buttons and other items in most dialog boxes. After the item you want has focus, you can press the Spacebar to select it, or select Enter to choose it.

In addition to these basic keyboard shortcuts for graphical environments, KDE also provides the shortcuts listed in Table 5.2.

TABLE 5.2 KEYBOARD SHORTCUTS IN KDE

Key Combination	Action
Alt+F1	Opens the K menu on the Panel
Alt+F2	Opens a mini-command line where you can execute any Linux command
Alt+F3	Opens the window control menu (described later in this hour)
Alt+F4	Closes the current window
Alt+Esc	Displays a dialog box with the window list, where you can select a window to switch to.
Ctrl+F1 to Ctrl+F4	Changes to desktop 1–4.

In addition to these shortcuts that you can use throughout KDE, most KDE applications use keyboard shortcuts to access menus items and dialog box options. Underlined letters indicate that you can hold the Alt key plus that letter to choose that item. Menu accelerator keys indicate a control key combination you can use to select an item without opening the menu.

For example, reviewing the KDE Help window shown in Figure 5.13, the following keyboard shortcuts apply:

FIGURE 5.13

Keyboard shortcuts can be used in most applications.

- Press Alt+F to open the File menu. (The letter F is underlined.)
- Use the arrow keys or press P to choose Print from the File menu.
- Without opening the File menu, press Ctrl+P to open the Print dialog box.

Using Multiple Desktops

A desktop in KDE contains icons, open application windows, and usually a background image of some type. KDE lets you have multiple desktops to help you arrange your working space.

Each desktop can be viewed separately, so that all the applications you opened in that desktop stay there. You can switch to a different desktop to open another set of applications, and then switch to the first set of applications and find them arranged and sized just as you left them.

Experimenting with multiple desktops and the arrangement of the applications that you commonly use will help you get the most productive use out of your KDE environment.

Caldera OpenLinux, described here, uses four desktops by default. Each of these desktops uses a different background (wallpaper) to help you tell instantly which desktop you're viewing. You'll learn in the coming hours how to change all these settings.

Switching Between Desktops

You can switch between desktops in KDE in several ways. All the places in this hour where the Window list was mentioned also list the desktops; you can select a desktop from the Window list to change to it.

To switch the current view to another desktop, you can

- Click the button for the new desktop on the Panel.
- Select a desktop by name from the Window list icon pop-up menu on the Panel.
- Press Ctrl+F2 for Desktop Two, Ctrl+F3 for Desktop Three, and so on. (If you change the names of the desktops, you'll have to remember what their number was to use this option.)

Renaming Desktops

The default desktop names of one, two, three and four are a good start. But if you're like me, you define one desktop for email reading windows, another for development, another for a word processor. You can name the desktops as Mail, Development, Writing, and Web so that those names appear in the Window list for you to select.

To change the names of desktops, follow these steps:

1. On the main menu, choose Settings, Applications, Panel.

2. In the KPanel configuration tool, choose the desktops tab (see Figure 5.14).

FIGURE 5.14

The Panel Configuration tool lets you rename desktops and increase or decrease the number of desktops.

3. Enter new names in each of the Desktop Name fields, where you see *one*, *two*, and so on.

 If you want to use more or less than the default four desktops, move the Visible slider below the names of the desktops. More Desktop Name fields are activated. When you close the dialog box, the additional desktops will appear.

Summary

This hour describes the key features of the KDE Desktop, including the main menu, taskbar, and Panel. You learned how to access each of these items. You also learned how to manipulate windows in KDE using the standard window controls, and how to access most of these features using the keyboard rather than the mouse. In the next hour, you learn more about the KDE Desktop, including details about how to configure the desktop items, such as the location of the taskbar and size of the Panel.

Questions and Answers

Q **Can I configure my KDE Desktop and windows to look like other graphical systems?**

A Yes, sort of. You can change KDE to use Windows 95 or Motif-style windows; you can place the Panel and taskbar in different locations; you can even emulate a Macintosh in many ways. Read the next few hours to see how to choose the options that will give you the look you want. Keep in mind, however, that some systems, such as NeXT or CDE, are only partially matched by a KDE look and feel—at least at this point.

Q **Can I switch between desktops just by moving the mouse to the edge of the screen instead of clicking on a desktop button on the Panel?**

A Yes. This feature is called Active Borders, and is described in Hour 9.

Q **I have so many open windows, I can't read the titles of them on the taskbar. How can I switch to an open window and tell which one I want?**

A First, try placing open windows on different desktops, so you can switch between desktops rather than minimizing all the windows to keep your screen uncluttered. Second, try using Alt+Tab to switch between windows instead of clicking on a taskbar icon. The Alt+Tab pop-up window shows you the full name of each window, making it easier to switch to the one you want. Pressing Alt+Esc displays a list of windows with full titles that you can choose from.

Exercises

1. Not all the buttons on the Panel are described in this hour because they vary depending on your Linux distribution and KDE installation. Explore the buttons on your Panel to see what application each one starts. Think about which ones you would add or remove. You'll learn how to do that later.

2. Explore the options on the Settings, Application menu to see if you can turn off the yellow pop-up hints that appear when you leave your mouse over a Panel or main menu item.

HOUR 6

Managing the KDE Environment

In this hour you continue to explore the desktop, but also work with applications—moving windows between desktops, switching between tasks, and so forth. You learn in this hour how to configure the basic appearance of your KDE environment, including where the Panel and taskbar appear, how windows operate, and similar options.

Working with Application Windows

Several later hours describe in detail how to use applications in KDE, both those that are included by default in KDE and those that you add to your system (both KDE and non-KDE applications).

Before then, however, you'll probably want to know how to work with the windows that fill your screen as you explore the KDE Desktop, configuration options, and start your own applications. In general, KDE uses standard graphical operations such as a Macintosh, Microsoft Windows, or other UNIX system based on the X Window System. Because all these systems are slightly different, however, and I can't know which one you use or prefer, the following sections define some common windowing operations in KDE. Later sections in this hour also describe how to configure the windows in KDE to suite your preferences.

> The windows in KDE are all controlled by the kwm program (the K window manager). If you're familiar with the setup on other Linux systems, the kwm program is similar to other window managers such as twm, fvwm, and so forth. KDE includes a lot of other integrated applications that start by default when kwm starts.

Switching Between Windows

Linux is a powerful multitasking operating system. If you're like me, you often have half a dozen open applications, many of which are working in the background as you type a letter, read email, or review a Web page.

When you have several application windows open, you can use several methods in KDE to switch between those windows.

The easiest might be to click on the title bar of the window you want to work in. This activates the window, brings it to the top (so it's visible), and directs all keystrokes to that window.

You can also use the Alt+Tab key combination to rotate between open windows. Hold down the Alt key and press Tab or Shift+Tab repeatedly to see a pop-up window listing open windows. (Alt+Shift+Tab scrolls through the window list in reverse.) When the title of the window you want to use is displayed, release all the keys (see Figure 6.1).

FIGURE 6.1

Using the Alt+Tab or Alt+Shift+Tab key combinations switches between open windows.

The Alt+Tab key combinations only rotate between open windows on the current desktop. To see applications on another desktop, change to that desktop, and then try the Alt+Tab keys again. The taskbar, however, displays windows from all desktops.

When you use the Panel buttons, Ctrl+*<function key>* combinations (F1 through F4, depending on which desktop the user is currently in), or the Window list to switch between desktops, the most recently visited application on that desktop becomes active.

You can also use the mouse to interact with windows via their title bars.

Clicking on the title bar of a window makes that window active and *raises* it (makes it fully visible on top of other windows on that desktop). Other mouse functions related to activating windows are as follows:

- Right-click the title bar to activate the window without raising it above other windows (leave it where it is).

Keystrokes that you type will always go to the active window, even if it's covered by other windows.

- Middle-click on the title bar (or click both mouse buttons, if you're using three-button emulation on a two-button mouse) to activate the window and *lower* it so that all other windows are on top of it.
- Hold down the Alt key and click anywhere in a window to move the window.
- Hold down the Alt key and right-click anywhere in a window to resize the window (as if dragged from the corner closest to the mouse pointer).

6

Using the Alt+click and Alt+right-click combinations is a big help when a window's edges are outside of the screen borders and you can't grab the title bar or corners to move and resize it.

Several of the features described here can be configured differently. The section "Defining Window Policies," later in this hour describes how to set configuration options for KDE windows.

Moving Applications Between Desktops

As you begin to work more with multiple desktops in KDE, you'll probably define different desktops for different parts of your work, for example, one for an email reader, one with several terminal windows, one for an office suite or word processor, and so on.

When you start an application, you might need to move it to another desktop, depending on how you're trying to arrange your workspace.

Some applications are composed of many different windows.

You can easily move any window to another desktop by opening the window control menu (with the mouse or by pressing Alt+F3). Then choose the To Desktop item. A submenu appears where you can select which desktop to move the window to (see Figure 6.2).

FIGURE 6.2

The To Desktop submenu of the window Control menu lets you move any window to any of the KDE Desktops.

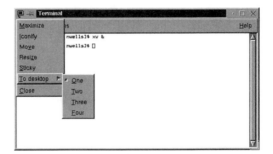

You can change the names of the desktops shown on the To Desktop submenu. This procedure is described later in this hour and also in Hour 5, "Exploring the Desktop."

Introducing the KDE Control Center

The KDE Control Center is a collection of configuration tools for KDE and for certain other applications. The KDE Control Center provides a convenient place to access many different configuration options, but it actually launches different configuration utilities, depending on which options you select.

The same options that you configure in the KDE Control Center can also be selected and configured by running the individual configuration tool, either from a command line or from the main menu. You'll see an example of this in the next section.

You can start the KDE Control Center either by choosing KDE Control Center on the main menu or by choosing the KDE Control Center icon on the Panel. The Control Center initial screen is shown in Figure 6.3.

FIGURE 6.3

The initial screen of the KDE Control Center displays basic information about your computer system.

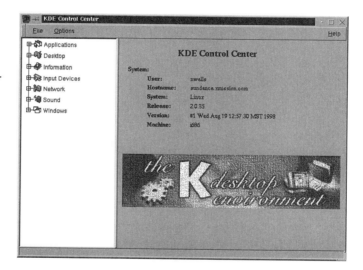

Setting Panel and Taskbar Options

Because the Panel and taskbar are the parts of the desktop that you'll work with constantly, you should place them where it makes the most sense for you.

KDE provides several configuration options for how the Panel and taskbar are displayed. Some of these options relate to the main menu as well. I'll describe these here, although further configuration of the main menu will be described in Hour 7, "Configuring KDE Options."

The Panel and taskbar are both part of a single KDE application called kpanel. You can see this process running if you use the ps command from a terminal window.

6

To start configuring the Panel and taskbar, open the kpanel configuration tool using either of these methods:

- Choose Settings, Applications, Panel from the main menu.
- Open the KDE Control Center. Open the Applications list by clicking the plus sign, and then choose Panel. The configuration options appear in the right side of the Control Center.
- Enter the command kcmkpanel from a terminal window.

Setting the Location of the Taskbar and Panel

The KPanel Configuration dialog box, shown in Figure 6.4, shows the dialog as started from the Settings menu or from the command line, not within the Control Center. The operation of the dialog box is identical in the Control Center.

FIGURE 6.4

The KPanel Configuration dialog box presents three tabs with options to set up the kpanel application.

In the Panel tab, you can set the location and style of the Panel and taskbar. The Location field refers to the location of the Panel. It can be on the top, left, or bottom of your KDE screen.

The Taskbar field refers to the location of the taskbar. You can place the taskbar on the top, bottom, or top left corner of your screen. Or you can hide the taskbar completely. Hiding the taskbar frees up more room on your screen for your applications. If you hide the taskbar, however, you'll have to use the Alt+Tab key combination or the Window list icon on the Panel to switch between open applications. A better idea for most users is to choose the Auto Hide Taskbar option, described later in this hour.

The Top Left corner option for the taskbar is shown in Figure 6.5.

FIGURE 6.5

The taskbar can be positioned as a list of buttons in the top left corner of the KDE screen.

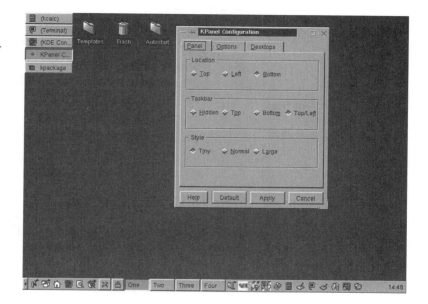

Setting the Panel Size

The Panel can be set to tiny, normal, or large size using the Style field of the Panel tab (still in the KPanel Configuration dialog box).

The Tiny option uses smaller icons for items on the Panel and spreads out the desktop buttons so the Panel is not as tall. The Tiny style is a good way to free up some desktop real estate for your applications. Another benefit of the Tiny option (shown in Figure 6.6) is that more icons are visible on the Panel, so you can have more items immediately available there.

The Normal and Large styles both use the same size icons, but the Large option places them in a larger box, so the Panel is taller and fewer icons fit across the screen, but the icons might be easier to see. The Large style might be best if you're using a 1600×1200 screen resolution and want to be able to see the Panel icons a better.

6

FIGURE 6.6

The Panel provides a Tiny option to use smaller icons, giving more desktop space for applications and more horizontal space for Panel icons.

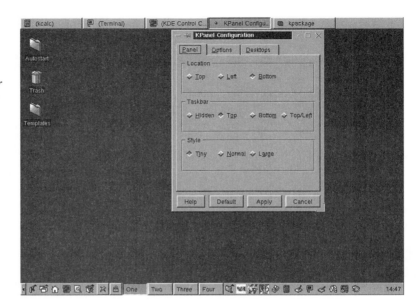

Setting Other Panel and Taskbar Options

The Options tab of the KPanel Configuration dialog box (shown in Figure 6.7) lets you select some additional features for the Panel and taskbar.

FIGURE 6.7

The Options tab controls pop-up hints and options to hide the taskbar and Panel.

In the Menu Tooltips field, you uncheck the check box to stop the yellow pop-up hints from appearing next to menu items and Panel icons. These hints are helpful, but can get in the way of reading the menu items, especially after you've become familiar with KDE.

The Delay slider determines how long KDE waits before displaying the pop-up hint (the ToolTip). The default of 1,000 ms (milliseconds) indicates that you must leave your mouse sitting on a menu item or icon for one second before the ToolTip appears.

> The KPanel Configuration dialog box only controls the taskbar and Panel. Other applications (such as StarOffice) will also provide pop-up menus or icon hints, which you can turn on or off separately from those described here.

The Others field provides three useful options:

The Personal First check box changes the arrangement of the main menu so that the items in the Personal submenu are listed first, and the default main menu items appear as a submenu. Figure 6.8 shows how the menus might appear with the Personal First option selected.

FIGURE 6.8

The Personal First option displays your applications first on the main menu.

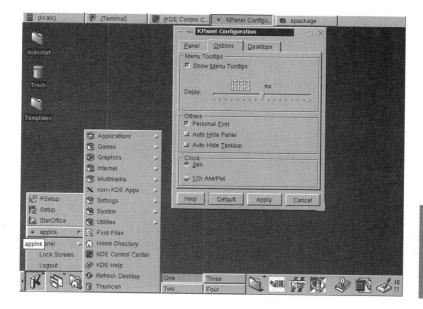

The Personal First check box is a useful option once you have some applications installed that you use frequently and once you know your way around the KDE menus and options.

Don't select the Personal First check box now or the instructions in this book for finding KDE options won't apply.

The Auto Hide Panel and Auto Hide Taskbar are useful options if you're short on screen space or prefer to work on an uncluttered blank screen. When these check boxes are selected, the Panel or taskbar, respectively, changes to a thin line, about five pixels high. To make the Panel or taskbar reappear, move the mouse pointer to that edge of the screen.

Finally, the Clock field allows you to choose between a 12-hour and a 24-hour clock format. The time can be displayed in various places in KDE; this option determines which format it is displayed in.

Clearing Your Desktop

So, what options should you select if you want to work on a clear desktop, rather than the default desktop showing a large Panel and taskbar?

Two good options are as follows:

- Choose Auto Hide Panel and Auto Hide Taskbar in the Options tab.
- On the Panel tab, choose Hidden in the Taskbar field and Tiny in the Style field. After closing the dialog box, choose the Hide arrow on the far left of the Panel. You're left with a tiny square to access the Panel.

As mentioned previously, if you really don't want to see the Panel and taskbar, you can kill the kpanel application from a terminal window. Just be certain you know how to start the applications and tools you need from a command line.

Adding Desktops

Hour 5 describes how to use more than the four default desktops. To review those options, change to the Desktops tab (see Figure 6.9).

The number of desktops used by KDE is controlled by the Visible slider. Move it to the right to add desktops (up to eight). Move it to the left to reduce the number of desktops.

Desktops are added and removed in twos. Each additional desktop will use some memory on your system, depending on what you have displayed on that desktop and how it is configured. Adding complex themes requires more memory. (Themes are described in Hour 8, "Using KDE Themes.").

FIGURE 6.9

The Desktops tab lets you add, remove, and rename the desktops of KDE.

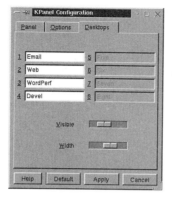

If you have applications on a desktop (such as Desktop Four) and reduce the Visible slider so only two desktops are listed, you won't be able to access the application window on Desktop Four. The application will still be running (check with the ps command), but you can't see the window. To remedy this, return to the KPanel Configuration dialog box and change back to four desktops. The application will be where you left it.

You can click on the name of any active desktop to enter a new name for that desktop. The names are used in the Window lists and on the Panel.

The Width slider determines how wide the desktop labels are on the Panel. Making the width smaller leaves more space for application icons if you have named your desktops *1*, *2*, *3*, and *4*. Making the width larger lets you put names such as *Development* on the buttons and still read them. However, one button can't be wide or narrower than another button.

The Panel always includes buttons for the different desktops you define. But if you hide the Panel, you can switch between desktops using the key combination Ctrl+F1 for the first desktop, Ctrl+F2 for the second desktop, and so forth.

6

Changing How KDE Windows Appear and Operate

All the descriptions thus far in this hour assume that you're using a default installation of KDE on Caldera OpenLinux.

However, KDE allows you to easily change many of the settings described here. This is done by choosing items from the Settings, Windows submenu on the main menu, or by opening the list of Windows options in the Control Center.

The descriptions and figures that follow use the Control Center. This is a little more convenient than the items in the Settings, Windows submenu, which must each be chosen separately instead of working within a single dialog box with multiple tabs.

> Most of what follows in these sections is part of a KDE *Theme*—a collection of definitions that define a *look* for your KDE environment. By installing or selecting a theme, you can alter all the KDE look-and-feel options at the same time. (Themes are described in Hour 8.) This section teaches you how individual components are controlled and what your options are.

Changing Which Buttons Are on the Title Bar

The Buttons item in the Windows list of the Control Center is shown in Figure 6.10.

FIGURE 6.10

The Buttons tab lets you define which buttons are used on all KDE windows.

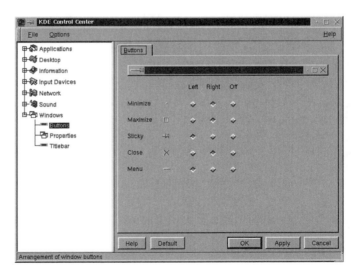

You see in this dialog box a list of the buttons that are on either end of the title bar for any KDE window. A sample title bar is also shown above the list.

Each of these buttons can be moved to a different location on the title bar or turned off completely. This setting applies to all windows for all applications that use the standard window manager—kwm in this case—to create their windows.

Some applications, such as StarOffice for Linux, include their own window-drawing routines, and so do not rely on KDE to create windows for the application. The settings here will have no affect on these applications.

For example, if you prefer a cleaner title bar with only a Close button on the left side of the title bar, select Off for all buttons except Close. Select Left for Close, and then choose the Apply button below the list. The resulting window will appear, as in Figure 6.11.

FIGURE 6.11

Buttons included on the title bar of each window can be reconfigured as needed.

If you remove some or all of the buttons on the title bar, you can still access the window Control menu by right-clicking your mouse on a window's title bar. All the control options remain on the pop-up menu; none are removed by selecting items in the Buttons tab.

Defining a New Title Bar

The next window item to explore is how the title bar of each window is defined. Choose Titlebar in the Windows list of the Control Center (see Figure 6.12).

The Titlebar Appearance field is the most straightforward of the options shown. The title bar for your windows can be shaded vertically or horizontally; it can be plain (using the selected color scheme), or it can be a *pixmap* (a graphic image).

If you select the Pixmap option, the Pixmap field becomes active. You should define a pixmap for the title bar when the window is active and another for when the window is inactive.

6

To select a pixmap, click on the empty button next to Active Pixmap or Inactive Pixmap. A file-browsing window opens where you can select a file (in xpm format) to use as the pixmap for the title bar. The image file that you select in this dialog box is used as the pixmap for the title bar. A few samples are included in the directory /opt/kde/share/apps/kwm/pics (or a similar path, depending on where KDE is installed on your system), as shown in Figure 6.13.

FIGURE 6.12

The Titlebar dialog box lets you define how title bars appear on all KDE windows.

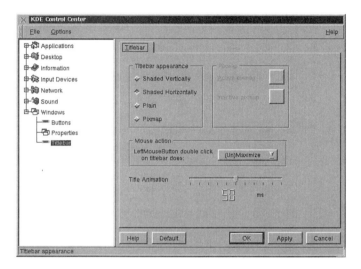

FIGURE 6.13

You can select any xpm format image as the title bar. Be sure the title is still readable through the graphic!

The Mouse Action field defines what will appear when you double-click your mouse button on the title bar of a window. By default, the window will be maximized, and then restored if you double-click again on the title bar.

The drop-down list provides nine choices from which you can select what you'd like to happen.

> One useful option in the Mouse Action field is the (Un)Shade option. This option causes double-clicking on the title bar to roll up the window like a window shade, so that only its title bar is visible. The window is restored (reopened) when you double-click again on the title bar.

You probably don't need to change the Mouse Action field.

Finally, the Title Animation field defines how quickly the window title in the title bar scrolls back and forth when the window is too small to display the entire title at once.

If you choose a higher number on the slider, the title will race back and forth. If you choose a lower number, the title crawls. You can even choose *0* to prevent the animation altogether. This means, however, that you can't read the full title on some windows.

Defining Window Policies

The Properties item on the Windows list of the Control Center defines several options for how windows interact with users. In particular, these options define how windows receive focus.

If you haven't worked with other Linux or UNIX systems, these options might seem strange to you. But if you're accustomed to working on another Linux or UNIX system, you'll be happy to know you can probably configure KDE to behave like your old, familiar system.

The Properties options, which are displayed in the Windows tab, are shown in Figure 6.14.

FIGURE 6.14

The Windows tab displays options for setting up the properties of KDE windows.

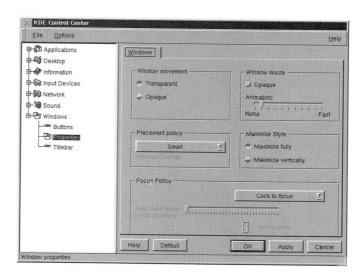

6

The Window Movement field allows you to define how windows are displayed as they are moved. If you select Transparent, the window's new location is shown as an outline during the move.

If you select Opaque, the entire window moves as you drag it, with all its contents remaining visible during the move.

> Using Opaque window moves gives an impressive display of graphical computing power, but you might find that computing power better used in other ways. Redrawing windows during moves will draw CPU cycles from other running programs.

The Window Resize field is similar to the Window Movement field; it provides for Opaque window resizing, where you can see how the contents of the window change as you drag the mouse to resize it.

The Animation slider determines the speed of redrawing as you resize windows. Faster animation (moving the slider further to the right) will make the resize operation look nicer, but will use more CPU cycles to resize the window.

> As with moving windows, be careful about using the Opaque option to resize windows if you're worried about drawing CPU cycles from other programs (or users) running on your system.

The Maximize Style field determines how windows will be redrawn when you choose the Maximize button on a window's title bar (or in a window's Control menu).

Windows can be maximized fully, (in both directions, filling all available screen space), or vertically (expanding vertically to the top and bottom of the screen, but not expanding sideways).

Using the Maximize Vertically option is helpful when you work with text-based programs (terminal windows, text editors, and Web browsers). In these programs, you often want to see the longest block of text possible, but you don't want to make the window any wider than necessary because the margins of your document don't extend that far.

The Placement Policy area defines where new windows are placed onscreen as they are opened. For example, when you choose KDE Help from the main menu, KDE must determine where to place the KDE Help window. This field selects how the location is determined. The default policy is Smart. This means that KDE opens the window and places it where it chooses.

The other options display an outline of the new window. As you move the mouse, the outline moves. You click the mouse button to *drop* the window so that it is completely displayed.

> You can also use the arrow keys to move the window outline if you're not using Smart window placement. Press Enter when the window is placed where you'd like it.

The Focus Policy provides users of other Linux or UNIX systems with some options they might already be accustomed to. First, I'll define a couple of terms: The *focus* is another way to say *the active window*. When a window receives focus, it becomes the active window, so that keystrokes are sent to that window.

To *raise* a window is to bring it to the top of the pile of windows on the desktop, so that the window is fully visible—none of it is obscured by other windows. Note that a window can have focus but not be on top of other windows. Keystrokes might appear in the window that has focus, even though part (or most) of the window is covered by other windows.

For your purposes here, assume that the two relevant options from the drop-down list in the Focus Policy field are Click to Focus or Classic Focus Follows Mouse.

> The operation of the Classic Sloppy Focus allows focus to change to the background (preventing further typing in the active window) if the mouse pointer drifted out of the current window into the background. KDE doesn't use the sloppy part of this (focus remains with the window if the mouse moves to the background), thus the Classic Focus Follows Mouse choice is basically equivalent.

6

The default setting, Click to Focus, activates a window when you click on the window's title bar. At that time, the window is also raised. This is familiar to users of Macintosh or MS Windows systems.

If you select Classic Focus Follows Mouse, the active window is changed to whichever window the mouse pointer is sitting in. This makes it easier to move between multiple terminal windows, for example, entering different commands or clicking browser links, without moving up to the title bar of each window to activate it.

Although a window can have focus (be active) without being raised, you probably want to raise a window to the top of the desktop if you're going to continue working in it. The Auto Raise Delay slider will automatically raise a window after a specified delay.

- If you set the delay to a low value, the windows on your desktop will immediately raise as you move your mouse around the screen.
- If you choose a higher value (up to 3,000 milliseconds, or 3 seconds), you can work in a window by moving your mouse over it, but the window will not raise for up to 3 seconds. This option is useful if you want to jump momentarily to another window to enter something, but then return to the window where you were working previously.

Choose the Apply or OK button in the Control Center to apply your configuration changes. If you use the Apply button, the dialog box remains visible, so you can see the effect of your new configuration and change it again if needed.

Summary

This hour describes how to move between KDE applications and configure the look and feel of your KDE environment. You learned how to set preferences for the Panel and taskbar, and configure how all KDE windows appear, including how you can use your mouse to move between active windows. In the next hour you will learn about more KDE configuration options. You also explore the KDE Control Center in much more detail.

Questions and Answers

Q **Can I add buttons to the title bar that use different graphics from the standard icons?**

A Yes, but that's a more advanced topic not covered in this book. If you read the discussion in Hour 8, and review how a few themes are created, you can probably do it without much trouble.

Q **Can I just drag the Panel or taskbar to a new location on the desktop, or must I use the Configuration dialog box?**

A You must use the Configuration dialog box. However, menus in all KDE applications are detachable by default. Click and drag on the tab to the left of any menu or toolbar.

Exercises

1. Rename the KDE Desktops according to the functional activities that you spend most of your time on, such as development, word processing, Web, and email. Add programs to the Autostart folder to launch these applications automatically. Can you make the applications stay on the desktop on which you place them?

2. Experiment with the Mouse Focus policy, trying the Click to Focus and Sloppy Focus with various delays for raising windows. Which settings do you prefer? Have you found anything on a non-UNIX/Linux system that resembles this feature?

6

HOUR 7

Configuring KDE Options

In this hour, you learn how to configure KDE options to fit your personal preferences. These options include some settings for the appearance of KDE, such as the screensaver and wallpaper, as well as operational settings for things such as the language used by KDE menus and help screens, and the items listed on the KDE main menu.

Most of the options described in this hour are set using the KDE Control Center or equivalent main menu items.

Choosing Colors and Wallpaper

Each user in KDE can select the preferred background color for the KDE Desktop, a wallpaper graphic if desired, and other aspects of the color scheme. The sections that follow describe using the KDE Control Center to select these options.

Most of the settings described in this hour can also be set all at once using a KDE Theme, as described in Hour 8, "Using KDE Themes."

Setting the Background Color

The background color is the color that fills the KDE Desktop. The background is *behind* everything else, so it is often covered by wallpaper or open KDE windows and dialog boxes.

The background you select is always composed of one or two colors, with several blending options if you select two colors.

To set the background color, open the KDE Control Center from the main menu and choose Background from the Desktop list (see Figure 7.1).

FIGURE 7.1

Use the KDE Control Center to set background color and wallpaper options.

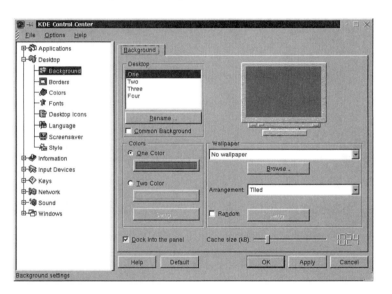

The background color is set using the Colors area of the dialog box. You can select one color or two colors using the radio buttons.

All the color and wallpaper options described in this hour can be different for each KDE Desktop. Select the name of the desktop you want to set up from the Desktop list. Hour 5, "Exploring the Desktop," describes how to set up other features of the KDE Desktops.

For either of the colors shown in the Colors area, you can click on the colored bar and open a Select Color dialog box, as shown in Figure 7.2.

FIGURE 7.2

You can define a precise background color using the Select Color dialog box.

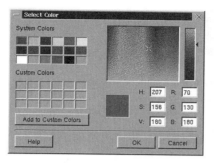

In the Select Color dialog box, you can define new colors using the Rainbow box, the Hue, Saturation, Value fields (H, S, V), or the Red, Green, Blue fields (R, G, B).

> You can click and drag your mouse in the Rainbow box; the defined color changes as you move the mouse.

After you have a color defined, you can add it to the Custom Colors area by choosing the Add to Custom Colors button. Custom colors are color definitions that are remembered every time you open a Select Color dialog box.

You can select a predefined color from the Custom Color area (which you must have defined or loaded previously), or from the System Colors area. Clicking on a box in either area makes the large color box change to match that color.

When the color you want is selected, choose OK to close the Select Color dialog box. The Preview window in the upper-right part of the Background dialog box shows how the desktop background will appear with the colors that you've selected.

If you only want a single color desktop, you only need to set the color bar under the One Color option. If you want a two color desktop, select both colors by clicking on both color bars and selecting two colors (one at a time).

> Two-color desktops are generally formed by different shades of the same color. Start with one color you like, and then define the other color using the same H, S, V numbers, but with a lower value for S (Saturation).

7

With the Two Color option selected, you can choose the Setup button to define how the
two colors that you've selected interact to form a background for your desktop. The Two
Color backgrounds dialog box is shown in Figure 7.3.

FIGURE 7.3

The interaction of two desktop colors is configured using the Two Color Backgrounds dialog box. Several shading and pattern options are provided.

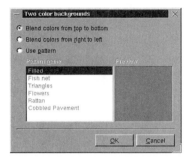

The two colors that you selected can be blended either from top to bottom or from side
to side. When you select either of these radio buttons, you must choose the OK button
and close the dialog box to see a preview of your actions in the Background dialog box.

You can only blend from the top color to the bottom color. If you want to
reverse the order of the blending, you must use the Select Color dialog box
to reverse the order of the selected colors.

Choosing a pattern gives you several attractive options for blending the two selected colors. When you select an option from the Pattern Name list, the colors are shown blended
using that pattern in the Preview window to the right of the Pattern Name list (see
Figure 7.4). Choose OK to use the selected pattern; it appears in the larger Preview window of the Background dialog box.

FIGURE 7.4

Patterns can be applied to blend two colors for your KDE background.

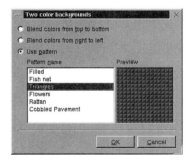

After you have the background colors as you want them, choose Apply to make them active on your desktop or click OK from the main Background window in the Control Center.

> The KDE Control Center stays open when you choose OK. To close the Control Center, use the Close Window icon on the title bar, or choose File, Exit from the Control Center menu.

If you want to define the desktop color for another of the KDE Desktops, choose the named desktop from the Desktop list in the Background dialog box. Repeat the above process to select a background for that desktop.

Choosing Wallpaper

Wallpaper is a graphic image that is placed *on top of* your KDE Desktop background. A wallpaper image can be displayed in many ways. The options available in the Arrangement drop-down list are described here:

- *Tiled.* Fills the desktop with a repeating pattern of the image.
- *Mirrored.* Fills the desktop with a repeating pattern of the image, but uses a mirror image of every other copy of the image.
- *Center Tiled.* Tiles the desktop with a repeating pattern of the image, but centers the image rather than starting in the upper-left corner (as with the Tiled option).
- *Centered.* Centers a single copy of the graphic file in the middle of the desktop (useful for pictures more than textures and patterns).
- *Centered Brick.* Centers a single copy of the graphic file in the middle of the desktop; the rest of the background being a brick pattern.
- *Centered Warp.* Centers a single copy of the graphic file in the middle of the desktop; the rest of the background being a *warp* pattern.
- *Centered Maxaspect.* Centers a single copy of the image in the middle of the desktop, but enlarged it as much as possible without distorting its aspect ratio (part of the background color will thus be visible on two sides for most graphic files).
- *Symmetrical Tiled.* Fills the desktop with a repeating pattern of the image, but tiles the image symmetrically, providing a slightly different image than other Tile options.
- *Symmetrical Mirrored.* Tiles the image to fill the desktop, combining the Symmetrical and Mirrored options to alter how the tiles are arranged.
- *Scaled.* Enlarges or reduces the image file to precisely fit the desktop screen.

If you use the Scaled or Centered Maxaspect option to make a small graphic fill the entire screen, it might become jagged or pixelated and unattractive.

These options are selected in the Wallpaper area of the Background dialog box, using the drop-down list provided.

To select which image you want to use for your wallpaper, click on the top drop-down list (displaying no wallpaper by default). About 140 wallpaper graphics are included with KDE. You can select any of these to see it in the Preview window (see Figure 7.5).

FIGURE 7.5

About 140 wallpaper patterns are included with KDE. Any one can be selected from the drop-down list.

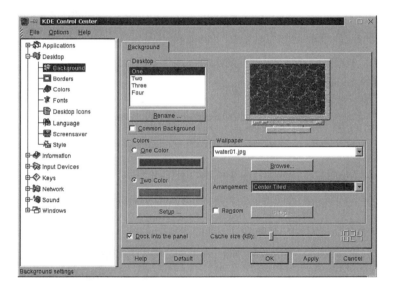

Most of the wallpaper options supplied with KDE are intended as patterns that use one of the Tiled options to fill the screen.

The list of wallpapers in the drop-down list is taken from the directory /opt/kde/share/wallpapers. If you want to use a wallpaper graphic that isn't included in the list, choose the Browse button. An Open dialog box appears (see Figure 7.6), where you can browse through your Linux file system to select any gif- or jpeg-format image to use as wallpaper, including the family picture you scanned in. You can also use xpm and bmp format images if you want to use an icon or other KDE or Windows graphic as wallpaper.

FIGURE 7.6

In the Open dialog box you can select any graphic file to use as wallpaper on your desktop.

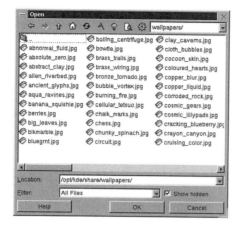

When you select a graphic file using the Open dialog box, that filename is added to the drop-down list of wallpapers that you can select from.

Using a Color Scheme

In addition to setting the background and wallpaper of KDE, you can select a color scheme for the borders and background of the windows that KDE uses for applications and utilities. Choose Colors from the desktop section of the KDE Control Center (see Figure 7.7).

FIGURE 7.7

The Colors dialog box lets you select a set of colors for the borders and background of windows and dialog boxes used in all KDE applications.

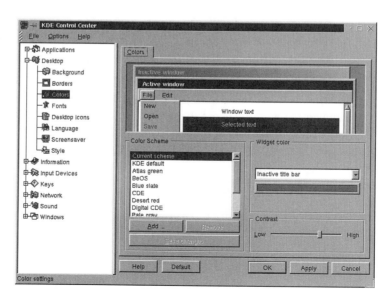

7

If you're familiar with the MS Windows Control Panel, you'll recognize this as a similar feature. KDE, however, allows additional flexibility in setting your color scheme, as described in this section.

The top part of this dialog box shows how the windows and dialog boxes in KDE will appear with the selected color scheme. The Preview area actually contains 12 different colors for the various *widgets*(a programming term for parts of a window). You can see a list of the various items by opening the Widget color drop-down list, which shows an inactive title bar by default.

The Color Scheme list shows predefined sets of colors that you can select for your KDE windows. The KDE default is used when you first install KDE. Other options for UNIX-savvy users include several CDE options. Color schemes based on reds, greens, and so forth are available in this list.

By clicking on one of the choices in the list, the preview window shows how windows will appear using that color scheme.

You can alter the selected color scheme by using the Widget color and Contrast fields of the dialog box:

- *To raise or lower the contrast of the entire color scheme:* Move the slider in the Contrast field to a lower or higher value. (Changing contrast can be helpful if you're using a laptop screen or have trouble distinguishing slight color variations.)
- *To change one of the colors in the selected scheme:* Choose a widget from the drop-down list and click on the color bar to open a Select Color dialog box where you can select a new color for that widget.

In addition, you can create a new color scheme from this dialog box, basing it on an existing color scheme. Choose the Add button below the Color Schemes list. The Add a Color Scheme dialog box appears (see Figure 7.8), where you can enter a name for your new color scheme.

FIGURE 7.8

The Add a Color Scheme dialog box allows you to define a name for a new color scheme. Colors are then defined using the Widget Color drop-down list.

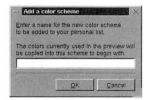

The name of a new color scheme can be a maximum of 18 characters in length.

With your new color scheme name shown in the Color Scheme list, you can define the colors that you want included in it. Select each of the widgets from the drop-down list and click on the color bar to set a color for that item.

When you have set all the colors for your new color scheme, choose the Save Changes button below the Color Scheme list.

 All color schemes are saved in preset configuration files in your home directory. You don't need to provide a filename to save your color scheme.

If you decide you want to remove a personal color scheme that you've created, select it from the list and choose Remove. It disappears from the list. Note that you can't remove the color schemes that come with KDE; the Remove and Save changes buttons are always gray when a preset KDE color scheme is selected.

Setting Up the Screensaver

Screensavers prevent monitor *burn-in* by constantly changing the image on your screen when you're not working at the keyboard. They also provide a visual feast for everyone passing by your computer and give you a chance to be a little creative.

 When using many types of laptop or energy-saving monitors, you might never see your screensaver. This is because the laptop screen or monitor switches to Standby mode before the screensaver starts.

KDE includes about 20 screensavers, with the option to easily add others if you choose to.

To select a screensaver, choose the Screensaver item in the Desktop section of the Control Center (see Figure 7.9).

7

FIGURE 7.9

You KDE screensaver is selected from the KDE Control Center using the Screensaver dialog box.

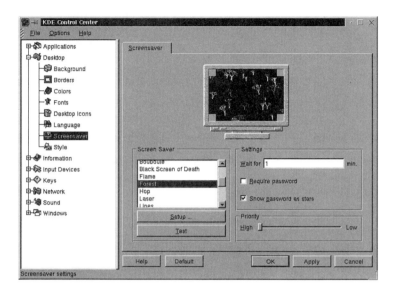

Notice that the Preview window always shows the currently selected screensaver, complete with animation.

The Settings area defines when the screensaver is started and how it can be stopped. The Wait For field lets you enter the number of minutes that KDE will wait with no keyboard or mouse movement before starting the screensaver that you select.

The Require Password check box allows you to select whether the screensaver will lock the screen for security when you step away from your computer, or only save the screen from video burn in.

If you select the Require Password check box, a pop-up window requests the current user's Linux password before an active screensaver will stop and display the regular KDE screen. In effect, this locks your KDE system if you leave it unattended for a while.

The Show Password as Stars check box makes it easier to see that you're entering your password correctly. Without this box checked, the pop-up window doesn't display any characters as you enter your password.

The slider in the Priority field lets you determine how much of your CPU the screensaver will use. Linux, being a true multitasking operating system, continues to run other programs even when the screensaver takes over the entire screen. This means that if you're compiling a program, calculating a spreadsheet, or sorting a database, the operation continues while the screensaver does its tricks.

The Priority slider determines whether the screensaver uses a lot of the computer's processing time for animation and so forth. If the priority is low, the screensaver animation might be uneven or jerky, but the programs that are still running will have more CPU time to complete your real work.

Selecting Screensavers

You can select any screensaver installed in KDE by clicking on it in the Screen Saver list. The Preview window displays the action of the selected screensaver.

You can test the selected screensaver on your entire screen by choosing the Test button under the list.

The Test button doesn't require a password to end the screensaver, even if the Require Password check box is selected. Press a key or move the mouse to end the test.

The Setup button lets you define information about the screensaver option that you selected. The Setup dialog box is different for each screensaver; the options it contains depend on the features of the selected screensaver.

For example, if you choose the Banner screensaver, the Setup kbanner dialog box lets you define the text of the banner, the color and font of the text, and the speed that the text scrolls across the screen (see Figure 7.10).

FIGURE 7.10

The Setup kbanner dialog box lets you define the font, color, and speed for a scrolling banner screensaver.

However, you might select the Science screensaver, which bounces a screen distortion around the KDE screen. The Setup Science dialog box (shown in Figure 7.11) lets you

7

define the shape and size of the bouncing distortion, the speed and angle of attack for each bounce, whether the KDE screen is hidden, and several other options.

FIGURE 7.11

The Setup Science dialog box defines how the KScience screensaver functions.

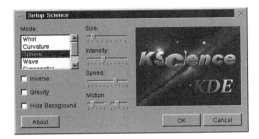

When you install other screensavers, each will include its own setup dialog box to set parameters for how it operates.

> If you find bouncing, rolling screensavers annoying, choose Blank Screen as your screensaver.

Adding Screensaver Options

Screensaver programs are included in the `opt/kde/bin` directory. Each one ends with the `.kss` file extension. You can find additional screensaver programs to add to this directory on various KDE archive sites (see Table 2.1 in Hour 2, "Installing KDE from Scratch").

Any screensaver programs that you place in the KDE binary directory are included in the list of available screensavers when you use the KDE Control Center.

Enabling Desktop Positioning Features

By using multiple desktops, as described in Hour 5, you can manage your workspace and applications in KDE. As with other Linux window managers, KDE provides the capability to move between desktops using the mouse (rather than selecting a desktop name from the Panel).

The Borders dialog box lets you define how these features operate. To see this dialog box, choose the Borders item from the Desktop list in the KDE Control Center (see Figure 7.12).

FIGURE 7.12

The Borders dialog box defines how windows are snapped into position on the desktop, and how your mouse moves between desktops.

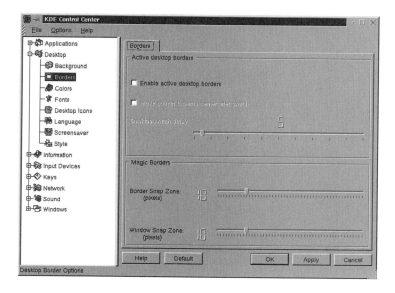

Using Active Desktop Borders

By default, you change to a new desktop in KDE by clicking on the Panel buttons or selecting a desktop from the Window List icon.

When you enable active borders, you can move to a new desktop by moving the mouse to the edge of the current desktop. The mouse then jumps to the *next* desktop. All four of the default desktops are arranged in a square, with Desktops Two and Four below Desktops One and Three, respectively.

 If your desktops have the same background, you'll have to watch the buttons on the Panel to see which desktop you're in until you become familiar with KDE. (KDE, as installed by Caldera OpenLinux, includes a different background for each of the four desktops.)

You enable active borders by choosing the corresponding check box in the Desktop dialog box.

The slider in the Desktop Switch Delay field determines how long you have to leave your mouse on the edge of one desktop before KDE switches you to the next desktop over.

7

If you move the slider to 0 ms (milliseconds), the Active Desktop border feature doesn't work. You must move the slider to a non-zero value. (1,000 milliseconds are equal to 1 second.)

The Desktop Switch Delay setting doesn't function on some Linux systems; if you choose a non-zero value on the slider, the switch to the next desktop is always instantaneous.

The Active Desktop borders features wraps from one desktop to the next. For example, if you are in Desktop Three and move to the right edge, your mouse pointer wraps back into Desktop One. The same rule applies in both directions, side to side and up and down.

Using Magic Borders

Magic Borders is a feature of KDE that snaps your windows onto an invisible grid. The sliders in the Magic Borders area of the dialog box define how large the squares are (how far apart the lines are) on that invisible grid.

By snapping windows to this invisible grid, the windows on your KDE Desktops will line up more precisely, and window resizing will always be done as a multiple of the Magic Border size.

The Snap Zone for Magic Borders can be defined as any size from 0–50 pixels. The smaller the number, the smoother the resizing motion of your windows, but the more likely that they won't *line up* as nicely.

Some graphical programs that display text lines won't respond correctly to the settings that control the Snap Zone. In this case, the bottom line of text in a window might be displayed incorrectly.

Choosing a Language

Hour 1, "Understanding the KDE Project," highlights the international nature of the KDE Project. In the Language section of the KDE Control Center, you see the result of hundreds of KDE translators working to localize parts of KDE into more than 30 languages.

Changing languages in KDE is easy. All applications are designed to read the languages' settings (described here) and use any available translated text as these settings direct.

The Locale dialog box is shown in Figure 7.13. You can view this dialog box by selecting Language from the Desktop section of the KDE Control Center.

FIGURE 7.13

The Locale dialog box defines the language used by all KDE applications and utilities.

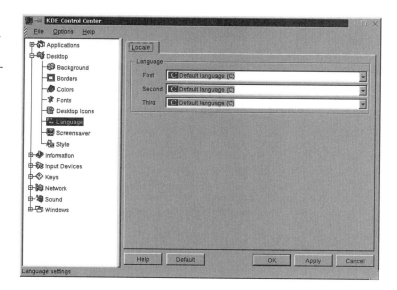

When a KDE application is launched, it reads these Locale settings to determine which language to use for displaying messages, menus, help screens, and dialog boxes.

Changes that you make to the Locale dialog box only affect applications launched after you make the changes. To see the changes reflected in the KDE main menu or other applications that are already running, restart those applications, or exit and restart KDE.

Different KDE applications have been translated into different sets of languages. Some applications are translated into 32 languages; others have text available in only three or four languages.

By providing a first, second, and third language choice, KDE applications can attempt to use your preferred language, and then use the second choice if the first is not available, or use the third if neither of the first two are available.

7

The default language refers to the default for an individual application, which is almost always English.

You can change the first, second, and third choices by clicking on any of the three drop-down lists (see Figure 7.14).

FIGURE 7.14

Many languages are supported by KDE applications.

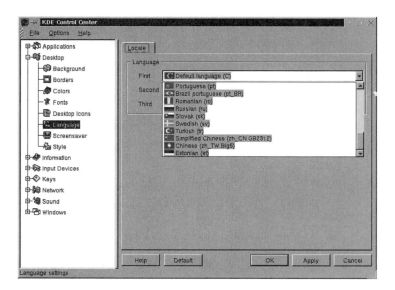

Each of the languages in the list is supported by some KDE applications. You must have the correct font installed, however, for some of the languages to function properly. (If you speak Chinese or Russian, you probably already know how to display the correct characters on your X Window System.)

Choose OK or Apply after selecting languages from the drop-down lists to make your selections take effect. A message box reminds you that the language choices only affect newly launched applications.

Because almost all KDE applications use English as the default, you might never need this dialog box. It is intended for people who speak several languages with different levels of familiarity.

Suppose, for example, that you live in Germany and have studied French. If an application can use German, you'd prefer that; if not, you would like any available French text to be used. If none is available, you'll work with the default English text. A screen showing the German version of the KDE main menu appears in Figure 7.15.

FIGURE 7.15

Changing to a new language for all parts of KDE, such as this German main menu, is easy in KDE.

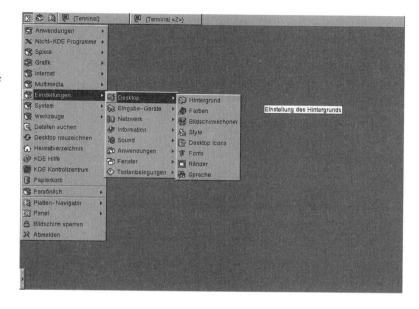

It's fun to play with the language settings, but be careful choosing languages you don't speak. If you can't read the menus and dialog boxes well enough to switch back to a language you know, you might have to edit the Locale section of the .kderc file in your home directory.

Selecting Display Fonts

The font used by KDE for displaying menu items, help text, and dialog box labels can be set using the Fonts dialog box (shown in Figure 7.16), which you can view by selecting the Fonts item from the Desktop list in the KDE Control Panel.

Five fonts are defined in KDE:

- *Genera.* Used for menu items, dialog box and button labels, and text messages.
- *Fixed.* Used for displaying monospaced items in tables or command examples.
- *Window title.* Used for displaying the application name or window description in the title bar of each window.
- *Panel button.* Used to display descriptive text for buttons on the Panel, including the names of desktops.
- *Panel clock.* Used to display the date and time on the right end of the Panel.

7

FIGURE 7.16

*Fonts for display in all
KDE applications are
selected in the Fonts
dialog box.*

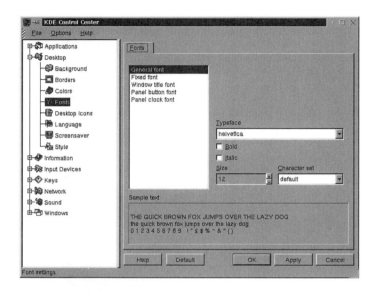

 The font displayed for help screens is set as part of the Preferences of the
KDE Help program. While viewing any help screen, choose General
Preferences from the Options menu.

The font you are most likely to want to alter is the General font. Changing this font will
affect nearly every KDE application.

 Some older KDE applications might not use the fonts that you define in this
dialog box. In addition, font updating might not occur in some windows
until that application or KDE is restarted.

Why change the General font?

- You want to use a bigger font or a bold font because you're using a high screen
  resolution or you have difficulty seeing the small characters.
- You're using a language setting that requires a different font.
- You think the default font is boring and want your KDE screen to be more customized.

The font that you select for the KDE General font can be any of the fonts installed in your X Window System. These are listed when you open the Typeface drop-down list (see Figure 7.17). Click on any font in this list to select it.

FIGURE 7.17

All the fonts on your Linux X Window System are available as the General font for KDE applications.

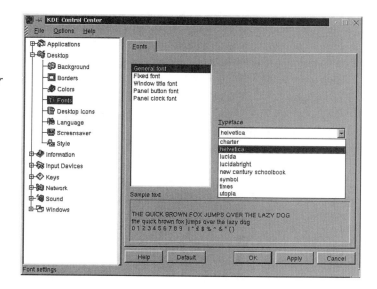

With a font selected, you can choose options for that font, such as Bold or Italic and the point size of the font. The default point size is 12. Larger point sizes such as 14 or 18 will make text easier to read.

Choose OK or Apply to make your new font selection immediately active in KDE.

Configuring Desktop Icons

The icons that appear on your KDE Desktop can be configured using the Desktop Icons section of the Desktop list in the Control Center (see Figure 7.18). Icons that appear by default on your desktop include the Autostart folder, Templates folder, and Trash can.

The following list describes the fields available in this dialog box to configure your desktop icons. These settings affect all icons that you place on any desktop, not just the default icons.

- *Horizontal Root Grid Spacing and Vertical Root Grid Spacing.* These two numbers refer to the number of pixels used to separate icons. You can increase these numbers to have your icons more spread out on the desktop, either horizontally or vertically.

7

- *Transparent Text for Desktop Icons.* This check box makes the text below an icon show the desktop background or wallpaper through a transparent background. If this check box is not selected, text below each icon appears as a colored box containing the icon description.

- *Icon Foreground Color and Icon Background Color.* These two color buttons allow you to define a foreground and background color for icons on the desktop. These two colors are used with the colors of the icon itself to make an icon blend or stand out from the desktop colors.

- *Show Hidden Files on Desktop.* If this check box is selected, any hidden files included in your Desktop directory (~/Desktop) will be displayed as icons on your KDE Desktop. Without this check box selected (the default), hidden files are not included on the desktop.

FIGURE 7.18

The Desktop Icons dialog box defines the arrangement and colors of the icons on your KDE Desktop.

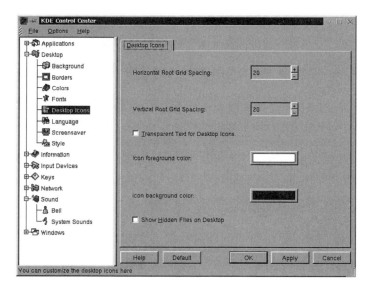

Using Style Options

KDE provides several additional style options for windows on your desktop. These can be set by viewing the Style dialog box in the Desktop section of the Control Center, as shown in Figure 7.19. Each of the three options is described here:

- *Draw Widgets in the Style of Windows 95.* Selected by default, this setting uses Windows 95-style widgets for KDE. This means that buttons, menus, and other graphical elements are displayed much as they would be in the latest Microsoft Windows operating systems.

FIGURE 7.19

KDE allows different styles to be used for your desktop, including Microsoft Windows 95-style widgets and Mac OS-style menus.

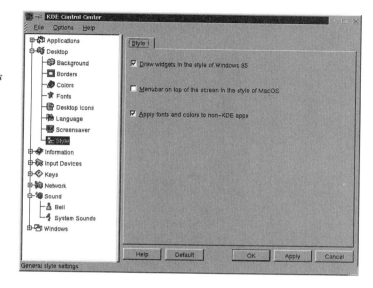

- *Menubar on the Top of the Screen in the Style of Mac OS.* If you're a fan of the Apple Macintosh, you can select this check box to have the menu of the active window always displayed at the top of the screen, like a Macintosh.

- *Apply Fonts and Colors to non-KDE Apps.* With this check box selected (the default), KDE attempts to make its resources and definitions available to all graphical (X Window System) applications. Although some applications might not use the KDE definitions, leaving this check box selected makes your graphical environment appear with a more consistent look and feel, no matter which applications you're running.

Configuring Sounds

As with other graphical systems, KDE lets you assign sounds to events, so you can use audio clues to know what's going on with your system.

KDE also uses a standard *bell*—which doesn't sound much like a bell—to indicate items such as an invalid selection.

Setting the Bell Sound

You can choose what you want the standard bell to sound like. Choose the Bell item in the Sound section of the KDE Control Center (see Figure 7.20).

7

FIGURE 7.20

The sound of the KDE bell can be selected in this dialog box.

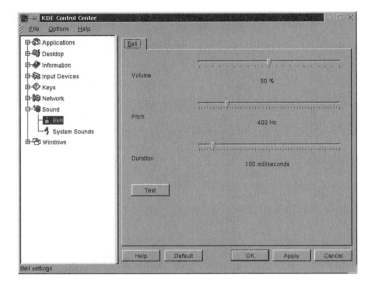

Use the sliders to select the volume, pitch (tone, high or low), and duration of the bell sound.

Click the Test button to hear what your slider settings will sound like when KDE sounds the bell.

Defining Sound Events

KDE also lets you define a specific sound for each of over two dozen events. To view the Sound dialog box, choose the System Sounds item in the Sound section of the Control Center (see Figure 7.21).

The Events list shows you which things you can assign a sound to. For example, if you assign a sound to the Logout event, that sound will play each time you choose Logout from the main menu (or another location).

All the sound files must be located in /opt/kde/share/sounds, and all sound files must be in wav format.

If the sound that you want isn't included in the correct directory, you can add it to the list of sounds in the Sound dialog box by dragging the .wav file from a file manager window (a kfm window) and dropping it in the Sounds list.

FIGURE 7.21

Sounds are linked to KDE events in the Sound dialog box.

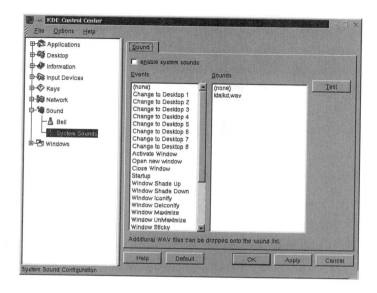

The only sound installed on your system might be the ktalkd.wav file, part of the kdenetwork package. You can download and install additional sounds from KDE and other Internet sites. (Refer to Hour 2 for a list of KDE FTP sites.)

To assign a sound to an event, follow these steps:

1. Choose an event from the Events list.
2. Choose a sound file from the Sounds list.
3. Choose the Test button if you want to hear what the sound file is like.
4. Repeat the first three steps for any event you want to have a sound associated with.
5. Choose OK or Apply to save your selections.

Having a sound assigned for too many of the events in the list can make working with KDE tedious—more like a circus than an operating system. Use the sounds sparingly.

7

Summary

In this hour you learned how to configure some of the many options available in KDE. The options you learned about focused on the appearance and operation of your desktop, including colors, wallpaper, screensavers, and language settings.

Questions and Answers

Q **Where are the system sound files located?**

A System sounds, which can be used by everyone, are located in the /opt/kde/share/sounds directory. You can also have sounds for your personal use. These are stored in ~/.kde/share/sounds directory. These directories might not exist on your system if you don't yet have any sound files installed.

Q **Is a screensaver with a password a secure way to leave my PC unattended?**

A No, not really. If you're concerned about passing strangers accessing your computer, the KDE screensaver can discourage them, but depending on how your X Window System is configured, pressing Ctrl+Alt+Backspace might exit X altogether, leaving a command prompt available to potential intruders. If you'll be away from your computer for a while or if your computer is located in an insecure area, the safest bet is to exit KDE and log out of Linux.

Q **If I modify a color scheme, how can I get back to the original version?**

A You can't, at least not easily. You can reinstall the package that included the color theme. The best choice is to never alter the color schemes that come with KDE. Instead, use the Add button to create a new color scheme based on a KDE-provided scheme. Then alter that color scheme. By the way, you might not be able to alter the KDE color schemes anyway, depending on the permissions granted to the user running KDE.

Exercises

1. Create your own color scheme using the Add button on the Colors dialog box. Define a color for each widget in the list.

2. Try the Random wallpaper option using the Setup dialog box to select which wallpaper graphics will be rotated randomly.

HOUR **8**

Using KDE Themes

In this hour, you learn how to use KDE themes to quickly change the appearance and operation of your KDE environment using predefined graphics and configuration files that you can download from KDE sites on the Internet.

The information in Hour 7, "Configuring KDE Options," is a prerequisite to this hour because a KDE theme changes many of the display elements that you learned about in the previous hour.

Understanding KDE Themes

A KDE theme is a set of graphic files and configuration information that give KDE a certain look and feel. To some degree, a KDE theme can even give KDE the look and feel of a NeXT, Macintosh, Sun workstation, or Windows NT system.

More often, however, KDE themes are centered around a graphical motif such as *Star Trek* or another movie or television show, or some other visual motif, such as space-flight or the arctic. The theme will generally provide a nice wallpaper image, graphics for buttons, title bars, and perhaps additional options. Specifically, a KDE theme can include:

- New window border graphics
- New button graphics (such as the minimize and close buttons)
- New title bar graphics
- Wallpaper images
- Graphics that will appear in the Panel or as a Panel background
- Background images for file browser windows (kfm windows)
- Sounds (.wav files)
- Icons
- Color scheme definition files
- Replacements or additions to several of your KDE configuration files
- Instructions or a README file
- An installation script

Of course, most themes only include some of the items on this list.

Setting up a KDE theme can be a challenging if you're new to Linux and haven't explored the KDE configuration files or used a UNIX text editor. I'll walk you through the process, however.

> Themes do exist that mimic OpenLook and other UNIX systems. Try these if you want to make KDE as close as possible to another UNIX system that you're familiar with.

The biggest challenge is that KDE themes modify many parts of KDE—parts that you can't modify from the dialog boxes alone. Beyond the configuration options described in previous hours, you can modify KDE in other ways by directly editing the configuration files. KDE themes often rely on this fact.

On the positive side, some KDE themes include an installation script that prepares all the files for you. All you have to do after running the installation script is select the new color scheme and wallpaper from the respective sections of the Control Center.

> A graphical theme manager is available to install and manage themes on your KDE system. While the theme manager is considered to be fairly stable, it isn't yet included in the default KDE distribution. See Hour 21, "Finding and Installing Additional KDE Applications," for more information.

Most installation scripts for KDE themes are not very careful about the files that they overwrite. If you have KDE configured just as you like it, I suggest learning about themes using a theme that requires you to copy files manually, rather than using an installation script. This will let you learn what files are involved in using the theme and make backup files along the way. This hour walks you through just such a theme.

8

KDE themes are created (generally in just a few hours) by people with in-depth knowledge of KDE, some graphical skills, and an idea that they want to see onscreen. Later in this hour you'll learn how to join their ranks if you'd like to.

Future releases of KDE and the Qt libraries on which it is based will include additional configuration options. Thus, KDE themes will come to play a larger role as customization of your KDE environment becomes more powerful.

Finding a KDE Theme

KDE themes are becoming more popular all the time, as more people learn to use and configure KDE. Because the concept of a theme for a graphical operating system isn't new, some Web sites have appeared that specialize in KDE themes. The sections that follow take you through some prime locations for spotting cool KDE themes.

Searching for Themes

KDE themes are currently found on two main archive sites. The first, and most up-to-date of these, is `kde.themes.org`.

The site `www.themes.org` is a collection of themes for many different operating systems. KDE themes are just part of the collection.

The `kde.themes.org` site is linked from the home page of KDE, at `www.kde.org`. As of this writing, the `kde.themes.org` site holds about 75 themes.

The second site for themes is `http://home.clara.net/george.russell/` `kdescreenshots.html`. This site is maintained by George Russell, who has created many

KDE themes. It isn't maintained as actively as the `kde.themes.org` site, but still contains about 50 themes (with some overlap to the `kde.themes.org` site).

I'll focus here on the `kde.themes.org` site, but you'll still find a lot of useful information and links on George Russell's site.

The `kde.themes.org` site includes information on the following:

- How to install themes
- How to create your own theme
- Details of recent, relevant KDE developments
- Information about and links to the theme installation tools
- Information about and links to the Ktheme utility (part of current KDE development, but not included with KDE 1.0)
- A gallery of available themes, complete with a small graphic screenshot of the theme

Because this hour walks you through the installation process, you can start your visit to `kde.themes.org` at the Gallery, exploring the available themes and choosing a screenshot that appeals to you. Figure 8.1 shows one view of the Gallery on this Web site.

FIGURE 8.1

The Gallery shows KDE themes on the `kde.themes.org` *Web site.*

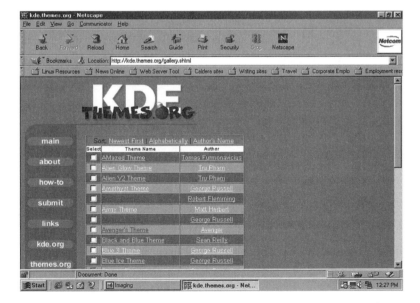

Downloading a Theme

You can download a KDE theme just as you would download any other file in your Web browser. Click the Download link shown on the Themes Web page and enter a filename for the locally saved file (see Figure 8.2).

FIGURE 8.2

A KDE theme can be downloaded using any Web browser, and then installed into KDE.

If your browser doesn't recognize the format of the theme file and tries to display it, hold down the Shift key while clicking on the download link.

Themes can be downloaded in any Web browser, and then installed on KDE. The file format for most themes that you will download is a *gzipped tarball* file.

Now to explain the term gzipped tarball, in case it isn't familiar to you: A theme is a collection of many files, such as graphics, configuration files, instructions, and so forth. The UNIX `tar` command puts all these files into a single file. The `gzip` command then compresses the archive file. These two UNIX commands can be used together to create a single compressed archive file of an entire collection of files.

If you had a set of files in a directory, you could use this command to create a compressed archive of everything in the directory (using the asterisk as a wildcard to represent all the files in the directory):

```
$ tar cvfz archive.tgz *
```

The .tgz file extension indicates a gzipped tar archive file. Another file extension used for these files is tar.gz, which you'll see on most KDE themes that you download. For example, a KDE theme could be uncompressed and unarchived using this command:

```
$ tar xvfz starwars.tar.gz
```

The complete process of unarchiving and installing the compressed archive for a KDE theme is the subject of the next section.

 Some themes are stored in a Linux ZIP file. Use the unzip command to decompress these files.

Installing a KDE Theme

This section describes how to install a KDE theme that you have downloaded so that it is active in your KDE environment. The sample theme in this example is the Arctic theme, which doesn't use an installation script. It also includes a fair number of steps, so you'll learn a lot about installing a theme by following along on this one.

 Some tools for installing any KDE theme are available on kde.themes.org. They are not fully tested yet, so I won't describe their use. Some themes come with their own installation script; these are described later in this hour.

As you learn to install the Arctic theme, you'll also learn more about how KDE configuration files operate.

Preparing the Archive

Once you have downloaded a theme archive file (and copied it to your Linux system if necessary), move the archive file to a temporary location such as /tmp.

```
$ mv ~/download/arctic.tar.gz /tmp
```

With the archive in a working area such as /tmp, you can untar and uncompress the file. It will create its own subdirectory containing all the files that comprise the new theme. The command to untar and uncompress is shown here, along with the resulting display of all the files contained in the archive:

```
$ cd /tmp
$ tar xvfz arctic.tar.gz
```

8

```
Arctic/
Arctic/ArcticTheme.kcsrc
Arctic/README
Arctic/activetitlebar.xpm
Arctic/arctic-background.jpg
Arctic/close.xpm
Arctic/iconify.xpm
Arctic/inactivetitlebar.xpm
Arctic/kde-theme00002.tar.gz
Arctic/kwmrc.arctic
Arctic/maximize.xpm
Arctic/maximizedown.xpm
Arctic/menu.xpm
Arctic/wm_bottom.xpm
Arctic/wm_bottomleft.xpm
Arctic/wm_bottomright.xpm
Arctic/wm_left.xpm
Arctic/wm_right.xpm
Arctic/wm_top.xpm
Arctic/wm_top2.xpm
Arctic/wm_topleft.xpm
Arctic/wm_topleft2.xpm
Arctic/wm_topright.xpm
Arctic/wm_topright2.xpm
```

Reviewing the README File

With the files that make up the theme available in a separate directory, your next step is to review the README file or other installation instructions for the theme. (Sometimes this will be a file named theme.install.)

The Arctic theme provides a set of simple instructions that you can follow here to install the theme. The instructions in the README file are listed here:

```
Arctic Spring 1.0 - rflemming@iname.com
Background by Peter Bukowinski - pbuko@uclink4.berkeley.edu


...

Install:

copy all xpms to ~/.kde/share/apps/kwm/pics
copy background jpg to ~/.kde/share/wallpapers
copy ArcticTheme.kcsrc to ~/.kde/share/apps/kdisplay/color-schemes

modify values in ~/.kde/share/config/kwmrc to match those of kwmrc.arctic

Use the KDE Control Center to set the color scheme and background image.

restart KDE and enjoy.
```

If you download a theme and the README file instructs you to run an installation script that comes with the theme. See the description later in this section on how to protect your system while using the installation script.

The installation instructions in the README file fall into a few general categories:

- Create needed directories in the .kde directory
- Copy graphics files to the correct directories
- Edit configuration files to include information provided in the theme archive
- Use the KDE Control Center to select the wallpaper and color scheme files that you copied into your KDE directories
- Restart KDE to see the theme

Creating KDE Directories

KDE uses standard directories to locate graphic files for all KDE users on your Linux system. If certain files are included in your home directory, however, those files are used instead of the default KDE files. For example, if you have certain button graphics in your .kde directory, the default KDE buttons from /opt/kde/share/apps won't be used.

To prepare for working with themes, you should create the following four directories. These directories are not part of a default KDE installation, because the default installation doesn't provide per-user graphics files like a theme does. The commands to create the directories are given here:

```
$ mkdir ~/.kde/share/apps/kwm
$ mkdir ~/.kde/share/apps/kwm/pics
$ mkdir ~/.kde/share/apps/kpanel
$ mkdir ~/.kde/share/apps/kpanel/pics
$ mkdir ~/.kde/share/apps/kdisplay
$ mkdir ~/.kde/share/apps/kdisplay/color-schemes
$ mkdir ~/.kde/share/wallpapers
```

Copying Graphics Files

The theme instructions usually give explicit instructions for where to copy the graphics files that the theme includes. The Arctic theme instructions tell you exactly what to do:

```
copy all xpms to ~/.kde/share/apps/kwm/pics
copy background jpg to ~/.kde/share/wallpapers
copy ArcticTheme.kcsrc to ~/.kde/share/apps/kdisplay/color-schemes
```

The directories named in these instructions don't exist when you first install KDE. Thus they were created in the previous section.

8

To copy the files as directed, use these commands:

```
$ cp /tmp/Arctic/*xpm ~/.kde/share/apps/kwm/pics
$ cp /tmp/Arctic/*jpg ~/.kde/share/wallpapers
$ cp /tmp/Arctic/ArcticTheme.kcsrc ~/.kde/share/apps/kdisplay/
↪color-schemes
```

The .xpm files that are placed in the kwm/pics directory are graphics that define new buttons and borders. Some of the names from the listing should be recognizable to you:

```
close.xpm
iconify.xpm
inactivetitlebar.xpm
wm_left.xpm
wm_right.xpm
```

These graphics replace the default KDE graphics for the user in whose home directory they are placed.

The wallpaper graphic (in jpeg format) can really be stored anywhere; the Wallpapers directory is a good standard location to place them. You will use the file browser to locate the graphic file you want as your wallpaper later in this hour.

Finally, the .kcsrc file defines a KDE color scheme. You can look at the contents of this file to get an idea of how KDE configuration files are set up.

In other themes, you might also copy icon files, sounds, or other graphics into these or other directories, as instructed in the README file for each theme.

Updating the Configuration Files

The most challenging part of installing your new theme is altering the KDE configuration files to use the new graphic images that you've just placed in your KDE directories.

The file you're most likely to modify when installing a theme is the kwmrc file—the configuration file for the KDE window manager, kwm. This file is located at ~/.kde/share/config/kwmrc.

You can use any text editor to modify these configuration files. The KEdit program is described in Hour 18, "Using KDE Text Utilities."

By modifying this configuration file, you can alter many parts of KDE that cannot be altered using the graphical configuration tools (such as the Control Center).

Installing configuration changes for a theme can be difficult because you don't just replace an existing configuration file with a new file. Instead, you must merge the additions or changes that the theme requires into your existing configuration file.

Let's see how this is done for the Arctic theme. The README file instructs you to modify the values in the ~/.kde/share/config/kwmrc file to match those of the kwmrc.arctic file that comes with the Arctic theme.

The first step is to make a backup copy of your existing configuration file, so you can backup and start over if problems occur:

```
$ cd ~/.kde/share/config
$ cp kwmrc kwmrc.backup
```

Now review the kwmrc.arctic file to see what changes you have to incorporate into your existing configuration:

```
$ more /tmp/Arctic/kwmrc.arctic
[General]
ShapePixmapTopRight=wm_topright.xpm
ShapePixmapRight=wm_right.xpm
ShapePixmapBottom=wm_bottom.xpm
ShapePixmapLeft=wm_left.xpm
TitlebarPixmapActive=activetitlebar.xpm
TitlebarPixmapInactive=inactivetitlebar.xpm
ShapePixmapTopLeft=wm_topleft.xpm
ShapePixmapBottomRight=wm_bottomright.xpm
TitlebarLook=pixmap
ShapePixmapBottomLeft=wm_bottomleft.xpm
ShapeMode=on
ShapePixmapTop=wm_top.xpm
[Buttons]
ButtonC=Off
ButtonD=Close
ButtonE=Maximize
ButtonF=Iconify
ButtonA=Menu
ButtonB=Off
```

Looking at this file, you know you have to review the [General] section and the [Buttons] section of the original kwmrc file, because those are the only sections referred to in kwmrc.arctic.

Review the original kwmrc file and you find a large [Desktops] section and a [Session] section. You can leave these unaltered.

You find that the [General] section of kwmrc looks like this:

```
[General]
WindowMoveType=Transparent
AltTabMode=KDE
TitlebarDoubleClickCommand=winMaximize
WindowSnapZone=10
ElectricBorderPointerWarp=FullWarp
FocusPolicy=ClickToFocus
ControlTab=on
RstartProtocol=rstart -v
Button3Grab=on
WindowResizeType=Transparent
AutoRaise=0
TraverseAll=off
ElectricBorderMovePointer=off
BorderSnapZone=10
WindowsPlacement=smart
MaximizeOnlyVertically=off
TitlebarLook=shadedHorizontal
TitleAnimation=50
ElectricBorder=-1
ShapeMode=off
ElectricBorderNumberOfPushes=5
ResizeAnimation=1
```

You can probably recognize several of these options as the settings discussed in Hour 6, "Managing the KDE Environment." For example, BorderSnapZone for Magic Border settings, and FocusPolicy to determine how window focus is set.

Many of these options, however, can be altered only by editing this configuration file. But that is not covered in this book.

Notice that the original [General] section of kwmrc and the [General] section of kwmrc.arctic have few common lines. You can insert the lines from the [General] section of kwmrc.arctic into the [General] section of the kwmrc file, or you can replace the original file's [General] section with the [General] section from the theme. This is often the surest way to install the theme. Remember, you have a backup file if things go badly wrong.

Next, reviewing the [Buttons] section, you see that all the lines are the same in both files, except that the Arctic version has ButtonB=Off instead of ButtonB=Sticky, as shown in this listing from kwmrc (compare to the kwmrc.arctic listing given previously).

```
[Buttons]
ButtonC=Off
ButtonD=Close
ButtonE=Maximize
ButtonF=Iconify
ButtonA=Menu
ButtonB=Sticky
```

You can alter the ButtonB line to match the kwmrc.arctic file.

Save the kwmrc file with your changes in it.

Other changes to the kwmrc file or changes to other configuration files might be necessary to install some themes. The same principles apply, however.

- Always make a backup of the configuration file before you change it (most installation scripts will do this for you).
- Carefully review the differences between the theme file and the original file, adding or changing lines as needed.

> Some theme instructions tell you to run the krdb program. This KDE program attempts to make all of the KDE changes that you've made for a theme available to all graphical programs using the X Window System resources. It won't work for all programs, of course, but feel free to use the krdb program when instructed to do so.

Choosing the Theme in the Control Center

You've made several changes to your KDE configuration files and added graphics to key directories to replace default KDE graphics for buttons, title bars, and so forth.

Although you could also edit a configuration file to finish the configuration, most people use the KDE Control Center for the final steps:

- Choosing the theme wallpaper for your background
- Choosing the theme color scheme

The following steps guide you through this:

1. Open the KDE Control Center and choose the Colors item in the Desktop section. The Colors dialog box appears, as shown in Figure 8.3.
2. Scroll down in the Color Scheme list to see the Arctic Theme at the end of the list.
3. Click on the Arctic Theme in the list and Choose Apply.
4. Choose Background from the Desktop section (see Figure 8.4).
5. Choose the Browse button in the Wallpaper section of the dialog box. The Open dialog box appears.

   The default location for the Wallpaper graphics is /opt/kde/share/wallpapers. The graphics included in this directory are shown in the Open dialog box.
6. Click in the Folders list (on the left side of the Open dialog box) to back up to the root directory, and then click on the directory names to reach your home directory.

7. Add .kde to the Location field and press Enter. (Because .kde is a hidden directory, it doesn't appear automatically in the Folders list. You can click the Show hidden button in the bottom-right corner of the screen.)

8. Choose Wallpapers to see the Arctic wallpaper shown in the Contents section (see Figure 8.5).

FIGURE 8.3

The Colors dialog box allows you to choose the new color scheme that you installed for this theme.

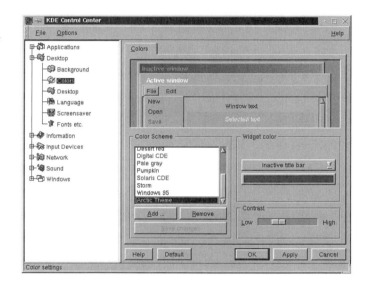

FIGURE 8.4

The Background dialog box lets you choose the new wallpaper image that you installed for this theme.

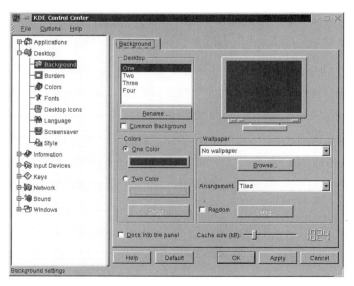

FIGURE 8.5

The wallpaper graphic that you installed must be selected in the Open dialog box.

9. Click on `arctic-background.jpg` and choose OK to close the Open dialog box.

10. The Arctic background appears in the Preview area of the Background dialog box (see Figure 8.6).

FIGURE 8.6

The newly selected wallpaper appears in the Preview area after you select it in the Open dialog box.

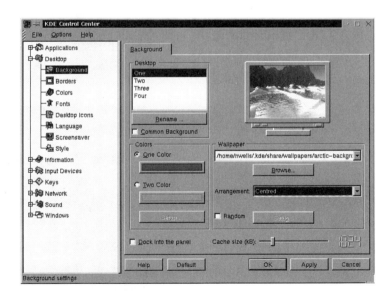

11. Choose the Centred radio button for your wallpaper.

The wallpaper images included with KDE are small and are designed for the Tiled option. The full-screen images used for most themes will take several seconds to load after you close the Open dialog box.

8

12. Choose OK to apply your background settings.

13. Close the KDE Control Center by choosing File, Exit.

Restarting KDE

Although the wallpaper and color scheme choices that you select for a new theme should appear onscreen immediately, the additional graphics and configuration settings will only be used when you restart KDE.

To restart KDE, use the Logout command (on the main menu or use a Panel button), and then use the same command you always use to start KDE (usually kde or startx). KDE launches, reading all the updated configuration and graphics files that you've installed.

Figure 8.7 shows the Arctic theme with a few windows open and the Arctic wallpaper in the background.

FIGURE 8.7

After the Arctic theme is installed, it affects every KDE window. The Arctic wallpaper forms the background image.

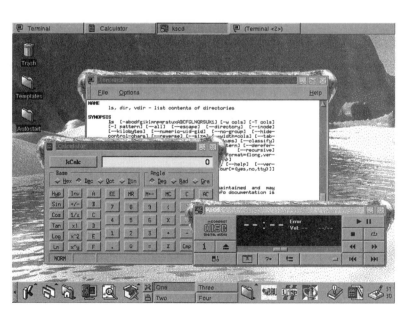

Notice all the changes made by this theme:

- A nice full-screen wallpaper graphic
- New border and title bar graphics
- New buttons on the title bar
- A new *cold* color scheme

Using Installation Scripts

I've offered some words of warning about using installation scripts for themes. They can, of course, make it easier to install themes. But a little caution can keep you from being stuck with a theme you don't like because you're not sure what the installation script did to your set up.

To make installation scripts a little safer, I recommend reviewing the script before you execute it. Check which files it alters and be certain that it makes backup copies of those files before altering them. If it doesn't, make backups yourself before running the script.

For example, the Avenger theme (available on kde.themes.org) includes an installation script named install-theme. This simple file makes it easy to use the Avenger theme because it does all the file copying for you. All you have to do is choose the new Avenger color scheme in the Control Center.

However, the install-theme script overwrites any existing configuration or graphics files with the same names.

By reviewing the script (or other similar installation scripts that you come across in themes), you can either install the theme elements manually, using the script as a guide, or you can make backup copies of existing configuration files and then run the script.

This listing shows the core of the install-theme script for the Avenger theme.

```
#!/bin/sh
KDEROOT=$HOME/.kde/share
KWM=$KDEROOT/apps/kwm
KWMPICS=$KWM/pics
KDISPLAY=$KDEROOT/apps/kdisplay
KCOLOUR=$KDISPLAY/color-schemes
KCONFIG=$KDEROOT/config

mkdir $KWM >/dev/null
mkdir $KWMPICS >/dev/null
mkdir $KDISPLAY >/dev/null
mkdir $KCOLOUR >/dev/null
mkdir $KCONFIG >/dev/null
```

```
cp -vf *.xpm $KWMPICS
cp -vf *.kcsrc $KCOLOUR
cp -vf kdisplayrc $KDISPLAY
cp -vf kwmrc $KCONFIG
```

This script does three things:

- *Defines the directories where the theme elements will be placed.* (These directories are the same as those listed earlier in this hour.)

- *Makes the directories if they don't exist.* (If they exist already, the error message is ignored.)

- *Copies the files from the current directory (where the install script is being run from) to the correct KDE directories.*

After reviewing this script, you can make the installation a little safer by doing the following before running the script:

- Check to see if any `.xpm` files in the `~/.kde/share/apps/kwm/pics` directory will be overwritten by the those in the Avenger theme. (Do they have the same filename?)

- Check to see if the Avenger color scheme (the `.kcsrc` file) is named the same as an existing color scheme (this is unlikely, however).

- Make a backup of the `kdisplayrc` file in `~/.kde/share/apps/kdisplay`.

- Make a backup of the `kwmrc` file in `~/.kde/share/config`.

Themes can be a lot of fun, but until KDE includes a graphical Theme Installation tool, install them with care or you risk altering your KDE environment in ways that you're not sure how to undo.

Getting Rid of a Theme

Getting rid of a theme that you've installed can be as difficult as the installation itself.

The easy part is choosing new wallpaper and color scheme selections in the KDE Control Center. These take effect immediately.

More difficult is the process of undoing any changes you've made to your configuration files. This is why I recommend making a backup copy of your configuration files before installing theme changes in them. Then restoring the old configuration is as easy as this:

```
$ cd ~/.kde/share/config
$ cp -f kwmrc.backup kwmrc
$ cd ../apps/kdisplay
$ cp -f kdisplayrc.backup kdisplayrc
```

The `-f` option on the `copy` command forces the copy to overwrite an existing version of the file; in this case, the version altered for the theme is overwritten by the backup copy.

You might have altered other configuration files, of course, but the backup files make it easy to revert to the previous configuration. If you don't have backup files, use the README file for the theme that you installed to back out the changes that you made to the files.

One final note on removing themes. The graphics files that you copy into directories such as `~./kde/share/apps/kwm/pics` are used by KDE because they have certain filenames, not because of any configuration file settings. To stop these graphics from being used, you must delete or move the graphics files so that KDE doesn't see them.

Remember to restart KDE after uninstalling a theme. You won't see the changes until you do.

Creating Your Own KDE Theme

If editing configuration files doesn't bother you, and you have an idea you'd like to bring to life as a KDE theme, the following steps might help you get started.

Detailed instructions for creating KDE themes are provided on the two KDE theme Web sites mentioned earlier in this hour.

1. Come up with a motif or idea for your theme.
2. Start creating graphics using GIMP or another bitmapped drawing program. Use the graphics that come with a downloaded KDE theme to see the size that you'll need for title bars, buttons, Panel backgrounds, and so on.
3. Save your screen elements as indexed xpm format graphics.
4. Find or create a nice background wallpaper image (usually in jpeg format).
5. Update your configuration files as other themes have done, to refer to the new graphics you've created.

6. Use the Control Center to choose your new color scheme and wallpaper.

7. Restart KDE to test your new theme.

8. If you want to send in your theme for others to enjoy, make a tar gzipped file of all the theme components, test it a few more times, and send it to the folks at `kde.themes.org`.

Many good graphics programs in Linux can be used to create new theme elements and screenshots of your theme. GIMP and XV are included in most Linux distributions. The KDE paint program, kpaint, is included with KDE and is described in Hour 17, "Using Graphics Utilities in KDE."

Summary

This hour describes how to use KDE themes to change the look and feel of your graphical environment. You learned how to locate an interesting theme and install it using a script or manually (by copying files from the command line). You also learned about some of the technical details behind a theme, including some general steps for creating a theme of your own.

Questions and Answers

Q Isn't there an easier way to install themes?

A Yes, the theme manager installs as part of your KDE Control Center and lets you install new themes and then choose among them. The theme manager must be downloaded and compiled on your system before you can use it, however. See Hour 21 for details.

Q How can I learn about all the options in the configuration files?

A It isn't easy. The documentation that comes with most KDE applications is incomplete—most developers focus on the software and have little time for documentation. You can check the online help for hints, study the files themselves (in the `config` or `apps` directories), or even look at the source code if you're comfortable doing that sort of thing. One great resource is the KDE mailing lists, where you can search the archives for answers or ask questions of the developers themselves. See the KDE Web site for details on the mailing lists.

Q Can I alter and redistribute a KDE theme?

A You should check the license if one is provided, or contact the author before redistributing a theme based on someone else's work. Most themes are distributed under the GPL, so redistribution of altered versions isn't a problem. In every case, crediting the original author, at least as inspiration, will win points.

Exercise

1. Create a new KDE theme that changes at least three graphical elements or place-ment options. Write a simple shell script that automates both the installation and removal of your theme (using command-line parameters or similar options). Compare your theme files and script with some that you've downloaded. What conventions must be followed for all KDE themes? Which are optional?

HOUR 9

Managing Files in KDE

This hour shows you how to use the file manager utility in KDE. This utility, called kfm, lets you browse local and network resources, providing file typing, drag and drop, and other powerful features that you might have used to manage your file system on other operating systems such as Macintosh and Microsoft Windows.

Understanding the KDE File Manager

The KDE file manager is the graphical tool that you use to view the directories and files on your Linux system within the KDE environment. The KDE file manager is a program called kfm.

kfm is also a complete Web browser. All the information you see displayed in a kfm window is created internally using HTML. kfm can thus be used to browse the Internet (Web and FTP sites) if you have an Internet connection established for your Linux system.

In addition to the kfm graphical file manager, KDE includes a program called Disk Navigator, which can help you quickly open a kfm window showing a part of your file system or view or launch a file. The Disk Navigator is also described briefly in this hour.

Integrating kfm and the Disk Navigator into KDE

kfm and the Disk Navigator are installed as part of the core KDE distribution and are both used as integral parts of the KDE environment. Whenever you view file listings, they appear in a kfm window. The Disk Navigator is always available from the main menu or taskbar (if the Panel is not visible).

The kfm program is divided into a client portion and a server portion. The server is integrated into many parts of KDE. For example, when you right-click on the KDE background, the pop-up menu includes the Bookmarks option (described later in this hour). The KPanel application opens kfm windows when you choose the Home Directory button on the Panel.

You'll use kfm almost exclusively from the graphical interface, so the client/server nature of kfm might not matter much to you. It does, however, make it easier for KDE to provide many types of services through any KDE-aware application. You'll see this illustrated during this hour.

How kfm Is Used

The best way to open a kfm window is to choose Home Directory from the main menu, or click the Home Directory icon on the Panel (see Figure 9.1). A kfm window appears showing the contents of your home directory. The sections that follow describe the components of the kfm window and how to use them to browse your local file system and the Internet.

FIGURE 9.1

The easiest way to open a kfm window is to select Home Directory from the main menu or Panel.

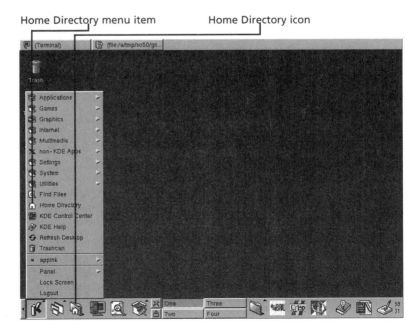

How the Disk Navigator Is Used

To explore the Disk Navigator, choose Disk Navigator from the main menu. A list of options appears as shown in Figure 7.2.

FIGURE 9.2

The Disk Navigator provides submenus to access several areas of your local file system.

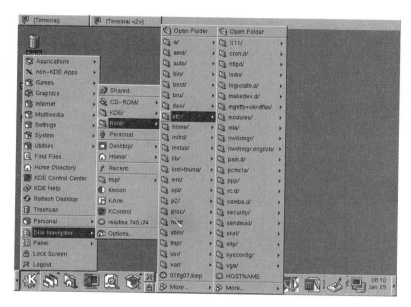

When you select one of the options in the Disk Navigator submenu, further submenus show you the contents of that directory. If you choose the Open Folder item at the top of any submenu, a kfm window opens displaying the contents of the directory that you selected.

For example, if you select Disk Navigator, Home, you see the contents of your home directory, where you can select other subdirectories. If you choose Disk Navigator, Home, Open Folder, the contents of your home directory appear in a kfm window. This hour describes working with kfm windows.

If you choose submenus to locate a file and then choose a file, KDE attempts to open that file using the file typing tools in kfm, as described in this hour.

The Disk Navigator also includes a Recent section where you can select programs or directories that you've recently accessed. Options for the Disk Navigator are configured by choosing Disk Navigator, Options.

Browsing Your Local File System

Although you can open kfm from a command line (see the next section), most users prefer to open a window with their home directory and browse from that point. Figure 9.3 shows the kfm window with a user's home directory. Key parts of the window are identified in the following figure.

FIGURE 9.3

Each kfm window includes a menu, toolbar, and status bar, in addition to the content area.

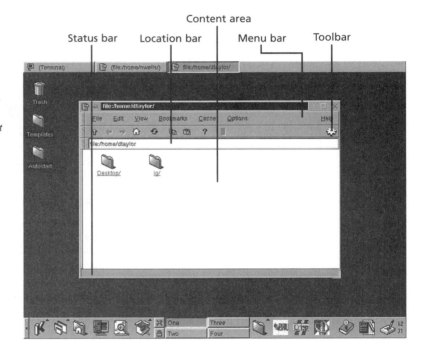

You can choose which parts of the kfm window are visible by choosing items on the Options menu. Other configuration settings are described later in this hour.

The location bar contains a URL-style description of the contents of the window. If you're viewing part of your local file system, the location URL begins with `file:/`; if you're viewing a Web page, it begins with `http://`.

You can click in the location bar and enter a new URL (leaving the `file:/` designator for local file system access), and then press Enter to update the contents of the kfm window.

Some basic operations in a kfm window might be obvious to you:

Double-clicking isn't required in kfm. One click will do it for all the operations described here.

- Click on the icon for a text file to open and view it in the KEdit text editor.
- Click on a directory folder to change to that directory (the current contents of the window are always described by the location bar).
- Click on the up arrow on the left end of the toolbar to change to the parent directory.
- Click on the Home icon on the toolbar to return to your home directory.

Some operations are just as simple, but may not be as obvious to you:

- To open a new window (handy for drag-and-drop operations), choose File, New Window.
- To select an icon without trying to open or view it, hold down the Ctrl key while clicking on it.
- To select files based on a pattern (such as all .gif files), choose Edit, Select, f and enter a pattern as requested.
- To move a selected icon or icons to the KDE Trash bin, choose Move to Trash from the Edit menu. (The desktop Trash icon doesn't need to be visible to do this.)
- To print the contents of any kfm window, choose Print from the File menu.
- To see a pop-up menu of options for a specific icon, right-click on any icon.

Because kfm is also a Web browser, if you view a directory that contains an index.html file, that file will be displayed instead of the files in the directory. To see this, you can visit the /home/httpd/html directory on most Linux distributions (see Figure 9.4).

To see the files in the directory instead of the index.html file, uncheck HTML View in the View menu.

With an HTML document displayed, you can use the Copy and Paste options on the Edit menu (or the buttons on the toolbar). This places the text in the KDE buffer, from which it can be pasted into other KDE applications.

FIGURE 9.4

*A kfm window can
view HTML documents
such as this default
index.html file on
Caldera's OpenLinux.*

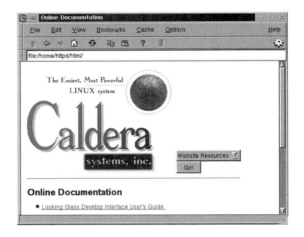

> Hidden files and directories (such as the .kde directory in your home direc-
> tory) don't appear in kfm windows unless you select Show Dot Files in the
> View menu.

Running Programs from kfm

When you have a kfm window open, each file in the window is assigned a type based on
the file extension or other information. The type assigned to a file determines the icon
used to display it, the options listed on the right-click menu for the icon, and what happens when you click on the icon.

KDE uses MIME file typing (a UNIX standard) to define data types that can be assigned
to files. When you open a directory containing text files, click on a file icon to open that
file in the default text editor, KEdit.

When you view a directory containing graphic files, click on the icon for a file to display
that graphic in the Image Viewer, KView.

However, if you click on a file icon for which kfm has found no corresponding MIME
type, you see a dialog box asking which application should be used to open or view this
file (see Figure 9.5). This is also true if you click on a program executable.

FIGURE 9.5

*When kfm cannot
determine how to open
a file, a dialog box lets
you select an applica-
tion to use.*

kfm isn't really intended as a place from which you can launch all programs. Instead, you must define an application that you want to run and assign a few basic properties to it. This is described in the next section.

Defining an Application in kfm

In order for kfm to launch an application, you must define the application using a `kdelnk` file. This file includes all the information that KDE and kfm need to successfully launch and manage your application.

To create a link so you can launch an application from your home directory (or any other location you choose), follow these steps:

1. Open a kfm window containing your home directory (choose Home Directory from the main menu).

2. Choose File, New, Application, in the kfm window. (The options on the New sub-menu are defined in the Templates directory of your desktop.)

3. In the pop-up dialog box that appears, enter a name for the application link that you want to create. The default is `Program.kdelnk`. Change the Program portion but leave the `.kdelnk` extension. I'll create an example called `gimp.kdelnk`.

4. When you choose OK, an icon appears in the directory with the name you entered.

5. Right-click the new icon and choose Properties from the pop-up menu.

6. The Properties dialog box contains different tabs depending on the type of icon for which you are viewing properties.

7. The General tab shows the name of the Application link. You can change the file's name here if you choose (see Figure 9.6).

FIGURE 9.6

The General tab of an applications link lets you define a name for the link.

8. Change to the Execute tab (see Figure 9.7) and enter the full path to the application binary in the Execute field. (If your PATH is configured to locate the binary, you can use just the executable name. Use the Browse button if you want to browse through your file system to find it.)

FIGURE 9.7

The Execute tab defines which program is launched when this kdelnk *file is selected.*

9. Enter a working directory for this application if applicable in the Working Directory field.

10. If you want to change the icon used to display this application, click on the icon (initially a gear) and choose an icon from the hundreds in the Select Icon dialog box (see Figure 9.8).

FIGURE 9.8

The Select Icon dialog box lets you choose an icon for a new application link from hundreds of icons included with KDE.

This hour doesn't explore the other options in the Execute tab.

You can choose OK to close the dialog box. Now click your new icon to run the application.

11. Click on the Application tab (see Figure 9.9) to assign MIME types that this application can read.

FIGURE 9.9

The Application tab defines which MIME types this application can edit or view.

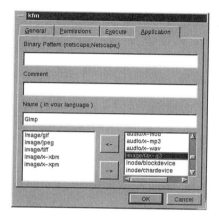

12. In the Binary Pattern field, enter the name of the application as it would be started from a command line, including a parameter for a filename to view or edit. For example, to start the XV Viewer with a filename, enter the following in the Binary Pattern field:

```
xv %f
```

13. Enter a comment and name in the respective fields to describe the application.

14. In the list of MIME types, select each one that this application can read (such as different text or graphic formats), and choose the arrow button to add them to the list on the left side.

15. When you see an icon of this type in a kfm window, the right-click menu for that file will include the application that you are now defining.

16. Choose OK to close the dialog box when you have finished.

The kdelnk file that you created is not a copy of the application that you wanted to launch. Rather, it is an information file that tells kfm how to launch the application and let other files use the application. If you view the contents of the gimp.kdelnk object (file) that was just created, you see that it contains properties values used by kfm and other KDE applications:

```
$ more ~/gimp.kdelnk
# KDE Config File
[KDE Desktop Entry]
Comment[C]=The Gnu Image Manipulation Program
Comment[pt]=Aplicacão
```

```
Comment[fi]=Sovellus
SwallowExec=
SwallowTitle=
Comment[fr]=Application
BinaryPattern=gimp %f;
Comment[sk]=Aplikácia
Name[C]=gimp
MimeType=image/gif;image/jpeg;image/tiff;image/x-xbm;image/x-xpm;
Exec=gimp
Comment[pt_BR]=Aplicacão
Icon=5floppy_mount.xpm
TerminalOptions=
Path=/tmp
Type=Application
Comment[it]=Applicazione
Terminal=0
```

In this listing, notice the Exec line, which indicates the program to launch, the name of
the icon graphic, the type (an application), and the MIME types supported by this application.

> You must create application links (application-type kdelnk files) in order to
> complete many configuration tasks in KDE, including adding icons to the
> Panel or main menu or placing programs in your Autostart folder.

You can also create new MIME types and define the files that use that type definition,
and define which application is used to read them (see Figure 9.10). Other types of
kdelkn files are used to access many types of resources in kfm files and throughout
KDE.

FIGURE 9.10

*New MIME type defin-
itions use the Binding
tab to define which file
extensions are included
in the MIME type.*

Later hours describe using `kdelnk` files for other purposes, but you can start to learn about them by creating other types of new objects from the File, New menu in a kfm window.

Use the Properties item on the right-click menu to edit the properties of each object type.

> The MIME Types and Applications items on the Edit menu display the `mimelnk` and `applnk` subdirectories of your local KDE directory (`~/.kde/share/`). These subdirectories provide a storage area for MIME types and application links that you create for your own use (rather than for all users on your Linux system).

9

Using Drag and Drop

Because kfm is so nicely integrated in KDE, you can drag icons from a kfm window and drop them in many other KDE applications. The MIME types described in the previous section are assigned to all files by kfm (to the degree possible); applications also register the MIME types that they can read.

Table 9.1 lists some ways that you can use drag and drop within KDE. You might find others that are convenient for you. It never hurts to try dragging an icon and dropping where you want it. A message will tell you if the operation can't be completed.

TABLE 9.1 SAMPLE DRAG-AND-DROP OPERATIONS IN KDE

Drag an Icon of This Type from a kfm Window	Drop the Icon Here
Any application link (such as the `gimp.kdelnk` created in the previous example)	The Panel (right-click on any Panel icon to shift or remove it
Any application link	The desktop (see Hour 10, "Managing your Files in KDE," for more detail)
Any text file	An open copy of the KEdit Text editor
Any graphics file	An open copy of the KView image viewer
Any PostScript document file	An open copy of the PS Viewer program
Any icon	A terminal window (to enter the full path of the dragged icon as if typed into the terminal)

Using kfm Bookmarks

Bookmarks are a common part of all Web browsers. A bookmark, or *hotlist*, contains pointers or links to Web pages that you have visited and want to be able to easily return to later.

These bookmarks are actually URLs, of course. In kfm, a bookmark can refer to a local file, a Web page, or anything else that kfm can display, including many types of `kdelnk` files.

To add a bookmark in kfm, view the page or directory that you want to bookmark, and then select Add Bookmark from the Bookmarks menu. The URL for the current location is added to the Bookmarks menu.

If you want to edit the list of bookmarks, choose Edit Bookmarks from the Bookmarks menu. The directory where bookmarks are stored—`~/.kde/share/apps/kfm/ bookmarks`—is shown in a new kfm window (see Figure 9.11).

FIGURE 9.11

Bookmarks are edited in a kfm window by deleting, moving, or changing the properties of a bookmark.

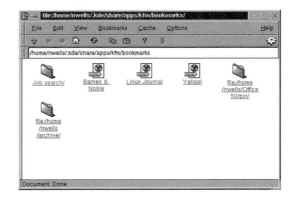

From this window, you can open the Properties dialog box for any bookmark (using the right-click menu) and change the URL that it refers to. You can also delete the bookmark.

If you want to create multilevel bookmark lists, add a subdirectory to the Bookmarks directory that you're viewing by choosing File, New, Folder and entering a new folder name.

Multiple levels of bookmarks are displayed in the Bookmarks menu using submenus (see Figure 9.12).

FIGURE 9.12

The Bookmarks menu can include submenus, defined by subdirectories in the share/bookmarks *directory.*

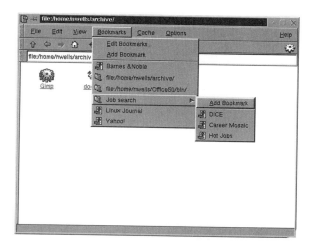

After you have several sublevels in your Bookmarks directory, you can move bookmarks by dragging their icons between kfm windows.

Bookmarks stored in the system-wide KDE directory (/opt/kde/share/apps/ kfm/bookmarks) are also added to your Bookmarks menu after those in your local Bookmarks directory.

Configuring kfm

kfm includes many configuration options to let you set the display of objects as you prefer. The sections that follow describe how to set these options.

Choosing How to View Objects

The default Icon view has been used in the figures so far, but kfm can display objects using several methods. All these are listed in the View menu of each kfm.

The second set of items in the View menu determines the base viewing method for objects in the window. The options are

- *Icon view.* Uses large icons in a grid.
- *Text view.* Displays a line for each object, as if created in a directory listing using the ls -1 command (see Figure 9.13).
- *Long view.* Displays the same information as the Text view, but with a small icon to the left of the object name (see Figure 9.14).

FIGURE 9.13

The Text view shows directory contents as a list of files, similar to the ls -l *command.*

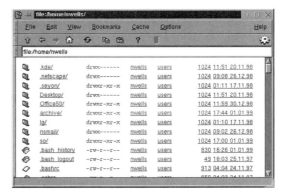

FIGURE 9.14

The Long view is similar to the Text view, except an icon is included, which can be dragged and dropped in other applications.

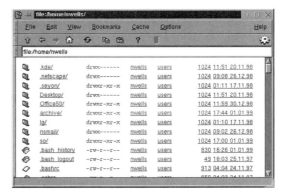

- *Short view.* Also has a small icon to the left of the object, but with only the object name shown (see Figure 9.15).

FIGURE 9.15

The Short view is similar to the Long view, except only the icon and object name are shown.

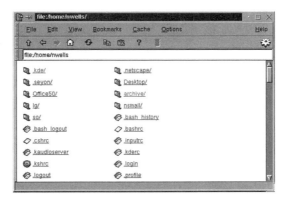

In any of these views, you can click on objects to choose them, or right-click on the text or icon for an object to see a pop-up menu of options.

The options at the top of the View menu let you select how to view objects:

- *To view all hidden files when viewing a directory, choose Show Hidden Files.* For example, your .kde directory will not appear in your home directory unless Show Hidden Files is selected.

- *To view a split window view of your file system, choose Show Tree.* This shows the directory structure on the left side of the window, with the contents of the current directory on the right side (see Figure 9.16)

9

FIGURE 9.16

With Show Tree selected, a file struc-ture tree is shown in a separate frame on the left of the kfm window.

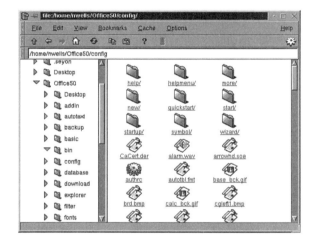

The Show Tree view is very helpful if you need to browse many areas of your file system. Don't be confused by the items in the tree frame, however. The right side always displays the contents of the directory listed in the URL field below the tool-bar. Click on any directory name in the left side of the Tree view to see the con-tents of that directory. Click on the small arrow to open or close that directory, which will show the subdirectories that it contains.

- If the HTML view is selected, kfm searches for an index.html file in each direc-tory that it displays. If the index.html file is found, it is displayed. To display the files in the directory instead of the index.html file, deselect the HTML View option. You can still click on the index.html icon to display it, of course.

The next three options on the View menu are used when something has been changed or updated on your system. Suppose, for example, that you had a kfm window open, but then mounted a new device in another window. To update the display in a kfm window, select Reload Tree from the View menu.

If you're viewing a document (such as an HTML file), choose Reload Document to reload the file from its source (disk or network).

> The Reload Document item is just like the Reload button on a Web browser.

The Rescan Bindings option lets you revise the rules used for kfm. This option is only useful if you've altered the kfm configuration files (described later in this section).

The last two options on the View menu let you view the source for an HTML document that you're viewing in a kfm window. The HTML source appears in a KEdit window when you choose Document Source from the View menu.

If you're viewing an HTML document with frames, click in the frame for which you want to view source text, and then choose View Frame Source.

> The Frame Source and Document Source options work by sending the URL to the KEdit program. If you're viewing the contents of a directory using the HTML View option (so that the index.html file is viewed automatically), the URL still shows the directory name. View Document Source will not work in this case because the filename, index.html, is not passed to the text editor for viewing. To view the file, turn off HTML View in the View menu, select the index.html file among the files in the directory, and then choose View Document Source again.

Selecting Cache Settings

When you visit Web pages in a kfm window, the files that are downloaded (both HTML and graphics) are stored on your local hard drive in the *cache*.

If you revisit the same location, kfm can save time by loading the files from the locally stored cache instead of reloading them from the Internet.

kfm provides several options for controlling the cache from the Cache menu of each kfm window.

> The options that you select in one kfm window apply to that window. Other kfm windows can use different cache options.

The first two options on the Cache menu allow you to view saved information in the current kfm window. If you choose Show History, a listing of all the locations you have viewed in kfm windows is displayed, including directories, files, Web sites, and so forth (see Figure 9.17).

FIGURE 9.17

Choosing Show History opens a kfm window with a list of all the URLs—local and networked—that you have visited.

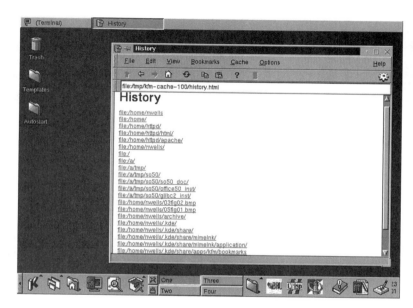

The History list is also shown as items on the Go menu.

This History listing shows you the URLs that you would visit if you used the back arrow repeatedly. By choosing this menu option, you can click on any item in the History list without stepping back through them one at a time using the back arrow on the toolbar.

Similarly, the Show Cache option shows you all the files that are stored in the cache. You can drag an icon for a cached file to a new kfm window to move it, or click on the name of the item to open it in the current kfm window.

Suppose, for example, that you had downloaded a page containing a graphical table of information, but you didn't remember the name of the URL, so you couldn't locate it in the History list.

Using the Show Cache item, you could browse the graphics files that kfm had cached on your system and drag the correct image to your home directory for review.

The Clear Cache option has a different purpose. Choosing this option deletes all the files that kfm has cached. There should be no harm in this, except that it means you must be connected to the Internet and wait for a download if you revisit a Web page.

> If you want to force a reload of a page you're viewing, choose Reload Document or press the Reload button on the toolbar. You don't need to use Clear Cache unless you want all documents to be reloaded.

The last four items on the Cache menu actually behave like two items.

Always Look in Cache or Never Look in cache: When you select one of these, the other is deselected.

These options select whether the cache is used when Web pages are requested. If you choose Never Look in Cache, all pages will be reloaded when requested. If you choose Always Look in Cache, pages that have been viewed previously (since the cache was cleared) will be loaded from the cache instead of from the Internet.

Working with the Always/Never Look in Cache option is the Always/Never Save Cache option. If Always is selected, each page that you view from the Internet is stored in the cache.

> Local files are not stored in the cache.

> You can use these two options independently. For example, when your cache contains many files, you can turn off Always Save Cache for a while, rather than clear the cache. Or, you could select Always Save Cache, with Never Look in Cache, to build up a new set of cached documents to replace older versions.

Configuring the Browser Options

The Proxy tab (see Figure 9.18) and HTTP tab both allow you to define options for the networking used by kfm to load Web pages.

FIGURE 9.18

The Proxy tab lets you define a proxy server and associated port if your network uses a proxy to access Web or FTP servers.

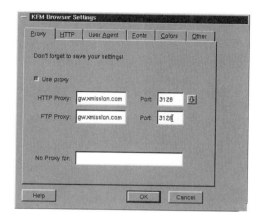

9

If you're using a proxy on your local network to reach the Web, you can enter the proxy server name and port number in the Proxy tab. Proxy for HTTP (Web) and FTP are supported.

The HTTP tab (see Figure 9.19) allows you to define the character set and languages supported when viewing Web pages. You can generally leave these settings as they are because they will be modified for you if you select new languages for KDE.

FIGURE 9.19

The HTTP tab defines which languages and character sets are used to display HTML pages in a kfm window.

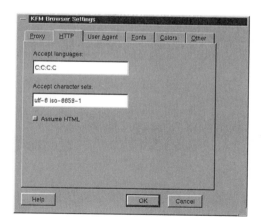

When the Assume HTML check box is selected, any file retrieved from the Internet is assumed to be HTML if no other file type can be determined for it. This is helpful if you're reading files with unexpected file extensions and prefer that kfm attempt to display the contents of the file.

Reviewing the kfm Configuration Files

As you learned in Hour 8, "Using KDE Themes," KDE uses configuration files to store settings for each KDE application. Most of the configuration for kfm, however, can be done using the menus described in this section.

Any configuration you do for kfm by editing text files is likely to be centered around the kdelnk files and MIME type files described earlier in this hour.

If you do want to review the kfm configuration files, check these two files in any text editor:

```
/opt/kde/share/config/kfmrc
~/.kde/share/config/kfmrc
```

Some additional files are located in the `/opt/kde/apps/kfm` directory, but these are files stored for the use of kfm; they should not be edited directly in a text editor.

You can change the icons used by kfm to display various file types by changing the filenames in the MIME type files (review `/opt/kde/share/mimelnk`) or change the graphics in `/opt/kde/share/apps/kfm/pics`.

Summary

This hour describes how to use the Disk Navigator menu and the kfm file management windows to access your Linux file system in KDE. You learned about changing the way files and directories are viewed, working with file types (based on MIME types), and how to configure parts of the kfm program. You also learned a little about the kdelnk files that are used by many KDE applications.

Questions and Answers

Q Why doesn't the CD-ROM option on the Disk Navigator menu show anything?

A Before accessing the CD-ROM drive, you must mount a CD-ROM using a command such as this one at a command line:

```
$ mount /mnt/cdrom
```

The command depends on how your hardware is configured, and might be more complicated than this example. In addition, you may not have permission to mount devices unless you're logged in as root.

Q **How can I change the items shown in the Disk Navigator menu?**

A The Shared section of the Disk Navigator menu is determined by the contents of the `/opt/kde/share/apps/kdisknav` directory. The Personal section is determined by the contents of the `~/.kde/share/apps/kdisknav` directory. Both of these directories must contain `kdelnk` files to provide KDE (and the Disk Navigator program) the information needed to work with the items.

Q **Can I define other drag-and-drop operations?**

A Sort of. The drag-and-drop operations are defined by two things. Each KDE application must be programmed to access dropped files or *sent* dragged files to other operations. You can't alter that part of the program, nor should you expect non-KDE applications to interact with KDE applications using drag and drop. If a program already allows drag and drop, you might be able to use additional file types by changing how the MIME types are defined for your KDE system. However, this is a pretty advanced topic.

Exercises

1. Use the Disk Navigator options to turn off display of the Recent section of the Disk Navigator menu.

2. Convert a few of the bookmarks from your Web browser into bookmarks for kfm by creating URL-style kdelnk files and subdirectories to define categories. The bookmarks should be placed in `~/.kde/share/apps/kfm/bookmarks`.

HOUR 10

Learning More KDE File Management

In this hour you learn how to manage your files using the graphical utilities provided by KDE. You learn how to make the best use of the KDE Desktop and how to place and remove files from the desktop. The use of the Autostart folder is also explained.

Creating KDE Links

The secret to managing your files in KDE is to understand a little about KDE Link files. These files, which I've described in previous hours, have a .kdelnk file extension. They contain information about a program, device, or other system resource that allows KDE applications to work with that resource.

For example, items in the main menu or on the Panel must be kdelnk files. Applications in your Autostart folder also must be kdelnk files.

To create a KDE link, you can use the New menu in any kfm file browsing window. You can also right-click on the desktop background of KDE and choose New from the pop-up menu that appears.

The items on the New submenu are defined by the templates in KDE. These templates provide a shell that you can use to quickly define a new KDE link for an application, device, Web address, and so forth. Create a couple of links to see how this is done.

Creating a Program Link

First, create a link to an application program.

1. Open a kfm window showing your home directory by choosing Home Directory from the main menu.

2. Choose File, New, Application.

3. A small dialog box lets you enter the name of the application program (see Figure 10.1).

FIGURE 10.1

Enter the name of the KDE link for the new application you want to refer to.

 Don't remove the .kdelnk extension. Only change the *program* portion of the name in the dialog box.

4. Choose OK. After a moment, a Gear icon appears in your home directory with the name you entered.

5. Right-click on the icon and choose Properties from the pop-up menu. A dialog box appears where you can change the properties of this KDE Link (see Figure 10.2).

6. The General tab contains the name of the link you've created. Before you can use this link, you must define which application it refers to. To do this, select the Execute tab (see Figure 10.3).

7. Enter the application name that this link should launch in the Execute field. (Use the Browse button if necessary to locate the application in your file system.)

8. If you want to change the icon used for this link, click the Gear icon and choose a new icon from the Select Icon dialog box.

FIGURE 10.2

Use this dialog box to change the properties of the new KDE link that you created.

FIGURE 10.3

The Execute tab defines the application that this program link will run when you click on its icon.

The Swallowing on Panel options let an application's window become part of the KDE Panel when it's run. This is similar to the date and time window that is included on the Panel. Some utilities, such as CPU usage monitors, are designed to be *swallowed* by the Panel. Only KDE applications that are designed to appear on the Panel can use this option. Refer to the online documentation for an application to determine if it is intended to be swallowed on the Panel.

9. You can explore the Permissions and Application tabs if you want. When you're finished, choose OK to close this dialog box.

Now, if you click on this icon, the application you entered in the Execute tab will be launched.

To see how this link helps KDE, open a terminal window and use this command in your home directory to see the contents of the link you just created (substitute the name of your link).

```
$ more ~/Netscape.kdelnk
# KDE Config File
[KDE Desktop Entry]
Comment[C]=Netscape Communicator browser
Comment[pt]=Aplicacão
Comment[fi]=Sovellus
SwallowTitle=
SwallowExec=
Comment[fr]=Application
BinaryPattern=netscape;Netscape;
Comment[sk]=Aplikácia
Name[C]=Netscape
MimeType=text/html;
Exec=netscape
Comment[pt_BR]=Aplicacão
Icon=www.xpm
TerminalOptions=
Path=~
Type=Application
Comment[it]=Applicazione
Terminal=0
```

The values assigned in this file tell KDE how to launch this application, which icon to use when displaying it, which file types it can edit (if you edited the Applications tab), and other information. Multiple language descriptions can also be provided.

Remember that a link isn't a copy of an application, it's only a pointer to the application so KDE can use it. If you delete the link file, it has no effect on the application, only on KDE's capability to graphically launch it.

Use this application link in the following sections about the Autostart folder and the KDE menu and Panel.

Creating a Device Link

Many types of system resources can be accessed or managed via KDE links, including a system device such as a hard drive, floppy drive, or CD-ROM drive.

A device link makes it easy to work with a device graphically. For example, if you want to begin using your CD-ROM drive or a floppy drive in Linux, you must first mount either device into your file system. A KDE link lets you do this with a click, instead of using a complex mount command.

To create a KDE link to your floppy drive, follow these steps:

1. Open a kfm window with your home directory in it.
2. Choose File, New, File System Device.
3. Enter a name for the device (leaving the `.kdelnk` extension unchanged).
4. Choose OK to close the dialog box. An icon appears in your home directory with the name you entered.
5. Right-click on the new icon and choose Properties. A dialog box appears with the properties of this link. The tabs are different than the application program in the previous section because this is a device.
6. Change to the Device tab (see Figure 10.4).

10

FIGURE 10.4

The Device tab lets you define how to mount and use the device that this KDE link describes.

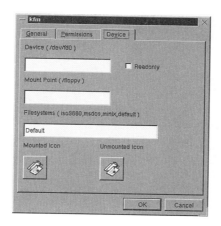

7. Enter the device location in the Device field. For example, your CD-ROM drive might be `/dev/cdrom`, and your floppy drive `/dev/fd0`. This examle uses `/dev/fd0`.
8. Select the Read Only check box if this device should not allow data to be written.
9. Enter a directory name in the Mount Point field. This might be something such as `/floppy` or `/mnt/floppy` for the floppy disk drive; but it can be any directory you define.

If your system is not set up to allow all users to mount devices, you'll have to log in as root or change the values in your /etc/fstab and /etc/mtab files so that all users can mount the floppy drive.

10. Enter a file system for the device (you can generally leave this set to the default).

You could create two separate KDE links: one to mount and unmount a MS-DOS format disk and another to use Linux-format disks (using the ext2 file system).

11. Choose icons for the device icon. One is shown when the device is mounted, another when it's unmounted. Figure 10.5 shows the filled-in Device tab for a floppy drive on an OpenLinux system. I have selected icons I think are appropriate.

FIGURE 10.5

The information in this Device tab refers to a floppy disk drive.

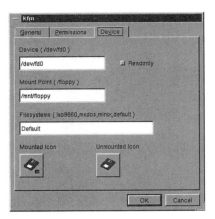

12. With the Device tab filled in, choose OK to close the dialog box.
13. Insert a floppy disk in the disk drive.
14. Now right-click again on the icon and choose Mount. The device is mounted.

If the Mount item is not visible on the right-click menu, choose View, Reload Document, to refresh the kfm window.

15. Double-click on the icon. A kfm window appears showing the contents of the disk drive, which you can work with just as you do files in other kfm windows.

16. In your home directory, right-click the Device Link icon and choose Unmount. You can now eject the floppy disk safety.

Looking at the KDE link file for a device is also interesting. In your home directory, you can use this command (substituting the name of the device link file you created).

```
$ more ~/floppy.kdelnk
# KDE Config File
[KDE Desktop Entry]
UnmountIcon=3floppy_unmount.xpm
Comment[pt]=Dispositivo com Sistema de Ficheiros
Comment[fi]=Tiedostosysteemi
Comment[fr]=Pèriphèrique système de fichiers
Comment[sk]=Zariadenie súborovèho systèmu (File System Device)
Comment[es]=Dispositivo con sistema de ficheros
MountPoint=/mnt/floppy
Comment=File System Device
Comment[pt_BR]=Dispositivo com Sistema de Arquivos
Comment[pl]=Urz±dzenie
Icon=3floppy_mount.xpm
Dev=/dev/fd0
ReadOnly=0
FSType=msdos
Comment[it]=Dispositivo con Sistema File
Type=FSDevice
Comment[de]=Dateisystem
```

You can also create links that refer to a Web page, an FTP site, or a file on your local system.

Links can be created in any kfm window. But a link is only a regular file with a special meaning to KDE applications. You'll see how to use them in the following sections.

Using the Autostart Folder

After you know how to create KDE links, KDE provides all sorts of great tools for managing your files.

The Autostart folder lets you place KDE links to applications or files that you want started automatically when you launch KDE.

If you add a data file to the Autostart folder, KDE attempts to start the correct application to view or edit that data file. For example, if you place a StarOffice document you're working on in the Autostart folder, KDE starts StarOffice and loads the document file automatically when you launch KDE.

Initially, the Autostart folder is displayed on your desktop, but it's empty. To see the contents of the folder, click on it. It appears in a kfm browsing window.

You can add an item to the Autostart folder in three ways:

- Create a new KDE Link using the File, New menu as described earlier in this hour.
- Use a terminal window to enter commands to move, link or copy the kdelnk file to another location.

> The contents displayed in the AutoStart folder are actually the contents of the directory ~/Desktop/Autostart.

- Drag and drop an existing KDE Link file into the Autostart folder.

You can use a KDE link file from anywhere and drag and drop it on the Autostart folder. For example, the new Netscape application link created in the preceding example (in the previous section) can be dragged to the Autostart folder.

> You can drag and drop KDE Link icons onto the Autostart folder on the desktop without opening the folder (so it's visible in a kfm window).

Each time you drag and drop a KDE Link icon, you see a small selection menu that you must select from before the drop operation is completed (see Figure 10.6).

Remember: A KDE Link is just a regular file that has special meaning to KDE applications (including the core of KDE that examines the Autostart folder at startup).

The pop-up menu gives you three choices when you drop a KDE Link in a new location:

- *Copy the KDE link file to the new location.* This allows the link to be edited independently if needed. (Each KDE link file takes up only a few bytes.)
- *Move the KDE link file to the new location.* The link will no longer exist in the previous location. (The location of the application itself, as referred to in the KDE link file, remains unchanged.)
- *Link the existing KDE link file to the new location you're dropping on, using a symbolic link.* This means that only one copy of the KDE link file exists; a pointer in the new location refers to the original when it is launched. This means that if you edit the KDE link from either location, the same physical file is updated.

FIGURE 10.6

Dropping a KDE Link lets you choose to Copy, Move, or Link it in the new location.

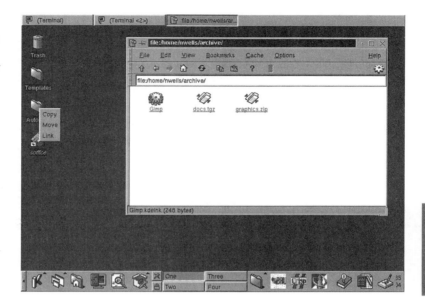

The Link option on the drop-down menu creates a UNIX- or Linux-style symbolic link in your file system. Don't confuse this with the KDE link file, which contains pointer information (as seen in the listings in this hour) to a system resource, but can only be used by KDE applications.

After you choose Copy, Move, or Link, the drop operation is completed and the new KDE Link can be used.

If you decide to cancel the drag-and-drop operation after seeing the drop-down menu, move the mouse pointer to a blank area of your KDE Desktop and click to cancel the drop.

Placing Objects on the Desktop

Placing an object on the KDE Desktop is straightforward once you have a KDE link created for the object in question.

As with the Autostart folder, you can place icons on the KDE Desktop using any of three methods:

- Create a new KDE Link on the desktop by right-clicking and using the New submenu to create a KDE link (as described earlier in this hour).

KDE links created using the Desktop pop-up menu are placed in the ~/Desktop directory.

- Use a terminal window to enter commands to move, link, or copy the desired .kdelnk file to the Desktop directory.
- Drag and drop an existing KDE link file anywhere on the desktop.

If you have a KDE link created for any data file or application, device or URL, you can drag it from a kfm window (for the directory where it's currently located), dropping it anywhere on the KDE Desktop.

As with the Autostart folder described previously, when you drop a KDE link file on the desktop, you see a pop-up menu allowing you to copy, move, or link the KDE link on the desktop.

Items that you drop on the KDE Desktop are shown on *all* your KDE desktops. That is, if you change to Desktop Two, from Desktop Three (or whatever you've named them), the same icons appear on the desktop.

After you've copied or created new KDE links on your desktop, you can use the right-click Desktop menu (shown in Figure 10.7) to arrange icons on the desktop. This moves the icons, aligning them on the side of your screen.

In places like the Autostart folder or the Panel, it makes sense to place links to application programs that you use regularly. On the desktop, however, you can also place icons for documents, spreadsheets, or other data files that you are currently working on.

With these icons on your desktop, you can click to open the correct application and begin working on your file.

You must have correct MIME types defined in order for KDE to know which application to use to edit a given data file. These are described in more detail in Hour 9, "Managing Files in KDE."

To create a KDE link for a data file, use the right-click Desktop menu and choose New, URL. After you name the URL link and right-click on the new icon to open the Properties dialog box, choose the URL tab (see Figure 10.8).

FIGURE 10.7

The right-click KDE Desktop menu includes an option to arrange all the icons you've placed on the desktop.

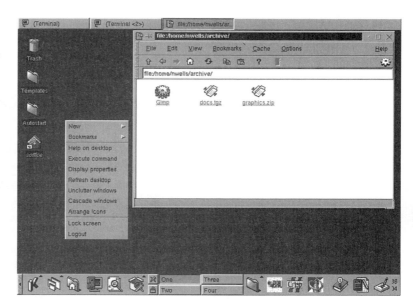

FIGURE 10.8

Any data or document file can be referenced by a KDE link using the New URL options. The URL tab defines the file that the Link points to.

In the URL field, enter the full path to the data file. (You don't need to start it with `file:`.)

Click on the default icon shown in the dialog box to select a different icon if you prefer.

Choose OK to close the dialog box. Now when you click on this desktop icon, KDE attempts to open the correct application and display this data file.

Modifying the Main Menu

Most of the items on the KDE main menu (shown in Figure 10.9) are defined by `kdelnk` files.

FIGURE 10.9

The KDE main menu contains many applications; most are accessed via KDE link files.

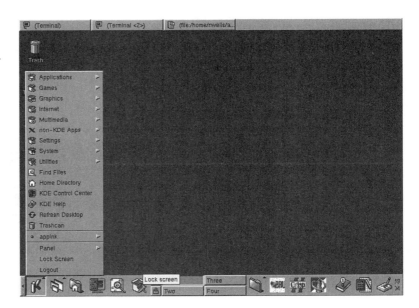

The KDE main menu is defined by the items found in the `/opt/kde/share/applnk` directory. To see this, open a terminal window and enter this command:

```
$ ls -l /opt/kde/share/applnk
total 20
drwxr-xr-x   2 root      root         1024 Dec 28 17:58 Applications
drwxr-xr-x   2 root      root         1024 Dec 28 17:54 Games
drwxr-xr-x   2 root      root         1024 Dec 28 17:56 Graphics
-rw-r--r--   1 root      root         1580 Oct  7 23:26 Help.kdelnk
-rw-r--r--   1 root      root         1800 Oct  7 23:26 Home.kdelnk
drwxr-xr-x   2 root      root         1024 Dec 28 17:56 Internet
-rw-r--r--   1 root      root         1300 Oct  7 23:26 KControl.kdelnk
-rw-r--r--   1 root      root         1418 Oct  7 23:26 Kfind.kdelnk
-rw-r--r--   1 root      root         1649 Oct  7 23:26 Krefresh.kdelnk
drwxr-xr-x   2 root      root         1024 Dec 28 17:54 Multimedia
drwxr-xr-x   9 root      root         1024 Dec 28 17:54 Settings
drwxr-xr-x   2 root      root         1024 Dec 28 17:56 System
-rw-r--r--   1 root      root         1624 Oct  7 23:26 Trash.kdelnk
drwxr-xr-x   2 root      root         1024 Dec 28 17:58 Utilities
```

This listing will vary slightly depending on your Linux distribution and on any modifications that you have made since installing Linux and KDE.

Notice in the listing that the directory names correspond to submenus on the main menu, such as Internet, Graphics, and Settings. The files with a `.kdelnk` extension are similar to items on the main menu, such as Kfind, Trash, and Kcontrol.

Some items on the main menu, such as the Panel submenu and the Logout option, are always included on the menu. They are not defined by the contents of the `applnk` directory or by KDE link files.

The actual name shown on the main menu is defined by a value within the `kdelnk` file. If you change to a subdirectory, such as Utilities, you can also find a `.directory` file, that contains the definition of how the directory name is displayed in the main menu (including the name of the submenu in many languages and the icon to use for it).

- *If you'd like to add an item to the main menu:* Copy, move, or link a KDE link file into the `/opt/kde/share/applnk` directory.
- *If you'd like to make a complete submenu on the main menu:* Create a directory in `/opt/kde/share/applnk` and populate it with a `.directory` file (copy from another and edit it) and kdelnk files to match the items you want to appear on the submenu.

The items on the main menu are always sorted by the label indicated in the `.kdelnk` or `.directory` file. Directories (submenus) are listed first, in alphabetical order, followed by individual links, also in alphabetical order.

Before you do this, however, keep in mind that the `/opt/kde/` menu structure is not intended for *normal* users to modify. If you are the only user on your Linux system or you are the system administrator, you can include new menu items in the `/opt/kde/share/applnk` directory. They will appear in the main menu for all KDE users on your Linux system.

Notice on the main menu that a submenu named Personal appears near the bottom. This submenu is intended for per-user changes to the main menu.

To place items on the Personal submenu (including more levels of submenus), copy, move, or link KDE link files to your ~/.kde/share/applnk directory. These additions will only appear when you log in to KDE. Other users will see only the system default main menu.

> Different installations of KDE will have different default configurations for the per-user Personal menu.

Now, if all this file copying is getting you down, choose Panel, Edit Menus from the main menu. The KmenuEdit utility appears, as shown in Figure 10.10.

FIGURE 10.10

Your KDE menus can be edited using the KmenuEdit program.

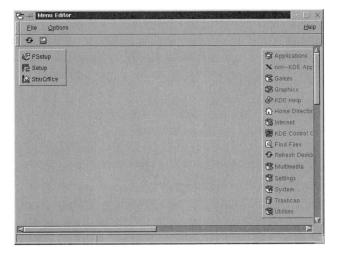

If you have permission to write files in the /opt/kde area, you can edit the main menu from here. Regular users will only edit the Personal submenu, displayed on the left side of the main KmenuEdit window.

To use KmenuEdit, use the right-click pop-up menu to choose New, Change, Delete, or other options. After you have a new item added to the menu, you can choose Change to modify its appearance, make it a submenu, rename it, and so forth. Figure 10.11 shows the dialog box where these options are selected.

FIGURE 10.11

The KmenuEdit program lets you modify newly added menu entries using this dialog box.

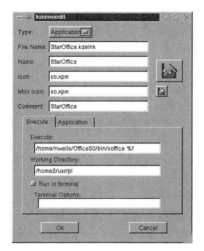

When you want to add applications to a menu, open a kfm window containing the KDE link that you have created to point to the application or other system resource. Drag the icon from the kfm window and drop it on the menu where you want it to appear. The kdelnk file is copied from the original directory to the appropriate directory (applnk or a subdirectory of it).

When you have finished editing your menus, choose File, Save, to save your changes, and then choose File, Quit to close the menu editing utility.

After editing the main menu, using the KmenuEdit utility or by moving files around, you should reload the main menu to see the results by choosing Panel, Restart on the main menu.

Modifying the Panel Icons

Changing the KDE Panel is a simple matter of dragging KDE link files and dropping them on the Panel.

Open a kfm window containing the .kdelnk file that refers to the program or device you want to add to the Panel. Drag the icon from the kfm window and drop it on the Panel in the location where you'd like it to be placed.

An icon on the Panel can cover up other icons. To move (or delete) an icon that is already on the Panel, right-click on the icon. If you choose Move, the icon moves as you move the mouse. Click to drop the icon in a new location.

If you choose the Properties item on the pop-up menu, a dialog box opens where you can set up information about this link. The dialog box should be familiar to you from earlier in this hour.

To create submenus on the Panel, you can drag a folder from a kfm window and drop it on the Panel. The folder should contain KDE link files; each will be shown on a pop-up menu when a user clicks on the folder on the Panel.

 As with the main menu, choose Panel, Restart, on the main menu after making any changes to the Panel to be sure they are visible and active.

If you prefer, you can also choose Panel, Add Application, on the main menu, and then select an application from the copy of the main menu, which appears to add it to the Panel (see Figure 10.12). The disadvantage of this method is that an item must be part of the main menu before it can be added to the Panel.

FIGURE 10.12

You can add items to the Panel by choosing Panel, Add Application.

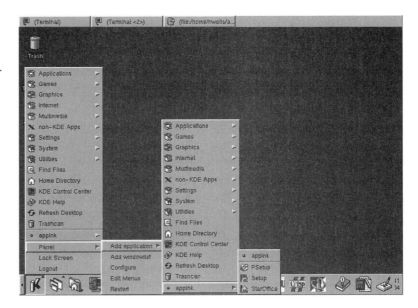

The Panel also has a configuration file that you can review. It contains many configuration options that you learned about in Hour 6, "Managing the KDE Environment," as well as a list of the buttons on the Panel.

The Panel configuration file is kpanelrc. It is located in the /opt/kde/share/config directory.

> Use caution when modifying the kpanelrc file by hand. Make a backup copy of the file first in case problems arise.

Changes to the Panel made by each user are stored in the ~/.kde/share/config/ kpanelrc file. The options in this file will override the settings in the system-wide file stored in the /opt/kde directories.

Summary

In this hour you continued learning about file management in KDE. You learned about KDE link files, practiced creating several of them, and learned how to use them on the KDE Desktop or Autostart folder, and in the main menu or Panel. You also learned how to modify or update Panel and main menu items.

Questions and Answers

Q Can I create link files without using the graphical system?

A Sure. You can use the templates provided in ~/Desktop/Templates as a basis and use any text editor to create a new KDE link file. Be certain to use the .kdelnk file extension. You can even use scripts to create new .kdelnk files automatically.

Q How can I change the Panel icon for the main menu (the K) or the fixed menu items such as the Trash can and home directory?

A Edit the source code for the KPanel program. If you develop a nice method to redefine some of these things, pass it back to the rest of the KDE community.

Q Why don't my screens match the figures in this book?

A Minor updates to KDE, different screen sizes (which cut off part of the Panel), and variations in the default KDE installation used by different Linux vendors all affect what you see onscreen. Because additional programs that you load automatically place themselves in the main menu, the Panel, or in other locations, you might not realize how customized your copy of KDE already is.

Q Can I make the Panel smaller or hide it?

A Yes. Choose Settings, Applications, Panel, on the main menu to change the size or other settings for the Panel. See Hour 6 for some additional information.

10

Exercises

1. Start the Moon Phase utility from the Utilities menu. Note how it appears on the Panel. This is an application *swallowed on Panel*. Right-click on the moon phase within the Panel and explore the options it provides.

2. Create a KDE device link for your CD-ROM drive (such as the floppy drive example in this hour). Choose New, File System Device, from a kfm window to get started. Add this KDE link to the Panel so you can access a CD by clicking on a Panel icon.

PART III

System Administration for KDE

Hour

11   Using KDE System Management Utilities

12   Using KDE Utilities

13   Managing Network Connections in KDE

14   Managing Printing in KDE

15   Accessing the Internet from KDE

16   Using the Command Line in KDE

Hour **11**

Using KDE System Management Utilities

In this hour you learn how to manage many different parts of your Linux system using the graphical utilities provided by the KDE environment.

KDE provides many utilities to manage parts of your Linux system such as CPU and memory usage, user accounts, installation of rpm-formatted software packages, and keyboard and mouse settings. In addition, KDE provides user-oriented tools to help locate files and perform other important system-related tasks.

> Changing most of the system settings described in this hour requires that you are logged in as the superuser, root. You can log in as root before starting KDE, or log in as su to root in a terminal window and start the named utilities from there. (Command-line names are given in each section.)

Setting Keyboard and Mouse Options

KDE provides configuration options to let you set up how your keyboard and mouse behave. You can set the keyboard repeat and key click volume options, define international keyboard options, and set a few options for your mouse.

Many of the keyboard and mouse settings shown here are controlled via the X Window System. While these KDE dialog boxes attempt to modify the settings of your X Window System, the options might not function as expected if your computer's BIOS (initial setup program) has disabled some functionality, such as the internal speaker for key clicks.

To configure the basic KDE keyboard options, choose Keyboard from the Input Devices section of the KDE Control Center (or from the main menu choose Settings, Input Devices, Keyboard). The Keyboard dialog box is shown in Figure 11.1.

FIGURE 11.1

The Keyboard dialog box provides simple configuration options for your KDE keyboard.

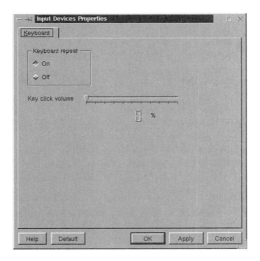

In the Keyboard Repeat field, you can select Off to disable keyboard repeat when you hold down a key. On is the default setting.

The key click volume slider determines how loudly the computer speaker clicks each time you press a key. This slider is set to 0% by default; the maximum value is 100%.

To review your mouse configuration settings, choose Mouse from the Input Devices section of the KDE Control Center (or choose Settings, Input Devices, Mouse, from the main menu). The Mouse dialog box is shown in Figure 11.2.

FIGURE 11.2

The Mouse dialog box adjusts for left- or right-handed users and controls accelerated mouse movement.

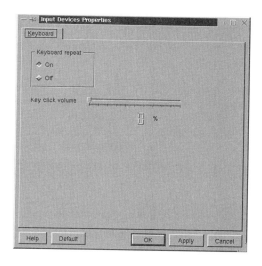

The Button Mapping field is used to indicate whether the user is right- or left-handed. When Right Handed is selected (the default setting), the main mouse button is the left mouse button; the right mouse button provides special functions such as pop-up menus.

When Left Handed is selected, the mapping of the right and left mouse buttons is reversed (the left mouse button is used for special functions such as pop-up menus).

The Acceleration and Threshold fields are used when you want to have the mouse be precise for small mouse movements and fast for larger mouse movements.

- *Acceleration slider:* Determines how fast the mouse will move when it switches to Accelerated mode. (Faster mouse movement means you move the mouse a little and the pointer onscreen moves a lot.)

- *Threshold slider:* Sets how far you have to move the mouse in a short period of time before it switches to Accelerated mode and moves more quickly (based on the Acceleration slider).

The idea behind this feature is that when you want to move the mouse pointer across the entire screen, you move the mouse quickly and the mouse pointer covers the entire distance. When you want to edit or choose precisely, you move the mouse slowly and the mouse pointer moves slowly as well.

If your mouse has a wheel for scrolling, you'll have to wait for the next release of KDE before the scrolling wheel will be recognized by KDE applications.

A few additional mouse options can also be configured using your X Window System configuration file (for example, /etc/XF86Config).

 If you choose a high acceleration rate and a low threshold, the mouse movement will be jerky and hard to work with. Adjust the values to find those that work best with your hand motions and work habits.

After setting any new values for the keyboard or mouse, choose OK or Apply to activate your settings.

Setting Up International Keyboards

Users of KDE outside the United States will be happy to know that KDE lets them configure their keyboard in many ways. To access the international keyboard configuration, choose International Keyboard from the Input Devices section of the Control Center, or choose Settings, Input Devices, International Keyboard, on the main menu.

This configuration dialog box sets up options for the kikbd utility, which you can start from the command line:

```
$ kikbd
```

or by choose Autostart in the Startup tab (described in this section). The kikbd program runs as a *daemon*—a process that manages the keyboard but otherwise doesn't make itself known except for a small window that appears in the Panel or on your desktop (depending on the Startup options). You can click in this window to switch to another configured international keyboard.

If you right-click on the kikbd window, a pop-up menu lets you choose from a list of configured keyboards or open the configuration dialog box described here.

The General tab, shown in Figure 11.3, allows you to select which international keyboard definitions are used by kikbd and how you can switch between these keyboards if several are defined in the Keyboard Maps list.

The keyboard maps that are available to kikbd are listed in the Keyboard Maps section. You can add additional keyboard maps to define various international keyboards by choosing Add. A dialog box appears where you can select from about 30 keyboard definitions. Each includes a brief description of that keyboard map.

The Up and Down buttons change the position of the selected keyboard map in the list. The top keyboard map listed is used as the default. If you want to use another of the keyboards listed as you work, you can use the Switch key defined in the Switch and Alt Switch field. Pressing the Switch key changes to the next keyboard in the list and updates the kikbd window to show you which keyboard is active. Pressing Alt plus the Switch key changes to the previous keyboard map in the list.

The Style tab lets you define the colors for the kikbd window on your Panel or desktop. You can click on any of the three color bars to change the color used for these notification features.

Finally, the StartUp tab defines how the kikbd program is launched (see Figure 11.4). If you've added an international keyboard in the General tab, you might want to check the Autostart check box so that the keyboard definition file is immediately available via kikbd when you launch KDE.

FIGURE 11.3

The General tab of the International Keyboard dialog box defines the keyboard maps that are used by the kikbd program.

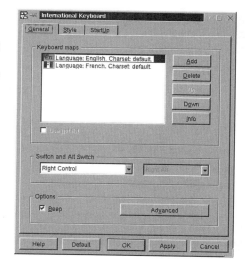

11

The Docked check box will cause kikbd to appear as a tiny window within the KDE Panel. If you prefer not to have it displayed on the Panel, you can display the kikbd window in any of the four corners of your desktop. To do this, uncheck the Docked check box and choose a location from the Place drop-down list.

When you have finished setting up the options in the International Keyboard dialog box, choose OK or Apply to save them. You can then run kikbd from a command line to see how the international keyboard features of KDE operate.

FIGURE 11.4

The options on the StartUp tab define where the kikbd program appears on your desktop, and whether it's started automatically when you launch KDE.

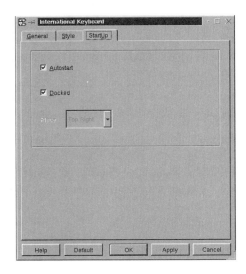

Using kfind to Locate Files

Finding what you want on a Linux system—especially a large or busy one—can be challenging. KDE includes a powerful searching utility called kfind that you can use to search for files on your system.

The Find Files window can be opened by choosing the Find icon on the Panel (a magnifying glass), choosing Find Files on the main menu, or entering the `kfind` command in a terminal window. Figure 11.5 shows the Find Files window.

FIGURE 11.5

The Find Files window lets you search your Linux system for files matching certain parameters, and then perform basic operations on those files.

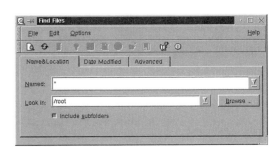

To perform a basic search, use the Name & Location tab. Enter a pattern to search for in the Named field, and enter a directory to search in the Look In field. If you don't want to search in subdirectories of the Look In directory, deselect the Include subfolders check box.

The toolbar in the Find Files window includes icons to start searching; update the search results list; open, archive, or delete a selected file; or open the directory in which a selected file is found. Leave the mouse pointer sitting on an icon to see a pop-up hint about it.

Choose the Start Search icon on the toolbar (or File, Start Search). As files are found, they are added to a listing at the bottom of the Find Files window (see Figure 11.6).

FIGURE 11.6

Files that match your search criteria are listed at the bottom of the Find Files window.

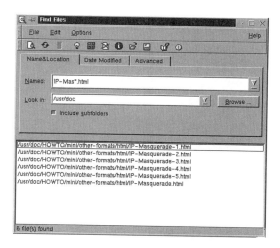

Working With the Files You Find

With a list of matching files shown, you can perform several operations on those files. To work on the list of files, first select the file or files that you want to use. You can click on multiple filenames to select them together.

The Edit menu contains several options, such as Select All and Invert Selection, to help you select multiple files.

Double-click on a filename to open the file. (If you use the kfm file typing system, a message asks you for the correct application if necessary.) Double-click on a directory name to open a kfm window, which shows the contents of that directory.

The selected files in the search results list can be added to a tar-format archive by choosing File, Add to Archive. This opens a file browsing window (see Figure 11.7), where you can either select an existing tar archive or enter the directory and name of a new tar archive, which kfind will create for you.

FIGURE 11.7

Archiving files located using kfind adds the files to an existing tar archive, or creates a new tar archive that you name.

Choosing File, Properties, or the Info icon on the toolbar opens a dialog box for the file or directory selected in the search results list (see Figure 11.8).

FIGURE 11.8

You can open a properties dialog box for any item in the search results list by choosing File, Properties.

You can select multiple items in the search results list, but the Properties dialog box only reflects information for the most recently selected item.

If you want to open a kfm window for the directory containing a file that you've selected in the search results list, choose File, Open Containing Folder.

You can even delete a file that you've selected in the list by choosing File, Delete.

Performing Advanced Searches

To search for files, you always need to enter information in the Named and Look In fields described previously. But often this yields too many files to make the search useful; or it yields none at all. kfind provides more advanced searching options on the Date Modified and Advanced tabs of the Find Files window.

The Date Modified tab (see Figure 11.9) lets you restrict the files included in the search results to those having a certain created or modified date.

FIGURE 11.9

The Date Modified tab lets you refine the search for files by filtering them by the created or modified date.

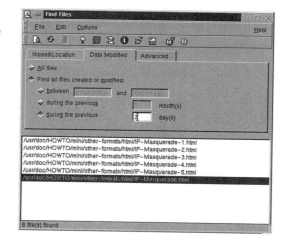

11

To use the Date Modified tab, choose the button labeled Find All Files Created or Modified. Then choose one of the three buttons to define the restrictions you want to place on the search. Find files created or updated

- Between two dates that you enter
- During the previous *x* months (you enter the number)
- During the previous *x* days (you enter the number)

With this information in place, you can start the search as before. The files listed in the search results include those with a filename and location that match the information in the Name & Location tab, but also have a created or modified date matching your specifications in the Date Modified tab.

The Advanced tab (see Figure 11.10) is the really powerful part of the kfind utility. Using the advanced options, you can restrict the files listed as search results to specific file types, sizes, or even by the contents.

FIGURE 11.10

The Advanced tab provides the capability to search for files based on file type, size, or contents.

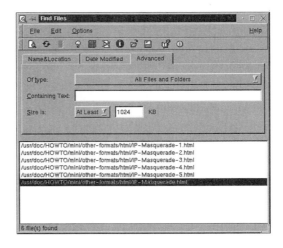

In the Of Type field, select the file type that you're searching for from the drop-down list; several dozen file types are listed. The list includes system descriptions such as symbolic links and folders (directories). It also includes many file data types, such as pdf, PostScript, C headers, HTML, and many others.

Leave the selection as All Files and Folders if you don't want to restrict your search by file type.

If you enter a text string in the Containing Text field, kfind searches within each file included by the other search criteria to see if the file contains the string.

If you use a containing text string within a large search space (such as starting the Look In field at the /usr directory with Include subfolders selected), the search will require a significant amount of time to complete. Also, searching from the root / will search all mounted file systems.

For example, suppose you have a directory full of HTML files that you have saved from the Internet and you want to find a file that describes diving expeditions in the South Pacific. You remember the title of the Web page is something such as *Palau Adventures*. All the files are HTML, and all are in the same directory.

You can enter Palau Adventures in the Containing Text field to find the file you want. (Assuming you also entered your archive directory in the Names & Locations tab.)

The Size Is field lets you filter the search by how large files are. To use this field, choose either At Least or At Most from the drop-down list. Then enter a value in the KB field.

> Remember that 1MB is 1,024KB. For example, if you want to search for files that are less than 1MB, select At Most and enter 1024 in the KB field.

As with the Date Modified tab, the Advanced tab works with the selections you've entered in the other two tabs. A file must meet the criteria given in all three tabs in order to be listed in the search results.

This also means that if you perform a complex search and then return to the same Find Files window to perform another search, you need to check the settings in all three tabs before you perform the next search. Otherwise you might restrict the search more than you intend to.

Using kpackage for Software Maintenance

The kpackage utility is a useful tool for anyone using a Linux system based on rpm software packages and it deserves a brief mention here.

> Caldera OpenLinux installs kpackage by default. If you don't have OpenLinux, your KDE distribution probably doesn't include kpackage. You can get it from the KDE FTP site. Hour 21, "Finding and Installing Additional KDE Applications," provides more details.

If you are using OpenLinux, start kpackage from the System submenu of the main menu. Otherwise, enter **kpackage** from a terminal window. The initial kpackage window is shown in Figure 11.11.

The rpm packages installed on your system are grouped into categories such as Desktop, Development, and so forth. You can view the contents of any of these categories and their subcategories to see the rpm packages that are installed on your system.

When you select a package name in the list, the right side of the window displays descriptive text about the package (see Figure 11.12), and displays a list of every file contained in that package, with its installed pathname (see Figure 11.13).

FIGURE 11.11

The initial kpackage window shows categories of software packages installed on your system.

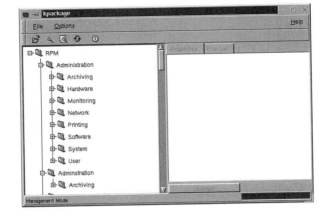

FIGURE 11.12

Selecting an rpm package in kpackage lets you see a descriptive page about that rpm.

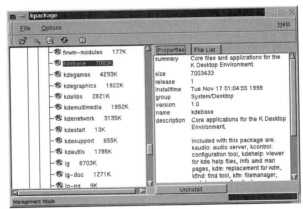

FIGURE 11.13

Information about an rpm package includes a list of every file included in that rpm.

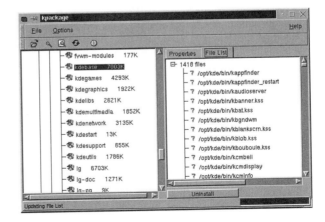

Although this information alone is helpful, kpackage provides additional features that

- Search for the rpm that *owns* any file on your system
- Install or update new rpms by browsing with kpackage
- Uninstall a selected rpm

Managing Initialization Scripts

Another useful tool that isn't included with the default KDE distribution is a utility to manage the available services on your Linux system.

If you've set up a Linux or UNIX system, you're aware of the structured and powerful design of the UNIX initialization process. Unfortunately, altering the process after you have installed a working Linux system can be tedious—changing scripts, checking for dependencies, and so forth.

The KDE utility called ksysv can be used to manage a key part of the initialization process: Determining which system services are started when you boot up or restart your system.

The default Red Hat KDE installation described in Hour 2, "Installing KDE from Scratch," includes this utility. If you are running Caldera OpenLinux, you won't have this utility installed. See Hour 21 "Finding and Installing Additional KDE Applications" for more details.

The ksysv utility described here is intended for systems using UNIX System V initialization scripts. If you're using another type, this utility won't be of any help to you.

You must be logged in as root to use the SysV Init Editor. To start the utility from a command line after you su to root, use the command ksysv.

Defining Some Terms

Before describing how to use the initialization script utility, I need to define a couple of terms.

Linux and UNIX can start up in different *Runlevels*. A Runlevel determines how the system is operating. For example

- *Runlevel 0*. Indicates that the system is halted (not running any programs, though the kernel is active)
- *Runlevel 1*. A single-user mode used by system administrators for testing and debugging the system
- *Runlevel 3*. The normal multiuser mode that your Linux system uses for everyday operation
- *Runlevel 5*. The same as Runlevel 3, except a graphical login is used (you never see a Character mode screen). This mode uses the xdm or kdm program, as described in Hour 3, "Starting and Exiting KDE."

Probably only Runlevel 3 and Runlevel 5 are of interest to you, but you'll see all seven (0–6) in the initialization script utility.

Another important term is *services*. A service is a program that provides a certain functionality to users and other programs. For example, a Web server is a service; the System Log tool is also a service. Dozens of services might be available on your Linux system. These are defined by the /etc/services file. However, you shouldn't need to even view that file.

When you start your Linux system, the initialization process uses a set of scripts based on the Runlevel that you are starting (usually 3 or 5) to initialize certain services. The entire process goes something like this:

1. The Linux or UNIX kernel starts the init program.
2. The init program runs the script /etc/rc.d/rc.sysinit.
3. The rc.sysinit script does a few housekeeping things, runs the rc.serial script (if it is found), and then exits.
4. The init program runs rc.local.
5. The init script runs the start script for all the services specified in the current Runlevel.

Obviously, you can edit any of the scripts mentioned in this process to change what your system does. The utility described in this section lets you graphically set up which services are started as part of each Runlevel by dragging and dropping icons.

If you want to run a program automatically at startup, don't use this utility; it only works with predefined Linux services. Instead, place a command in the /etc/rc.d/rc.local script, the /etc/profile script, or the .profile or .bashrc file (in a user's home directory). Better yet, use the Autostart folder described in Hour 10, "Learning More KDE File Management."

Running the SysV Init Editor

To start the utility to edit your initialization scripts, choose System, SysV Init Editor from the main menu of your Red Hat Linux KDE installation, or enter **ksysv** on a command line for any Linux on which ksysv is installed. The Init Editor window appears as in Figure 11.14.

FIGURE 11.14

The SysV Init Editor lets you select services to start in each Runlevel.

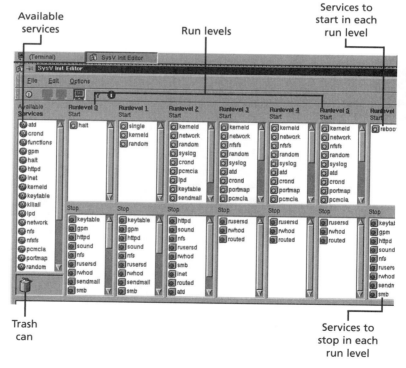

The main areas of this window are described here:

- The list of available services is shown down the left side of the window.
- The Trash can is where you drop unwanted services dragged from a Runlevel list.

- The Start lists for each Runlevel are on the top half of the window.
- The Stop lists for each Runlevel are on the bottom half of the window.

For example, in the Start list for Runlevel 3, you probably have services such as these (depending on your Linux distribution and how you've set it up): kerneld, random, syslog, crond, portmap, inet, and others.

From this window, you can use any of these procedures to change your initialization scripts:

- *To add a service from the list of available services:* Drag the service and drop it on the Start list for a Runlevel.
- *To change a service from the Stop list (not activated) to the Start list:* Drag the service's icon from the Stop list to the Start list.
- *To remove a service from the Start list of a Runlevel:* Drag it from the Start list and drop it either on the Stop list (for easy retrieval later), or on the Trash icon. (The icon appears the same after dropping an item on it.)

After you make any changes, two icons on the toolbar show a red X and a green check mark (see Figure 11.15).

FIGURE 11.15

After you have made changes in the initialization scripts, you can discard or save your changes.

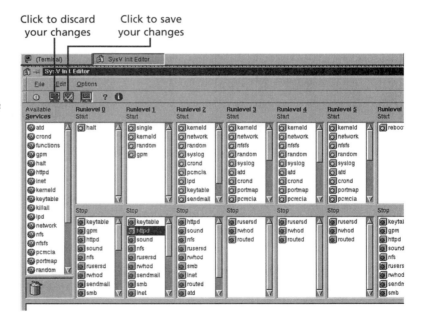

- Click the red X (or choose File, Clear Changes) to discard your changes to the initialization process and reload the existing scripts.
- Click the green check mark (or choose File, Accept Changes) to save your updates to initialization scripts.

When you've finished working with the initialization scripts, choose File, Exit, to close the SysV Init Editor.

Managing User Accounts

If you're acting as the system administrator for your Linux system, you probably spend some time managing the accounts of the users on your system. A user manager utility for KDE is available to help you maintain the user and group accounts on your Linux system.

To start this utility, choose System, User Manager, from the main menu of your Red Hat Linux KDE installation, or enter **kuser** from a command line for any Linux system on which kuser has been installed.

The default Red Hat KDE installation described in Hour 2 "Installing KDE From Scratch," includes this utility. Caldera OpenLinux does not. See Hour 21 "Finding and Installing Additional KDE Applications," for more details on obtaining and installing this utility.

You must be logged in as root to use the user manager utility.

The User Manager window is shown in Figure 11.16. User accounts are shown in the top part of the window; groups are shown in the bottom part.

If you're new to Linux, you'll be surprised by all the strange user accounts on your system. User accounts such as bin, daemon, sync, and halt are used by various Linux programs. You should avoid toying with these user accounts unless you're familiar with their purpose. The same applies to all the strange groups you see.

You can click on any column heading for the users and groups to sort each list by that column. For example, to sort the users by their full name, click on the Full Name column heading. To reverse the sort order, click a second time on the same column heading.

FIGURE 11.16

The user manager utility displays all the user and group accounts on your system and provides dialog boxes to edit their properties.

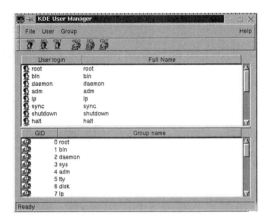

Adding and Modifying Users

To add a new user, choose User, Add, and enter a username of eight characters or less in the Enter Username dialog box. The new username appears in the user list. But you should also set up some additional information about the user.

To edit the properties of any user, double-click on the user's entry in the list or click on the username and choose File, Properties. The Edit User box appears (see Figure 11.17).

FIGURE 11.17

The Edit User dialog box lets you define information about a user account or the groups that the user is a member of.

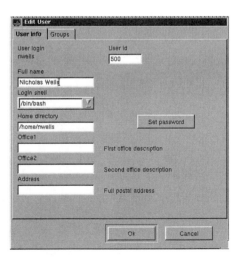

The User Info tab includes fields where you can enter the user's full name (for example, *Nicholas Wells*) and any descriptive information you choose (in the Office1, Office2, and Address fields).

The user ID, login shell, and home directory are set up automatically when the user account is created. You shouldn't need to alter them unless, for example, the user prefers to use the sh shell.

Be certain to set a password for the user by choosing the Set Password button and entering the password twice in the Enter Password dialog box.

The Groups tab (see Figure 11.18) lists all the groups on your Linux system. This user's primary group determines the group assignments when the user creates a file or performs other operations where a group name must be assigned. Each user can also be a member of other groups in order to grant access to additional resources (for example, to a POP server or PPP account).

FIGURE 11.18

The groups that a user belongs to are managed from the Groups tab of the Edit User dialog box.

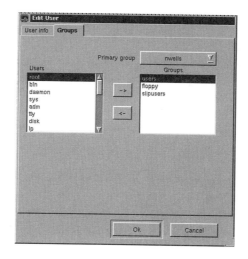

11

The current user's Primary group is shown in the Primary group drop-down list. You can choose a new group by selecting a group from the drop-down list.

> Some Linux distributions use a system called User-Private-Groups, in which each new user's primary group is a group containing only that user. (Hence the default primary group of a new user *nwells* is a new group—created at the same time—called *nwells*.) This provides some security benefits, but might require you to rearrange the group membership regularly to provide additional access.

You can add the current user to other groups by selecting them in the list of all Linux groups and moving them to the Groups list.

Managing Groups

Groups are managed much like users. To edit a group, double-click on the group name or choose Group, Edit. The Edit Groups dialog box appears (see Figure 11.19).

FIGURE 11.19

Group membership is edited in the Edit Groups dialog box.

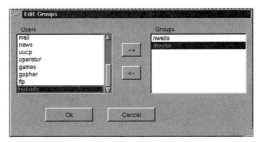

Users that belong to this group are listed on the right side; all other users on the system are listed on the left side. To change the membership of a group, select a user from either list and choose the arrow button to move the user to the other side.

Choose OK to close the Edit Groups dialog box and save your changes.

You shouldn't have to create a new group very often. When you do, choose Group, Add, and enter a group name in the Add Group dialog box (see Figure 11.20). The group number is automatically filled in. You can leave it as is, unless you have a specific number you want to use.

FIGURE 11.20

New groups are created by entering a group name in the Add Group dialog box.

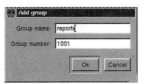

When you have finished modifying the users and groups in the user manager, choose File, Save, to update the appropriate Linux system files with your updates. Exit the user manager by choosing File, Exit.

Viewing System Information

A set of information utilities in KDE is provided to display details about how your system resources are being used. Although you can't change anything from these screens, they can provide important details about your system for installing new devices, improving and tuning performance, or troubleshooting your system.

The best way to view all the system information screens is within the Control Center. Choose the Information item to list the available screens. If you only want to view one of these items, you can choose it from the Settings, Information submenu on the main menu.

Not all the items listed under the Information section are discussed here. Some are discussed in later hours; others are not functional in this release of KDE.

The following list defines the KDE information screens available in the Control Center. (The Samba Status screen is discussed in Hour 13, "Managing Network Connections in KDE.")

The Devices tab (see Figure 11.21) lists the device types used by your Linux system. This information is useful if you need to define a new device that you've added to your system. The device numbers shown here correspond only to device types, however, not to specific devices. The actual devices on your Linux system are accessed through the /dev directory.

11

FIGURE 11.21

The Devices tab lists information about how character and block devices are defined on your system.

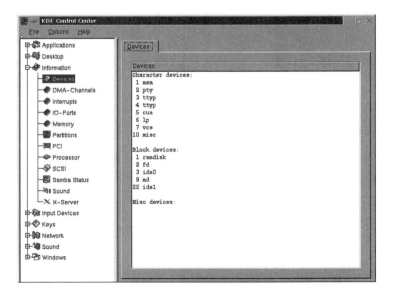

The DMA-Channels tab lists any DMA Channels that are set up on your system. This information is used by the Linux kernel and some devices to access your system memory.

The Interrupts tab (see Figure 11.22) lists some of the IRQ interrupts that are defined on your system. Unfortunately, this information doesn't include IRQ numbers for some of the devices that are likely to have conflicting IRQ numbers, for example, Ethernet cards, modems, external serial posts, and so forth. Nevertheless, this interrupt information can be helpful for some troubleshooting tasks.

FIGURE 11.22

The Interrupts tab lists some (but not all) of the IRQ interrupts on your system and how they are assigned.

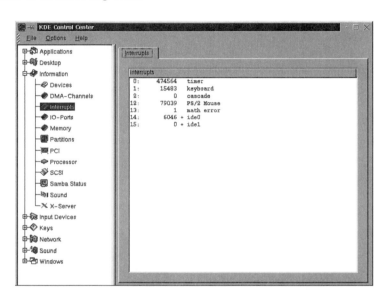

If you need to ascertain the IRQ and port information for a device, such as a serial port, use the setserial command with the device name. For example, to learn about Serial Port 1, enter this command:

```
$ setserial /dev/cua0
```

The IO-Ports tab (see Figure 11.23) lists information about how Input/Ouput memory ports are assigned. As with the Interrupt information, this can be helpful in diagnosing conflicts as you try to use devices on your system.

FIGURE 11.23

The IO-Ports tab shows how IO memory addresses are assigned on your system. Various devices use these port numbers to communicate with your Linux software.

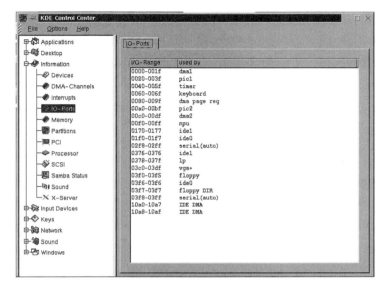

The Memory tab (see Figure 11.24) gives a dynamic display of how memory on your Linux system is being used. The items shown in the Memory tab include tracking the use of free system RAM, how much *swap space* (virtual memory) is used and available, and how much memory is used for shared resources and buffers.

FIGURE 11.24

The Memory tab shows a continually updated report on how RAM and virtual memory are being used on your system.

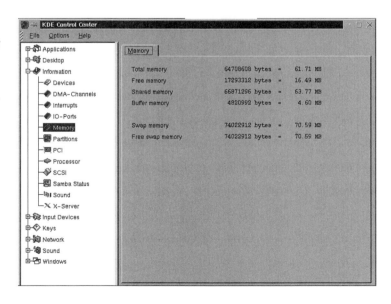

If you start the Memory dialog box from the Settings, Information menu rather than viewing it in the Control Center, you can resize and move the Memory dialog box to a corner of your desktop to continually watch the memory activity on your system.

The PCI tab provides a complete diagnostic report on the PCI slots in the back of your computer. This report includes a lot of technical detail that you can use to troubleshoot the devices in your system (if you're fairly familiar with the PCI bus) .

The Processor tab (see Figure 11.25) gives a summary of details about your microprocessor, including the manufacturer, speed, and details of which bugs are detected—and therefore avoided—in your particular processor.

FIGURE 11.25

The Processor tab shows the vendor, model, speed, and other information about the CPU installed in your Linux system.

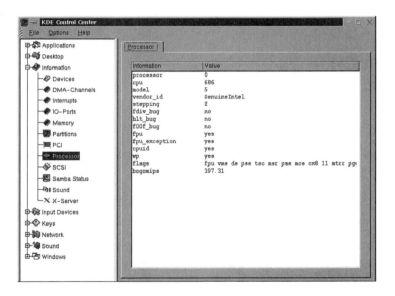

If you're interested in statistics about CPU usage or a dynamic display of CPU activity, check out the ktop or kpm programs, which are available from the KDE FTP site. (See Hour 21 for more information.)

The SCSI tab provides information about any SCSI devices installed on your Linux system.

Finally, the X-Server tab displays information about the X server that you're using (vendor and version) and the resolution of your screen (see Figure 11.26).

FIGURE 11.26

The X-Server tab shows which X server is being used on your Linux system, as well as the current display resolution and color depth.

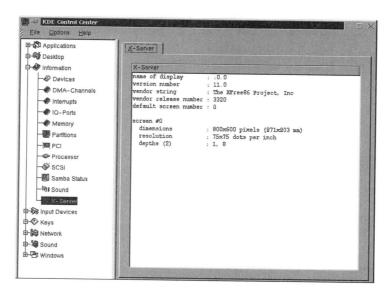

Summary

In this hour you learned how to use some of the system management utilities provided by KDE. Most of these utilities are intended solely for the system administrator or root user, but you can learn a lot about Linux and KDE by reviewing how they function. Any user can use the Find File utility. You learned about the kuser and ksysv utilities. The next hour describes some additional utilities that any user can use, such as the calculator, Text editor, and Archive tool.

Questions and Answers

Q Do I need to download the non-standard utilities such as ksysv and kuser?

A Not really. You can use other command-line or menu-based configuration tools, such as lisa in Caldera OpenLinux, to perform the same functions. These utilities are described in this hour because they are integrated, attractive KDE applications.

Q How can I use the scrolling wheel on my new mouse within KDE?

A I'm afraid you can't until the next release of KDE. Support should be included at that time.

Q **The keyboard map that I need isn't included in the list within the International Keyboards dialog box. What can I do?**

A Search for additional keyboard maps on the KDE FTP site or various Linux sites. You could also ask for help on the KDE mailing lists. Someone might have the keyboard map you need.

Q **How can I learn more about the initialization processes described for the ksysv utility?**

A Try a comprehensive book on Linux system administration, such as *Special Edition Using Linux, Fourth Edition*, from Que Publishing.

Exercises

1. Review the /etc/services file and the /etc/rc.d subdirectories for each run level. Compare the information you find with the list of services shown in the ksysv utility.

2. Use the Find utility to show a list of all files on your system that

   - Are located in the /usr subdirectory
   - Are less than 20KB in size
   - End with the HTML file extension
   - Have not been modified in the last month (or since you installed your Linux system)

3. Execute the sysinfo command from a terminal window. Compare the information that you see there with the details provided by the Information tabs in the Control Center. Where do they overlap? Review the online help for each Information tab to see how you can learn more about your Linux system.`

Hour **12**

Using KDE Utilities

In this hour you learn about other KDE utilities that are normally installed as part of a core KDE distribution. Although these tools are not essential to running KDE, you'll find them useful as you work day to day on your Linux system. The sections that follow describe the use of tools such as the KDE calculator, Hex editor, compression tools, and the note-taking utility.

Using the ark Archival Utility

If you've used a program such as WinZip for Microsoft Windows, you know how useful it can be to have a graphical interface to a good compression tool.

The ark archival utility lets you view the contents of compressed files, drag new icons from kfm windows to add them to an archive, and even view files contained in an archive without first extracting them to your file system.

The only downfall of the ark program is that is doesn't support all the common UNIX compression formats. In fact, ark supports only `.zip` and `.tgz` files. Those are good, useful formats, but `.gz` files and `.Z` files are not supported (`.gz` and `.Z` files are created by the gzip and compress programs, respectively).

The .tgz file format can also have the file extension .tar.gz. Either will work in ark. These are gzipped tarball files. However, neither .gz files, nor uncompressed .tar files are currently supported in ark.

The zip format in Linux is compatible with the zip or pkzip programs in other operating systems. So if you create a zip file in Windows, for example, you can extract it using ark.

To start the ark program, choose Utilities, Archiver, on the KDE main menu, or enter the ark command in a terminal window. The main ark window appears, as shown in Figure 12.1.

FIGURE 12.1

The ark utility provides a convenient graphical interface to extract and create compressed files.

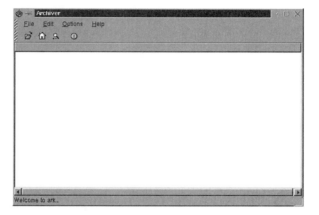

The toolbar includes four icons; they are described here as they appear on the toolbar from left to right:

- *File Folder icon:* Lets you open an archive file.
- *House icon:* Lists the files in your home or Archive directory.
- *Magnifying Glass icon:* Tries to extract the selected file.
- *Circle icon:* Exits ark.

Extracting Files from an Archive

To view or extract files from a compressed file archive, you first must open the archive file in ark. You can do this in one of two ways:

- You can click the Open icon (the File Folder icon) or choose File, Open, and then use the Open dialog box to select the archive file you want to explore or extract a file from.

  When you select a file to examine, the contents of the archive file are listed in the ark window, and the complete path and filename of the archive file are shown in the status line under the main window.

- You can also click the Home icon to see the files in your Home/Archive directory listed in the ark window. Click on the name of any archive file you want to work with. The contents of the archive file are listed in the main window, and the file-name is shown in the status line below (see Figure 12.2).

Contents of the
archive file

FIGURE 12.2

*After you have selected
an archive file to work
on, the contents of the
archive are listed in
the main ark window.*

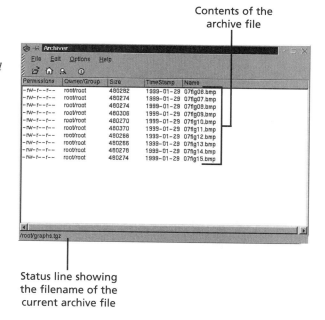

Status line showing
the filename of the
current archive file

12

The Home icon always shows the contents of the ark Archive directory. This is initially set to your home directory. You can change this to a directory where you store all your archive files (for example, /tmp or ~/download) by choosing Options, Set Archive Directory, and entering a new directory name.

If you click on a file that is not a supported archive type, you see a message on the status line that says Unknown archive format.

You can't change directories from the ark main window. If your archive file isn't in the Archive directory (which you see by clicking the Home icon), you must choose File, Open to browse the file system and select the file you want.

Although the contents of an archive are listed in the ark main window, the files themselves are still not extracted from the archive.

If you want to see one of the archived files, click on the filename in the ark window. ark uses the file typing provided by kfm to attempt to open the file and display its contents using the correct application. For example, using a text editor or image viewer. (see Hour 9, "Managing Files in KDE," for more about the kfm program and file typing with MIME types.)

Often, KDE won't be capable of displaying the contents of the file you want to view directly from the archive, because a matching MIME type is not set up. You'll see a message to this effect, which you can close and ignore.

After you have the contents of an archive file listed in the main ark window, you can extract some or all of the files in the archive by clicking the Magnifying Glass icon or choosing File, Extract To. The Extract dialog box appears (see Figure 12.3).

FIGURE 12.3

Files in an archive are saved in your local file system using the Extract dialog box.

If you want to extract the entire archive, choose the All Files option; if you have selected one or more files (using Shift+click or Ctrl+click) you can extract only Selected Files. The Pattern field lets you extract only certain files, based on a filename pattern such as *.doc or novem*.

Next, choose a Destination directory. This is where the extracted files will be written. You can type a directory name in the Destination field, or use the Browse button to use a simple file system browser to select a directory.

Finally, choose Preserve Permissions if you are extracting from an archive created on a UNIX or Linux system and you want to keep the same file permissions (who can read, write, and so on) as the original files. If this check box is not selected, ark will assign default permissions when creating the extracted files in the Destination directory. You might have to change some of them to make the files work correctly (such as the execute permission on programs or scripts).

 When you extract files from an archive, the archive file itself remains unchanged. It doesn't shrink or disappear when files are extracted from it.

With the extract options selected, choose OK to extract the files and close the Extract dialog box.

 You can also remove a file from an existing archive file by selecting it and choosing Edit, Delete.

Creating a New Archive

When you have a set of files you want to compress into a single archive file, the commands to create the archive can be challenging to learn. ark lets you use dialog boxes and drag and drop to create new compressed archives of your files.

To create a new compressed archive, choose File, New. A file browsing dialog box appears where you can change to the directory where the new archive should be stored and enter a name for the archive in the Location field.

For example, after browsing and entering an archive name, the Location field might contain the following:

`/home/nwells/reports/ann_report.tgz`

ark will create an archive file in `.tgz` format, storing it in the `/home/nwells/reports` directory. The file extension you enter determines what type of archive is created by ark.

 Remember to use only `.zip`, `.tgz`, or `.tar.gz` as file extensions when creating new archives. If you use other extensions, you'll see a message on the status line that reads: `Can't create archive of that type`.

12

When you choose OK to close the file browsing dialog box. The only evidence you see that you're ready to create a new archive is that the status line shows the name of the new archive. The new archive file is not created until you add at least one file to the archive.

Choose Options, File Adding Options (see Figure 12.4) to select whether the full path of files that you add is stored in the archive. This is useful if the archived files must be stored in a certain directory to work correctly.

FIGURE 12.4

Add File options let you determine what properties of a file are included in the new archive you create.

To add files to the archive, open a kfm window with the files you want to add. Click and drag the icons for those files, dropping them on the ark window. The files are added to the archive.

> Remember that you can easily select multiple files in a kfm window with Shift+click, Ctrl+click, click and drag to surround icons, or by choosing Edit, Select and entering a filename pattern.

Files are added to the new archive almost instantly (depending on their size). The files you add also remain in their original directory; they are copied into the archive, not moved into it.

You can immediately exit ark; the archive file has already been created. Or you can add additional files by dragging other icons from any kfm window and dropping them on the ark window.

If you have added a file you don't want in the archive, click to select it and choose Edit, Delete to remove it from the archive.

To rearrange the fields of information shown for each file, click and drag a column heading to a new location.

The Ratio field shows how much the file was compressed as part of the archive. A higher compression ratio (such as 80 percent) indicates that the file shrunk a great deal during compression. Compare the Length field (original size) with the Size field (compressed size).

Using the Scientific Calculator

A good calculator often comes in handy as you're working at your computer, preparing a report, or balancing your checkbook. The KDE calculator is so nice; you'll feel like you're back in high school wondering what all those buttons are for.

The KDE calculator is called kcalc. You can start it from the Panel, by choosing Utilities, Calculator on the main menu, or by entering **kcalc** in a terminal window. The Calculator window is shown in Figure 12.5.

FIGURE 12.5

kcalc provides a powerful scientific calculator for KDE.

While I can't pretend to teach you all about trigonometry and statistics (because I don't know them myself), I can explain what a lot of the buttons on the calculator are for, and how to set up the display options to fit your preferences.

Most of the buttons will be familiar to you if you've used even a simple calculator. Table 12.1 explains several areas of the kcalc window.

TABLE 12.1 PARTS OF THE KCALC WINDOW

Screen Element	Description
kCalc button	Click to open the kcalc configuration dialog box (described in the next section).
Display window	Shows the results of all calculations. (Change colors using the kCalc button.)
Base	Determines whether the numeric base for calculations is 16, 10, 8, or 2 (Hex, Dec, Oct, or Bin). Leave as Dec for normal use.

continues

TABLE 12.1   CONTINUED

Screen Element	Description
Angle	Determines whether angles are calculated using degrees (Deg), radians (Rad), or gradients (Gra).
The column of keys with letters A–F	Used for Hex (base 16) calculations (ignore for other work).
The MR, M+- and MC keys	Memory Recall, Memory Add, Memory Clear (as on desk calculators)
C and AC	Clear Entry and All Clear (as on desk calculators)

kcalc starts in Trigonometry mode. You can also change to Statistics mode, which changes the buttons such as Sin, Cos, Tan, and so forth to statistical functions.

kcalc supports some additional tricks you'll find useful:

- To enter Pi, click INV EE.
- To enter *e* (the Euler number), click 1 INV ln.
- Click in the display window to copy the current number shown to the KDE Clipboard (from which it can be pasted into other KDE applications).
- Right-click in the display to copy from the KDE Clipboard to the calculator.

If you try to paste a number to kcalc and the Clipboard doesn't contain a valid number, kcalc tries to use the valid portion of the number or ignores the paste operation. For example, if you copy and paste *23jan1998*, only *23* appears in kcalc.

- The online help for kcalc includes descriptions of all the trigonometry and statistics keys. View help by choosing kCalc, Help.
- kcalc works like a normal calculator; it doesn't use Reverse Polish Notation (RPN) like the scientific Hewlett-Packard calculators or xcalc. kcalc does however have a results stack. Each result of Enter or clicking equals (=) pushes a number to the stack. Use the up and down arrow keys to scroll through the stack.

The online help contains useful information about precision for kcalc, including setting the number of digits displayed, and how you can increase numeric precision if you need to.

To configure kcalc, choose the kCalc button. The Configuration dialog box appears with the Defaults tab selected (see Figure 12.6).

FIGURE 12.6

Configuring kcalc on the Defaults tab lets you choose colors and numeric precision, as well as the mode.

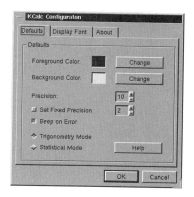

In the Defaults tab, you can select the color of the text and background by choosing one of the Change buttons.

You can also set the precision of the numbers displayed and the mode (trig or stats). The Help button opens the kcalc online help, which contains a lot of useful information.

Changing the precision of kcalc alters how numbers are displayed, not how they are stored internally.

The Beep on Error check box will alert you if you try to divide by 0 or perform some other mathematical no-no. The KDE system bell provides the beep sound (Hour 7, "Configuring KDE Options," explains how to configure the bell sound).

The Display Font tab (see Figure 12.7) lets you set the font used to display numbers in kcalc. Any font on your Linux system can be selected by choosing the Change button in the Display Font tab and using the Select Font dialog box to choose a typeface and style.

Some fonts appear jagged when displayed in kcalc. The kcalc online help provides suggestions for adjusting your X Window System fonts to prevent this from happening.

12

FIGURE 12.7

The Display Font tab lets you choose any font on your Linux system to display numbers in kcalc.

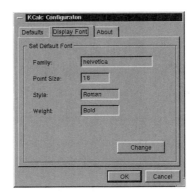

Using KNotes

The knotes program is a computerized version of the yellow Post-It sticky notes that cover everyone's desks and walls (and the edges of many monitors). knotes lets you easily place a graphical sticky note on your KDE Desktop, in which you can jot a note, set an alarm, show a calendar, and so forth.

To place the first note, click the yellow notepad on the Panel or choose Utilities, KNotes on the KDE main menu. A blank note appears on your desktop, ready for you to type (see Figure 12.8).

FIGURE 12.8

The first KNote that you display appears in yellow, ready to enter information.

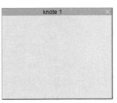

The simplest use of a KNote is to enter a reminder for later in the day or week: what to get at the store, a spur-of-the-moment meeting this afternoon, and so forth. Just type your message to use a KNote for things like this.

You can drag a file from a kfm window and drop it on a KNote to enter that text in the note. You can enter a URL in a KNote; when you double-click on the URL, a kfm window will appear and load that URL (local or from the Internet).

When you close a KNote by clicking the Close button on the title bar, the knote program is closed, but the notes are saved. The next time you start knote, the same messages will reappear on your desktop. KNotes don't appear in the KDE taskbar. Click the knote icon on the Panel to make a KNote visible.

KNotes are small, without a menu bar. To see the options available in a KNote, right-click on the note. The Operations submenu contains most of the features you'll use (see Figure 12.9).

FIGURE 12.9

The pop-up menu and Operations submenu of a knote provide many tools for your notes.

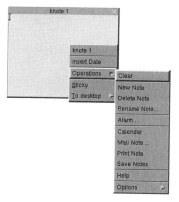

Pressing the knote icon on the Panel a second time doesn't create a second note. To do this, choose Operations, New Note from the pop-up menu.

To resize a KNote, hold down the Alt key, press the right mouse button, and move the mouse.

The names of all notes that you've created are listed at the top of the pop-up menu. Select the name of a note to make it active.

Table 12.2 shows how to use the other items in the knote pop-up menu. Note that all the settings apply only to the KNote that you click on and not to all open KNotes. The exception is the Change Defaults dialog box (see Figure 12.10), which is global to all KNotes (choose Operations, Options, Change Defaults).

12

FIGURE 12.10

The Change Defaults dialog box for all KNotes lets you set colors, fonts, and default commands for mail and printing.

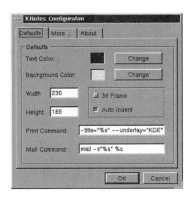

TABLE 12.2   SUMMARY OF COMMANDS ON A KNOTE POP-UP MENU

To Complete this Task	Do This
Change to another open KNote	Choose the name of the KNote from the top of the pop-up menu.
Insert the current date and time in a KNote	Choose Insert Date
Save the contents of your KNotes so you can close KNotes and have the same messages reappear next time you open it	Choose Operations, Save Notes
Make a KNote stick to the Desktop, so it appears in all KDE desktops	Choose Sticky
Move an unsticky KNote to a different KDE Desktop	Choose To Desktop and the desktop name
Rename a KNote (the new name appears in the title bar and pop-up menu)	Choose Operations, Rename
Delete a KNote (so it doesn't reappear when KNotes is opened or appear on the pop-up menu)	Choose Operations, Delete Note
Set an alarm that sounds a bell and pops open a message box at a certain day and time	Choose Operations, Alarm and set the date and time in the dialog box that appears (no indication of the alarm appears in your KNote)

To Complete this Task	Do This
Insert the current month's calendar in a KNote	Choose Operations, Calendar
Print a note	Choose Operations, Print Note (see the Online Help, Operations, Help, for more information on printing KNotes)
Email a KNote to someone	Choose Operations, Mail note and enter the recipient's email address
Change the current KNote to have a 3D frame (default is no frame)	Choose Operations, Options, 3D Frame
Change the font and colors used by the current KNote	Choose Operations, Options, Font or Colors

Learning About Other KDE Applications

This hour describes three very useful accessories that are included in the standard KDE distribution. Other utilities are also included that haven't been described here. Still others are available for download.

For example, KDE also includes the following:

- An address book, kab, which provides a simple database and attractive interface to store information about people.

- A Hex editor, which can edit any file (including a binary) one byte at a time (see Figure 12.11). Choose Utilities, Hex Editor on the KDE main menu.

12

FIGURE 12.11

The Hex editor lets an expert edit the contents of any file.

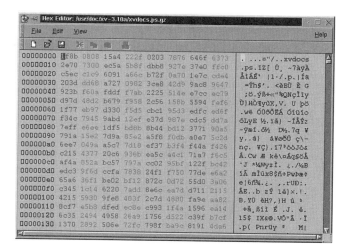

- A time and task manager, Karm, that you can find at Utilities, Karm
- A tool for using LaserJet printers (choose Utilities, Klaserjet)
- A screen capture utility, Ksnapshot (choose Utilities, Snapshot)
- A tool for graphically formatting floppy disks (choose Utilities, Kfloppy)

Many other KDE applications are available via the KDE Web site. Useful applications include the following:

- KIRC, a Chat program
- ktop, a system statistics program
- kpm, a process management tool
- Many additional games beyond the basic kdegames package

Hour 21, "Finding and Installing Additional KDE Applications," describes how to locate and install applications like these, so they become an integrated part of your KDE environment.

Summary

In this hour you learned how to use some key utilities that are included with KDE: the Archiver, ark, and the calculator, kcalc. You learned about creating new compressed archives and extracting files from an archive. In addition, you learned about the knotes program, which you can use to place handy reminders on your KDE Desktop. The next hour discusses network connectivity within KDE, including using KDE utilities to establish or examine your network connections.

Questions and Answers

Q How do I create archives or compress files from a command line?

A Linux includes several utilities for archival and compression. The compression tools usually take the name of the file to compress as a parameter. For example, here are two different compression commands:

```
gzip bigfile.doc
compress bigfile.doc
```

The compression programs add a file extension to the original filename (.gz and .z in the preceding examples). Archival programs are intended to place many files into a single archive file, compressing them along the way. You must provide a filename for the new archive file; the original files remain unaltered when you create an archive. Two commands for creating archives are:

```
tar cvfz archivename.tgz includedfiles.*
zip archivename.zip *.alldocs.*
```

The last part of each of these commands is a pattern that defines all the files to be included in the archive. You can learn more about these commands by reading the manual page for tar, zip, gzip, or compress.

Q Can I add a file to an archive in ark without dragging it from a kfm window?

A Not in the current release. If the drag-and-drop method doesn't appeal to you, try learning about the command-line methods described in the previous question. You can still examine and extract from these archive files using ark.

Q The kcalc calculator is nice, but I need more functions. Where can I find something else?

A Try running xcalc, which is included with most Linux products.

Q I see additional utilities that aren't described in this hour; what about them?

A Some of these utilities are more business related, and are discussed in Hour 19, "Using KDE Business Tools." Others are just for fun, or are simple to use. These include the moon phase tracker and the mouse pedometer. Explore these menu options to see what else KDE has to offer.

Exercises

1. Create a zip format archive of some files on your Linux system. If you have a Windows-based PC, unzip the archive within Windows. Do the long filenames from Linux carry over to Windows when you unzip the file?

2. Create a KNote with an alarm to remind you of an upcoming appointment. Shut down KDE and restart it. Does the alarm still appear on time? If not, how could you start KNote automatically each time you run KDE?

12

HOUR 13

Managing Network Connections in KDE

In this hour you learn how to manage some of your network connections using utilities provided with KDE. Although tools to manage the core Ethernet configuration are not yet included in KDE, you'll also learn a little about this part of networking in Linux as background.

The Kppp and Samba tools provided with KDE are also described. Understanding Kppp will help you establish an Internet connection to use the utilities described in Hour 15, "Accessing the Internet from KDE."

Understanding Linux Networking

Networking with Linux is a broad subject. Larger books than this one— many of them—have been written on Linux networking. This section attempts to provide an overview to using networking within KDE.

If you're not familiar with Linux networking, this information should make you feel more comfortable with the topics that follow. Don't feel like you should understand everything or that your networking systems will work flawlessly the first time around. Call your system administrator for assistance and read all the relevant documentation you can find.

Networking in Linux is based on *IP*—the Internet Protocol. The most well-known use of IP is for *TCP/IP*, or the Transmission Control Protocol running on IP. The TCP/IP protocol *stacks*, or drivers, are part of the Linux kernel. These networking capabilites can be added to, modified, or unloaded, but they are central to the design of Linux.

 Additional low-level protocols, such as IPX, are also included (or available for) Linux, depending on which Linux distribution you have installed.

TCP/IP packets travel across the network using a lower-level protocol. The most common of these is Ethernet. Others include FDDI and Token Ring. The Linux kernel must have the correct Ethernet (or Token Ring, and so on) device module installed and configured in order to send packets across your Ethernet network.

Higher level protocols that carry user data, such as the Web protocol HTTP, rely on TCP/IP as an underlying transport mechanism. Because TCP/IP is so well integrated into Linux, after you have your Ethernet connection established, standard Internet programs such as Netscape Communicator can use the TCP/IP protocol without any additional configuration.

Of course, things can become much more complicated, depending on your goals. The routing of IP packets across multiple network segments—such as when you use an Internet gateway or a PPP connection within a LAN—affects both your configuration and the security of your networks. However, I won't discuss those details in this book.

Checking Your Ethernet Connections

When you have an Ethernet card installed on your Linux system, you can use some of the utilities described in this section to be certain that your Ethernet connection is up and running. Once it is, the other Internet programs described in Hour 15 should work fine, assuming your Ethernet has a gateway to the Internet.

Unfortunately, KDE doesn't (yet) include many tools to configure and manage connections for TCP/IP over Ethernet, which makes up the core of most local networks.

As a consequence, you must rely on either the configuration tools that came with your Linux distribution or the basic Linux networking commands within a terminal window.

Fortunately, the major Linux distributions all include fairly comprehensive configuration tools. For example

- Caldera OpenLinux uses the lisa utility, which you can run from any command line.

- Red Hat Linux includes several strong graphical configuration tools, in addition to the complete LinuxConf tool set. All these tools are part of the applnk menu when you install KDE on Red Hat.

- SuSE Linux includes the YAST configuration utility.

To set up your Ethernet connection, you must use the correct kernel module for the type of Ethernet card installed in your computer. The configuration utilities should take care of the details for you.

After you have used these utilities to set up your Ethernet networking, Linux provides a few command-line tools to ensure that it's working correctly.

The first step to check your networking is to use the ping utility. ping sends a packet to the computer you indicate and awaits a response. First try this command. A typical response is shown:

```
$ ping localhost
PING localhost (127.0.0.1): 56 data bytes
64 bytes from 127.0.0.1: icmp_seq=0 ttl=64 time=2.5 ms
64 bytes from 127.0.0.1: icmp_seq=1 ttl=64 time=1.8 ms
64 bytes from 127.0.0.1: icmp_seq=2 ttl=64 time=1.7 ms
64 bytes from 127.0.0.1: icmp_seq=3 ttl=64 time=1.7 ms
64 bytes from 127.0.0.1: icmp_seq=4 ttl=64 time=1.9 ms
64 bytes from 127.0.0.1: icmp_seq=5 ttl=64 time=1.7 ms
64 bytes from 127.0.0.1: icmp_seq=6 ttl=64 time=1.7 ms
64 bytes from 127.0.0.1: icmp_seq=7 ttl=64 time=1.7 ms

--- localhost ping statistics ---
8 packets transmitted, 8 packets received, 0% packet loss
round-trip min/avg/max = 1.7/1.8/2.5 ms
```

13

 Press Ctrl+C to end the ping display. When you do, the summary information is shown as in the preceding listing.

When you ping localhost, you're verifying that the networking system is running. But because localhost is just another name for your computer, this is only a first step. Next, try using ping to reach another computer on your network. Use the IP address of that computer, which is similar to the following (although this is an Internet address):

```
$ ping 207.179.39.2
```

This should display the same type of response as the first ping command. Using the IP address shows that the networking is functioning, because packets of information are being passed between the two computers. Now try this command, using any complete hostname that you think of:

```
$ ping www.caldera.com
```

By using a hostname, you verify that the domain name service is working, because the domain name must be converted to an IP address before the ping command can reach the other computer.

Beyond experimenting with the vendor-specific configuration utilities provided with your Linux system, Linux provides two other utilities to show the status of your networking. These utilities are fairly complicated, but you can use them in their simplest form to see if networking is functioning.

The first of these commands is /sbin/ifconfig—the interface configuration. When you enter this command, Linux reports on the networking interfaces that are available for the kernel to use in transmitting data. A sample output for this command is shown here:

```
$ /sbin/ifconfig
lo        Link encap:Local Loopback
          inet addr:127.0.0.1  Bcast:127.255.255.255  Mask:255.0.0.0
          UP BROADCAST LOOPBACK RUNNING  MTU:3584  Metric:1
          RX packets:159 errors:0 dropped:0 overruns:0
          TX packets:159 errors:0 dropped:0 overruns:0

eth0      Link encap:Ethernet  HWaddr 00:20:AF:3D:80:8E
          inet addr:198.68.100.2  Bcast:198.68.100.255  Mask:255.255.255.0
          UP BROADCAST RUNNING MULTICAST  MTU:1500  Metric:1
          RX packets:363 errors:0 dropped:0 overruns:0
          TX packets:350 errors:0 dropped:0 overruns:0
          Interrupt:10 Base address:0x300
```

You should always see the localhost section. This example also includes an Ethernet section, indicating that the Ethernet card is configured and functioning.

Some types of problems can still occur after your Ethernet card is recognized by Linux. Network address conflicts and routing issues are common problems on large or multisegment networks.

The `ifconfig` command can also be used with parameters to set up the networking interfaces. For more details on this command, review the manual page (enter **man ifconfig**).

Another useful command is `/sbin/route`. When you enter this command, as shown in the following listing, you see the *routes* or paths that network packets take as they try to reach their destination. If only localhost is listed, your network connection doesn't extend outside of your computer.

```
$ /sbin/route
Kernel IP routing table
Destination     Gateway          Genmask          Flags Metric Ref   Use Iface
198.68.100.0    *                255.255.255.0    U     0      0       2 eth0
127.0.0.0       *                255.0.0.0        U     0      0       1 lo
default         sundance.xmissi  0.0.0.0          UG    1      0       4 eth0
```

The default route shown at the end of this listing is the first connection that the kernel tries when locating the destination for a packet. In this listing the two interfaces that the `route` command detects are `lo` (the localhost test loop), and `eth0` (the Ethernet card for a LAN). When you install the protocol PPP, the PPP interface is designated as the default route, so all network traffic is directed to that network connection.

> Routing becomes more complicated if you have both a modem with a PPP connection and an Ethernet card for access to a LAN (local area network) within the same computer. The IP Forwarding feature, required to make such a computer act as a gateway to the Internet, is generally turned off by default in the Linux kernel.

As with the `ifconfig` command, the `route` command can use many different parameters to alter the routing used to reach your network connections. See the `route` man page for more information.

After your Ethernet connection is established correctly, you can immediately start accessing any servers that are connected to your network. If your Ethernet network includes a gateway to the Internet, you can also start browsing the Web and reading email using the KDE Internet tools described in Hour 15 or a browser such as Netscape Communicator.

13

> Your LAN might be using other types of networking besides Ethernet, such as Token Ring. Contact your system administrator for details.

The Samba connectivity described later in this hour for Windows-to-Linux resource sharing also relies on an established network connection using Ethernet or another network system.

Establishing a PPP Connection

For users at home or in small offices, one of the most important protocols to know about is the *Point to Point Protocol (PPP)*. PPP establishes a dial-up connection using a modem that TCP/IP (or other protocols) can use to send packets between computers. To use a graphical Web browser or connect multiple PCs to one Internet connection, PPP is the protocol of choice.

Understanding PPP

The core of PPP is the PPP daemon, *pppd*. Using pppd can be straightforward, though dozens of options are also available.

Establishing a PPP connection involves several steps, as outlined here:

- Start the pppd daemon with the appropriate options for routing, modem use, and so forth.
- The pppd daemon uses the Chat program to establish a modem connection.
- The Chat program uses either command-line parameters or a chat script to exchange information with the PPP server that you're dialing in to.
- Depending on the security used by the server, various authentication tokens are exchanged to complete the login process.
- The Chat program closes, and the pppd daemon is left with a PPP connection to the server. A default route to the PPP server is normally established as part of the connection options so that all Internet traffic is routed to the PPP connection.

> PPP supports several authentication options, including standard script-based login (which isn't very secure), PAP, and CHAP. You should contact your Internet service provider (ISP) to determine which authentication method your PPP server expects when you connect.

Starting the Kppp Utility

KDE provides a convenient utility to configure and start a PPP connection. To start this utility, choose Internet, Kppp on the main menu, or enter **kppp** on a command line.

More and more ISPs are providing scripts to connect their customers who run Linux. Although Kppp is a powerful and easy-to-use utility, an ISP-provided Linux script might be a better choice. At any rate, you will need certain information from your ISP to determine how to configure Kppp.

The initial Kppp dialog box, shown in Figure 13.1, includes a drop-down list where you can select which account you want to connect to and a place to enter the username and password for that account. After you have your options and accounts set up, as described in the sections that follow, starting a PPP connection is as simple as entering a username and password, selecting an account, and choosing the Connect button.

FIGURE 13.1

The main Kppp window lets you choose an account, enter a username and password, and connect using PPP.

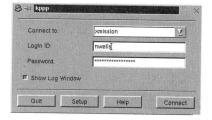

The Help button on the initial Kppp dialog box opens the Kppp online help, which provides a wealth of information on PPP and Kppp.

Configuring a Kppp Account

Before you can use Kppp, you must set up at least one account and review the Kppp configuration options.

An account in Kppp defines everything about how to connect to a certain PPP server, such as an ISP or office-based PPP server for telecommuters.

To begin defining an account for Kppp, choose the Setup button. The Configuration dialog box appears, as shown in Figure 13.2.

The Accounts tab allows you to manage multiple PPP connection accounts. To create a new account, choose New. The New Account dialog box appears, as in Figure 13.3).

13

Figure 13.2

In the Kppp Configuration dialog box, you define everything about your PPP connections.

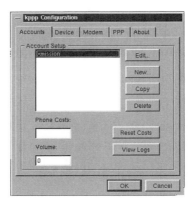

Figure 13.3

New PPP accounts are defined in the New Account dialog box, starting with the Dial tab.

The Dial tab is the most critical. In this tab you should complete the following fields:

- *Connection Name.* Enter a name for this connection, such as the name of your ISP.
- *Phone Number.* Enter the phone number to dial to reach this account.

> Kppp doesn't provide separate fields for things such as calling cards or dialing 9 for an outside line. Just enter the complete number to dial out in the Phone Number field. Adding a comma in the phone number causes a one-second pause during dialing.
>
> If you need to have multiple, similar accounts, use the Copy button in the Accounts tab of the Configuration dialog box to duplicate an existing account and modify the Phone Number field to include any additional extensions or codes required to dial out from that location.

- *Authentication drop-down list*. Choose the security method used by your PPP server. (You'll need to contact your ISP or system administrator to find out the correct setting.)

- *Store Password check box*. Select this option if you're not worried about others logging into your PPP account. Uncheck this box if you prefer to enter your password each time you log in.

- *Execute program Upon Connect*. If you want to start a program automatically when a PPP connection is established, such as a Web browser, enter the command to start that program this field.

  You can also execute a program when you disconnect by entering it in the corresponding field.

- *Edit pppd Arguments*. If you need to edit the parameters that are used to start pppd, choose this button. A dialog box appears (see Figure 13.4) where you can add or remove from the list of parameters. Don't change the default settings unless instructed by your system administrator or ISP.

FIGURE 13.4

The Customize pppd Arguments dialog box lets you define options for how the pppd daemon is started.

The IP tab of the New Account dialog box (see Figure 13.5) and the Gateway tab both define how your networking will be configured after a PPP connection is established. The preferred option is to leave the default options, with dynamic assignment of an IP address and use the default gateway. You can choose the Static IP or Static gateway option on the Gateway tab if your networking requires this.

In the DNS tab (see Figure 13.6) you define how name resolution is done after you are connected via PPP.

If you are running a single computer or a small network without a DNS name server, you should use the IP address of the name server given to you by your ISP or system administrator. Enter this IP address in the DNS IP address field and choose Add.

You can add several DNS servers by repeating this procedure; multiple DNS servers protect you in case one is unavailable to resolve a domain name.

13

Enter the domain name of your ISP or other remote PPP server in the Domain Name field. This information helps route packets correctly.

FIGURE 13.5

The IP tab of the New Account dialog box defines whether a dynamic or static IP address will be used with this account.

FIGURE 13.6

The DNS tab defines how your computer resolves domain names once your PPP connection is established.

If you're system is part of a network that includes a DNS name server and you're having trouble connecting using Kppp, select the check box to disable DNS on your computer during the PPP connection.

The Login Script tab of the New Account dialog box, shown in Figure 13.7, is the most complicated of the PPP configuration.

FIGURE 13.7

In the Login Script tab, you define the commands that the Chat program uses to communicate with the PPP server.

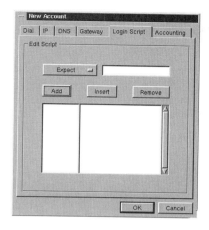

The Chat program uses the instructions in this dialog box to *chat*, or exchange information with the PPP server. The chat or login script is usually made up of *expect this* and *send this* items. Fortunately, Kppp takes care of the login script exchange, so you don't need to add anything to the fields in this tab unless you're having a problem accessing your ISP.

The Accounting tab, shown in Figure 13.8, is used to track how much money you're spending with your ISP.

FIGURE 13.8

The Accounting tab lets you track PPP costs based on the telecommunications system you're connected through.

13

To use the Accounting feature, choose the Enable Accounting check box, click on a country in the list, and choose a telecom system to track usage costs based on that provider.

The United States isn't listed here because dial-up connections in the U.S. are rarely charged by time units.

You can also track the volume of data that you're transmitting and receiving, which is sometimes the basis of your Internet account charges.

To use this feature, choose an option from the Volume Accounting drop-down list. Options include the following:

- *No Accounting.* The default
- *Bytes In.* Measures characters received
- *Bytes Out.* Measures characters sent
- *Bytes In and Out.* Measures traffic in both directions

Your accounting statistics (costs) are shown in the Accounts tab of the Configuration dialog box. Each account is tracked separately.

- *Phone Costs.* This field shows your cost based on the national telecom provider you selected from the list of countries on the Accounting tab.
- *Volume.* This field shows the number of characters (bytes) transmitted over your PPP connection.

These two fields are cumulative. You can reset the Phone Costs field by choosing the Reset Costs button.

Configuring Kppp Options

Options that apply to all Kppp accounts are configured using the other tabs in the Configuration dialog box. In the Device tab (see Figure 13.9) you define where the modem is located on your Linux system, and how it should be accessed.

The device is selected from the Modem Device drop-down list. If you're modem is located on the COM1 port, choose /dev/ttyS0. COM2 is located on /dev/ttyS1, and so forth. Other options might also apply depending on your Linux configuration. If you're not sure which port to use, try the /dev/modem device. Often this device name is a link to the correct port.

The only other two fields you need to worry about are the Connection Speed and the Modem Timeout.

Choose a connection speed from the drop-down list. The higher the number the faster the Internet connection. However, the modem might be limited by the quality of your phone connection. The modem will connect at the highest speed it can unless limited by the connection speed. Thus, you can use this field to limit the speed of your connection if bad phone lines are causing dropped connections.

The Modem Timeout field determines how long Kppp will wait for a connection. Longer times might be needed if your ISP has a slow system, but this also delays retries if you're having problems connecting.

The other fields in this tab should not be changed unless recommended by your system administrator.

The Modem tab, shown in Figure 13.10, lets you interact with the modem to troubleshoot problems with your connection. The Busy Wait field is the only part of this tab you need to worry about unless problems occur.

FIGURE 13.9

The Device tab of the Configuration dialog box defines which device Kppp uses to connect via PPP.

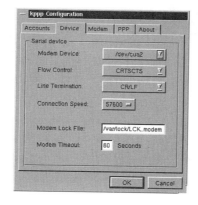

FIGURE 13.10

The Modem tab lets you interact with your modem to test it or change how Kppp interprets what it receives from the modem.

13

The Modem Commands button opens a dialog box where you can define the command strings sent to your modem and what Kppp should expect in return (see Figure 13.11).

FIGURE 13.11

The Edit Modem Commands dialog box defines how your modem model is initialized and how it responds to common situations such as busy signals.

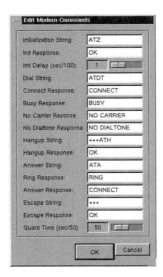

The Query Modem button opens a message box where the modem is queried to see if it responds. This is a quick way to see if you have selected the right modem device in the Device tab.

The Terminal button opens a simple terminal program where you can issue commands to the modem and interact with the responses. This is like a simplified version of the Linux program minicom (or Hyperterminal in Windows).

The PPP tab of the Configuration dialog box (see Figure 13.12) is where you define features for how Kppp operates:

FIGURE 13.12

The PPP tab defines various options for what happens when Kppp establishes or ends a PPP connection.

The pppd daemon Timeout field defines how many seconds pppd will wait before expecting a connection to be established. Increase this time if your connection takes longer to establish because of your phone system or ISP server.

- *Dock into Panel on Connect.* When this is selected, Kppp is minimized to your KDE panel after the PPP connection is established. You can still see that the connection is active, but the Kppp window doesn't take up space on your desktop.

- *Automatic Redial on Disconnect.* Causes Kppp to attempt to reestablish the PPP connection if it's dropped for any reason. This is useful if you're operating a dial-up server that operates unattended.

- *Show Clock on Caption.* Indicates that Kppp should include the connect time when minimized to the Panel after connecting.

- *Disconnect on X-server shutdown.* Causes Kppp to close your PPP connection if you close KDE.

- *Quit on Disconnect.* Closes the Kppp application when you close your PPP connection.

- *Minimize Window on Connect.* Causes Kppp to be minimized to the taskbar instead of docked to the KDE Panel after a connection is established. (You can unselect both of these options to leave Kppp open on your desktop after establishing a connection.)

When you've finished these configuration options, choose OK to close the Configuration dialog box. You're now ready to select an account on the main Kppp window, enter a name and password, and choose the Connect button.

When you have established a PPP connection, you can use the route and ifconfig utilities mentioned earlier in this hour to examine the PPP connection.

Reviewing Other KDE Connectivity Tools

The default installation of KDE doesn't include tools for some types of connectivity that may be useful to you. Table 13.1 lists some additional KDE networking utilities that you can find via the KDE Web site under Applications. Hour 21 provides more details on using these tools.

13

The utilities described in Table 13.1 are for the lower levels of networking connectivity. Additional tools for higher level protocols such as Internet Chat and Telnet are listed in Hour 15.

TABLE 13.1   ADDITIONAL NETWORKING TOOLS AVAILABLE VIA THE KDE WEB SITE

Utility	Description
Knetmon	A graphical front end to many networking tools, including Samba
KISDN	A graphical dialer, configuration utility, and monitor for ISDN connections
Kimon	A monitor for ISDN connections
Ksamba	A graphical interface for Samba server configuration
Kwin	A graphical front end to mount Windows file systems using the smb server described later in this hour
KModem	Displays the status of a modem over an Internet connection
KInetEd	A graphical utility for managing the inetd configuration file, which controls which protocols and services are available on your Linux system

Managing Samba Within KDE

Samba is almost as large a subject as Linux networking. Samba, or the *SMB* protocol, is used by dozens of different computer systems to share file systems and printers. When you have a Samba server running on your Linux system, it can replace services such as NFS and NetWare for file and print sharing.

Of course, you might still need these services installed in Linux, depending on what else is attached to your network. The most popular use of Samba on Linux is to share files and printers with Windows systems, including Window 95, Window 98, Windows for Workgroups, and Windows NT.

> The SMB (Server Message Block) protocol, is based on the LAN manager and NetBEUI protocols Microsoft products use.

Setting up a Samba server on Linux can be a daunting task. At any rate, it isn't discussed in this book. A number of Linux books cover Samba in greater detail to help get you started.

Unfortunately, no KDE utility exists at this point to automate this entire process or to connect to other servers as a Samba client.

After you have a Samba server running, however, KDE provides a utility to track how your Linux resources are being used via Samba connections.

Using the KDE Samba Monitor

The KDE Samba monitor displays the status of the Samba server running on your Linux system. You can view the Samba information by choosing Settings, Network, Samba on the main menu or choosing Samba in the Network section of the KDE Control Center. The Samba status window is shown in Figure 13.13.

FIGURE 13.13

The Samba status window tracks usage of your Linux resources by Samba clients.

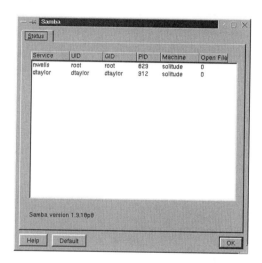

Because this utility is only a graphical display of the information provided by the smbstatus utility, you can't change anything in this window; it's for information only.

However, the Samba status window will be updated about once per second. So if you need to track who is accessing your Linux server using Samba, you can leave this window open and see constant updates of which users are connected and how many files they are accessing.

If you see a warning message in the Control Center or in the bottom of the Samba status window stating that Samba is not running, the window won't display any information. Start Samba as described earlier in this hour and try the utility again.

The fields in the Samba status window are described in the following list:

- *Service.* The Samba service that is being used on your Linux system by this user. This is normally a user's home directory or a printer, depending on how you have configured the access control for your Samba server.

13

- *UID*. The username of the account accessing your Linux system as a Samba server.
- *GID*. The group membership of the user accessing your Linux system as a Samba server.
- *PID*. The process ID number of the smb daemon on your Linux system that services the requests of this user.
- *Machine*. The hostname of the computer from which this user is accessing your Linux system using Samba.
- *Open File*. The number of files that this user has open. (If small files are being used one at a time, this might always show zero, even though work is being done.)

Summary

This hour describes how to use, review, and maintain your Linux networking connections within KDE. You learned about some basic diagnostic utilities provided by Linux. You also learned about setting up a PPP connection using the Kppp utility and about using the Samba status monitor to track who is using system resources via Samba from within KDE. The next hour describes some background on printing in Linux, including use of the HP LaserJet utility included with KDE.

Questions and Answers

Q Because KDE doesn't help me set up Samba, only check the status after it's running, how can I learn about using Samba?

A Samba is a large subject. Start with a visit to www.samba.org to do a little reading. Then pick up a book on Samba; *Sams Teach Yourself Samba in 24 Hours* would be a good choice. The man pages within Linux provide some guidance on the Samba utilities, but you'll need to have a basic understanding before you start to use them.

Q If I use a PPP script provided by my ISP, will it interfere with Kppp? Which should I use?

A First be certain the connection utility provided by your ISP is for Linux. If so, you should probably use that utility instead of Kppp. It should be simple to use because it's designed to connect to a single ISP, so there are no unknowns in the setup. If you have problems with it, you can fall back on Kppp. Or if you prefer the flexibility of Kppp to configure your connection, ask your ISP for the PPP details as described in the text, and then plug them into Kppp.

Q **I see some additional networking utilities on the main menu. What are they used for?**

A KDE is always adding new useful utilities to provide graphical access to Linux features or the configuration. Many of the networking tools that are becoming available for KDE are more complex or low-level network diagnostics than what I've described in this hour. However, you might also find graphical utilities for ping, route, and so forth, that make it easier to use these basic utilities. In general, these graphical utilities execute the text utility behind the scenes and feed the information into a convenient display format.

Exercises

1. Use some of the command-line Samba utilities to connect to a PC running Windows using Samba. At the same time, view the Samba status window in the KDE Control Panel. Does anything that you do as a Samba client to Windows affect the Samba status window? Why or why not?

2. What is involved in having a computer that is part of a LAN using an Ethernet card, but also connected to the Internet using a modem and PPP connection? What routing and security issues will arise? What capability does this provide for everyone on the LAN if the system is configured correctly?

13

HOUR 14

Managing Printing in KDE

In this hour you learn how to configure and manage printing using KDE. This includes a review of printing in Linux and your print configuration file. After that, you'll learn about K-LJet—the KDE utility for graphically configuring.

Printing in Linux or UNIX is a complex and important topic. This hour presents an overview of Linux printing that will help you prepare and troubleshoot so that you can print from KDE. You might need to consult your system administrator or Linux vendor for support if you're having serious trouble getting printing to work correctly on your system.

If printing is working correctly on your Linux system, you should be able to print from applications even before you use K-LJet.

Understanding Linux Printing

Because UNIX and Linux are multiuser systems, printing on UNIX and Linux is done differently than on systems such as DOS, Windows, or

Macintosh. The standard Linux printing system allows multiple users and multiple applications from each user to print files to the same or different printers, all without interfering with each other.

Linux printing uses a *print spool,* which is where files to print are stored until it's their turn to be printed. A Linux daemon (or background) process accepts new print jobs, stores them in the print spool area, and then sends them one at a time to the printer.

The components of the Linux printing system are listed here. As noted, some of the components are optional:

- A program called lpd that manages all print jobs from all users.
- A program called lpr that accepts each print job and submits it to the lpd program.
- A configuration file called /etc/printcap, which defines one or more printers and how lpr should send print jobs to those printers.
- Additional utilities (optional) for listing which print jobs are in the print spool; lpq for print queue and lprm for removing a job from print queue.
- A filter script to manage the formatting of print jobs for the specific printer you have (optional, although needed if you don't have a PostScript printer).
- A program to provide the formatted output to the filter script for different printers (optional; examples of this program are nenscript, enscript, and gs).
- Additional printer-specific drivers (these are unusual at this point; only a few programs such as WordPerfect for Linux provide them).

With that groundwork laid, the process of printing a file is straightforward:

1. An application submits a file to lpr for printing. This can be done using a Print dialog box or directly from a command line using a command such as this:

   `$ lpr textfile`

2. The lpr program reviews the printcap file to see how to process the file, including using a filter to format the file.

 One common print filter uses the gs or nenscript program to format a document in the PCL page description language for output to a Hewlett-Packard printer.

3. The formatted print job is submitted to the lpd program. After the print job is accepted by lpd, you can use the lpq and lprm utilities to manage that print job.

4. The lpd program sends each print job in turn to the physical or network printer specified by lpr when the print job was submitted.

> If you didn't indicate during your Linux installation that you wanted to run a print server (the lpd program), the lpr program can't submit print jobs for printing. Check your Linux installation guide or configuration utilities for directions on starting lpd on your system.

Reviewing Your Print Configuration

With all these complications—printcap file, lpr program, lpd program, filters—it's no surprise that most Linux vendors include a utility to set up your printing system for you.

Starting the lpd program (called the print server daemon) is generally done at startup. You can check your initialization scripts or review your Linux documentation. (See also Hour 11, "Using KDE System Management Utilities." Caldera OpenLinux users can run the lisa utility to specify that the print server should be started at startup.)

Using Linux Print Utilities

The lpr, lpq, and lprm commands are installed by default and will be used each time you print a file. You can learn more about any of these utilities by reading the man pages. For example, enter this command to learn about lprm:

```
$ man lprm
```

The lpr command is used automatically when you print from a Print dialog box within a graphical application. If you choose to use lpr directly from a command line, as the example in the previous section showed, you can add parameters to set the page size, number of copies, and many other options. In most cases, the application that you're printing from will manage these options, however.

Entering the lpq command lists the print jobs that the lpd print server has stored in the print queue. The output of lpq shows the owner of the print job, the filename and size, which printer it will be printed on, and a print job number. This print job number is important. You can use the print job number to manage that print job using the lpq or lprm commands.

14

If you use the `lpq` command without any options, as in the following example, it displays information about the default printer in the `printcap` file (the first one listed). To see information about other printers, use the `-P` option with the printer name you want to examine.

Sample output of the `lpq` command is shown in this listing:

```
$ lpq
Printer: ps@sundance
 Queue: 6 printable jobs
 Server: pid 1907 active
 Unspooler: pid 1908 active
 Status: printed all 279 bytes at 09:32:02
 Rank    Owner/ID                    Class Job
➡ Files             Size    Time
active   root@sundance+906              A  906
➡ (stdin)                12579  09:32:02
2        nwells@sundance+911           A  911
➡ /etc/fstab           376    09:32:43
3        nwells@sundance+915           A  915
➡ /…/nwells/report.txt 119274 09:33:13
4        dtaylor@sundance+920          A  920
➡ /…/dtaylor/expense.sdc 31279 09:33:14
5        jkoch@sundance+922            A  922
➡ (stdin)                227189 09:35:03
6        nwells@sundance+928           A  928
➡ /…/nwells/archive/summary.sdw 2232 09:35:04
```

If you wanted to remove the file `report.txt` from the print queue so that it didn't print, you could use this command:

```
$ lprm 915
```

You can only remove print jobs that you submitted for printing. The root user can remove and manage all print jobs.

The `printcap` file and printing filters are set up by a utility provided by your Linux vendor. For example, if you're running Caldera OpenLinux, the lisa utility includes a section where you choose a printer and configure how it's used. After you start the utility with this command:

```
$ lisa
```

select System Configuration, Hardware Configuration, Configure Printer, to begin this process. From this screen (shown in Figure 14.1) you can select from a list of several dozens printer models.

FIGURE 14.1

Caldera OpenLinux users can start the lisa utility to define a printer.

Red Hat Linux includes a similar printing tool that can be accessed from the Personal submenu of KDE after you have installed the KDE rpms as described in Hour 2, "Installing KDE from Scratch."

The `/etc/printcap` File

The `/etc/printcap` file contains cryptic descriptions of how lpr should process each print job. The `printcap` file can include definitions for several printers, and each print job can specify which printer it should be sent to. Although you hope to never edit `/etc/printcap` by hand (that's what all the fancy new Linux configuration utilities are for), I've included a simple `printcap` file below for review.

```
# /etc/printcap
#
# Don't edit this file directly unless you know what you are doing!
# Look at the printcap(5) man page for more info.
#
##PRINTTOOL## LOCAL ljet4 300x300 letter {}
ps:\
        :sd=/var/spool/lpd/ps:\
        :mx#0:\
        :lp=/dev/lp1:\
        :if=/var/spool/lpd/ps/filter:\
        :sh:
##PRINTTOOL## LOCAL
lp:\
   :sd=/var/spool/lpd/lp:\
   :mx#0:\
   :lp=/dev/lp1:\
   :sh:
```

14

The standard printer definitions that all `printcap` files include are `ps` and `lp`. They might both point to the same physical device but use different filters, for example, one for PostScript printing and one for text files.

> The `printcap` file can define several logical printers for one physical printer device. For example, you can create a printer called *letterhead* and another called *envelopes*. Sending print jobs to one of these different logical printer definitions lets you prepare your physical printer before printing from those print queues.

The `printcap` file uses a series of two-letter codes to define a printer. Only a couple are worth looking at here. The `lp` line indicates the physical printer to send files to `/dev/lp1` (in this example). The `sh` line indicates that the *banner page*—an initial page with the username and print job information—should not be used (that is, suppress the header).

Additional information would be included in the `printcap` file if you were using a networked printer. For example, the name of a remote print server or the address of the printer itself (if it includes a network port) might be included. The lpd program can process both local and network (remote) print jobs.

Using K-LJet to Configure Printing

Most KDE Print dialog boxes are simple. Figure 14.2 shows the Print dialog box from the KEdit program, described in Hour 18, "Using KDE Text Utilities." Notice that the many options available for printing are not listed in this box. These include how many copies to print, what paper size to use, what resolution to print, and so forth. These options are part of the printer's capabilities, and are also supported by the `lpr` command.

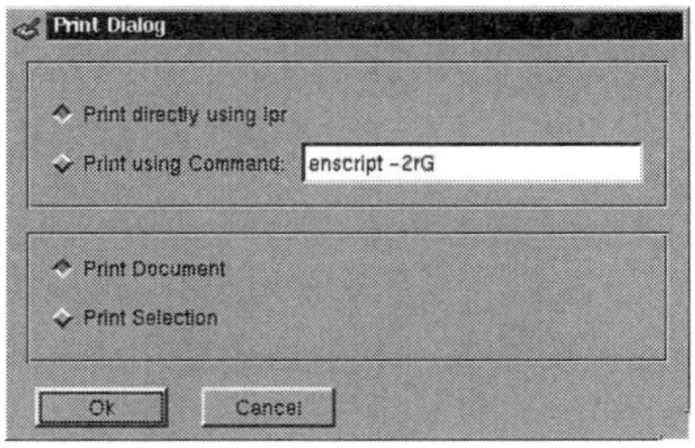

FIGURE 14.2

The Print dialog box for KEdit doesn't include options for things such as the number of copies and the print resolution.

To use the additional features that don't appear in many KDE Print dialogs, you can use the K-LJet utility to set printing options are used by all compliant KDE applications. To start this utility, choose Utilities, HP LaserJet Control Panel from the main menu, or enter **kljettool** in a terminal window. The initial K-LJet window is shown in Figure 14.3.

FIGURE 14.3

The K-LJet tool lets you configure how compliant KDE applications will print.

The K-LJet utility is intended for use with Hewlett-Packard LaserJet printers or compatibles. Although it might help with other printers as well, K-LJet uses the HP Printer Control Language (PCL) to manage the options that you select, so it might prove useless with your non-HP printer. In this case, resort to the printing tools that come with your Linux distribution to define a default printer and options. The KDE Print dialog boxes should then use the default printer.

The following sections describe the four tabs in the K-LJet utility.

The K-LJet tool might conflict with some printing utilities on your Linux system, particularly if your version of Linux includes sophisticated filters or print configuration tools. Choose Help on the Operations tab of K-LJet for more information about resolving these conflicts.

Setting Paper Options

The Paper tab lets you define basic information about KDE print jobs. The fields of the paper tab are described in the following list (refer to Figure 14.3):

- *Format drop-down list.* Defines the paper size. The standard size in the U.S. is Letter; in Europe, choose A4. Other paper sizes include Legal, Executive, and larger formats such as B5 and C5.

14

- *Copies field.* Defines how many copies of each print job are printed. For example, if you enter 3 in this field, every time you print from a KDE application, you'll get three copies.

- *Lines field.* Defines how many lines are on a page. This number is used to format the document that you're printing. It doesn't change, however, when you change paper sizes, so if you change to Legal or another longer paper size, you should change the Lines field as well or part of the page might not be used.

- *Orientation field.* Defines whether pages are printed as Portrait (the default), or Landscape (wider instead of taller).

- *Miscellaneous field.* Lets you select Manual Feed or Auto Continue (for continuous feed). The Manual Feed is useful for printing just a few pages on letterhead without defining a new printer and reconfiguring things. Continuous feed is the default.

Setting Printer Options

The Printer tab, shown in Figure 14.4, defines other information about your print job. The options in this tab are described in the list that follows:

FIGURE 14.4

The Printer tab of the K-LJet tool defines settings such as resolution and print density of graphics.

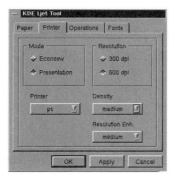

- *Mode field.* Sets the print quality to low or high. Lower quality printing (labeled Economy) takes less time and less toner or ink. Higher quality printing (labeled Presentation) provides a nicer printed page but takes longer and uses more toner or ink. Presentation quality is selected by default.

- *Resolution field.* Defines either 300dpi (dots per inch) or 600dpi. Again, the higher quality will take more time to print and use more toner or ink.

Selecting 600dpi when your printer doesn't support that high of resolution can produce strange results when you print.

- *Printer field.* Includes a drop-down list where you can select which printer to send all print jobs to by default. The printers listed in this field are taken from the definitions in the /etc/printcap file. The default printers are ps and lp; either one should work for most print jobs. Use your Linux configuration tools to define other printers in the printcap file.

- *Density field.* Defines how much *ink* should be used to render graphics. Higher density generally produces nicer graphics, though this depends on the image itself and how it is dithered for printing. Medium density is selected by default.

- *Resolution Enh. (Enhancement) field.* Lets you modify this setting for printers that use resolution enhancement technology to simulate higher dpi than they are actually capable of. Higher settings in this field will take longer to print and might use more toner. The default setting of Medium should be fine for most applications.

> Not all printers will respond to changes in the Density and Resolution Enhancement fields. The filter that you're using to print might not send commands specific to the printer model that you're working with.

Configuring Operations

The Operations tab, shown in Figure 14.5, includes buttons that immediately send commands to the printer. Each of the fields in the Operations tab are described in the following list.

FIGURE 14.5

The Operations tab includes buttons that immediately send commands to the printer.

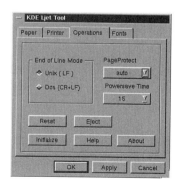

14

- *End of Line Mode field.* In this field, select whether the files that you're printing are UNIX-style or DOS-style files. The difference is in how the end of each line is marked. UNIX files use an LF (line feed) character; DOC files use both a CR and an LF character (carriage return and line feed). Choosing the appropriate setting in this field tells the print filters to accommodate the types of files you're printing.

UNIX files are selected by default. If you are printing UNIX files and select DOS, all the lines in your file will run together on the top of the page instead of flowing down. If you are printing DOS files and leave the default setting of UNIX, your documents will be double-spaced or behave strangely, depending on the type of printer you're using.

- *Page Protect field.* Lets you turn on the Page Protection feature for your documents. This feature is used when you print a page containing a lot of graphics information. Page Protection causes the entire graphic to appear on one page when otherwise the printer would run out of memory and print the graphic on multiple pages. The default of Auto is a good choice.

- *Powersave Time field.* Defines how many minutes your printer can sit idle without shutting down to Powersave mode. The Powersave mode is sort of like a laptop *going to sleep* to save power. Because printers are often left on all the time, this is a very useful feature. The shorter the time (the default is 15 minutes), the more you might have to wait for the printer to warm up before printing a print job.

- *Reset*, *Eject,* and *Initialize.* These three buttons are used to send a command to the printer immediately. The Initialize button sends the command string that is used to begin each print job. This can be useful if a print job is *stuck* and needs to be started or restarted.

  The Reset button resets all the features and options of your printer. It's sort of like turning the printer off and on again. Don't use this button unless you have a serious problem with your print jobs. It can affect other users waiting for their print jobs as well.

  The Eject button sends a page eject command to the printer. Because some print jobs don't include an End of Page character, a print job will sometimes be in the printer's memory, but not output because the printer is waiting for more information to finish the page. Choosing Eject will output the partial page stored in printer memory.

Because the K-LJet utility doesn't have a menu bar, the Help and About buttons are located in the Operations tab. They function as the Help, Contents and Help, About options would if K-LJet included a standard menu bar. The online help includes information about incorporating K-LJet with your Linux print configuration utilities.

Setting Font Options

The Fonts tab, shown in Figure 14.6, defines the characters used to print documents. The following list defines the fields in this tab.

FIGURE 14.6

The Fonts tab defines the printer language and which characters are used to print documents.

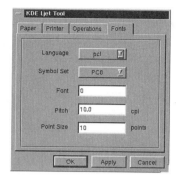

- *Language field.* Defines which page description language is used to process documents before they are sent to the printer. The default setting of PCL is the Hewlett-Packard standard language. If your HP printer supports PostScript, however, you might want to select this option.

- *Symbol Set field.* Lets you select the character set used for printing from a list of about 30. The default setting is PC8. Other symbol sets include ISO and Windows character sets. Choosing a different symbol set allows you to print files that contain non-English characters or different currency symbols.

- *Font field.* Defines the number of the font to use within the printer. Because most printers include several fonts (sometimes dozens), you can use this field to select from them without downloading new font details to the printer.

- *Pitch and Point Size fields.* Define how many characters will fit on each page of your documents. The Pitch defines how many characters per linear inch. The default setting is 10. Other settings, such as 12 or 15, produce compressed print, allowing more characters on each line. The Point Size field defines how large characters are. An inch is equal to 72 points. Another standard size is 10 points. This setting provides a baseline for your documents. Larger font sizes can still be defined within a document.

Additional KDE programs related to printing, such as utilities to send and view faxes, are described in Hour 19, "Using KDE Business Tools."

14

Summary

In this hour you learned about Linux printing, including the /etc/printcap file and the basic command-line utilities that are used to print files in Linux. You learned how to see and manage print queues using the lpq command. You also learned about the K-LJet utility in KDE, which enables you to manage how print jobs are sent to HP printers. In the next hour, you will learn how to connect to the Internet from within KDE and use basic Internet utilities to read email or newsgroup postings, browse the Web, or download files from FTP sites.

Questions and Answers

Q How can I learn about all the configuration options in the printcap file?

A You shouldn't really need to because the configuration utilities manage most of it for you, but you can read the manual page for printcap to learn all about the meaning of the configuration codes.

Q I've selected options in K-LJet but still can't print. Why not?

A You must configure Linux printing before K-LJet options can take effect. Use the configuration tools that come with your Linux product to create a printcap file with the appropriate filter definitions, hardware descriptions, and printing options.

Q How can I print to a network printer?

A The Linux printing system works just as well over a network as it does locally. If you have a printer connected to another computer running Linux (and the lpd print server daemon), you can define a network printer in the printcap file using your Linux print configuration tools.

Exercises

1. How does Linux standard printing differ from the print spooling that occurs in operating systems such as Microsoft Windows or Macintosh? (Think of multiuser ability, management tools, and automatic networking.)

2. After configuring the printcap file using the utilities included with your Linux system, define each of the two letter codes in the printer definition section of the printcap file by referring to the printcap manual page (enter **man printcap** for details). How is a network printer indicated?

HOUR 15

Accessing the Internet from KDE

In this hour you learn how to use some key Internet accessories that are included with KDE. After reviewing your Internet connection—based on your Ethernet or PPP connection—you will learn how to use the KDE graphical utilities to read email or browse newsgroups.

Checking Your Internet Connection

Before you can use the Internet utilities in KDE, you must have an Internet connection established. Your connection can be via your Ethernet (or similar) LAN (local area network) connection through an Internet gateway. Or you might be connected directly to an Internet service provider (ISP) using PPP.

Hour 13, "Managing Network Connections in KDE," discusses how to use the Kppp connection to establish a PPP connection to your ISP. You can use the information in Hour 13 to test and troubleshoot your Internet connection. To summarize those tests, you can use this command from a KDE terminal window:

```
$ ping www.mcp.com
```

If you see a response to this command, which shows the time each packet takes to reach the Web server, your Internet connection and domain name resolution are working fine.

Other issues might arise as you start to use the Internet utilities described in this hour. For example, your local network might use a firewall that doesn't allow you to access certain Internet sites or use certain protocols. You might also need to enter the address of a proxy server in order for your Web browser to reach the Internet.

Some of these issues are described in more detail as you learn about the KDE Internet utilities.

Reading Email with KMail

All Linux distributions include several products for reading email. Netscape Communicator is probably the most popular choice, but it's a large program if all you need is an email reader.

You could also use a text-based program such as elm or pine. These are powerful applications, but if you want to work with multiple open messages, easily add attachments, and graphically review the contents of mailboxes with Web integration, a text-based program won't do.

KDE includes a simple graphical email reader called KMail, which has most of the email functionality that you're likely to need. You can start KMail by choosing Internet, Mail client from the main menu, or enter `kmail` on a command line.

Configuring KMail

When you start KMail the first time, you should set up your account information in the Settings dialog box. This dialog box includes six tabs. The Identity tab is shown in Figure 15.1.

The Identity tab will have your name and email address filled in based on your Linux account name and your hostname. You should also review the other fields:

- *Organization.* Enter your company name here, if applicable.
- *Reply-To Address.* The Email Address field is taken from the hostname for the computer you're running on, but your email might come in through another mail server. Enter the address that you want mail to come to in this field.

  Some email systems won't process email messages if they can't contact the host that the message came from. This is a junk email (*spam*) prevention tool. Be sure to include a valid address in the Reply-To Address, especially if messages from your computer go to a main mail server on your network for forwarding.

FIGURE 15.1

In the Identity tab, you define your username, email address, and signature options.

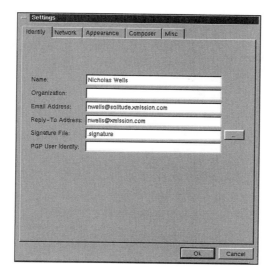

15

- *Signature File.* Enter the name of a file for your message signature. The contents of the file you name here are added to the end of every email message that you send out. Click on the ellipsis button (...) to open a file browser and select a file if you prefer.

A signature file should be in plain text. It should begin with `-- ` (dash, dash, space) on the first line, followed by no more than four lines of text. These lines normally include things such as your name, title, email address, perhaps your postal address, phone number, and sometimes a favorite quotation or personal cause.

The default setting is to include a signature file on messages you send. If you don't enter a file in this field and you leave the default setting in the Compose tab of the Settings dialog box, you will be prompted for a signature file when you try to create a message.

Switch to the Network tab of the Settings dialog box (see Figure 15.2), which is where you define how mail is sent and received.

FIGURE 15.2

The Network tab defines how messages are sent and received.

In the Sending Mail area, you can define either Sendmail or SMTP *(Simple Mail Transport Protocol)* as your mail agent. If you choose sendmail, you should be certain that the sendmail program is installed on your system. The filename for the sendmail program should be shown in the Location field.

If you prefer to have your messages forwarded on to another mail server for *processing and delivery*, choose SMTP. The mail server you name in the Server field can use a program such as sendmail or qmail (or dozens of other mail agents) to process your messages.

For example, you might need to enter a server name such as `mail.mycompany.com` to forward all messages to the central mail server for archiving and security reasons.

The default port of 25 for SMTP should be left as it is unless your system administrator informs you that the email server is using a different port.

In the Incoming Mail area, you can define multiple accounts for incoming mail. You must define at least one before you'll be able to read any messages. Choose the Add button to get started.

In the Select Account dialog box, choose Local Mailbox or POP3. Then choose OK.

- *Local Mailbox* reads mail messages directly from mail spool directories on your Linux system. Only use this account type if your email is arriving (directly or by SMTP forwarding) to your personal Linux machine.
- *POP3* allows you to specify a remote server from which messages are downloaded using the POP3 protocol.

After you choose an account type, the Configure Account dialog box appears. If you select a local mailbox, the dialog box appears as in Figure 15.3.

FIGURE 15.3

Use this dialog box to configure a local email account.

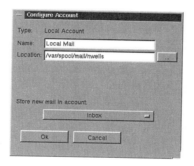

In this dialog box, you should enter a name for the account in the Name field (such as your username, the hostname of your computer, or Local Mail).

Unless you've altered your mail spooling system, the directory shown in the Location field shouldn't be changed. This is the file where incoming mail will be stored.

The Store New Mail in Account drop-down list includes all the mail folders defined in KMail. You can select which folder incoming (new) messages should appear in. This is normally the Inbox, but you can choose another if you prefer.

Messages in the Inbox are stored in the file ~/Mail by default. Other messages are stored in a file with the name of the mail folder you define.

After adding more folders, you can return to this dialog box and change which folder incoming messages are sent to.

If you select a POP3 account in the Select Account dialog box, the Configure Account dialog box that appears looks like Figure 15.4.

FIGURE 15.4

To configure a POP3 account you must specify the server and user information to retrieve your messages.

Check each of the fields in this dialog box:

- *Name.* This is the name of the email account, not your name.
- *Login.* Your username on the system where your email is stored.
- *Password.* Your password for your account on the POP3 mail server. (The Password field displays asterisks as you type.) Some ISPs require a separate authentication for your mail account, even if you're already logged in to their system.
- *Host.* The name of the server where your mail is stored, for example, `mail.xmission.com` or `popd.ix.netcom.com`.
- *Port.* The port number on the host server used to retrieve messages using POP3. Don't change this from the default of 110 unless instructed to by the system administrator of the mail server.
- *Delete Mail from Server* . Deselect this check box if you want a copy of your messages to remain on the mail server after downloading. This is appropriate if you are at a remote site and want to retrieve the messages on your main system later.

  It's not a good idea to leave all your messages on the ISP's mail server long-term, however. They might charge you for using extra disk space.
- *Show New Mail in Account.* As described for a local account, you can select from the drop-down list which mail folder your new messages should appear in. The default folder is the Inbox.

After setting up one or more accounts to receive mail, you can alter any account by double-clicking on it in the Accounts list or by clicking and choosing Modify.

The Appearance tab, shown in Figure 15.5, lets you define the font used for the list of messages and for the body text of a message.

FIGURE 15.5

The Appearance tab defines the fonts used for message text and the list of messages in a folder.

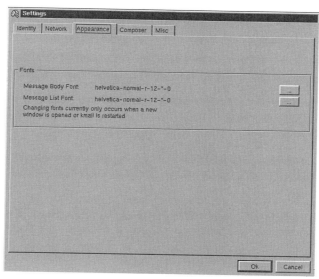

The current fonts are shown in standard X Window System font notation. You can select other fonts by choosing the ... button and using the standard KDE Select Font dialog box. The Composer tab lets you specify options to use when you compose a new message (see Figure 15.6).

FIGURE 15.6

The Composer tab defines the options you use when you compose a new email message.

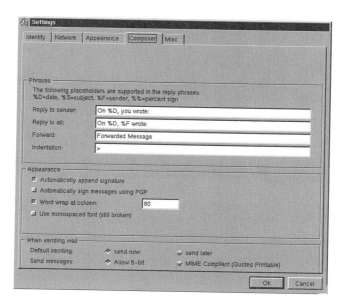

The fields in the Phrases section define what KMail will insert as part of a message when you forward or reply to a message.

The parameters, %S, %F, and so forth, listed at the top of the Phrases section, show how you can use parts of an original message to define part of the forward or reply message.

The Appearance section contains options for adding your signature file (which you defined in the Identity tab), using PGP, how long lines should be before wrapping to the next line, and whether to use a monospaced font for messages.

Finally, the When Sending Mail section lets you choose to send mail immediately or hold messages that have been composed until you choose File, Send Queued, to process the messages you've written.

This section also defines how message text is treated. You can choose to use 8-bit characters, which might not be readable on some text-based email readers, or a MIME-compliant format that places non-printing parts of the message in an attachment while the rest of the message can be read on any email system.

When you have configured everything in the Settings dialog box, choose OK to close the dialog box and start reading your email.

> You can change your settings, including adding or modifying accounts, by choosing File, Settings at any time.

Reading Messages

Before you can read your messages in KMail, you must retrieve them from the account where they're stored. This is true even for local email accounts. To retrieve messages, you can do any of the following:

- *Choose File, Check Mail.* This retrieves email from *all* your email accounts.
- *Choose File, Check Mail in, followed by the name of one of your email accounts.* This retrieves messages only from that account.
- *Click the icon on the toolbar showing an envelope with a question mark.* This also retrieves messages from *all* your email accounts.

The messages are added to your Inbox (or the folder you selected in the Settings dialog box). Figure 15.7 shows how a typical window might appear.

FIGURE 15.7

The KMail main window displays a list of mail folders, the messages in the selected folder, and the text of a selected message.

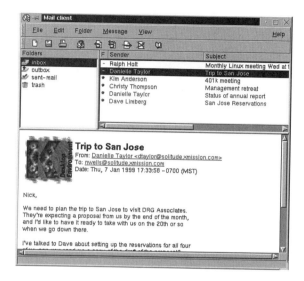

The Folders list shows your mail folders. When you click on a folder, the messages in that folder are displayed in the Messages list. The default folders include

- *Inbox.* This is where your messages arrive (by default).
- *Outbox.* This is where messages you have composed are stored until you send them using File, Send Queued (though they can be send immediately; see the Composer tab of the Settings dialog box).
- *Sent-mail.* This is where messages are copied after being sent (either immediately or from the Outbox).
- *Trash.* This is where messages that you delete are stored until you exit KMail (see the Misc tab of the Settings dialog box), or choose Folder, Empty.

> The Folder, Empty item deletes all the messages from your current folder. Be sure to select the Trash folder before selecting this item if you intend to empty the trash.

Some common folder operations include the following:

- Create a new folder by choosing Folder, Create.
- Modify the definitions for the currently selected folder by choosing Folder, Modify.

- Compress the contents of a folder by choosing Folder, Compact (especially useful for archive or mailing list folders).
- Move a selected message to a different folder by dragging and dropping it on the destination folder name or choosing Message, Move, and selecting a folder from the dialog box that appears.

 The File, Filters option lets you define mail filters that automatically store messages in different folders based on criteria such as the From and Subject headers.

You read an email message by clicking on its subject in the message list. The message text appears in the lower part of the window.

The status of a message is indicated by the icons to the left of the message subject. The most common status indicators are New, Unread, and Read. Other status indicators are for messages that have been Replied to, Queued (in the Outbox), or Sent (in the Sent Mail folder).

You can place the mouse pointer over each icon and see a pop-up hint describing what it is.

You can change the status of the current message by choosing an option from the Message, Set Status submenu.

As you're reading email, all the standard features you expect are available in KMail, both from the toolbar and within the Message menu. You can

- Reply to a message by clicking the icon with a page and curved arrow or choosing Message, Reply.
- Reply to all recipients of a message (adding those in the CC field) by clicking the icon with a page and two curved arrows or choosing Message, Reply All.
- Forward the message to another person by clicking the icon with a page and a straight arrow or choosing Message, Forward.
- Delete the message by clicking the icon with a page and an X or choosing Message, Delete (this moves the message to the Trash folder).
- Choose which message headers are displayed by selecting items on the View menu.
- Attempt to open an attachment by clicking on the attachment icon (opening attachments is governed by the kfm file typing system—see Hour 9, "Managing Files in KDE").

- Copy part of a message into the KDE Clipboard (for use in the KEdit program or other KDE applications) by dragging to select message text and choosing Edit, Copy.

- Save a message to a separate file by clicking the Disk icon or choosing File, Save As.

- Print a message by clicking the printer icon or choosing File, Print.

- Compose a new message by clicking the blank page icon or choosing File, New Composer.

In addition to these options, you can right-click in the message body to display a pop-up menu with Reply, Forward, and other commonly used functions.

Creating a New Message

When you click the blank page icon or choose File, New Composer, a blank message window appears (see Figure 15.8).

FIGURE 15.8

A blank message window appears when you want to send a new email message.

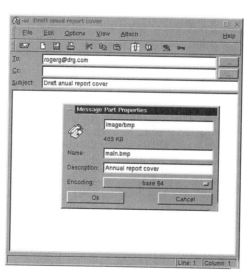

 The same type of window appears when you reply to or forward a message, but the text of the current message is inserted into the window.

Composing a message is a lot like using a Text editor; just be sure to include a person's email address in the To field and a message subject in the Subject field.

The KMail Address Book, which appears when you click the ... button next to the To or CC fields, is not functional in this version of KMail. When it is (in a future release), you can select a name from the pop-up Address Book, or add people to the Address Book by choosing File, Address Book in the Mail Reader window.

When you completed your message, click the moving envelope icon or choose File, Send to send your message.

You can enter information for other common email headers such as the Reply To and BCC (blind carbon copy) fields by choosing them from the View menu.

You can also set some headers by choosing them from the Options menu. You are not required to enter information; these headers use your email address as the response address. They include the following:

- *Urgent.* Marks the message as Priority: Urgent.
- *Confirm Delivery.* Sends a message back to you when the message you created is stored in the recipient's mailbox.
- *Confirm Read.* Sends a message back to you when the message you created is opened by the recipient.

These three options are nice, but they might not be honored by all email systems. Give your recipients the benefit of the doubt until you have confirmed that their email server responds to these standard email headers.

Many of the same options available in the Mail Reader window area are also available in the Composer window. For example, you can save or print a message that you're composing, or use the Cut, Copy, and Paste features to move text around (and between other KDE applications).

Attaching files in the Composer window is done by choosing Attach, Attach or by clicking on the Paper Clip icon. A file-browsing window appears where you can select a file to attach.

You can also drag a File icon from any open kfm window and drop it on a Composer window to add it as an email attachment.

After you select a file, a Message Part Properties dialog box appears (see Figure 15.9), where you can indicate basic information about the attached file to make it easier for recipients to use.

FIGURE 15.9

When you attach a file in the Composer window, you can describe the attached file in the Message Part Properties dialog box.

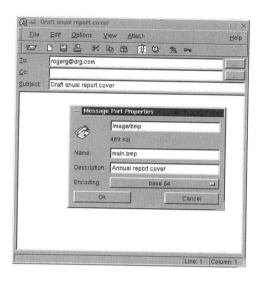

 For most files, you can choose OK in this dialog box and use the default settings. If you need to review them, choose Attach, Properties.

- The MIME type for the file is shown in the top of the dialog box. You can edit this field if needed.
- The Name field shows the name of the file as it is stored on your file system. You can change this name if you want the attachment recorded under a different name (so that the recipient does not see what the file was called on your system).
- A description can be included to describe the attached file for the recipient.
- Finally, the Encoding field specifies how the attachment is attached. The Base 64 option provides a common binary format, but might be difficult for some recipients to access (generally those using text-based email readers). You can choose None or Quoted Printable to use a simpler encoding scheme.

The Quoted Printable option converts all the information in the attachment into characters that can be printed (no control or special characters). The attachment is then included as text at the end of the message. This feature is similar to the UUEncode command.

You can also use the File, Insert File option to add a local file as text within your message.

After you have attached a file, it appears in a list box at the bottom of your message. You can use the Attach menu options operate on the attachment, or right-click on the attachment name to see a pop-up menu of attachment options (see Figure 15.10).

FIGURE 15.10

Right-click on an attachment in the Composer or Mail Reader windows to bring up a list of possible operations for the attachment.

If you're using PGP security for your email, click the Key icon to encrypt your message using your PGP key. PGP information is defined in the PGP tab of the Settings dialog box.

A message Composer window closes when you send the message.

When you close the Mail Reader window, your messages stay intact until the next time you open KMail because they're stored in your local home directory.

Browsing Newsgroups

Newsgroups are Internet-based discussion groups. A user who wants to participate in a newsgroup dedicated to a certain subject attaches to a news server—using a program that understands the NNTP protocol—and downloads the messages that have been sent to that newsgroup. If the user wants to respond to any of the messages, he or she composes a message, much like writing an email message, and posts it to the news server.

All the news servers in the world mirror different selected newsgroups. All the servers that mirror the newsgroup that the user posted to will soon have a copy of the message that was sent, so that others reading the discussion will see the additional comments and continue the discussion.

Newsgroups are divided into larger categories and then smaller categories. Some of the top-level categories include *comp* for computer discussions, *rec* for recreational discussions, and *sci* for science topics. Hundreds of top-level categories are available on large news servers. Within each top-level category are many more subcategories.

An example of a subcategory is `comp.os.linux.announce`. This could be written out as `Computer topics:Operating Systems:Linux-related:Announcements`.

Some newsgroups are moderated, meaning you can send a message to the newsgroup, but it doesn't get posted to the news server for everyone to read until a moderator decides that the content is relevant to the newsgroup it's posted to.

> Most newsgroups are a complete free-for-all. The few moderated newsgroups are often for announcements or more serious discussions.

To read newsgroup messages, you need a news reader program (a news client) that can access the news server, display messages, and post your responses. Many news readers are available for Linux, such as trn, tin, (both text-based and difficult to learn) and Netscape Communicator's Discussion feature.

KDE includes a nice graphical news client that will have you reading and posting messages in no time. To start the KDE news client, choose Internet, News Client on the main menu, or enter **krn** at a command line.

Configuring the KDE News Client

The first time you start the KDE news client, several small dialog boxes appear to inform you that you haven't configured the program. You can't use a news reader without defining some configuration details. Enter the information requested into the dialog boxes:

- Enter your email address; use the one you want people to use to send you messages—this is your Reply To address. (See Figure 15.11.)

FIGURE 15.11

You must supply initial configuration information the first time you start the KRN news client.

- Enter your full name (this is an important part of newsgroup posting—people like to see more than an email alias).

- Enter your organization's name, if appropriate; otherwise, click OK without entering anything.

- Enter the name of your primary news server (called your NNTP Server in the dialog box). This is the server that the news client accesses to retrieve and post messages. It might be a server on your local network or a server at your ISP's location. Check with your ISP or system administrator.

- Enter the name of your primary SMTP email server. Responses to newsgroup posting can be *public* (back to the newsgroup) or *private* (to another user's email address). The news client uses the news server to process these messages.

After entering this information, the Group List window appears, as shown in Figure 15.12. Because so many newsgroups are available, news clients simplify things by maintaining a list of *subscribed* newsgroups—those from which you want to regularly read messages.

FIGURE 15.12

The Group List window is the starting point from which you select newsgroups to subscribe to.

Reading Newsgroup Messages

Before you can access the server to retrieve a list of groups or messages, you must define the username and password for your account on the news server. To do this, choose Options, NNTP Options (see Figure 15.13).

FIGURE 15.13

The NNTP Options dialog box contains the name of your news server and your account information for that server.

The password that you enter in the NNTP Options dialog box is shown in clear text.

Enter your username and password in the NNTP Options dialog box and select any additional options that you want.

- *Connect on Startup.* Attempt to connect to the NNTP news server defined in the Settings dialog box as soon as the news client program is started.

- *Connect Without Asking.* Attempt to connect to the NNTP news server defined in the Settings dialog box whenever needed without a request to display a confirmation dialog box beforehand. This choice is easier if you have a constant or stable Internet connection.

- *Authenticate.* When connecting to the NNTP server, log in using the username and password in this dialog box.

To start defining your list of subscribed newsgroups, click the red icon on the toolbar or choose File, Connect to Server to connect to the news server that you defined when you starting the news client. Then click the icon to get the active newsgroup list or choose File, Get Active List. This will retrieve the list of available newsgroups from the server.

It might take some time to download a list of all the newsgroups. The news server at my ISP contains 26,000 newsgroups.

After the list of active newsgroups has been downloaded, you can open the All Newsgroups folder, scroll through it, and select a newsgroup that you're interested in by clicking on it.

Choose Newsgroup, Subscribe, to add the selected newsgroup to your Subscribed Newsgroups folder. Repeat this process to add as many newsgroups as you'd like.

With a list of newsgroups in your Subscribed Newsgroups folder, you're ready to read the messages in those groups.

First, you must retrieve the messages by choosing Newsgroup, Subscribed, Get Subjects, or choose Newsgroup, Subscribed, Get Articles. Choosing Get Subjects will take less time, especially for busy newsgroups. But then you must download messages that you want to read individually, which can be tedious. After selecting either option, a list of messages will appear. Click on the subject line of any message to read it.

As you read news messages, you'll probably want to respond to some of them, either privately via email or publicly back to the newsgroup. Before you start posting with wild abandon on a newsgroup that sounds interesting, follow these steps:

- Look for a FAQ posting that answers Frequently Asked Questions related to the topic at hand. (A good place to start looking is at `http://www.faq.org`.)

- Read some rules of Netiquette about how to act online. (For example, avoid flame wars and do not use all capital letters in messages.)

- Read the newsgroup for a few days before posting to determine it's tone, technical level, acceptance of new folks, and so forth.

 You can also initiate a new thread rather than responding to an existing message; choose Newsgroup, Post New Article.

The KDE news client includes many additional options. Some key features are listed here:

- To mark all the messages that you've downloaded as Read so only newly posted messages will appear, choose Newsgroup, Catchup.

- To retrieve the articles for subject lines that you've tagged to be read, choose Newsgroup, Tagged, Get Articles.

- To determine how long old articles should be saved, choose Options, Expire Settings.

15

- To set up how the news client prints messages (when you choose File, Print from the Message List window), choose Options, Print Settings.
- To send messages to the news server that you've written but not yet sent, choose Newsgroup, Post All Queued Articles.

Using a graphical news client is a convenient way to sort through the thousands of messages that accumulate daily in newsgroups. As you work with the KDE news client, you'll discover other useful tools it provides to manage newsgroup that you want to keep track of.

Summary

In this hour, you learned how to use some basic Internet tools that are included with KDE. You learned how to start and configure KMail for reading and sending Internet email messages. As part of that configuration, you learned a little about how email systems function. You also learned how to use the news client to read and post messages to Internet newsgroups. In the next hour, you will learn about the Linux command line and how to use a terminal window in KDE to access the Linux shell.

Questions and Answers

Q When I'm using a news reader, what's the difference between a public and a private reply?

A A public reply is sent back to the same newsgroup as the message you're replying to. A private reply is an email message sent to the personal email address of the person who sent the original message. The windows to create these two types of replies might look similar in many news reader programs. Always check where or to whom a message is being sent before sending it off!

Q I'm looking for certain newsgroups I've heard about; why aren't they listed in the available newsgroups?

A The news server that you're connecting to for downloading messages determines which newsgroups it will carry. The larger the ISP, the more newsgroups they're likely to carry. You can try to find other news servers that will let you connect, but be aware that most news servers are accessible only to their own clients or employees.

Q **I sent some email messages, saving them for later delivery. Why have they bounced back as undeliverable before I've even connected to the Internet?**

A This is a *feature* of the sendmail program, which your Linux system is probably using to process your email. If a message sits for more than five days without being forwarded, sendmail assumes something is wrong and returns it as undeliverable. Try sending the message again but connect to the Internet to upload queued mail messages within a day or two of writing the message.

Exercises

1. Try running the trn text-based news reader. Use the same news server information that you entered to configure the KDE news client. Can you see why graphical news clients are so popular?

2. Review the headers in a few of your email messages by choosing View, All Headers, in the main KMail window. What can you learn from these headers about how email messages are processed? Who or what reads which of these headers? (Think of the sender, the receiver, the mail clients and the mail server/Mail Transfer Agent.)

HOUR 16

Using the Command Line in KDE

In this hour you learn how to use the command-line interface in KDE using the kvt terminal emulator. You'll learn how to open terminal windows, work with multiple terminal windows, and set up configuration options for kvt.

Understanding the Command Line

A command line in Linux is actually a program called the *shell*. This program provides a command-line interface where users enter commands and do a lot of other things.

Each user on a Linux system is assigned a default shell program. The standard shell for Linux is called bash. bash is an acronym for the Bourne Again SHell, a revision of the Bourne shell. Other shells include sh, csh, and tsh.

If you look at the /etc/passwd file, you'll see each user's home directory and shell name. For example, one line might look like this (you might not have permission to view this file on your Linux system):

```
nwells:!!:500:500::/home/nwells:/bin/bash
```

The last item indicates that whenever nwells requests a command-line interface (a shell), program /bin/bash starts.

> If you want to see how powerful the shell really is, enter the command **man bash** to see a 50-page instruction manual on the bash shell.

When you first log in to Linux, you're probably at the Linux console. The console is the Character-mode screen connected to the CPU where Linux is running. Because Linux is a multitasking, networked operating system, however, you can also log in to Linux via a serial connection. This type of connection could be called a terminal connection, because dumb terminals are often used for this purpose.

The result of all this discussion is this: When you want a command-line interface in KDE, you open a terminal emulator window (a fake dumb terminal), which in turn starts the bash shell (or another shell defined for your user account).

The program in KDE that provides a terminal emulator window is called kvt.

> A terminal emulator window displayed on a graphical screen within the X Window System—which KDE uses—is often called an *xterm*. I'll use this term at times during this hour.

Many new users of Linux won't be very comfortable using the command line, but because many tasks in Linux still require that you work from a command line, this hour helps you become familiar with starting and using the kvt program in KDE.

> This hour doesn't teach you much about *what* to enter on a command line, only how to start a command-line window. For details on using bash commands and editing configuration information, refer to a book such as *Sams Teach Yourself UNIX in 24 Hours* or *Sams Teach Yourself Linux in 24 Hours*, both from Sams publishing.

Opening Terminal Emulator Windows

KDE provides several methods of starting a terminal window. The easiest method is to click the Terminal Emulator button on the Panel (see Figure 16.1).

FIGURE 16.1

Terminal Emulator button

16

You can click the Terminal Emulator button repeatedly to open multiple terminal windows.

The same function is also provided on the KDE main menu. Choose Utilities, Terminal to open a terminal window from the main menu.

When you use the Panel button or the Main Menu option, a terminal window appears, as shown in Figure 16.2.

FIGURE 16.2

A terminal window appears when you use the Panel or Main Menu options described.

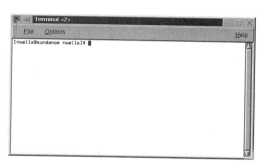

When a new terminal window opens, it is always sized to 80 characters by 24 rows. This is the size of a standard Character-mode display.

You can resize any terminal window using the mouse on the corner of the window (or by using Alt+right-click).

With the terminal window open, you can enter commands to interact with your Linux system.

Starting from Another Terminal Window

You can open a terminal window from within another terminal window that you've already opened. Choose File, New Terminal.

If you prefer, you can also enter this command to open a new terminal:

```
$ kvt &
```

The ampersand (&) following a command runs the command in the background and returns you to the shell prompt so you can continue working in the terminal window.

For variety, you can also start the standard xterm program from any terminal window. Enter this command:

```
$ xterm &
```

The xterm program is provided as part of the X Window System. It uses different colors by default and doesn't include the configuration options available with a kvt terminal window. But if you're used to xterm, you can use it.

 You can copy any text to the KDE Clipboard by highlighting it in a kvt window (click and drag over it). To paste text from the KDE Clipboard into a kvt window, press both mouse buttons at the same time, (or press the middle button of a three-button mouse).

You can have several terminal windows open at the same time. The active terminal window receives keystrokes you type in. Each terminal window executes commands separately from other terminal windows.

If you use the ps command within a terminal window, you'll see two entries for each terminal window that you have open in KDE. One entry (process) is the kvt program, the other is the bash shell that kvt runs to provide a command-line interface.

 You can *freeze* a window so that all keystrokes go to that window, no matter which KDE window is active. The configuration section later in this hour discusses this Secure Keyboard option.

Using the Single-Command Entry

The KDE window manager provides a handy option for starting any program without resorting to the Panel, main menu, or another terminal window.

At any time as you use KDE, you can press Alt+F2 to see a small command window (see Figure 16.3). In this window you can enter a command and KDE will execute it.

To start a terminal window from the pop-up command window, enter **kvt** and press Enter. You can also launch other programs from the pop-up command window. For example, enter **kcalc** to start the KDE calculator.

FIGURE 16.3

KDE provides a pop-up command window that you can use to start a terminal window or any other program.

Don't try to enter anything too complex in the command window. It's intended mainly for quickly launching programs that don't have a Panel button or menu entry.

Using the Character-mode Console

Sometimes, you might want to revert back to the Character-mode Linux console without exiting from KDE; the X Window System provides this feature, which you can use within KDE.

Most Linux systems include six *virtual terminals* that you can access by pressing Alt+F1 (the default login screen), Alt+F2, and so forth to Alt+F6. Each virtual terminal is like a separate dumb terminal attached to your computer.

When you start the X Window System and KDE, one of these terminals is busy running the graphical system. But you can switch back to the other five virtual terminals by pressing Alt+Ctrl+F2, through Alt+Ctrl+F6. When you do this, you'll have to log in again to begin using the command line.

After you've used the Character-mode terminal, you can switch back to the graphical environment of KDE by pressing Alt+F7.

When you switch back to KDE using Alt+F7, any processes you started in the Character-mode terminals continue to execute. If you return to the Character mode (with Alt+Ctrl+F2, for example), your screen will be just as you left it.

Configuring kvt

The bash shell doesn't provide any graphical configuration settings like KDE programs. It only receives input from a command line and processes that input.

The kvt program, however, lets you set up your terminal window in many different ways. The following sections describe those configuration options.

The configuration options of kvt can be accessed from the menu bar (using the Options menu), or by right-clicking anywhere in the terminal window.

> The settings that you choose within a terminal window are specific to that window only. If you save your settings, however, by choosing Options, Save Options, any new terminal windows you start will use the new configuration settings.

Setting Color and Font Options

Users who are accustomed to other Linux or UNIX systems may prefer a different color scheme when working at a command line.

kvt provides five default color settings that you can apply to a terminal window. These include the following:

- Black text on a white background (the default)
- White text on a black background
- Green text on a black background (similar to a dumb terminal—see Figure 16.4)

FIGURE 16.4

The kvt color options let you configure a terminal window to look like a traditional dumb terminal.

- Black text on a light yellow background (similar to the default setting of black on white, but not quite as harsh)
- Linux Console, which provides gray text on a black background

You can choose any of these color settings by selecting Options, Color, and choosing a setting.

If you prefer to set other colors for your text and background, you can also choose Options, Color, Custom Colors, and choose then Foreground Color (to set the text color) or Background color. When you select one of these options, a Select Color dialog box appears where you can choose a color (see Figure 16.5).

FIGURE 16.5

The KDE Select Color dialog box can be used to select custom colors for your terminal window text and background.

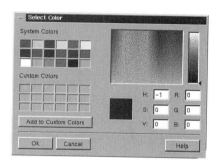

16

The font size and typeface within a terminal window can also be set from the Options menu. The standard size options included on the Font size submenu are Normal, Tiny, Small, Medium, Large, and Huge.

Changing to a smaller size than Normal (Tiny or Small) is helpful if you have a low-resolution screen or have really good eyes and want to fit a lot of information onscreen at once.

Changing to a larger size (Medium, Large, or Huge) is helpful if you have poor eyesight or a very high-resolution screen.

If you want more precise control over the font used to display text in a terminal window, choose Options, Font. This opens a Select Font dialog box (see Figure 16.6) where you can select the typeface, size, style, and character set for the terminal window.

FIGURE 16.6

A Select Font dialog box lets you choose exactly which font to use for a terminal window.

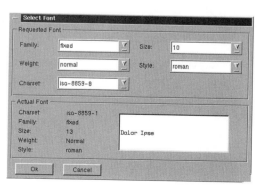

If you choose a proportionally spaced font, much of what you do in a terminal window won't look good because tabs won't be capable of lining up columns of information. When you choose a fixed-width font (such as Fixed, Courier, or Terminal) each character in the font is the same width. For example, the letters *i* and *m* both use the same amount of horizontal space on a line.

Setting Input and Display Options

Several other options are available within a kvt window.

If you choose Options, Hide Menubar, the menu at the top of the terminal window disappears. This gives you more space on your KDE Desktop. You can always right-click in the terminal window to view the Options menu, which includes the option of showing the menu bar again.

The Secure Keyboard option lets you tie all keyboard input to the current terminal window. If you choose Options, Secure keyboard, all keyboard input will be sent to that terminal window. If you click on other KDE windows—even other terminal windows—to make them active, keyboard input still appears in the *secured* terminal window.

 When you choose Secure Keyboard, the background of the terminal window changes to bright red. This can make it hard to read the text in some color configurations.

To end the Secure Keyboard mode, choose Options, Secure Keyboard again.

You can modify the appearance of a terminal window by moving or hiding the scrollbar. Choose Options, Scrollbar to choose Hide, Left, or Right. The default setting shows the scrollbar on the right edge of the Terminal window.

While you can resize any terminal window graphically using the mouse, the terminal window can also be resized to precise settings that match standard Character-mode displays. Each of the size settings refers to the number of characters by the number of rows. The settings on the Options, Size submenu include:

- *80×24*. This is the default setting. You can use this menu item to restore it after resizing using the mouse.

- *80×52*. Provides a standard width display of 80 characters, but with about twice the number of visible lines. This setting is suitable for a 1024×768 resolution screen (using normal font size).

- *96×24.* Similar to the 80×24 size, but shows a few additional characters on each line.

- *96×52.* Similar to the 80×52 settings, but shows a few additional characters on each line.

Finally, the Terminal Options dialog box (see Figure 16.7) lets you set additional configuration options for how the terminal window interacts with your keystrokes. To open this dialog box, choose Options, Terminal.

FIGURE 16.7

The Terminal Options dialog box selects various input options for the terminal window.

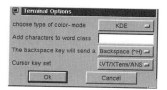

In the Terminal Options dialog box, you can choose the Color mode, the backspace action, and the cursor key set. The cursor key set determines which set of control or escape sequences are used to control the cursor movement in the terminal window.

These options provide flexibility for the many types of computers running KDE and with which a kvt terminal window might need to interact. For most standard Intel-based PCs, however, changing these options will not be necessary.

Summary

In this hour you learned about using a command-line interface within KDE. You also learned about the kvt program, which provides a terminal emulator window running a shell program such as bash. You learned how to start, configure, and copy or paste within a kvt window. You also learned how to access the quick command box by pressing Alt+F2. The next hour describes the core graphical utilities that are included with KDE, such as the KView image viewer and the KPaint drawing tool.

Questions and Answers

Q I've heard about another program, similar to kvt, called konsole. Can I use this instead?

A Sure. The konsole program is similar to kvt. It provides a few options that differ, but it is provided with the standard KDE distribution.

Q How can I mix the KDE Clipboard with the X Window System Clipboard that I'm used to (where selected text is placed)?

A KDE and the kwm window manager actually use a single Clipboard. When you highlight any text, it's placed in the KDE Clipboard. When you click both mouse buttons, the text that you see pasted is coming from the KDE Clipboard as well. If you're using a program that has an Edit menu with Copy or Paste options, these also access the KDE Clipboard. So you could copy highlighted text from a KEdit file using the Edit, Copy menu item, and then paste it into a kvt window by pressing both mouse buttons. You can review the contents and history of the Clipboard by right-clicking the docked Clipboard History icon on the Panel. (Choose Utilities, Cut & Paste History from the main menu if you don't see the Clipboard on the Panel.)

Q You described multiple virtual terminals, accessible from Alt+F1 through Alt+F6. Can I also have multiple graphical environments running?

A Unfortunately, no. The X Window System cannot be running twice on the same system. You can, of course, use remote terminals to have many graphical displays. To have more graphical space on your main system, use the multiple desktops provided by KDE.

Exercise

1. Change the Cursor Key Set field in the Terminal Options dialog box. Can you identify and differences as you work? Try launching a program that creates menus or windows onscreen in Character mode (lisa is a good example if you're using OpenLinux). Can you see a difference now?

PART IV

Using Additional KDE Applications

Hour

17   Using Graphics Utilities in KDE

18   Using KDE Text Utilities

19   Using KDE Business Tools

20   Using KDE for Entertainment

21   Finding and Installing Additional KDE Applications

22   Integrating Non-KDE Applications into KDE

Hour 17

Using Graphics Utilities in KDE

In this hour, you learn how to use the graphics utilities that come with KDE to view and create or edit bitmapped graphics.

Several other graphics utilities for KDE are also mentioned in this hour. Some of these other utilities, however, are not included with a standard KDE distribution. You will need to download and install these utilities if you want to use them. Hour 21, "Finding and Installing Additional KDE Applications," provides some additional direction on doing this.

Using KView to View Graphics Files

An image viewer is a key part of any graphical operating system, especially now that we're all browsing the Web regularly. While a Web browser itself can display some graphic formats (usually gif and jpeg), the KView image viewer that comes with KDE lets you view many additional formats and provides additional features that make it convenient to view and track multiple images.

You can start KView by choosing Graphics, Image Viewer, from the main menu, or by clicking on a graphics file in a kfm window.

In addition, you can start KView from a command line. This is most useful if you want to review a set of graphics files. Use a command such as this one:

```
$ kview /opt/kde/share/wallpapers/*
```

Although kfm can act like a Web browser, when you click on a separate image file, kfm sends the image to KView for display.

The supported graphics formats in KView include the following (additional formats are forthcoming in future releases):

- jpeg
- gif
- xpm
- xbm
- pnm
- bmp
- pcx
- ilbm
- tga
- eps

These formats should fill most of your graphics needs, as they include UNIX resource formats for icons, PC standards, Web standards, and even eps for viewing vector-based drawings saved in many popular design packages.

When KView is first launched, an empty window appears, as shown in Figure 17.1.

If you've launched KView from a command line with multiple image filenames as parameters, only the first image is shown in the window. The next section describes how to use the Image list to view the additional images specified on the command line.

From an open kfm window, you can drag and drop the icon for an image file in the viewing area of the KView window. This image file is then immediately displayed.

FIGURE 17.1

The initial KView window is empty unless KView is started with a graphic filename as a parameter.

Manipulating an Image

KView provides many options to manipulate the image that you're viewing. All these options are accessed via the menu bar. Each menu that you use to manipulate the image is described in this section. As you make changes to an image, remember to choose File, Save if you want to store your changes.

The Edit menu provides the following options:

- *Full screen.* Displays the image in full-screen format. Press Esc to cancel this mode and return to the normal KDE window.

- *Crop.* Click and drag the mouse to outline a region of the image, and then choose this item to crop to the selected rectangle.

- *Reset.* Displays the image as it was when first loaded or at the time it was last saved. Choosing Reset cancels any operations such as Crop, Flip, or Resize.

- *Preferences.* Opens a configuration dialog box. The Preferences dialog box includes two tabs. In the Keys tab you can redefine the accelerator keys used to access KView features. The Options tab (see Figure 17.2) includes settings for whether the image or the viewing window should be resized, and how to run the slide show feature (described in the next section).

FIGURE 17.2

In the KView Preferences dialog box, you can select options such as how long each slide is displayed and how to size and display newly loaded images.

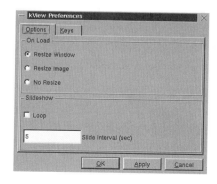

The Zoom menu lets you control the view of the image. Using a Zoom option doesn't change the image itself, only how you are seeing it. Options on the Zoom menu can be used repeatedly to select a certain zoom factor to view an image. Options on the Zoom menu include the following:

- *Zoom.* Opens a dialog box where you can enter a percentage to view the image. For example, entering 200% makes the image twice as large; entering 50% cuts the size of the image in half.
- *Zoom in 10%.* Makes the image 10 percent larger.
- *Zoom out 10%.* Makes the image 10 percent smaller; more of the image is thus visible in the same sized KView window.
- *Double Size.* Makes the image twice as large.

 The pixels of the image are interpolated to increase the image size (KView guesses what a larger image will look like); choosing Double Size repeatedly for a small image will greatly reduce the image quality.

- *Half size.* Makes the image half as large.
- *Max size.* Maximizes the size of the image so that it fills your KDE Desktop. If the ratio of height to width (the *aspect ratio*) for the image doesn't match that of the KDE Desktop (which would have a ratio of 800×600, 1024×768, or something similar), the image will be distorted.
- *Max/Aspect.* Maximizes the size of the image, but keeps it correctly proportioned so that no distortion takes place. This leaves a blank area at the sides or top and bottom to compensate for the difference in aspect ratios.

While the Zoom menu only changes how you are seeing the image in the KView window, the items on the Transform menu change the image. This means that if you use a Transform option and save the image, it will appear with the transformation next time the image is loaded. Options on the Transform menu include the following:

- *Rotate Clockwise.* Rotates the image 90 degrees clockwise.
- *Rotate Anti-clockwise.* Rotates the image 90 degrees counter-clockwise. (Anti-clockwise is British English for counter-clockwise).
- *Flip Horizontal.* Flips the image horizontally, creating a mirror image.
- *Flip Vertical.* Flips the image vertically, making a mirror image top to bottom.

The To Desktop menu is used to make the current image your KDE Desktop wallpaper. This feature only places the image in the current desktop, however, and only until you change to a different desktop. When you switch back, the image will be gone.

The image can be tiled on your desktop (choose Tile), resized to fill the desktop background (choose Max Size), or resized to fill the desktop without changing the aspect ratio (choose Max/Aspect).

Future releases of KView are expected to allow saving images in different formats, printing images, and support for additional image formats. Until that time, you'll need to use another image viewer (such as GIMP or xv) to perform those tasks.

Using the Image List and Slide Show Features

If you load multiple images into KView, either by repeatedly choosing File, Open or by including them on the command line as a parameter when you start KView, you can use the Images menu to work with all those images as a group.

To change to the next or previous image that you have loaded, choose Images, Next or Images, Previous, respectively.

If you want to run a slide show, rotating among all the images that you have loaded, choose Images, Slideshow. The settings in the Edit, Preferences, Options tab dictate how long each image is displayed and whether the slideshow loops continuously.

All the items on the Images menu are also available by right-clicking the image itself.

When working with multiple images, the Image List window provides a convenient reference. Choose Images, List, to open this window, as shown in Figure 17.3.

This list shows you all the filenames that have been loaded into KView. You can use the Prev and Next buttons to switch the viewing window to the previous or next file in the list, respectively.

The Start Slide button starts a slideshow for all the loaded images, just like choosing Images, Slideshow.

If you want to randomly rearrange the images in the list, choose the Shuffle button.

17

FIGURE 17.3

The Image List window shows all the images that you can work with in KView.

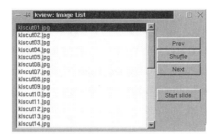

When multiple images are shown in the Image List window or have been loaded using File, Open, KView maintains a list of the image filenames, but only one file is loaded into memory at a time. Including a long list of images does not use all your system resources.

Using KPaint to Create Bitmapped Images

KPaint is a simple bitmap drawing program that you can use to create or edit bitmapped graphics files. Although KPaint doesn't have some of the features of more full-featured programs such as GIMP, KPaint is included with KDE, so it's always easy to access. It also doesn't use the system resources required by a larger, more complex program.

You can start KPaint by choosing Graphics, Paint from the main menu, or by entering **kpaint** on a command line in KDE. The initial KPaint window provides a blank drawing canvas of 300×200 pixels (see Figure 17.4).

FIGURE 17.4

KPaint opens with a blank image canvas of 300×200 pixels.

If you start KPaint from a command line, you can include the name of a graphics file to begin working on. Be certain that you use the full path to the graphic file or KPaint might have trouble loading the file.

Manipulating an Entire Image

To load an image in KPaint, choose File, Open, and then choose a filename from the file-browsing window. The following graphics formats are supported:

- gif
- jpeg
- bmp
- xbm
- xpm
- pnm

When you load an image, the size of the KPaint window doesn't change, so you'll only see a portion of a large graphic. A thumbnail version of the entire image is shown in the box on the right side of the KPaint window (see Figure 17.5).

17

FIGURE 17.5

As you work with any image in KPaint, a thumbnail of the complete image is shown on the right side of the KPaint window.

KPaint provides several tools for manipulating an entire image that are not included with the KView program described previously in this hour. These features are described in this section. The list that follows assumes that you have a graphic image loaded in KPaint. Later in this section you'll learn about creating a new image.

- To change the format of an image, choose File, Image Format, and select a format from the drop-down list (see Figure 17.6). You must still choose File, Save Image, to save the image in the new format.

FIGURE 17.6

The format of an image can be changed in the Image Format dialog box.

- *To change the name of the image, select File, Save Image As.* This dialog box doesn't allow you to change the image format, only to save the image using a different name.

- *To change the magnification of the image, choose Edit, Zoom In or Edit, Zoom Out.* Icons on the toolbar can also be used to zoom in or out. This action doesn't change the size of the KPaint window, so you might need to resize the window after zooming. The status bar displays the current zoom percentage for the image.

- *To view color and size information about the image, choose Image, Information.* A dialog box shows you the color depth, the number of colors used in the image, and the image width and height.

- *To change the image size, choose Image, Resize, and enter a new width and height for the image in pixels.* (See Figure 17.7.)

FIGURE 17.7

You can resize an image by entering new pixel dimensions in the Canvas Size dialog box.

> The Zoom item on the Edit menu changes the view of the image, but not its size. Choose Image, Resize to change the size of the image; it will appear smaller or larger without changing the Zoom setting.

- *To change the color palette used by the image, choose Image, Edit Palette.* A palette appears (see Figure 17.8) showing a square for each color in the image. You can change any color by clicking on its square and selecting a new color from the KDE Select Color dialog box.

FIGURE 17.8

The color palette used by the image is displayed in this dialog box. You can alter any color by clicking on it.

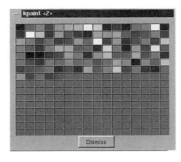

- *To change the color depth of the image (the storage space used for each pixel in the image), choose Image, Change Color Depth.* From the dialog box that appears, you can select 1 bit (black and white), 8 bit (256 colors), or 24 bit (TrueColor).

> After making any changes, be certain to save your image by choosing File, Save Image. Because KPaint doesn't have an Undo feature, small mistakes can waste a lot of editing time.

Drawing a New Image

To create a new image in KPaint, choose File, New Image. In the dialog box that appears, enter the pixel dimensions of the image you want to create.

17

> If you are creating a small image, you might want to use Edit, Zoom In immediately after creating the new image, so you have a better view of what you're drawing.

KPaint includes a simple set of drawing tools. You can select any tool from the Tool menu or click on its icon on the toolbar. The tools—in the order they appear on the toolbar from left to right—are as follows:

- Ellipse
- Circle
- Pen (draws a freehand line)
- Rectangle
- Line (draws a straight line between two points by clicking and dragging)
- Spray can (draws with a diffused set of dots)
- Select area (outlines a rectangular area of the image that you want to work with)
- Round Angle (draws a rectangle with rounded corners)

Some of these tools can be configured by choosing Tool, Tool Properties. In the Tool Properties dialog box that appears (see Figure 17.9) you can set the width and style of the lines used for drawing. The line style you select is applied to all objects that you draw, including circles, ellipses, and rectangles.

FIGURE 17.9

The Line Properties tab lets you define the line used to draw objects in KPaint.

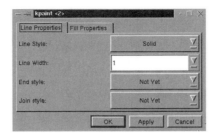

The most useful part of the Tool Properties is the Fill Properties tab (shown in Figure 17.10). From the Fill Pattern drop-down list, you can choose how rectangles, circles, ellipses, and rounded rectangles are filled in.

FIGURE 17.10

The Fill Properties tab lets you define how objects that you draw are filled—using a solid color or a pattern.

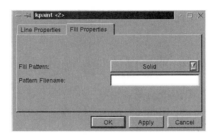

The default fill setting is None. You can select Solid to fill in a solid color matching the object's outline, or you can choose from several patterns included in the list. You can even specify a filename for a pattern that will be applied to the objects you draw.

Choosing Object Colors

KPaint can use two drawing colors. The two colors are shown in small boxes on the right side of the KPaint window. The first color (used by default) is usually red; the second is usually green.

To draw an object, such as a line or circle, click on that tool in the toolbar, and then click and drag in the image canvas. If you click and drag with the right mouse button, the first color (red) is used. If you click and drag with the left mouse button, the second color (green) is used.

You can change either of the two drawing colors by clicking one of the color boxes on the right side of the KPaint window.

Using Cut and Paste

The Area Selection tool lets you define a part of the image canvas by clicking and dragging a rectangle around it.

With an area selected, you can use Edit, Cut or Edit, Copy to place the selected area on the KPaint Clipboard. Then choose Edit, Paste to place the copied portion of the image in another part of your image.

Exploring Other KDE Graphics Utilities

Many graphics utilities are available for Linux and UNIX systems, including the venerable xv and the popular GIMP drawing program. These tools are generally included with any Linux product that you purchase. Hints for integrating these tools into your KDE environment are provided in Hour 22, "Integrating Non-KDE Applications into KDE."

Although the KDE-aware tools described in the first part of this hour are not as powerful as many other Linux graphics tools, many other useful tools are also available for KDE. Some of these tools are described in this section.

Most of the tools described in this section are not included with the default KDE distribution. See Hour 21 for information about using these and other tools.

As with many other KDE applications, as well as free software in general, these graphical applications are in various states of readiness. Some are considered stable and ready to use on KDE 1.1; others are openly labeled *pre-alpha code*.

Of course, it doesn't hurt to spend a few minutes trying a program that sounds interesting or useful, even if you find it isn't far enough along to be of much help to you.

Table 17.1 presents a list of some interesting and useful graphics-related programs available for KDE. These applications can be downloaded via a link on the Applications page of the KDE Web site (www.kde.org).

An application page, which details the function of the program and provides screen shots, is available for many of these utilities. The KDE Web site includes links to these pages.

17

TABLE 17.1 ADDITIONAL GRAPHICS-RELATED APPLICATIONS FOR KDE

Application	Description
kiconedit	An icon editing program used to prepare standard KDE icons (in the default KDE format and size). Included with KDE; choose Graphics, Icon Editor.
ksnapshot	A screen capture utility for use within KDE. Included with KDE; choose Graphics, Snapshot.
kfract	A simple fractal generating program with Mandelbrot and Julia series; provides many configuration options. (This tool is actually included with KDE; choose Graphics, Fractal Generator on the KDE main menu.)
kmandel	A fractal utility.
kray	A simple ray tracing program for KDE.
KDEicons	Additional icons for KDE; provides nice designs for things such as DVD and GIMP.
k3de	A 3D editor for KDE; actually a programming widget that generates source for POV ray tracing.
kshow	Another image viewer; provides a directory-structure view of multiple images.
ksciplot	A function plotting tool.
KPlot	Another function plotting tool.
kfourier	An image processing utility.
KuickShow	An image browsing utility.
killustrator	Intended as a *clone* of Adobe Illustrator; part of the KOffice suite, which is soon to be released for KDE.

Summary

This hour describes how to use the graphical utilities that come with KDE. You learned about how to view and manipulate multiple images in KView. You also learned the basics of creating new bitmapped images using KPaint. Several additional KDE graphical utilities are also mentioned for reference. In the next hour you learn about the text utilities that are included with KDE, such as the text editor KEdit and text viewers for PostScript, DVI, and RDF files.

Questions and Answers

Q **I need to view or edit a graphic file in a format that isn't supported by KView or KPaint. How can I do it?**

A You'll need to convert the format of the image. This can be done using a variety of other graphics programs or utilities. Depending on the format that your file is in, you can try GIMP (enter `gimp`), Ghostscript (enter `gs` to start it, but see the man page for details), the Image Magik package, or the netpbm package (both available from popular Linux archive FTP sites such as `ftp.caldera.com`).

Q **What is a color palette?**

A A *palette* is a set of colors. Each image file will have a palette; the more colors in the image, the larger the palette. The maximum size of an image's palette is defined by the number of bits used to store each picture element (*pixel*) of the image. More bits means more colors are possible. Similarly, reducing the color palette of an image can reduce the amount of space needed to store it (this is a common operation for images destined for the Web). In drawing programs, one or more default palettes are provided so you can choose which colors to include in your image. In most KDE programs you can use the Select Color dialog box to select from or add to the palette of available colors.

Q **I see some graphics formats that I've never heard of, such as xpm and ppm. What are they?**

A Because UNIX and Linux systems might be used for a variety of graphics and image processing tasks, you'll find that Linux graphics programs often include support for a diverse set of formats, such as Macintosh, Windows, SGI, Sun, and professional printing or design (CAD) formats. Several additional formats (such as xpm) are used by the X Window System for icons or internal storage of images.

Exercises

1. Try the Icon Editor program (on the Graphics menu). Make a copy of a few icons from the `/opt/kde/share/icons` directory and edit them using the Icon editor. How could you use this utility to help create a new KDE theme? Why would you use the Icon editor instead of KPaint to create icons?

2. Try the screen-capture utility, Ksnapshot (also on the Graphics menu). How does it compare to xv, GIMP, the xwd utility, or other screen-capture utilities that you have used?

Hour **18**

Using KDE Text Utilities

In this hour you learn how to use the text utilities that come with KDE. You'll learn about the KDE text editor as well as utilities for viewing and processing some common document types that you can create on Linux or other types of computer systems.

The information in Hour 14, "Managing Printing in KDE," relates to several of the topics in this hour, such as viewing text files and PostScript files.

Using the KDE Text Editor

Text files are basic to any UNIX or Linux operating system. Many configuration files, option files, and scripts are nothing but plain text files. Although KDE provides a graphical interface to review and edit many configuration details on your Linux system, learning how to use a text editor for creating scripts and updating configuration files can be very helpful.

Experienced Linux users often rely on standard UNIX tools such as the vi editor and the emacs editor. While these are powerful tools, they aren't easy to learn.

KDE includes an integrated graphical text editor named KEdit. The sections that follow describe how to launch and use KEdit within KDE.

 When I say a *graphical* text editor, I'm referring to an editor that runs in the X Window System and includes menus and dialog boxes for editing and con-figuration options. The text files that you create in a text editor such as KEdit can't include graphics, different fonts, or even bold and italic text.

Starting the Text Editor

The default installation of KDE includes a button on the Panel to start the KEdit. Each time you click on this button, a copy of KEdit is started.

 Caldera OpenLinux also includes another text editor called CRiSP. To use KEdit in OpenLinux, you might have to use the Applications menu instead of the Panel.

Choosing Applications, Editor on the main menu is also an easy way to start KEdit, especially when you have the Panel hidden. Figure 18.1 shows the KEdit window as it appears when you first launch it.

FIGURE 18.1

The KEdit text editor appears with a blank screen, ready to enter text.

If you're working from a command line (a terminal window, as described in Hour 16, "Using the Command Line in KDE," you can enter this command to start the editor:

```
$ kedit &
```

FIGURE 18.2

From a kfm window you can start an editor by clicking on any text file.

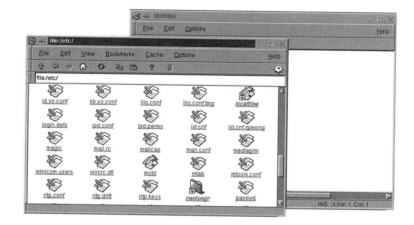

The ampersand runs the command in the background and returns you to the command-line prompt so you can enter other commands.

You can also start the editor from a kfm window. If you are viewing the contents of a directory (as shown in Figure 18.2), click on an icon representing a text file to open that file in a copy of KEdit.

If you click on an icon in a kfm window that doesn't have a file type associated with it, you see a message asking what program you want to use to open this file. If you enter **kedit**, the file is opened in an editor window.

If you click on a binary or other non-text file and try to use KEdit to view it, you could damage the file if you save any changes to it. To review the contents of a binary file, use the Hex editor program (choose Utilities, Hex Editor).

18

Finally, if you have a kfm window open and a copy of the editor, you can drag the icon for a text file from the kfm window and drop it on the editor window.

- *If the KEdit window is empty*: the file you dropped appears in that window.
- *If the KEdit window already contains a file*: KEdit clones itself and the file you dropped appears in a new KEdit window; the file in the original window is unchanged.

Each copy of KEdit works on only one file at a time. Starting several copies of KEdit is a great way to compare files or copy and paste between them. Of course, each copy of KEdit also uses more of your system memory.

Using Basic KEdit Features

With a text file open in KEdit, you can use the Backspace, Delete, arrow keys to move around in the file and change the text. Several additional keys are useful in moving around larger text files:

- *Page Up.* Moves toward the beginning of the file by one screen of text.
- *Page Down.* Moves toward the end of the file by one screen of text.
- *Shift+arrow keys or Shift+Page Up or Page Down.* Selects the next character, line, or screen of text.
- *Home.* Moves to the beginning of the current line.
- *End.* Moves to the end of the current line.

The KEdit File menu includes standard items such as New, Open, and Print. The Open Recent item contains a submenu listing files that have recently been opened in KEdit (see Figure 18.3). When you select an item from the Open Recent submenu, that file is opened in the current KEdit window.

The File, Open URL option lets you enter a URL for a `file:/`, `ftp://`, or `http://` location and directly open that text file. If you have permission, you can even save the updated version of the file to the same network URL.

Saving or uploading to a Web site can become complicated, especially if you have a firewall. Ask your system administrator for assistance if you think you have permission to upload files but the operation is failing.

FIGURE 18.3

The Open Recent sub-menu contains a list of files that have recently been edited. Choose any one to open it.

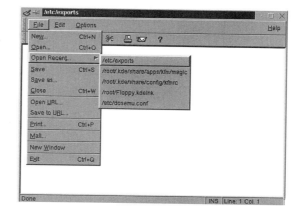

 Local URLs can use the full path to the file without the `file:/` designator. Of course, using File, Open with the file-browsing window might be easier.

Anytime you use File, Open, File, New, File, Open Recent or File, Open URL, KEdit warns you if you have made changes to the current file before discarding it and loading the new file that you've requested.

Choosing File, Print opens a Print dialog box (see Figure 18.4) where you can select how to print the file and which part of the document to print. Hour 14 provides additional information about how you might use the Print Using Command field in this dialog box.

FIGURE 18.4

The Print dialog box lets you choose how to print the text file and which part of it to print.

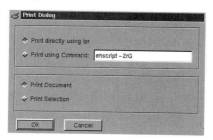

Because KEdit is integrated with other parts of KDE (as shown by the Drag-and-Drop feature from a kfm window), you can directly email a text file from within the KEdit

18

window. When you choose File, Mail, a Mailing dialog box appears (see Figure 18.5) where you can enter the full email address of the person to receive the text file and the subject line of the message.

FIGURE 18.5

You can email a text file within KEdit. The recipient's email address and a subject line can be entered in the Mailing dialog box.

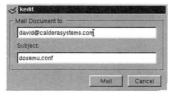

The recipient's email address should be a complete address, such as `nwells@xmission.com`, unless the recipient is on your local network, in which case you might be able to use an abbreviated form. The subject of the message is the name if the text file when you open the Mailing dialog box. You can enter additional information in the field, which is generally a good idea.

Text files that you email are sent as the body of the email message, not as an attachment. You can't enter any explanation at the beginning of the message (although you can include something as part of the text file in the KEdit window).

The Emailing feature uses a standard Linux `mail` command to send your message. This command can be configured as described in the next section by choosing Options, KEdit Options, but in order for the command to work, you must have an email server and a network/Internet connection for your Linux system.

> The sendmail or qmail mail agent is generally started as part of your Linux installation and configuration. You might need to review your Linux configuration if your mail messages seem to be going into a black hole. This command will tell you if sendmail is running on your system:
>
> `$ ps aux ¦ grep sendmail`

KEdit includes search-and-replace features. Choose Edit, Find to enter a search string and locate a string; choose Edit, Replace to enter both a search and a replace string (see Figure 18.6). For repeated use of the search or search and replace functions, use the accelerator keys shown in the Edit menu.

FIGURE 18.6

KEdit includes search-and-replace features. Only simple text string searches are possible— no pattern matching is provided.

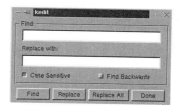

If you're working with a large text file, the Edit, Goto Line feature can help you jump to a specific line number. The right side of the status line below the text file shows you the current line number and column of the cursor.

You can insert another file into the file you're working on by choosing Edit, Insert File, and selecting a filename from the file-browsing window that appears. The Edit, Insert Date function inserts the complete time and date into your text file. This feature is useful when you update configuration files and want to time-stamp the update.

The Cut, Copy, and Paste features in KEdit work as they do in most word processors and editors. You can select a block of text using Shift+arrow keys, or click and drag using the mouse. The selected text appears in reverse (white text on a black background).

- To remove the text from the file, choose Edit, Cut, or press Ctrl+X. The text disappears and is stored in KDE's internal Clipboard buffer.

- If you prefer to copy the selected text, choose Edit, Copy, or press Ctrl+C. The text is copied into the Clipboard but remains in your file.

- To paste a copy of the Clipboard contents at the current cursor position, choose Edit, Paste, or press Ctrl+V.

Using Copy and Paste is the easiest way to copy text from one KEdit window to another KEdit window or to other open KDE applications. Because all KDE applications have access to the Clipboard, you can use the Edit, Paste command on any KDE application that supports its use.

The KDE window manager also supports the X Window System standard for Copy and Paste. You can drag to select any text on the screen; the text is placed in the KDE Clipboard. When you press both mouse buttons at the same time (or press the middle button of a three-button mouse), the text from the KDE Clipboard is pasted at the current cursor location.

18

Most of the basic features of KEdit described so far can be accessed from the toolbar. These include New, Open, Save, Cut, Copy, Paste, Print, and Mail. The Online help for KEdit is also available from the toolbar question mark icon, or by choosing Help, Contents, or by pressing F1.

In addition to the standard menus, you can right-click on the main text window at any time to see a list of basic options taken from the menu bar. This right-click menu is shown in Figure 18.7.

FIGURE 18.7

When you right-click on the KEdit text window, a pop-up menu of basic options appears.

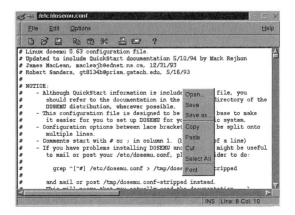

Setting Up KEdit Options

KEdit provides several configuration options. All are available on the Options menu. The options that you select in the Options menu apply only to the current KEdit window. If you want the options you select to apply to all KEdit windows, choose Options, Save Options. All KEdit windows opened *after* you save the options will use those options. (KEdit windows that are currently open are not affected.)

The font used to display text, and the color of the text and background, can be selected by choosing Options, Font; Options, Colors, Foreground Color; or Options, Colors, Background Color, respectively. These selections open the standard KDE Select Font dialog box or Select Color dialog box, where you can define the font and color that you prefer.

If you want to reduce the amount of space used by each KEdit window, you can hide the toolbar and status bar by choosing Options, Hide Tool Bar or Options, Hide Status Bar.

The font and colors that you select have no affect on the contents of the text files that you edit. A plain text file cannot include font information or color information. The font and color settings are only to make the display of the text files fit your preferences. For example, if you prefer to work with green text on a black background or use a larger or smaller font, you can choose these settings.

The AutoIndent option, which can be toggled on or off by selecting Options, AutoIndent, automatically indents lines each time you press Enter on a blank line. This is useful if you are using KEdit to enter something such as a script, which is much easier to read when sections of the script (such as loops) are indented.

Additional KEdit options can be configured by choosing Options, KEdit Options; this opens a dialog box where you can set up several configuration options (see Figure 18.8).

FIGURE 18.8

The KEdit Options dialog box includes several configuration settings.

You can set the following options in the KEdit Options dialog box:

- *Fill-Column.* This field determines how many characters are allowed on one line. If you set this to a larger number (79 is the default), KEdit will allow longer lines of text, scrolling to the right as you type, before moving you to the next line.

- *Word Wrap.* This check box determines whether KEdit moves an entire word to the next line when you reach the end of a line (as determined by the Fill-Column number). If Word Wrap is not checked, the text that you are typing breaks at exactly the 79th character and begins on a new line. If you're in the middle of typing a word, the word is split into two parts.

- *Mail Command.* This field shows the Linux command line used to send a text file as a mail message when you choose File, Mail, and enter a recipient email address and subject. The default setting uses the `mail` command, with the first parameter (`%s`) being the Subject field from the Mailing dialog box and the second parameter being the recipient's email address.

You can modify the Mail Command field to include other options in the `mail` command, such as always adding a CC to your own mailing address. Or you can use a different command, such as `elm`, if you prefer.

> Don't modify the Mail Command field unless you are familiar with the Linux `mail` command. Otherwise the Mailing feature might not work. To learn about the `mail` command, enter this command in a terminal window.
>
> `$ man mail`

Viewing Text Documents

If you need to view a text document without editing it, Linux provides several handy commands to do so. If you already have a KEdit text editor window open, it might be easier to open a file in KEdit.

If you don't have KEdit open but do have a terminal window open, it's easier to use a simple Linux command. My favorite is the `less` command; use this command with the name of the text file you want to view. For example

`$ less /etc/services`

This command displays the file in the terminal window, one screenful of data at a time. The `less` command supports many keystrokes to move up or down in the file:

- Press the Spacebar to scroll down to the next screenful of data.
- Press Enter to scroll down one line.
- Press the up or down arrow keys to move up or down one line.
- Press the Page Up or Page Down keys to move up or down by one screen.
- Press j or k to move up or down by one line (these are keys used in some other UNIX programs).
- To stop viewing the file, press q to Quit.

If you don't have `less` installed on your Linux system, the `more` command is also useful, although it doesn't give you as much flexibility. This is an example of the `more` command:

`$ more /etc/services`

If you're familiar with DOS commands, using the more command is like using this command in DOS:

```
$ type filename ¦ more
```

After you execute this command, you can use these keys to view the text file:

- Press Enter to scroll down one line.
- Press the Spacebar to scroll down to the next screenful of data.
- Press b to back up by one screenful of data.
- Press q to exit the more command.

Both less and more support many other keystrokes, which you can review by reading the man page for either command.

Linux products often include many other text editors besides the KEdit application described here. For example vi, emacs, pico, and joe are all popular text editors included with some Linux systems.

If you're accustomed to using one of these other text editors, you can easily continue to use it in KDE by adding an icon to the Panel that launches your preferred editor, adding an icon to the desktop, or just starting it from a command line. Hour 22, "Integrating Non-KDE Applications into KDE," provides some direction for making your preferred editor a part of your KDE environment.

18

Viewing Other Document Types

Text files aren't the only type of document you'll want to view on your Linux system. This section describes KDE tools to help you view two common document types: PostScript and DVI files.

Using the PostScript Viewer

PostScript is a standard page description language produced by Adobe. PostScript is used to control printers by defining the way a file appears on the printed page.

Most UNIX and Linux systems use PostScript as the default printing system (see Hour 14). Instead of printing to a PostScript printer, however, you can send the same information to a file. The PostScript file can then be sent to a printer at a later time; or you can send the PostScript file to another person to print on their printer. PostScript files use the file extension .ps.

The file extension .eps indicates an encapsulated PostScript file. These files include additional reference information beyond a simple PostScript file to allow them to be inserted into another image (such as an Adobe Illustrator drawing), but they can also be viewed using the KDE PS Viewer.

PostScript files are the method used to distribute a lot of documentation for UNIX and Linux systems. PostScript files can create attractive pages, they don't cost as much as paper manuals to produce (because the PostScript file can be added to the CD-ROM containing a product), and they can't be easily edited.

The following listing shows you what the beginning of a PostScript file looks like:

```
%!PS-Adobe-2.0
%%Creator: dvipsk 5.58f Copyright 1986, 1994 Radical Eye Software
%%Title: tech.dvi
%%Pages: 8
%%PageOrder: Ascend
%%BoundingBox: 0 0 612 792
%%DocumentPaperSizes: Letter
%%EndComments
%DVIPSCommandLine: dvips tech.dvi -o Technical_Guide.ps
%DVIPSParameters: dpi=600, comments removed
%DVIPSSource:  TeX output 1998.05.07:1505
%%BeginProcSet: tex.pro
/TeXDict 250 dict def TeXDict begin /N{def}def /B{bind def}N /S{exch}N
/X{S N}B /TR{translate}N /isls false N /vsize 11 72 mul N /hsize 8.5 72
mul N /landplus90{false}def /@rigin{isls{[0 landplus90{1 -1}{-1 1}
ifelse 0 0 0]concat}if 72 Resolution div 72 VResolution div neg scale
isls{landplus90{VResolution 72 div vsize mul 0 exch}{Resolution -72 div
hsize mul 0}ifelse TR}if Resolution VResolution vsize -72 div 1 add mul
TR[matrix currentmatrix{dup dup round sub abs 0.00001 lt{round}if}
forall round exch round exch]setmatrix}N /@landscape{/isls true N}B
/@manualfeed{statusdict /manualfeed true put}B /@copies{/#copies X}B
/FMat[1 0 0 -1 0 0]N /FBB[0 0 0 0]N /nn 0 N /IE 0 N /ctr 0 N /df-tail{
/nn 8 dict N nn begin /FontType 3 N /FontMatrix fntrx N /FontBBox FBB N
```

If you have a PostScript file for a user manual or other document, KDE provides a program that lets you view the document onscreen, a page at a time, or without printing the entire file on paper. You can then choose which pages to print, if any.

To open this program, choose Graphics, PS Viewer from the KDE main menu. The initial window of this application is shown in Figure 18.9. You can also start the PS Viewer by entering **kghostview** in a terminal window.

FIGURE **18.9**

From the initial window of the PS Viewer you can open and view a PostScript file.

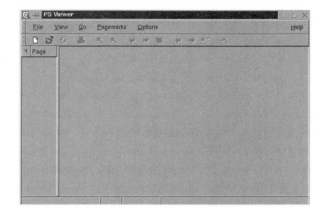

The KDE PS Viewer is based on the popular GhostView program, which is also probably included with your Linux system.

18

Documents can be loaded into the PS Viewer by choosing File, Open, File, Open Recent, or by using the Folder icon on the toolbar.

If you click on a PostScript file in a kfm window, the file is opened in the PS Viewer. You can also drag the icon for a PostScript file from a kfm window and drop it on an open PS Viewer window.

When you load a PostScript file into the PS Viewer, the first page appears, with the page numbers of the document shown in a list along the left side of the screen (see Figure 18.10). The toolbar becomes active with many icons that make the PS Viewer a convenient way to browse through even large documents.

FIGURE 18.10

After a document is loaded into the PS Viewer, most of the toolbar icons become active and the pages in the document are listed along the left side of the screen.

The PS Viewer is a complete online viewing tool. The following list describes some basic operations that you can use to view a document.

- Click the Paging icon in the middle of the toolbar (the little book with the waving pages) to scroll down to the next screen of the document. If you're at the top of a page, you move down the page; if you're at the bottom of a page, you move up to the next page. Clicking this button repeatedly is a good way to read and scroll through an entire document.

- Click on a page number in the list on the left side of the window to jump to that page.

- Click on the Magnifying Glass icons to increase or decrease the size of the page you're viewing (or choose the Zoom options on the View menu).

- Use the Page Up and Page Down keys to move to the previous or next page of the document.

The PS Viewer also allows you to mark pages in a document for printing. You can mark the page you're viewing by clicking the Pagemark icon in the toolbar (a red flag) or by choosing Pagemarks, Mark Current Page. A red flag then appears next to the current page in the page list on the left of the window.

The Pagemarks menu—or right-clicking in the page list—gives you other options for marking a set of pages.

If you prefer not to view the list of pages, choose Options, Show Page List.

PostScript documents can include color. If you want to configure whether the document you're viewing is shown in color, grayscale, or black and white, you can review PostScript options by choosing Options, Configure Interpreter (see Figure 18.11).

FIGURE 18.11

The Configure Interpreter dialog box lets you set up a few PostScript options, including the use of color.

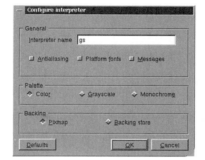

One of the principle uses of the PS Viewer is to print on paper the pages that you need from a long document. After you have used the Pagemarks to define the pages you need to print (if not all the pages are needed), choose File, Print. The Print dialog box includes options to print all the pages in the document, the current page, a range of pages, or only those pages that you have marked (see Figure 18.12).

FIGURE 18.12

The Print dialog box lets you print all pages in the document or only a selection of the pages.

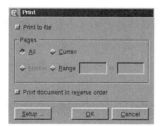

The File, Page Setup option lets you define the paper size and page orientation before printing.

18

Check boxes in the Print dialog box let you print the pages out in reverse order (this is useful for some printers), or print to another PostScript file. Printing to another PostScript file only makes sense if you aren't printing all the pages of the current PostScript file.

> Future releases of the PS Viewer are expected to support Adobe PDF files. PDF is another popular document format for distributing manuals, brochures, and so forth on the Web or to others. Until that time, you can find a PDF Viewer for Linux (AcroRead) on the Adobe Web site at
> `http://www.adobe.com/prodindex/acrobat/readstep.html`.

Using the DVI Viewer

For years, one of the most popular document formats on UNIX and Linux systems has been TeX. TeX is a page description system like PostScript, but it is used to write documents from scratch, like a word processor, while inserting explicit formatting commands in a text editor.

> Preparing a document in TeX is sort of like writing a paper in WordPerfect using the Reveal Codes option.

After you create a TeX file, you can generate a DVI file that shows the output of the TeX commands that you entered. Because TeX is a popular UNIX tool, DVI files are sometimes used to distribute documentation for things such as UNIX utilities as well as some professional documents.

KDE includes a DVI Viewer to show you these files onscreen, much as the PS Viewer displays PostScript files.

You can use the same methods to start the DVI Viewer as you did the PS Viewer:

- Choose Graphics, DVI Viewer from the main menu.
- Click on a `dvi` file in a kfm window.
- Drag and drop a DVI icon from a kfm window to an open DVI window.
- Enter **kdvi** in a terminal window.

The initial DVI Viewer window is shown in Figure 18.13.

FIGURE 18.13

The DVI Viewer lets you preview DVI files onscreen.

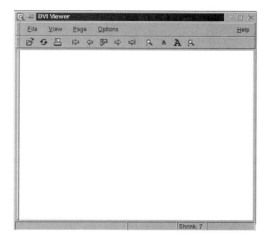

The DVI Viewer provides many of the same features as the PS Viewer, including zooming, jumping between pages, and configuring which pages to print to paper.

Configuration options for the DVI Viewer can be set up by selecting Options, Preferences. Choosing File, Print opens the Print dialog box where you can select which pages to print and where to print them. (A Print to File option is not provided—it doesn't make much sense for a DVI file—but you can choose to print two or four pages of the file on each sheet of paper.) The DVI Viewer Print dialog box is shown in Figure 18.14.

18

FIGURE 18.14

In the Print dialog box for the DVI Viewer, you can select which pages to print to paper and how to print them.

Summary

In this hour you learned how to use the basic text utilities included with KDE. You learned about using and configuring the KEdit text editor and the document viewing tools for PostScript and DVI files. You learned how to create and edit text files in KEdit, and how to print paper copies of files that you view in the PostScript or DVI Viewers. The next hour is devoted to business utilities that are part of KDE. You will learn about time tracking and schedule organizer utilities, as well as information about other business tools such as fax utilities.

Questions and Answers

Q I try to email documents in KEdit, but it doesn't work. Why not?

A KEdit relies on the email infrastructure of Linux. Ensure that your email is working by using other programs to read email (such as KMail) or send email (mail, elm, and pine are all standard Linux mail programs). If you can use email within other Linux programs, KEdit should be capable of mailing documents. If not, check the configuration options to be certain that you're using a valid command to send the email messages.

Q I've been playing with the configuration options for KEdit and I've made a mess. How can I restore the options to what they were originally?

A The simplest method is to delete the configuration file for KEdit, located in ~/.kde/share/config. Of course, this will remove *all* the configuration information, so you'll really be starting from scratch. KEdit will use its internal defaults the next time you start it.

Q Can I change the way keys are used to move around and edit text within KEdit?

A You might be able to depending on what you want to do. The action associated with standard keys such as Page Up or the arrows can't be changed within KEdit, but you might be able to make the changes in the Key Binding section of the KDE Control Center.

Q I've seen others use the cat command to view files. Why haven't you mentioned this command?

A The cat command doesn't provide interactive options to page or search in a file as you view it. The cat command *dumps* the file to the screen, without pausing.

Exercises

1. Open two KEdit windows. Copy and paste some text between the two windows. Try this using both the standard Copy and Paste commands on the Edit menu, and the X Window System method, selecting text and then pressing both mouse buttons to paste that text. Which method do you prefer? Why would you need to use one method over another in some circumstances?

2. Locate a PostScript file (extension .ps) in the /usr/doc directory of your Linux system or on the Web. Open it using the PS Viewer program. The text describes why a company might prefer to send out a PostScript file instead of a printed manual. As a user, why might you also prefer a PostScript Viewer instead of a printed manual? When would you want the paper manual?

18

Hour **19**

Using KDE Business Tools

In this hour you learn how to use some key business tools (or *applets*) that accompany KDE. While anyone might find these tools useful, they relate primarily to things such as faxing documents, managing your daily schedule, and so forth.

KDE includes several convenient tools for users who work in an office. This hour describes how to use those tools, as well as lists some additional business-related applications that are not included with the base KDE distribution but are available for download.

Using the Address Book

KDE provides a simple address book program that you can use like a card file to store names and contact information. The KDE address book program, called kab, isn't sophisticated, but it is easy to use and doesn't use a lot of disk space or system resources.

To launch the Address Book application, choose Utilities, Address Book from the main menu, or enter the command **kab** in a terminal window. The initial address book window appears, as shown in Figure 19.1.

FIGURE 19.1

When the Address Book is first launched, you see the window where information will be displayed.

Each time you start the address book, all your entries are displayed in the main window. Entries that you add or change can be saved to disk, so that the next time you start the address book, all the information is available.

Adding and Managing Entries

To add a new entry to the address book, choose Edit, Add Entry, press Ctrl+N (with the Address Book window active), or click on the Add Entry icon on the toolbar (third from the right). A new entry window appears, as shown in Figure 19.2.

FIGURE 19.2

In the address book you enter information about a person by filling in the fields on each tab of the Edit the Current Entry dialog box.

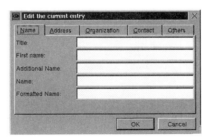

Enter information in each of the fields according to what you know or want to record about the person referred to in the address book entry. None of the fields are required, but you should have at least one of the Name fields filled in (any one will do) to provide a way to recognize this entry in the future.

The Name field is intended for the person's last name. The Additional Name field is for a middle or second name.

Switch to the Address tab and enter any postal address information you have for this person. Then enter information in the Organization tab as appropriate.

The Contact tab contains fields to enter phone and Internet contact information, including numbers for fax, modem, and voice lines, as well as Web, email, and talk addresses.

> The talk protocol is similar to a person-to-person irc Internet Chat, where you can exchange messages in realtime with other users (mostly on UNIX or Linux system) who are logged in and working at a command prompt. The talk protocol is rarely used these days.

You must click on either the Edit Email Addresses or Edit Talk Addresses button before you can enter any email or talk address information. If you click on the Edit Email Addresses button, a small dialog box appears where you can enter one or more email addresses for this person (see Figure 19.3). Click on the X icon to enable a text entry box for each email address that you want to add.

FIGURE 19.3

Email addresses are added one at a time by choosing the X icon.

After you have entered all the email addresses, choose OK to close this dialog box. Unfortunately, you must re-open this dialog box to review the email addresses that you entered. A future release might have the email addresses accessible in a drop-down list for quicker access.

The final information tab for an address book entry is the Others tab. In this tab you can enter any additional information that you want to record about this person, such as notes on a recent phone call, a list of projects this person is working on, or where they like to eat out.

A nice feature of this tab is the Birthday field. Double-click on the blank Birthday field to pop up a calendar where you can select the day (and year, if you like) of this person's birthday. No alarm features are provided here, however. You'll need to use the KOrganizer for that.

19

After you have entered all the information applicable to this person, choose OK to close the dialog box. Because this is the only address in the address book, it is selected in the drop-down list, and much of the information that you entered is displayed in the viewing window (see Figure 19.4).

FIGURE 19.4

Information about the selected contact is displayed in the viewing area of the address book.

Once you have entered information for a person, you can edit or add to that information any time by choosing Edit, Edit Entry or pressing the Edit button on the toolbar (second from the right).

After you have added multiple names to your address book, choose the card that you want to view in the main window of the address book by selecting a name from the drop-down list below the menu bar.

> You can also use the arrow keys on the toolbar to scroll through names, viewing the complete information for each person in the Viewing area.

Any entry can be deleted by choosing Edit, Remove Entry or pressing the Trash bin icon on the toolbar.

After you have added or changed the information in your address book, choose File, Save to update the information on your hard disk. The information that you enter is stored in a text file named `addressbook.database`, located at `~/.kde/share/apps/kab`.

Using Address Book Entries

After you have a collection of information about people stored in your address book, how can you use that information beyond simply opening the address book and reviewing the information onscreen?

The address book program provides a number of features to integrate the information in the address book with other work that you might be doing in KDE. The following list shows the key features available:

- Print one, many, or all the cards in the address book by choosing File, Print and selecting options from the address book Print dialog box (see Figure 19.5).

FIGURE 19.5

Many printing options are available to output the fields contained in address book entries.

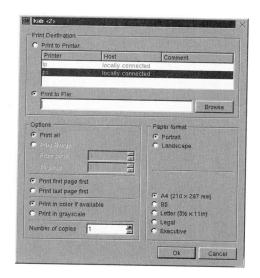

- Export the contents of the address book to an HTML table by choosing File, Export, HTML Table. A dialog box appears where you can select which fields from the address book cards to include in the HTML table.
- Jump to the URL associated with a person (as stored on the Contact tab) by choosing Edit, Browse. This opens a kfm window and loads the home page indicated in the currently viewed card.
- Send an email to this person by choosing Edit, Mail. This opens a KMail window where you can compose a message and send it to the person.
- Search among all the entries in the address book for matching information. Choose File, Search Entries or choose the Binoculars icon on the toolbar. A Search Entries dialog box appears where you can select a field to search and enter a pattern to match (see Figure 19.6).

FIGURE 19.6

You can search for a pattern in any of the address book fields.

19

Using the KOrganizer

If you've used a program such as Microsoft Outlook on Windows or StarSchedule for Linux, you know how useful a complete calendar and organizer program can be. KDE 1.1 includes a program similar to Outlook called KOrganizer. KOrganizer includes task lists and event calendars with many options to set up and manage your day.

To start the Organizer, choose Applications, Organizer on the main menu, or enter the command **korganizer** in a terminal window. The initial KOrganizer window is shown in Figure 19.7.

FIGURE 19.7

The initial KOrganizer window uses the Day view to show a reference calendar, To-do list, and daily event calendar.

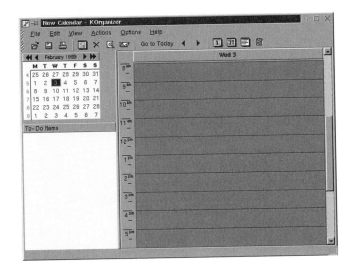

The KOrganizer can also be used on the 3Com PalmPilot. The online help provides additional information. You'll need to use the KPilot tools to get KDE ready for use with your PalmPilot. Visit the KDE Web site for information.

Exploring the KOrganizer

The default KOrganizer screen is divided into three sections:

- Reference calendar
- List of tasks (a To-do list)
- Daily calendar of appointments and events

KOrganizer keeps lists of tasks in the To-do list. This list is not associated with any particular day. The next section, "Creating a To-do Task List," shows how to enter items into the To-do list. KOrganizer also keeps track of appointments or events that you schedule for a day and time.

You can change the view of the main KOrganizer window using the View menu or the icons on the toolbar. The view options include:

- *List view.* Displays all the appointments for one day in a compact list, with times, alarms, and recurring events noted by columns in the list. This view is helpful if your appointments are spread throughout the day and you want to see them all listed together.

- *Day view.* Shows the event calendar for one day, with times and events noted. This is the default view when you start KOrganizer.

- *Week and Work Week views.* Formatted as the Day view, but with either seven or five days shown across the window, with times and events noted for each day. This view is useful to see an overview of how busy your week is, although it might not provide enough screen space to see the full description of your appointments.

- *Month view.* Shows a full month calendar, with appointments noted (very briefly) on each day. Unlike the Day, Week, and Work Week views, the Month view doesn't display the To-do list.

- *To-do list view.* Displays the To-do list in the full window, without any daily calendar or reference calendar shown.

The icons to change to any of these views are located on the toolbar (see Figure 19.8).

19

FIGURE 19.8

Several different views of KOrganizer can be selected from the toolbar.

To-do List view
List view
Month view
Schedule view

The icon labeled Schedule View switches between the Day, Week, and Work Week views when you press it repeatedly.

Creating a To-do Task List

To add items to the To-do list, follow these steps:

1. Right-click your mouse in the To-do list area of the KOrganizer window.
2. From the pop-up menu that appears, choose New To-do.

   An item is added to the To-do list. The new item is selected (highlighted).
3. Double-click on the new item in the To-do list. A cursor appears.
4. Enter a description of the to-do item.

> The description that you enter can extend beyond the right edge of the to-do area. If you need to see a larger size list of to-do items, choose the To-do List view as described previously in this hour.

5. Press Enter to complete entry of the To-do list item.
6. Repeat as often as needed to add items to the list.

After you have items added to the To-do list, you can edit the properties of any item in the list. All items are marked as high priority and uncompleted when you create them. To update information about an item in the To-do list, right-click on that item and choose Edit To Do. The Edit Todo dialog box appears, as shown in Figure 19.9.

FIGURE 19.9

Information about each To-do list task can be edited in the Edit To-do dialog box.

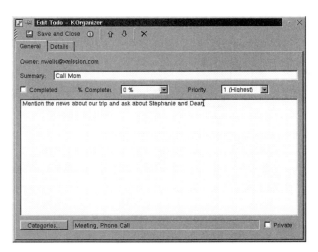

The Edit Todo dialog box includes two tabs: General and Details. In the General tab, you can do any of the following tasks:

- Edit the text of the to-do item in the Summary field.
- Check the completed check box if this task has been done.
- Enter a percentage complete if the task is partially done.
- Change the priority of this task, selecting any number from 1 (highest) to 5 (lowest) priority. The priority that you enter is shown next to task in the To-do list. (Filtering by priority is not yet available.)
- Enter any notes associated with this task (a list of items to purchase, preferred times for a flight, notes from a previous meeting, and so forth).
- Select a category for this task.

By default, tasks don't have a category associated with them. You can choose the Categories button to open a dialog box from which you can select one or more categories to apply to this task.

The Categories dialog box is shown in Figure 19.10.

FIGURE 19.10

You can select one or more categories that apply to each task from the predefined category list. You can also add new categories.

19

You can also create new categories in this dialog box if the predefined list doesn't include categories that fit your needs. For example, you can define categories for each of your school classes or for each work project that you're assigned to.

When you have finished updating information in the General tab, you can choose the Save and Close button to close the dialog box, or choose the Details tab, as described next.

Some of the information that you enter in the General tab is shown in the Brief view of the To-do list. Specifically, the priority of each task is indicated by a number on the far left of the item. A check box also indicates if the task is marked as completed.

You can delete all to-do tasks that have been marked as completed by right-clicking anywhere in the To-do list and choosing Purge Completed from the pop-up menu.

In the Details tab of the Edit Todo dialog box (see Figure 19.11) you define information about whom is involved in the task that you have defined.

FIGURE 19.11

In the Details tab you define who is to be involved in completing the task.

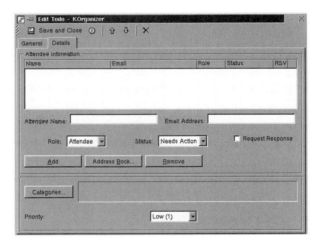

You can update the Attendee Information list by entering a name in the Attendee Name field, filling in the other information (such as email address and role), and pressing the Add button.

The information in this tab is suited more to appointments, and in fact matches the Details tab for appointments that you'll see in the section, "Managing Appointments," later in this hour. For that reason, you might not use this tab much for To-do list tasks.

Any To-do List item can be deleted by right-clicking on that item and choosing Delete To Do from the pop-up menu.

The Priority field listed in this tab uses the reverse order from the Priority field in the General tab. (Priority 1 is lowest in the Details tab; Priority 1 is highest in the General tab.) Because sorting and filtering based on priorities are not yet included in KOrganizer, I suggest not using the Priority field in the Details tab.

Saving Information

After you have a To-do list defined and organized, you must save it to a file. KOrganizer permits you to have multiple lists and calendars each saved with a different filename. Different calendars can be used for different individuals who use KOrganizer, different projects, and so forth.

Both the To-do list and the calendar appointments described in the following section are saved in the same file. To save a KOrganizer file, choose File, Save and enter a filename for the list and calendar.

The information you save in KOrganizer is stored by default in the directory `~/.kde/share/apps/korganizer`. The file format uses a `.vcs` extension. Information is stored in plain text.

When you restart KOrganizer, you can choose File, Open and select the file that you saved this information in.

19

You can also start KOrganizer from a command line with the name of a calendar file. For example, enter a command like this one:

```
$ korganizer ~/.kde/share/apps/korganizer/nicholas.vcs
```

Managing Appointments

Items that you add to the To-do list are not associated with a particular date and time; they just need to be done. Items that you enter in the calendar are associated with a particular date and time.

Each appointment or event that you add to the calendar can have various details associated with it. Events can also have an Alarm set so that a pop-up message appears and optionally a musical tone sounds at a set interval before the appointment time.

To add an appointment to the calendar day that you're viewing, use either of these methods:

- Choose Actions, New Appointment from the main KOrganizer dialog box or click the New Appointment icon on the toolbar (fourth from the left) to open a dialog box where you can define a new appointment.
- Double-click on the time slot where you want to place an appointment. When a cursor appears, type a summary description of the appointment.

If you use the second method to quickly add an appointment to your calendar, you can then right-click on that appointment to edit the appointment details. This opens the same dialog box that you see if you choose Actions, New Appointment to create the new appointment.

From the right-click menu on a calendar day, you can also toggle the alarm for an appointment. If the alarm is turned on, a small Bell icon appears next to the appointment in your calendar.

The three tabs of the New Appointment or Edit Appointment dialog box let you define information about the appointment, including defining recurring appointments. The General tab is shown in Figure 19.12.

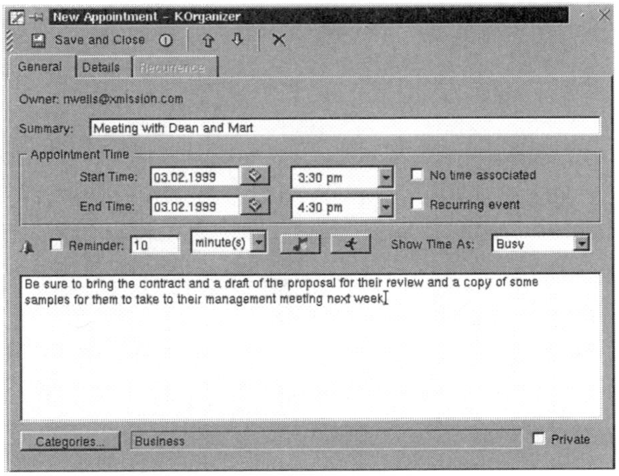

FIGURE 19.12

In the General tab of the New Appointment dialog box you define the title, time, and other basic information for a calendar event.

In the General tab, you can enter or edit a description of the appointment as it will appear on the calendar using the Summary field.

> Unless you create a new appointment by double-clicking on a calendar time slot, new appointments always use 12:00 as the default start time for the event. You can change this default using the Configuration dialog box described later in this section.

The Appointment Time field defines when the appointment starts and ends. By default, the date and time to start and end the appointment are shown. Two additional options are provided, however:

- *If you select No Time Associated:* The start and end date remain but the time fields disappear. The appointment will be floating on the specified day.
- *If you select Recurring event:* The start and end time remain but the date disappears. The Recurrence tab also becomes active, where you can set the schedule of recurrence for this event.

Next to the small Bell icon you can select a check box to activate the alarm for this appointment. If you select the check box, the Reminder field defines how long before the scheduled time the alarm reminds you of the appointment. You can also specify other actions besides a pop-up reminder window to occur when the alarm goes off:

- *Click on the music note button.* This selects a sound file to play when the alarm goes off.
- *Click the running man button.* This selects a program to execute when the alarm goes off.

You can add any notes related to the appointment by entering text in the large text box. A category for this appointment is defined by choosing the Categories button and choosing one or more categories that apply to this appointment, much the same way as you selected categories for tasks in the To-do list.

The Details tab for an appointment is identical to the Details tab for a To-do list task. On this tab you define a list of individuals that will participate in the appointment, for example, a list of attendees at a scheduled meeting.

If you check Recurring event in the Appointment Time section of the General tab, you can also select the Recurrence tab (see Figure 19.13) to define exactly when this appointment will be automatically added to your calendar in the future.

19

FIGURE 19.13

FIGURE **19.13**

*For recurring events,
you can define in the
Recurrence tab
exactly when the
recurring event should
be scheduled.*

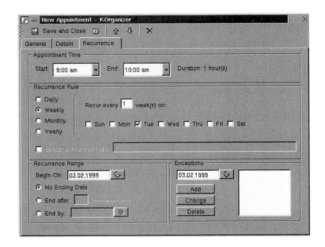

The Recurrence tab is very flexible. You can select a start and end time for the appointment, how often it will recur (daily, weekly, monthly, or yearly), which day or date, and even the range of time to continue the appointment, with exceptions for holidays or special occasions.

Configuring KOrganizer Options

The KOrganizer includes more features than this book can cover. One final area I want to describe, however, is how to set key options for the KOrganizer. These are all configured from a single dialog box that you access by choosing Options, Edit Options. In the KOrganizer Configuration Options dialog box, choose any of the categories of options to configure from the list on the left side of the dialog box. The Personal section is shown in Figure 19.14.

From this section of the Configuration dialog box you can set the following information:

- Your full name and email address (these are taken from your Linux configuration, but you can edit them if necessary)

- An additional email address if needed

- Whether a confirmation dialog box appears when you delete an appointment or To-do list item

- Whether to auto-save the calendar information

- Which nations' holidays should be marked on the calendar

FIGURE 19.14

The Personal section of the KOrganizer Configuration dialog box contains descriptions of you and your working environment.

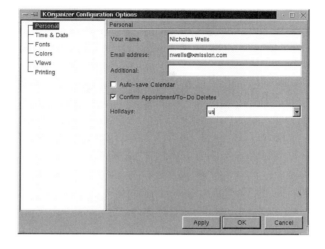

FIGURE 19.15

The Time & Dates section of the KOrganizer Configuration dialog box defines your time zone, date format preferences, and related information.

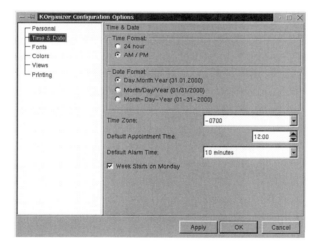

19

The Time & Date section of the Configuration dialog box, shown in Figure 19.15, enables you to set the following options:

- Select between 24-hour or 12-hour time format (using a.m. and p.m.)
- Select the date format to match your preference and national convention
- Specify your time zone (this should be set correctly by your Linux system)
- Choose a default time for newly created appointments
- Choose how long before an event is scheduled to sound a reminder alarm (only for events on which you have placed an alarm)
- Select to start the week on Monday (or on Sunday, if the check box is not selected)

In the Fonts and Colors sections of the Configuration dialog box you can configure which fonts are used for different parts of the KOrganizer displays, such as the To-do list, as well as what colors to use for backgrounds, selected items, appointments, and so forth.

The Views section enables you to define how early in the day to begin the appointment calendar (the default is 8:00 a.m.) and how wide to make the display for each hour when viewing a daily or weekly schedule.

The larger your screen resolution, the larger you can make the hour display in the Views section. This leaves plenty of room to read all the appointment information for that day. Increasing the display width for each hour also provides more space if you need to increase the font size for appointments.

Using the Time Tracker

KDE includes a handy utility for tracking how much time you spend on projects. Imagine that you have several reports that you're writing or several programming projects that you're developing, and you want to keep track of how much time you spend on each one, either for billing purposes or to know why your days disappear so fast.

The karm utility enables you to define a task then start and stop a timer as you work to add up the time that you spend on that task. Tasks and times are saved in a configuration file, so you can exit and restart KDE, and then add time to the tasks that you've defined.

To start the time tracker, choose Utilities, Personal Time Tracker, or enter the command **karm** in a terminal window.

Defining a Task

To define a new task in the time tracker, choose Task, New, or click the Blank Page icon on the toolbar.

In the dialog box that appears, enter a description of the task in the Task Name field. You can also enter a number in the Time Accumulated field. This number will be a starting point for the time accumulation for this task.

In the Time Accumulated field you must enter the total number of minutes of time spent thus far on this task. The number that you enter is converted to an hours:minutes number in the main window display.

When you press OK, the task is listed in the main karm window with the accumulated time shown in the left column. (If you don't enter a number in the Time Accumulated field, the time starts at 0.)

Figure 19.16 shows the karm window with several tasks defined.

FIGURE 19.16

With the time tracker utility you can define tasks and easily track how much time you spend on each task.

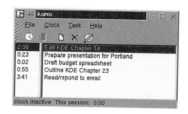

If you exit the time tracker (or even KDE), the tasks are restored the next time you start the program. You can delete a task by choosing Task, Delete or clicking the X icon on the toolbar. A confirmation dialog box asks if you really want to delete the task.

If you need to make the time column wider, move the mouse pointer to the dividing line between the time and task name. When the mouse pointer changes to a double horizontal arrow, click and drag to change the size of the columns. You can also resize the entire time tracker window using standard KDE windowing operations.

Tracking Time for Tasks

19

After you have tasks defined that you want to track time for, follow these steps to use the time tracker:

1. Click on the task in the list that you are going to work on.
2. Click the Clock icon on the toolbar (or choose Clock, Start, or press Ctrl+S).

   The time tracker begins timing. The status bar of the window shows you that the clock is active. Each minute, the accumulated time increases by one.

You can minimize the Time Tracker window to free up space on your desktop. The timer continues running. Just don't forget about it when you've finished working on the task.

3. Work on the task.

4. When you're finished working on this task, return to the time tracker window and choose the Stoplight icon on the toolbar (or choose Clock, Stop, or press Ctrl+T). The clock stops timing.

5. If you have another task to work on, click on that task in the list and restart the timer.

 You can edit the name or accumulated time numbers for any task by choosing Task, Edit, or by clicking the Pencil icon on the toolbar.

Using Fax Features

A fax machine is part of nearly every business office. Unfortunately, KDE's fax tools are not quite finished. KDE 1.1 includes a program called KFax, which you can start by choosing Graphics, Fax Viewer on the main menu.

However, KFax does not yet send or receive faxes. Rather, it provides a place to view fax files (graphics files in a facsimile format) within KDE. Using KFax, you can do the following:

- Drag a fax graphic file from a kfm window and drop it on KFax for viewing
- Rotate, mirror, and zoom fax pages
- Read files in most common fax formats, including g3, g32d, and g4
- Print out fax graphics to a printer, page by page

Future versions of KFax will no doubt include the capability to send and receive faxes from the modem on your Linux computer. In the meantime, you can try any of the following options:

- The mgetty/sendfax package, available freely at `ftp://ftp.leo.org/pub/comp/networking/communication/modem/mgetty`. For information about this package, visit `http://www.leo.org/~doering/mgetty`.
- The HylaFAX package, available freely at `ftp://sgi.com/sgi/fax`. For information about this package, visit `http://info-sys.home.vix.com/flexfax/toc.html`.
- ksendfax, another KDE utility, is not as far developed as KFax (ksendfax was at version 0.3 at last count). But it does include a graphical interface to configure and manage the sending of faxes using hylafax or another installed fax-transmission software package.

Summary

This hour describes using several business-oriented utilities that come with KDE. You learned how to manage your day with the KOrganizer (a program similar to Microsoft Outlook) and the time tracker. You also learned to manage contacts or other lists of names and personal information using the address book, kab. The next hour describes the entertainment features of KDE: games and multimedia.

Questions and Answers

Q How can I get a fax-format graphic file to try out KFax before I have a fax send/receive program installed?

A You can use image conversion utilities (such as Image Magik or the netpbm set of filters) to convert most image formats to g3, a common fax format. The better option is to print a file from a word processor to a PostScript file, and then use GhostScript to create a fax-format file. This gives you page-sized output that looks like a real fax. If you have GhostScript installed, try this command:

```
$ gs -sDEVICE=faxg3 -sOutputFile=/tmp/fax.g3.%d document_file.ps
```

Each page will be saved as a separate file (such as fax.g3.1, fax.g3.2, and so forth in this example)

Q I need to use the address book entries like a database; how can I extract the information in the database?

A No commands are provided in the kab program for things such as this. You can export to an HTML table, which might provide a useful intermediate format. Beyond that, you'll need to write a script to extract the information from the file where the database is stored. Something as simple as this command will extract information from the database:

```
$ grep name= addressbook.database
```

Be sure you're in the directory ~/.kde/share/apps/kab before using this command.

Q The KOrganizer looks a lot like other scheduling programs, but it seems to be missing some features such as filtering and sharing across the network.

A Yes, but you can expect to see more of these features in forthcoming releases of KOrganizer. In the meantime, you can also try the Scheduling features of StarOffice for Linux. They include both filtering integration with Internet features and sharing data across the network.

19

Exercises

1. Write a script to insert a collection of records that you already have into the address book database file.

2. Use what you know about creating `kdelnk` files to create a Panel or Desktop icon that starts the KOrganizer with a calendar file that you've saved.

HOUR 20

Using KDE for Entertainment

In this hour you learn how KDE can help you have fun with your computer. KDE includes utilities to play audio CD-ROMs and manage some of the multimedia aspects of your Linux system.

In addition, KDE includes a nice collection of arcade and strategy games, all available directly from the main menu (if you've installed the KDE Games package). This hour explores some of the entertainment offerings included with KDE. It also lists a few of the additional programs that are available for download.

Reviewing Your Sound Card and Related Devices

The sound system is not a standard part of most Linux distributions. By that I mean that when you installed Linux, it probably didn't search for, recognize, and install software support for your sound card or other sound or music devices.

Before you can use all the sound-producing utilities described in this hour (such as the wav file players and the CD Player), you must install sound support in your Linux system. Because sound card devices are not as standardized as hard disks or CD-ROM drives, you should consult the documentation that came with your sound card or computer system, and the documentation or technical support pages from your Linux vendor.

> If you're running Linux on a dual-boot system, you might be able to use your sound card in Windows but not in Linux. Windows provides default drivers; you must install a driver so that Linux can access the device.

Beyond the standard sound drivers, you might also want to check out the Open Sound System at http://www.opensound.com. They provide an evaluation copy of their driver software for Linux.

Using the CD Player

KDE includes a complete audio CD Player utility called kscd. You can start this utility by choosing Multimedia, CD Player on the main menu, or by entering **kscd** on a command line. The initial window is shown in Figure 20.1.

FIGURE 20.1

When you launch the CD Player it automatically checks for a CD and displays any information that it discovers.

When you start the CD Player, it immediately looks at the /dev/cdrom device, gathers information about the CD, and prepares to play it.

You don't have to mount an audio CD before starting the CD Player. The program takes care of that for you if the user that you're logged in as has permission to mount the CD-ROM device. If you don't, log in as root and execute this command (or change the settings in the /etc/fstab file to include *user*):

```
chmod a+r /dev/cdrom
```

The Display Screen

The display screen of the CD Player shows information about the current CD, including the following:

- Whether the CD is stopped, ejected, playing, or ready to play
- The total time of the CD
- How full the CD is
- The volume level set for the CD drive output
- The elapsed playing time (while playing a track)
- The remaining playing time on the entire CD
- The remaining playing time on the current track

The button to the left of the display screen with the compact disc logo switches the display between the following three modes. Click it repeatedly to change modes:

- Display elapsed playing time for the current track (starts with 0:00)
- Display the remaining playing time for the current track (starts with the length of the current track)
- Display the remaining playing time for the entire CD (starts with the length of the CD and counts backward during play)

You can configure additional options for the display screen using the configuration dialog box described later in this section.

Adding CDDB Information

The Compact Disc Database (CDDB) is a distributed, worldwide networked database of CD titles and track information. If you're connected to the Internet, the CD Player will query one of the known CDDB servers to see if a record is found for the CD that you have inserted in your CD drive. If a record is found, the artist and title appear in the display screen, and a name for each track appears in the drop-down list below the display screen.

20

You must enable remote CDDB access in the configuration dialog box before the CD Player will attempt to access the network to find CD information.

The CD Player will also check your local kscd configuration files to see if you have stored information about this CD.

If you are not connected to the Internet, the CDDB server cannot be contacted, or your CD isn't included in the local database, you can enter information about the CD that you're listening to. The information that you enter is stored locally so that each time you pop in this disc, the artist, title, and track information appears in the CD Player.

To enter information about the CD that you're listening to, click the CDDB button (the File Drawer icon) just below the display screen on the left side. The CD Database Editor dialog box appears, as shown in Figure 20.2. If you're not connected to the Internet, you might see a brief error message in the Artist/Title field as the CD player attempts to find the correct CD information.

FIGURE 20.2

The CD Database Editor provides fields to describe the artist/title and each track of the CD you have inserted.

Informational items are displayed on the right side of the dialog box. These include the ID code for the CD. This is a unique identifier, which allows the CD Player to locate the correct database information the next time you play this CD. The total playing time of the CD is also noted. The number of tracks on the CD and the length of each track are shown in the Track/Time/Title list. The other information fields are blank.

If you have information about this CD stored in a non-default location on your system or network, choose the Load button and select the directory where the CD information can be found and loaded into this dialog box. If you can find the information in this way, you shouldn't have to enter any information as described here.

To enter information about the current CD, follow these steps:

1. Select and erase the `No matching entry` message, and then enter the artist and title of the CD in the Disc Artist/Title field.

   This should follow the format shown in the field name, with a space-slash-space between the artist and title. For example, The Pretenders / The Singles.

2. If you want to add extra information about this title, choose Ext Info. Click in the editing window and type your additional text. This information is stored with the database for your reference. It is not displayed anywhere.

3. Click on track 1 in the Track/Time/Title list.

4. Click in the Edit Track Title field below the Track/Time/Title list.

5. Type the title of track 1 and press Enter. The selection bar in the Track/Time/Title list moves to track 2.

> You can choose Ext Info to add notes to any individual track. Click on a track number in the list to edit the title again or add extra information using the Ext Info button.

6. If you want to change the default order that the tracks of this particular CD are played in, click in the Play List Editor field and enter a comma-separated list of track numbers to define the play order. For example, if you don't like two of the tracks on this CD, you can enter the following in the Play List Editor field:

   1,2,4,5,7,8,9

7. If you are connected to the Internet and don't see information about your CD because it isn't contained in the CDDB server records, choose Upload to share your information with all the other people in the world who have this CD and a CD Player that accesses the CDDB database. This service allows everyone to enter information on only a few of their CDs, instead of all of them.

8. Choose Save to record the information about this CD in your local `kscd` configuration files (a local CD database).

20

When you create a new CDDB record for a CD and save it locally, it is saved
to the master KDE directory, not in your local kde directory. This allows all
users to access it. The default CDDB directory is
/opt/kde/share/apps/kscd/cddb.

9. Select a category for this CD from the list shown. If no categories are shown or if
   you don't want to define a category for this CD, choose Cancel. The other information is still saved.

10. Choose Close to close the dialog box.

Configuring the CD Player

The CD Player includes many configuration options. To access the configuration dialog
box, choose the icon with a hammer and screwdriver, below the display window.

In the CDDB tab, shown in Figure 20.3, you define how the CD Player accesses local
and remote CD database information. The fields in this tab are outlined as follows:

FIGURE 20.3

*The CDDB tab of the
configuration dialog
box defines how infor-
mation is retrieved
and saved for the CD
database.*

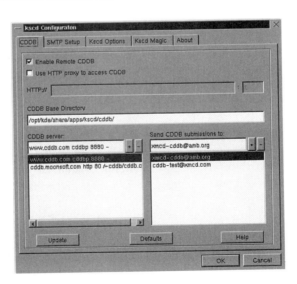

- *Enable Remote CDDB.* Select this check box to have the CD Player attempt to
  query a CDDB server on the network.
- *Use HTTP Proxy to Access CDDB.* Select this check box if your computer is
  located behind a firewall that only allows certain types of data to pass. Because
  Web traffic is usually passed through the firewall, you can indicate a Web URL

and port number in the HTTP:// field to use as a proxy to reach the Web and a CDDB server.

- *CDDB Base Directory.* This field defines where local CDDB information is stored.

- *CDDB Server.* A list of servers where CDDB information can be queried. To add a CDDB server to the list, enter the server name and press the + button.

- *Send CDDB Submissions to.* A list of email addresses that accept submissions of CDDB data. The submission will then be processed and included in the CDDB database that is shared around the world.

- *Update.* Choose this button to update the information in this dialog box from the nearest CDDB server.

- *Defaults.* Choose this button to reset the servers and email addresses in this tab to their default values.

- *Help.* Opens the online help. This might be obvious from this point, but it isn't obvious how to reach the online help for the CD Player when you first launch it.

The SMTP Setup tab is used to define email protocols so that CDDB submissions can be emailed to the addresses in the CDDB tab. The SMTP (email) server and your email address are included in this tab. You should review these fields before submitting any new CDDB information; the default settings should work for users who are running sendmail (the default on most Linux systems).

In the Kscd Options tab (see Figure 20.4) you can configure many options for how the CD Player operates. The fields in this tab are described here:

FIGURE 20.4

Additional options for the CD Player are selected in the Kscd tab of the configuration dialog box.

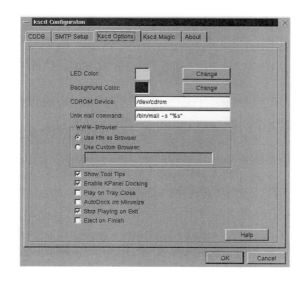

20

- *LED Color.* Displays the color of the text in the display screen. Click the Change button to select a new color for the text from a standard KDE Select Color dialog box.

- *Background Color.* Displays the color of the background of the display screen. Click the Change button to select a new background color.

- *CD-ROM Device.* The device that the CD Player accesses to locate and play a CD-ROM. Because most Linux systems will use a link to /dev/cdrom, the default should be fine. If your CD-ROM is located at a different device, change this field.

- *UNIX Mail Command.* Defines the command-line syntax used to send an email message. The standard mail command should work fine, but you can change or add to it if you need to for your local email system.

- *WWW-Browser.* The Artist Information button (described later in this section) accesses the Web to display various information about music and CDs. The CD Player uses either kfm (the default) or a custom browser that you define to view the Web pages that it accesses. If you choose Use Custom Browser, enter the command line to start the browser in the Text field.

- *Show ToolTips.* Displays pop-up hints on each part of the CD Player when the mouse pointer sits in one place for a few seconds.

- *Enable KPanel Docking.* When this check box is selected (the default), the CD Player shows both the main CD Playerwindow and a small icon on the Panel. You can turn the main window off by clicking on the CD icon on the Panel. Click again to view the CD Player window. This makes it convenient to have the CD Player running in the background as you work, but only have it onscreen when you want to use the CD controls.

- *Play on Tray Close.* The CD drive always detects when you insert a new CD and close the drive. If this check box is selected, the CD Player starts playing as soon as you close the drive.

- *AutoDock on Minimize.* If this is selected, the CD Player becomes an icon docked on the Panel when you choose the Minimize icon.

- *Stop Playing on Edit.* When you exit the CD Player, the program will stop the CD from playing as it exits. If you deselect this check box, the CD will continue to play after you exit the CD Player. You must restart the CD Player or use some other means to stop the disc from playing.

- *Eject on Finish.* If this check box is selected, the CD Player automatically ejects a CD when it has played to the end.

An additional feature of the CD Player is the i button, for information. When you click on this button, a pop-up menu appears where you can select from Performances, Purchases, or Information. Each of these items displays a submenu of Web sites. When you choose an item, a Web browser is launched with the selected music resource site.

Exploring the Rest of the CD Player

Most of the buttons on the CD Player are probably familiar to you, but some are specific to this program. The set of buttons on the right side of the window is the easiest to understand. These buttons include the following:

- *Play/Pause (the top-right button).* Press this button to start playing the CD. When the CD is playing, press this button to pause the CD; press it again to take it off of pause.
- *Stop (a square).* Stop playing the CD. This does not, however, close the CD Player.
- *Loop (a circle of arrows).* Set Loop mode so the CD will play continuously, starting over when it reaches the end (for those extra-long sessions at your PC).
- *Skip backward and forward buttons.* Go quickly back or forward within the current track.
- *Skip a track backward and forward buttons.* Change to the previous or next track on the CD, while it still playing.

To exit the CD Player, choose the button in the lower-left corner on the CD Player window, showing a small switch with a 1 and 0.

Do not close the CD Player by clicking the X on the title bar. You might not be able to access the CD drive for other (non-audio) CDs. Always use the Exit button in the lower-left corner.

20

In the drop-down list below the display screen you can select by name one of the tracks to play. This can be faster than using the forward or back arrows to move to the track you want to listen to.

Just below the display window is a long horizontal slider. This slider sets the volume of the CD drive output. The Vol field in the display screen shows the volume as a percentage.

Several other factors affect the final volume that you hear, such as the settings of your sound card and the volume knob on your speakers.

The button with a question mark is for Random Play. When you click this button, the CD plays the tracks in random order. Click the Stop button to end play.

The Eject button is located just to the left of the display window. It contains an up arrow with a bar under it. You can use this button or the Eject button located on your CD drive.

Using Other Multimedia Tools

KDE includes several other multimedia utilities. These are mainly devoted to digitized music in either wav or midi format.

The Media Player can be accessed from the Multimedia submenu on the main menu. The Media Player is used to play wav format sound files, which you can download from many different Web sites.

The MIDI Player is also accessed from the Multimedia submenu (see Figure 20.5). By their similar appearance, you might recognize that the MIDI Player was created by the same developer as the CD Player (and of many other KDE utilities, actually).

FIGURE 20.5

The MIDI player sends MIDI digital sound files to a midi device on your computer system.

While audio CDs and wav sound files are played through a standard PC sound card, the MIDI format requires that you have a special MIDI hardware device installed on your Linux PC. If you have a MIDI device, both the MIDI digital audio Player and the MIDI/Karaoke Player (see Figure 20.6) are available to help you make music on your Linux PC.

If you have additional sound hardware, a Sound Mixer Panel is also available from the Multimedia menu.

Video players for mpeg, avi, and QuickTime formats are also available for KDE. Try aKtion, a player based on the xanim program. Other utilities such as kwintv and ktvision, which will both allow KDE to support a TV Tuner card, are in various stages of development.

FIGURE 20.6

The MIDI/Karaoke Player controls a special sound device for MIDI files.

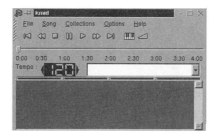

Playing Arcade Games

KDE includes a collection of more than a dozen games. This section highlights a few of the action or arcade-style games, which are included in the kdegames package mentioned in the KDE installation of Hour 2, "Installing KDE from Scratch." (Caldera OpenLinux and SuSE both include the kdegames package in their default KDE installations.)

These games are launched from the Games submenu on the main menu.

One of my personal favorites, Asteroids, was an arcade kit for years. The KDE version has attractive, smooth graphics. You control a rocket ship, blasting asteroids into smaller and smaller pieces until they disappear. More asteroids and faster asteroids appear as you clear each set of rocks.

Choose File, New Game to start a game (see Figure 20.7). Press Enter to begin.

FIGURE 20.7

Asteroids is a popular arcade game included with KDE.

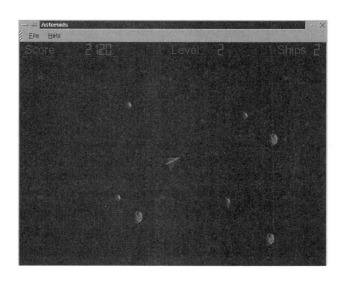

20

The following keys control the rocket:

- *Left arrow.* Rotates counter-clockwise
- *Right arrow.* Rotates clockwise
- *Up arrow.* Moves the rocket ship forward (thrust)
- *Spacebar.* Fires weapon

KDE includes two versions of Tetris. In this game, you try to arrange falling blocks so that each row is completely filled in. Each completed row disappears. The game ends when the blocks pile up to the top of the window because rows were not completed. Sirtet, shown in Figure 20.8, is a traditional version of Tetris. To control each falling block use these keys:

FIGURE 20.8

Sirtet is a version of Tetris in which you try to keep falling blocks from building up to the top of the window.

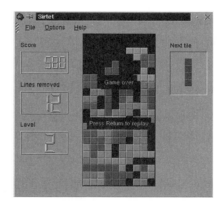

- *Left arrow.* Moves the block left
- *Right arrow.* Moves the block right
- *Up arrow.* Rotates the block to the best position
- *Down arrow.* Drops the block immediately

The other version of Tetris is a little cuter and would be appropriate for children because it has animated pictures on the blocks. The goal of the game is the same. In Smiletris, (see Figure 20.9), you can use either the Up or Down arrow key to rotate the block; the Spacebar drops the block immediately onto the pile below.

FIGURE 20.9

Smiletris is a milder version of Tetris with slower play and more visual treats during play. Kids should enjoy this version.

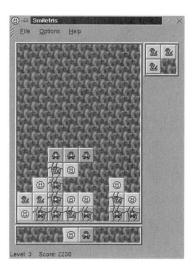

Snake Race is an arcade game, similar to Centipede, in which you try to eat up everything onscreen by controlling a fast-moving snake without running into any walls or dangerous enemies. Snake Race is shown in Figure 20.10.

FIGURE 20.10

Snake Race is similar to Centipede. You race around the board eating things while trying not to get caught by enemies.

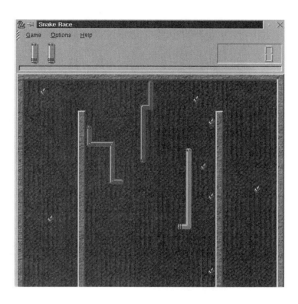

20

Several additional action games are available from the KDE Web site, including Block Out and a nice implementation of Pac Man.

Playing Other Games

Most of the games included in KDE are not action games, but card or strategy games. This list describes the titles included with KDE. For most of these games, additional online help provides a description of the game's objective and rules of play.

- *Abalone.* Like Chinese checkers, you move your pieces across the board. Play against the computer or another player on the same computer (see Figure 20.11).

FIGURE 20.11

Abalone is like Chinese checkers. You jump and move pieces to cross the board before your opponent.

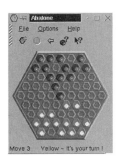

- *KBlackBox.* A graphical game of hide and seek. Use your logic to find hidden balls on the playing field. The computer is your opponent.
- *Konquest.* A space warfare strategy game in which you plan battles against multiple opponents (see Figure 20.12).

FIGURE 20.12

Konquest is a space strategy game; similar versions have been popular for decades.

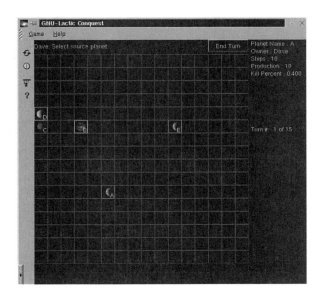

- *Mahjongg.* KDE's version of the popular board game. Excellent graphics (see Figure 20.13).

FIGURE 20.13

The KDE version of the board game Mahjongg includes attractive graphics.

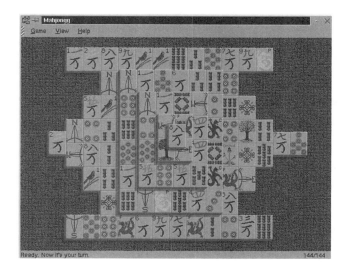

- *Minesweeper.* KDE's version of the game made popular on Windows. Try to clear the board without landing on a mine (see Figure 20.14).

FIGURE 20.14

In Minesweeper, made popular on Windows, you try to clear the minefield without landing on a mine.

20

- *Patience.* A card game for one player.
- *Poker.* If you're not familiar with this one, I'm sure a friend will teach it to you.
- *Reversi.* A nice version of Othello in which you surround the opponent's pieces to convert them to your color.

- *Same Game.* A strategy game in which you try to clear the board of colored balls in the fewest possible moves.
- *Shisen-Sho.* A Japanese game that uses Mahjongg tiles but with slightly different play.
- *Sokoban.* A Japanese game based on the popular Warehouse Keeper. You try to move items around a warehouse without being crushed in the process.

Additional strategy games for KDE include the following, all available from the KDE Web site:

- *krubik.* A graphical Rubik's Cube
- *freecell.* Based on the Windows card game
- *kblackjack.* Another card game
- *kgo.* A KDE version of the Japanese game Go
- *krossword.* For computer crossword puzzles
- *qchess.* A simple chess program

Summary

In this hour you learned a little about the sound and other multimedia systems on your Linux system and how you can access those devices using KDE utilities. You also explored the games that KDE includes. The next hour describes in detail how to locate, download, compile, and install additional KDE applications that you find on the Internet.

Questions and Answers

Q Can I use games from any other systems on KDE?

A Not exactly on KDE. You can run many DOS games (including graphical games) in Linux using the DOS emulator. This is installed by default in OpenLinux and available on other Linux systems but requires a licensed copy of DOS.

Q The CD Player appears to be accessing the CD, showing track times and everything, but no sound comes out. Why not?

A The CD Player accesses the CD drive and sends the information to the sound system on Linux. If that system isn't installed and working correctly, the CD Player can't tell the difference, but you won't hear anything. Get your Linux sound system working first by adding and configuring necessary kernel modules or other settings, according to your Linux vendor's directions.

Q Are any networked games available for KDE?

A None are described here or included with KDE, but several networked Linux games are available (including Doom), in addition to the networked DOS games that you can run on Linux. Networked games specific to KDE are likely to arrive soon.

Exercises

1. Visit one of the Web sites where CDDB information is stored (such as www.cddb.com) to see what it contains and learn more about this database.

2. Visit the KDE Web site and see what other games sound interesting to you. The next hour describes how to download and run other KDE applications.

20

HOUR **21**

Finding and Installing Additional KDE Applications

In this hour you learn how to locate, download, and install KDE applications that you're interested in using, but that aren't part of the core KDE distribution (and therefore are not installed by default). This hour describes where to find additional applications, how the download sites are organized, and how to use the tools provided with your Linux distribution to prepare and start using applications that you download.

Adding KDE applications to your system, particularly the very latest developments, usually involves downloading source code and compiling it for your Linux system. This hour describes how to perform these steps as well.

Locating Additional KDE Applications

Although the standard KDE distribution includes dozens of great utilities, as you've seen in previous hours, new applications are continually being developed. When useful KDE applications reach a stable state, most are included in the standard KDE distribution, usually in one of the application packages such as kdenetwork, kdegames, kdemultimedia, and so forth.

Between releases of KDE versions, you might want to download additional applications that are waiting to be included in the next KDE release. Also, some applications that are not considered completely stable might still be of interest to you.

Because of the nature of Linux, trying an *unstable* KDE application isn't all that dangerous. Running an early version of a KDE application that ends up crashing will very rarely have any affect on other running programs. Just be certain that you aren't logged in as root when you try new KDE programs.

KDE applications are developed by people all over the world. These developers often have a Web site dedicated to their KDE application. All completed KDE applications, however, are best accessed directly from the KDE Web site (for information) or KDE FTP site (for downloading the application). By going directly to the KDE sites, you are assured of getting the latest version that has been declared safe and ready for public use.

The KDE Web site, referred to throughout this book, includes tables that are automatically updated to include all KDE applications that can be freely downloaded.

Some applications that are commercial (such as StarOffice for Linux) might recognize and integrate with a KDE environment, but they are not mentioned in the KDE Web site because they cannot be downloaded from the KDE FTP site.

You can review lists of KDE applications in each category by visiting http://www.kde.org/applications.html . The applications shown include those that are part of the standard KDE distribution. That is, you will see listed applications such as kedit, which are already installed on your KDE system.

The tables of applications are divided into stable and unstable programs. Watch the version numbers. Applications with version numbers below 1.0 might have serious problems performing their intended functions. Nevertheless, you will find a wide variation in the meaning of these terms: some *stable* applications will crash regularly if a certain function is selected; some *unstable* programs run without a hitch, but the author of the program doesn't consider them well-tested enough to be labeled *stable*.

The tables of applications include short descriptions of the program, but these might not be entirely helpful. Most KDE applications are less than 1MB, so you can download several and try them without wasting too much time on those that end up not meeting your needs.

After you have selected an application to try, the table will link you to the KDE FTP site. You can also go directly to the FTP site and explore the KDE applications by entering the URL `ftp://ftp.kde.org/pub/kde`. A few of the worldwide mirrors for this busy site are listed in Table 2.1 in Hour 2, "Installing KDE from Scratch".

Downloading KDE Applications

The structure of the FTP site is arranged into stable and unstable areas.

The stable directory contains the standard KDE distribution for different Linux vendors and formats, as described in Hour 2. Additional applications considered to be stable are placed in the `apps` subdirectory. You can search in a directory such as `/pub/kde/stable/1.1/apps/network` to locate networking applications that have recently been declared stable and ready for general use.

Both the stable and unstable `apps` subdirectories contain additional subdirectories for different types of applications. These include the following:

- `admin`. Administrative utilities
- `comm`. Communication utilities
- `database`. Database accessories, integration programs, and so forth
- `games`. Entertainment (all kinds)
- `graphics`. Tools for creating and viewing bitmapped and vector graphics
- `multimedia`. Applications devoted to music files, sound files, video boards, software video players, and various CD devices
- `network`. Utilities to manage networking on your Linux system
- `office`. Pieces of the KOffice application suite
- `scientific`. Specialized scientific applications
- `themes`. Themes and theme-management tools
- `utils`. Various other utilities that didn't fit well into another category

21

Several other directories are part of the FTP site, such as snapshots, CVS, and incoming. These other directories shouldn't be of interest unless you start working with KDE software development.

When you enter one of these subject subdirectories, such as games, you see a list of the applications available. Notice that each application seems to include two files:

- One file with the extension .lsm that is quite small (less than 1KB)
- One file with the extension .tar.gz or .tgz

While the KDE distribution packages that you used in Hour 2 were probably in rpm or deb package format, the additional applications that you download are in gzipped tarballs. They are also source code, not binaries. The next section describes how to compile the source code.

The .tar.gz and .tgz formats are two file-naming conventions for the same compressed tar archive format.

The lsm file is a descriptive file for the application. You can click on that filename in your browser to read more information about the application. You don't need to download a copy of the lsm; it's just for reference. For example, the lsm file for KVoice is shown here:

```
Begin3
Title:          kvoice - frontend for voice and fax modems
Version:        0.3.1
Entered-date:   1.10.98
Description:    Graphical frontend for easy handling of voice mails
                and faxes. Uses the mgetty package for sending and
                receiving fax and voice mails. Allows configuring
                of the mgetty package via gui
Keywords:       KDE, QT, modem, voice, fax, mgetty, vgetty, sendfax
Author:         Lars Knoll <knoll@mpi-hd.mpg.de>
Maintained-by:  Lars Knoll <knoll@mpi-hd.mpg.de>
Primary-site:   ftp://xpc56.mpi-hd.mpg.de/pub/kde/kvoice
Alternate-Site: ftp://ftp.kde.org/pub/kde/stable/1.0/apps/comm
Platform:       unix (only tested on Linux), KDE >= beta4, Qt >= 1.33
Copying-policy: GPL
End
```

Notice that from this listing you can read

- The version currently available
- The date this application was updated for download
- A description of the application (often longer than the information in the table on the KDE Web site)
- The home page where the author might maintain additional information about this application
- Platforms on which this application has been compiled or tested (Linux is generally the first one listed.)
- The copying policy for the application (usually GPL)

After reading the lsm for an application, you can download the application by clicking on the link for the .tar.gz or .gz file.

> If you see garbage on your screen when you click on the filename, hold down Shift+click to indicate to your browser that you want to download and save the file rather than view it.

Save the downloaded application archive in a working area of your Linux system such as /tmp or in your home directory (under something such as /home/nwells/new_kde/). The next section describes how to use the application archive that you have downloaded.

Preparing New KDE Applications

After you have located and downloaded the KDE application that you want to try, the fun begins. Because virtually all the KDE applications that are not part of the standard KDE distribution are source code, you must follow these steps to run the downloaded application:

- Unpack the archive of the source code tree
- Configure the source code so it can be compiled
- Make (compile and link) the source code files
- Install the binary files into KDE

If everything goes smoothly, this entire process takes only two or three minutes. The rest of this hour tries to provide enough details so that it does go smoothly.

21

First, you need to understand a few concepts. When a programmer creates a new application for KDE, the programmer writes instructions in a programming language called C++. The instructions that the programmer writes must be converted into code that the CPU of your Linux system can use. This process is called *compiling the source code*.

A related step called *linking* combines the compiled source code that the programmer has written with library functions (pre-built components) that the source code accesses. By linking the source code and its related components, a completed executable is created.

Hour 23, "Getting Started with KDE Development," and Hour 24, "Developing for KDE," include much more detail about how programs are written for KDE.

Compiling and linking the source code of a program usually involves many steps. To automate all these steps, a utility called make is often used. All the files involved in creating a program are part of the source tree. This is the directory structure that you will create from the compressed archive file that you downloaded. The make utility examines all the files in the source tree and completes all the necessary work, starting a compiler, moving files around, and so forth.

Before running the make utility, use another program called configure that examines your system, locates all the resources needed to compile the program, and prepares instructions for the make utility.

Once the make utility has successfully compiled the application, you will have a binary program that can be run on your Linux system.

Checking for Development Libraries

Compiling an application requires certain standard components beyond the files that you downloaded for a particular program. For example, every KDE program uses the Qt graphics library described in Hour 1, "Understanding the KDE Project." Many other libraries contain functions used by KDE applications. When you installed your Linux system, you probably didn't install these libraries unless you intended on using development software.

In order to compile new KDE programs that you download as source code (the .tgz files described in the previous section), you must have the following packages installed:

- *libg++-devel.* Development libraries for the C++ compiler (not just libg++, which is a separate package). This package should be included with your Linux distribution.

- *XFree86-devel.* Development libraries for the X Window System. This package should be included with your Linux distribution.

- *kdelibs-devel.* Development version of the KDE libraries (download from the KDE site)

- *kdesupport-devel.* Development version of additional KDE libraries (download from the KDE site)

- *qt-devel-1_4_2.* Development libraries for Qt version 1.42. (Download from the KDE site; using older versions of the Qt libraries will cause some KDE applications to malfunction or not compile when launched)

To check to see if one of these packages is installed on your system, use a command such as this one:

```
$ rpm -q packagename
```

To install any of these packages that are missing from your system, follow this example. (The options indicate to install, showing hash marks to indicate progress, with verbose output of messages):

```
$ rpm -ihv packagename
```

Unpack the Application Archive

To unpack the source code tree archive that you downloaded, move the .tgz or .tar.gz file to a working directory and execute this command:

```
$ tar xvfz filename
```

The tar command creates a subdirectory for the application source code tree and fills it with all the files needed to create the application. You see a list of these files as the archive is unpacked.

After running the tar command, the original archive file (the .tgz or .tar.gz file) remains unchanged. If you have a problem with the application source code tree, you can delete it completely and use the tar command again to start over.

The typical source code tree for a KDE application is composed of many files, including among others

- A README file, which might describe the application or how to install it
- An INSTALL file, which might describe how to install the application
- Several configuration files
- A subdirectory named for the application (where the actual source code is located)

21

Make the Source Tree

To prepare to compile the source code using the make utility, you must first run the configure script to prepare instructions for make. Change to the directory that you unpacked, where you see files such as configure, INSTALL, README, and Makefile. Execute this command:

```
$ ./configure
```

You see many lines of text scroll down the screen as the configure script examines your system. The script is building up information that it uses to prepare a Makefile. The Makefile is used by the make utility.

You will probably see dozens (even hundreds) of lines of text (depending on the application) as the configure script runs. It might take several minutes to run, depending on the speed of your computer. If the last line before you see the command prompt again contains Error, you have a problem. Review the message and see if you can determine where the problem is. Unfortunately, the complexity of Linux software development makes it impossible to give a simple list of troubleshooting fixes here.

> You may see Warning on several of the lines from the configure script. Itís a good idea to note these in case a problem occurs with the next step (using the make utility). Often, however, warnings wonít cause a problem. The configure script will stop immediately if an error is detected. Youíll have to resolve the error before proceeding.

If the configure script completes successfully, you're ready to use the make utility. Enter this command:

```
$ make
```

You see more lines scrolling down your screen as make works. As with the configure script, if you don't see an error message on the last line of the output from make, you can assume that it completed the operation successfully.

Because the make utility is running a C++ compiler for the components of the KDE application, it can take several minutes to run make for a larger application. Compiling some of the KOffice applications on a slower PC might take 30 minutes. You should see messages occasionally during that time, however, as different steps are executed.

One reason that you use make instead of running the compiler directly is that it detects which parts of the program need to be compiled and which are already in an intermediate format. If you run make again in the same source code tree, it will take less time to complete.

Installing the New Application

When you use the rpm command to install an rpm-format software package, each of the files is placed in the correct location, scripts might be run, the environment updated, and so forth.

After creating the binary (executable) program by running make, you use a similar command to place the binary in its default location, set up environment variables or graphic files, and generally get things ready so you can type the name of the application to run it.

To complete this step, you might need to be logged in as root (use the su command to switch temporarily to root access). This is because KDE applications generally are placed in the main KDE directories, which are not accessible by all users. Use this command to install the application:

```
$ make install
```

Why are you using the make command again? The parameter for make (install in this case) indicates what you want make to do. The instructions in the Makefile indicate how to install the application after a *plain* make compiles it.

Unfortunately, using this command is not as clean as using rpm to install a package. If you install an application using rpm, you can easily query to find out where it placed each file, and uninstall or erase the package and all its files if needed. Still, using make install is easier than copying the files by hand.

Many Makefiles also include an Uninstall option that removes the files copied by the Install option.

Running the Application

Depending on the application that you download and install, executing make install may add the application to one of the submenus on the KDE main menu. In any case, it should move the binary for the application to the default KDE binary directory, /opt/kde/bin.

21

To run the application, you should be able to execute the application name. For example

```
$ kpacman &
```

If this doesn't work, go to the directory where you executed the `configure` and `make` commands, and change to the subdirectory named for the application. For example, I used the following two commands for the kpacman application, first to change to the directory where the `.tgz` file was unpacked, and then to change to the directory where the binary created by `make` is stored:

```
$ cd kpacman-0.2.4
$ cd kpacman
```

Then try to run the binary directly

```
$ ./kpacman &
```

This won't always work, depending on what other files are needed by the application (such as graphics or configuration files), but it can give you some hints as to where problems are.

Summary

In this hour you've learned how to download, prepare, and install new KDE applications. You learned how to install additional development packages so that KDE applications could be compiled and how to run the `make` utility to compile them. You learned many programming concepts that will be helpful if you continue to explore KDE software development in Hours 23 and 24. In the next hour you learn how to integrate non-KDE applications more fully into a KDE environment, including creating icons for them and placing them on your desktop or Panel.

Questions and Answers

Q How can I determine which versions of the Qt graphical library are needed to run the application that I want to use?

A Review the `lsm` file for the application. On the Platform line you should see something like this: `Qt >= 1.33`, or `Qt >= 1.42`. This indicates which version of the Qt libraries you must have installed to compile and run this application.

Q The application that I've downloaded appears to be a binary not a source code tree. How can I get it installed and running?

A It should be easier than the steps in this hour for a source code tree, but you'll have to look for a README or INSTALL file in the application directory created by the tarball archive. You might be able to use the `make install` command to install the program. This isn't as smooth as using rpm, but should make the application ready to run in the KDE directories. Check the instructions that come with the binary for details.

Q I'm seeing errors related to my X includes. Why?

A If you're using an X server besides XFree86, the XFree-devel package described in this hour might not work correctly. You might need a development library for the X server that you're using.

Exercises

1. You installed the devel packages for Qt and libg++. Other packages named devel-static are also available. What are these static packages used for? Read a little in the gcc man page or ask a friend who is a programmer.

2. As you review the messages from the configure script, what things do you think the script is determining about your system? You can review the script itself with this command: **less configure**.

21

HOUR **22**

Integrating Non-KDE Applications into KDE

In this hour, you will learn to add other Linux applications to KDE so that they are integrated into your graphical environment. Of course, non-KDE applications can't provide all the drag and drop and file compatibility of KDE applications. But using the instructions in this hour, you'll learn how to make non-KDE applications appear on your KDE menus, on the KDE Panel, and generally fit in with your KDE workspace.

Reviewing a Few Non-KDE Applications

When you start using KDE, you probably notice that several non-KDE applications are included on the KDE menus. For example, if you have installed the Red Hat KDE packages, you can find standard Red Hat administration utilities, additional graphical tools, and games on the various submenus of the main menu.

If you are running Caldera OpenLinux, the KDE Applications submenu of the main menu includes many programs that are included with OpenLinux that are not part of the KDE distribution. These include the following:

- *Netscape Communicator.* The popular Web browser for Linux
- *DR-DOS.* A DOS emulator that allows you to run DOS applications
- *BRU.* A backup and restore utility with a graphical interface
- *CRiSP.* A graphical text editor similar to the KEdit and KWrite programs

In addition, Caldera OpenLinux is configured to include a non-KDE submenu on the KDE main menu. This submenu includes standard Linux graphical applications, as shown in Figure 22.1.

FIGURE 22.1

Many non-KDE applications are included for your convenience on the main menu of most KDE distributions.

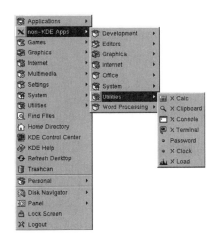

All these non-KDE applications are integrated with KDE to some degree. As you learned in previous hours, an application must have a KDE link file in order to appear on the KDE main menu. These KDE link files, each with a `.kdelnk` extension, are information files that KDE uses to access and run the application.

You might have many other Linux applications that you want to integrate with KDE to a greater or lesser degree. These applications can include the following:

- WordPerfect for Linux
- GIMP (graphics program)
- Database clients or configuration utilities

- NetWare administration tools
- Proprietary connection software for your ISP
- Character-based programs that you are running in a terminal window

These applications can all be integrated into KDE in several ways, including

- Placing them on the main menu or a submenu of your choice (if you have sufficient access rights on your Linux system)
- Including them on your Panel
- Including them in your Autostart folder
- Including them on your desktop
- Making KDE understand the data types supported by these programs

> Drag-and-drop interaction with KDE applications canít be added to non-KDE applications. The Cut and Paste features should work in most applications, however, because all standard X applications rely on the same window manager Clipboard.

If you use the default settings in the Style dialog box (choose Settings, Desktop, Style), the check box to apply KDE fonts and colors to non-KDE applications is selected. With this option set, the non-KDE applications that you run will have the same look and feel as your KDE Desktop and applications.

> Some graphical applications might not use the KDE fonts and colors even with this style option selected. Applications that don't conform to standard programming practices to define these items may appear with their own unique look and feel.

The following sections describe how to select and integrate a non-KDE application into KDE. The example application that I've chosen is the GIMP, a popular graphics tool for Linux, which is similar to Adobe Photoshop.

Locating Applications to Integrate with KDE

Before you can run an application from a KDE menu, you have to know how to run it from a command line. You will enter this command line in the KDE link file for the application.

The command line to run a program is simply the name of the program. But command line or startup options are often available to let you refine how the application starts. You can usually see these options by using the `--help` parameter. For example, the GIMP application provides several startup options, as shown here:

```
[nwells@sundance Applications]# gimp --help
Usage: gimp [option ...] [files ...]
Valid options are:
  -h --help                 Output this help.
  -v --version              Output version info.
  -b --batch <commands>     Run in batch mode.
  -n --no-interface         Run without a user interface.
  --no-data                 Do not load patterns, gradients.
  --verbose                 Show startup messages.
  --no-splash               Do not show the startup window.
  --no-splash-image         Do not add an image to the startup window.
  --no-shm                  Do not use shared memory bet. GIMP and plugins.
  --no-xshm                 Do not use the X Shared Memory extension.
  --console-messages        Display warnings to console, not a dialog box.
  --debug-handlers          Enable debugging signal handlers.
  --display <display>       Use the designated X display.

[nwells@sundance Applications]#
```

If you want to start the GIMP without showing the splash screen, you can include the `--no-splash` option when you designate how to start the application. Other applications will have different startup options.

You might also need to know where the application is located in your Linux file system. If it is stored in a directory that is always accessible to you because it is part of your PATH environment variable, you can use just the name of the application when defining how to start it:

```
gimp
```

If the application is stored in a directory that can't be accessed via the PATH variable, you need to use the entire path to reach the application:

```
/opt/gimp/gimp
```

You can determine if the first example (without the complete path) will work by trying to launch the application from a terminal window.

Another important piece of information about an application is what types of files it supports. Some of these formats are obvious (StarOffice supports the .sdc StarWriter document format). Many others might not be obvious, but are important for you to know so that you can make the application as useful as possible in KDE.

The first step in this process is determining the file types that the application supports. You can often do this by starting the application and reviewing the Save As dialog box, the File, Export option (if it exists in the application), or the Import Filter that appears when you try to open an incompatible file format.

> All these methods won't work with every application. You might need to explore the application, try opening several types of files, or even read the documentation to determine what file types are supported.

If you have loaded WordPerfect for Linux, for example, you can review the Save As dialog box to see what document types WordPerfect can read. By knowing these, you can instruct KDE (later in this hour) to send documents of any of those types to WordPerfect.

For the current example, Figure 22.2 shows the Save as dialog box for the GIMP, with the Save Options dialog box open to show the graphics file types that are supported. (Note that some are gray because the correct filters are not available on my system.)

FIGURE 22.2

Explore the Save As dialog box of graphical applications to determine which file formats they support.

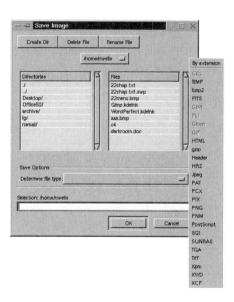

22

As you discover the file formats that are supported by the application you want to add to KDE, make a list of them.

The next step is to determine how to systematically identify file types. This is usually done by examining the file extension. For example, each graphic format has a standard file extension used on files with that format: `.cgm` for Computer Graphics Metafiles, `.tiff` for Tagged Image File Format, `.xbm` for X Window System Bitmap, and so forth.

Gather information about how the file types supported by the application you want to add to KDE are defined by their file extension.

> Files can also be identified using information in the magic file, located at `/opt/kde/share/mimelnk/magic`. This file contains an encoded description used to check the contents of a file to identify the data type of the file. For example, the magic file might indicate that any file that contains a certain string of letters within the first 100 characters is a WordPerfect file. The WordPerfect MIME type could then be assigned to the file. Review the KDE magic file and the magic man page for details on setting up this advanced feature.

Creating Application Links

Once you know how to start an application and what file types if supports, you can create a complete KDE link to access it.

To do this, open a `kfm` directory window (choose Home Directory on the main menu). You can create the KDE link for the application anywhere. After the KDE link is created, it can be copied to various places (as described in the next section) to add it to menus, the desktop, and so forth.

1. Within an open kfm window, choose File, New, Application. A message box appears with a new KDE link name shown: `Program.kdelnk`.

2. Edit the name of the KDE link in the message box so that it reflects the name of the application you want to access in KDE.

> Leave the `.kdelnk` file extension on the name of the KDE link.

3. Choose OK. The message box closes and a Gear icon (representing an executable application) appears in the kfm window, labeled with the name you assigned to the new KDE link.

4. Right-click on the new icon and choose Properties. The General tab appears showing the creation date and time for the KDE link file and the name that you just assigned to it.

5. You shouldn't need to change anything on the Permissions tab, but you can review it if you'd like. The permissions assigned to newly created files are determined by your Linux system. See your Linux documentation for details.

6. Click on the Execute tab (see Figure 22.3).

FIGURE 22.3

The Execute tab defines how to launch the application for which you created this KDE link file.

7. In the Execute field, enter the command to start this application as you would enter it from the command line in a terminal window.

If you need to search for the exact program name or path, choose the Browse button. You can't try the application or check available parameters from the Browse button however.

8. All applications use a standard Gear icon. To change this icon, click on the Gear icon. A Select Icon dialog box appears, as shown in Figure 22.4.

FIGURE 22.4

You can select the icon assigned to an application from hundreds included with KDE.

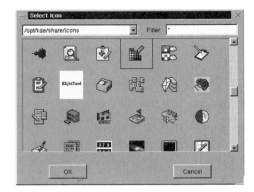

9. All the icons in the `/opt/kde/share/icons` directory are shown in the dialog box. You can select from the list by double-clicking on an icon. To view other icons, select a different directory from the drop-down list shown at the top of the dialog box. When you double-click on an icon or click on an icon and choose OK, the dialog box closes and the icon you selected appears below the Execute field.

10. If this application can be displayed in a very small window, you can designate it to be swallowed on the KDE Panel. In the Swallowing on Panel, Execute field, enter the command to start the program as a very small window. (This might be the same as the command in the Execute field.)

11. If you entered a command in the Swallowing on Panel, Execute field, enter a window title to identify the application when it is part of the Panel. (The GIMP example used here shouldn't be swallowed on the Panel because it doesn't have a small status window. It is intended for active, full window use.)

12. If this application should be run in a terminal window, select the Run in Terminal check box and enter any terminal options that apply to this application in the Terminal Options field.

 Applications that would be run in a terminal include character-based applications or graphical applications that print messages to Linux Standard Output. Using a terminal window allows you to review these messages as the application is running.

Finally, change to the Application tab and fill in each field:

- *Binary Pattern.* Enter the program name for this application. Don't include the parameters that you used on the Execute tab to start the application; include only the program executable name.

- *Comment.* Enter a descriptive sentence about this application. This comment is used for pop-up hints when the icon for this application is included on the Panel, desktop, or similar situations.

- *Name.* Enter a brief description of the application. This should be shorter than the Comment field (something like you would use as a menu item).

The two lists at the bottom of the Application tab are the MIME types supported by your KDE system. To choose which MIME types are supported by the application you are creating a KDE link for, follow these steps:

1. Choose a MIME type from the list on the right side.

2. Choose the Left arrow button (<) to move the MIME type to the left side.

3. Repeat for each of the MIME types supported by this application.

If you determine that this application supports a certain list of MIME types (as described in the preceding section), but those MIME types are not all listed in the Application tab, follow these steps to list all the MIME types that do apply to this application. You can add more MIME types to this list later, after you have defined them on your system. It's better to define the application first, add MIME types as necessary, and then update the Application tab. This allows you to specify this new application as a default application for the new MIME types that you create.

After you have entered all the information in the Applications tab (see Figure 22.5 for the GIMP application), choose OK to close the dialog box.

FIGURE 22.5

The Applications tab defines additional information for a KDE link file, such as which data formats this application supports.

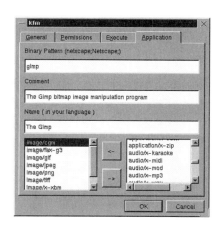

Adding to the Desktop, Panel, and Menus

With a KDE link file defined for a non-KDE application, you can add the application to different parts of KDE to make it easily accessible.

You can do this by copying the new KDE link file that you created into certain key directories that KDE uses, or by using the graphical interface to drag and drop the application in the locations where you want it to appear.

Most of these operations are outlined in previous hours as I described setting up the Autostart folder and Desktop, Configuring the Panel, and so forth. The sections that follow provide a review of those options and steps.

> The next section describes how to add a new MIME type to your KDE system to support additional data formats (such as WordPerfect files or new graphics formats). In order to specify a non-KDE application as the default application for a new MIME type that you create, you must include the non-KDE application on the KDE main menu (or a submenu). The sections that follow describe how to do that.

Adding an Application to the Desktop

To add a non-KDE application to the KDE Desktop after creating a KDE link file for the application, use any of these methods.

- Drag the KDE link file for the application from the kfm window in which it was created to the KDE Desktop. When you drop the icon, choose Move, Copy, or Link, depending on whether you want to move, duplicate or create a link to the KDE link file. (This doesn't affect the application itself, only the KDE Link file that refers to it.)

- Open two kfm windows, one for the directory where the KDE link file is located and the other for the ~/Desktop directory. Drag and drop the KDE link file from its original location to the ~/Desktop directory.

- Using a command line, copy the KDE link file from its original location to the ~/Desktop directory. For example

  `$ cp /tmp/Gimp.kdelnk ~/Desktop`

  After copying the KDE link file, you can drag the icon on the desktop to place it where you like.

Adding an Application to the Main Menu

You can update the main menu by either using kfm windows or the command line to move or copy the KDE link file.

Depending on whether you want the new application on the main menu or on the Personal menu, select one of the methods in this list:

- If you want to make a non-KDE application available to all user accounts on your system, you must be logged in as root. Drag the KDE link file from the location where you created it and drop it in the /opt/kde/share/applnk directory.

    You can also use a command like this:

    ```
    $ cp newapp.kdelnk /opt/kde/share/applnk
    ```

- If you are not logged in as root or want to make a non-KDE application available only as part of a user's Personal submenu, drag the KDE link file from the location where you created it to the ~/.kde/share/applnk directory.

    You can also use a command like this:

    ```
    $ cp newapp.kdelnk ~/.kde/share/applnk
    ```

If you prefer, you can use the graphical Menu editor utility.

To use the Menu editor utility, start by opening a kfm window containing the new KDE link file that you've created.

Choose Panel, Edit Menus from the main menu. The main window is shown in Figure 22.6. The Personal menu is shown on the left side of the Menu Editor window. If you haven't placed anything in your Personal menu yet, the only item you see is *Empty*.

FIGURE 22.6

When you open the Menu editor, the Personal menu on the left probably contains only "Empty." You must be root to edit the main menu on the right.

22

To add your application to the Personal menu, drag the icon for the KDE link file from the kfm window and drop it on the Empty item (see Figure 22.7). The new application is added, with a default icon and the name *Application*.

FIGURE 22.7

The KDE link that you drop on the Personal menu is added as "Application." You can then edit the name of the menu item.

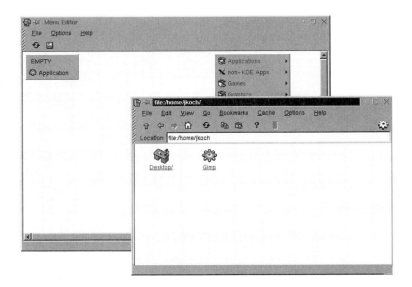

Now you'll want to remove the Empty item and rename the menu item to match your application's name.

Right-click on the Empty item. Choose Cut from the pop-up menu that appears. The Empty item is removed from the Personal menu.

Right-click on the Application item that you added. Choose Change from the pop-up menu. A menu editing dialog box appears, as shown in Figure 22.8.

Enter a new name for this menu item in the Name field. (You can also review the other fields, but the information you entered when you created the KDE link should all be inserted and ready to use.)

Close the dialog box and choose File, Save to save your changes to the menus.

Now when you use the menu, your new item has been added (see Figure 22.9).

You can only modify the main menu if you're logged in as root. If you're logged in as a regular user, you can only modify the Personal menu.

FIGURE 22.8

You can edit the properties of each item in the Personal menu by choosing Change from the right-click pop-up menu.

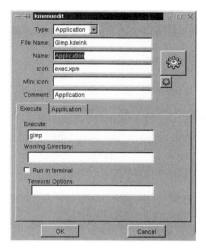

22

FIGURE 22.9

New items that you add with the Menu editor appear immediately when you view the main menu.

Adding an Application to the Panel

To add an application to the Panel, drag the KDE link file from an open kfm window and drop it on the Panel in the location where you'd like it included. It appears on the Panel.

You can adjust where it appears on the Panel by right-clicking on the icon and choosing Move. Slide the mouse from side to side until the icon is positioned as you want it, and then click the mouse.

The contents of the Panel are defined by the KDE link files named in the file `~/.kde/share/config/kpanelrc`, or, if that file doesn't exist, in the file `/opt/kde/share/config/kpanelrc`.

Adding MIME Types

If all the data types or formats supported by the non-KDE application that you added are not already defined in KDE, you can add additional MIME type definitions so that KDE will use the new application to access those data files.

Defining these additional MIME types should be done after you have added a new non-KDE application to your main menu or Panel, so that the non-KDE application is listed as an option when defining a default application to use for the new data type. Only applications (KDE links to applications) located in the applnk directories are scanned and used automatically with new MIME types that you create.

When creating a KDE link for an application, use the %f parameter to launch the application. Otherwise KDE canít automatically launch the application when you click on a data file with the new MIME type that you define. For example, to start GIMP, use this command in the Execute tab of the KDE link definition:

`gimp %f`

KDE includes definitions for more than 60 different MIME types. The list of available MIME types is in the Application tab of the properties dialog box for the KDE link file that you created. You can also review the different MIME types that are defined within KDE by visiting the `/opt/kde/share/mimelnk` directory. This directory contains subdirectories for each of the major data types that MIME types are created for, such as audio, video, and image.

MIME types that are defined only for your current user account are listed in the `~/.kde/share/mimelnk` directory. When you visit this directory in a kfm window, however, kfm displays the contents of the system-wide MIME type directory and your personal MIME type directory, combined together as if they were both physically stored in your personal MIME type directory. This makes all those MIME types available to all applications that you launch.

Change to the image subdirectory and list the files it contains with the ls command. You see a .kdelnk file for the image formats that KDE supports:

- cgm
- fax-g3
- gif
- jpeg
- png
- tiff
- x-xbm
- x-xpm

Each of these .kdelnk files is based on the MIME type template located in ~/Desktop/Templates. You can use the MIME Template is that directory or copy one of the files in the /opt/kde/share/mimelnk directory, and then modify it to create a new MIME type definition.

MIME type definitions (that is, .kdelnk files based on the MIME type template), must be placed either in the /opt/kde/share/mimelnk directory for all users to see or in your local MIME directory, ~/.kde/share/mimelnk. If you create a new MIME type definition and place it anywhere besides these two directories, KDE cannot use it.

A key part of fully integrating other applications with KDE is defining the data types that those applications work with so that KDE can tie together the application with the files that it can operate on. For example, if you want to integrate the GIMP graphics program, you should make several additional graphics formats supported in KDE.

As another example, if you are installing WordPerfect for Linux, you should define a MIME type that will allow KDE to launch WordPerfect when you click on a WordPerfect document file.

Defining a New MIME Type

While you can define a MIME type by copying an existing MIME type file from the mimelnk directory and modifying it, it is much easier and less error-prone to use the graphical dialog boxes provided by KDE.

To create a new MIME type, follow these steps:

1. Open a kfm window and browse to your `mimelnk` directory,
   `~/.kde/share/mimelnk`. (You must have View, Show Hidden Files selected to see
   the `.kde` directory.)

> If you are logged in as root and want to make the new MIME type available
> to all users, open the kfm window to `/opt/kde/share/mimelnk`.

2. Choose the subdirectory under the `mimelnk` directory that matches the type of data
   that you are defining as a new MIME type (for example, video, image, or text).

> If you don't create the new MIME type in one of the `mimelnk` directories
> (or move it there after you create it), the new MIME type will have no affect
> on KDE.

3. Choose File, New, MIME Type. A message dialog box appears.

4. Change the name of the file to match the format that you are defining as a new
   MIME data type. For example, change the name to `bmp.kdelnk`.

> The MIME type definition that you are creating is actually another KDE link
> file, with a `.kdelnk` file extension. The KDE link template used to create a
> MIME type includes different lines of information than a KDE link for an
> application, device, and so forth.

5. Choose OK. You might see an error message stating that the new MIME type does-
   n't include the needed definitions. Ignore it; you're about to fix that problem.

   An icon for the new MIME type appears in the kfm window.

6. Right-click on the new MIME type icon and choose Properties from the pop-up
   menu. The properties dialog box appears.

7. The General tab and Permissions tab are the same as those associated with the new
   Application KDE link file you created in the previous section. You don't need to
   alter these tabs.

8. Change to the Binding tab. In this tab you define the new MIME type.

9. In the Pattern field, enter the filename pattern that defines the MIME type. For example, a bmp graphic file has a certain file extension. You can include several possibilities, separated by semicolons:

    `*.bmp;*.BMP`

10. In the Mime Type field, enter a descriptive text line for the MIME type that you're defining. For example

    `image/bmp`

    or

    `text/wordperfect`

    The first part of this description should match the subdirectory of the `mimelnk` directory where you store this MIME type definition.

11. In the Comment field enter a descriptive sentence about this data type. For example

    `MS Windows BMP bitmapped graphics file`

12. In the Default Application field, choose the new application that you defined from the drop-down list.

> If you haven't included an application in the KDE main menu or Panel, it doesn't appear in the Default Application drop-down list as an option. You can leave this field blank if the correct application isn't shown and return to this dialog box later to specify.

13. To define an icon that will be used for all files that match this MIME type, click the icon next to the Default Application field and choose a new icon from the Select Icon dialog box that appears.

    An example of the Bindings tab with all fields filled in is shown in Figure 22.10.

14. Choose OK to close the dialog box. The MIME type that you defined is now active on your KDE system.

> You might want to return to the Application tab of the new application KDE link file that you defined and add the new MIME type as a supported data type.

FIGURE 22.10

The fields in the Bindings tab define how KDE will recognize and act on files of this data type.

Summary

In this hour you learned the details about how to integrate a non-KDE application into KDE by creating a detailed profile of the application in a KDE link file and adding that KDE link file to key locations with your KDE environment, such as the main menu or Panel. You also learned how to define a new MIME type for a data format that is supported by one of your applications but which KDE doesn't know about by default. In the next hour you learn the basics of KDE development, including what tools you need to get started with a KDE software development project.

Questions and Answers

Q Does it make sense to add non-graphical applications to KDE?

A Generally yes, if you use the application regularly. By creating a KDE link file for a text-based application, you can start it easily from the Panel or menu, and define MIME types that will be associated with the application in KDE. The application is run in a terminal window.

Q Do some applications take care of all these integration steps for me?

A Yes, and hopefully more will in the near future. StarOffice 5.0 for Linux is the best current example. If you select the KDE integration option during installation, it adds itself to your Personal menu, creates a set of StarOffice MIME types, adds icons, and so forth.

Q I added a new MIME type as directed. Why do I still have to enter the application name when I click on icons for that data type?

A The application that you want to run must include instructions for how to start with a data file. This is generally done by including the `%f` parameter in the Execute field of the application's KDE link file (the one located in the `applnk` directory). All menu directories are scanned to determine which applications are accessible for auto-launching from a data-file icon. For example, instead of starting WordPerfect like this in the Execute tab of the KDE link file:

```
wp
```

Start it like this:

```
wp %f
```

See the online help for the kfm file manager for additional details.

Q Can't I use the executable file to refer to a program instead of creating KDE link files.

A No. A KDE link file is required so that KDE can refer to the application from multiple locations, include descriptive text in multiple languages, and generally include meta-information about the application that is separate—and therefore not dependent on—the binary itself. This provides more flexibility within KDE, although it's a bit more work when dealing with non-KDE applications.

Exercises

1. Create another MIME type for Microsoft Word documents. Should this MIME type go in the Application or Text area? If you have StarOffice 5.0, assign it as the default option to open Word documents.

2. Examine the `.kdelnk` files for the new application link and the new MIME type that you created. What are the differences? What do they have in common? Why would it be a challenge to create these files by hand in a text editor?

PART V
Developing for KDE

Hour

23 Getting Started with KDE Development

24 Developing for KDE

Hour **23**

Getting Started with KDE Development

If you've been wondering how to become more involved in the KDE Project, writing new KDE applications or code for KDE itself, this hour will get you started. You will learn how a KDE application is organized, how to start a simple KDE application project from a framework, and how to begin modifying and extending that framework.

Although this hour doesn't assume any Linux programming experience, you should be familiar with C++ programming and the basic concepts that it depends on (such as objects, inheritance, classes, and so forth). If you want to pursue KDE programming but you don't know C++, you should begin with a book such as *Sams Teach Yourself C++ in 21 Days*. This is particularly true as you move on to Hour 24, "Developing for KDE."

Reviewing Software Development Concepts

In Hour 21, "Finding and Installing Additional KDE Applications," you learned about using `configure` and `make` to convert the source code for a KDE application into a binary executable. These commands are only a small part of the software development process in Linux. In order to develop a KDE application or even modify the source code for an existing program, you need to understand some additional concepts.

KDE applications are created in an object-oriented programming language called C++. Object-oriented programming in C++ involves some concepts that many people who have programmed in non-object-oriented languages find very foreign. These concepts include the following:

- *Object classes*
- *Objects* (instances of an object class)
- *Methods* (functions associated with an object class)
- *Inheritance* (the capability of one class to automatically include the data and functions of another class)

Beyond object-oriented programming concepts, you should understand how programming libraries function before diving into the rest of this hour.

Because programs can be written much faster by reusing common functions, libraries of these functions are precompiled into an intermediate format. This library format isn't directly executable as a program, but it provides a function that programs can use for things such as opening files, choosing a color, and so forth.

When you write a program for KDE, you rely on many (hundreds) of these library functions. These functions are grouped together in files that you refer to at the beginning of your application source code.

Examples of the library files that Linux and KDE use include the following. You might include or refer to any of these in a KDE program that you write:

- Qt graphical functions
- KDE standard dialog boxes (Open File, Select Font, and so forth)
- Standard X Window System functions
- Linux kernel functions to access devices
- Programming functions that are built into a library of commonly-used tools

When you compile your program using the `make` utility, the libraries are blended into the binary application. This process is called *linking*.

> The library functions can be embedded in your application. This is called *static linking*. They can also be referred to without being included in your application. This is called *dynamic linking*. Dynamic linking has several advantages, such as smaller code and easier maintenance, but it requires that the library files be installed on a system before your application can be executed.

23

Using KAppTemplate

The easiest way to learn any type of software development is to start with an idea for a project you'd like to create, and then learn the things you need to make that project a reality. The problem with this approach is that it can take so long to get the development system up and running that you lose interest in the project.

The easiest way I've found to start a new KDE application is the KAppTemplate package. You can find this tool on the KDE Web site in the Developer's Library section, or you can directly visit http://home.sprintmail.com/~granroth/kapptemplate/ to download a copy of it.

Installing KAppTemplate

KAppTemplate isn't a KDE program. It's a script that creates an application framework, from which you can expand functionality to create the project you have in mind.

The KAppTemplate package that you download is a gzipped tarball. Place it in a temporary location such as /tmp and extract the package using this command:

```
$ tar xvfz kapptemplate-0.3.tar.gz
```

After the archive is expanded, change to the KAppTemplate installation directory.

```
$ cd kapptemplate-0.3
```

You can review the README file in a text editor, or immediately install KAppTemplate with this command:

```
$ ./install-me
```

The installation script asks you several questions. Answer each question, pressing Enter after your response (the default response is shown in brackets after each question). Questions include the following:

- Your name
- Your email address

- Where to create apps (`/usr/src`)
- Where to install apptemplate (`opt/kde/bin`)
- Where to install kapptemplate files (`/opt/kde/share/apps/kapptemplate`)

> You can't install KAppTemplate to the default location unless you are logged in as root or have been granted rights to create files in the default directories (such as `/usr/src` and `/opt/kde/bin`). If you don't have permission, enter subdirectories in your home directory to place the components of KAppTemplate.

Once you enter this information, you see messages as the installation process creates directories for KAppTemplate and installs the package. This process, however, only installs the KAppTemplate scripts.

Running **KAppTemplate**

When you have KAppTemplate installed, you can run the `kapptemplate` program (actually a script) anytime you want to create a KDE application. Follow these steps:

If you didn't install KAppTemplate in the default location (`/opt/kde/bin`) or another location that is included in your PATH variable, change to the directory where you instructed the installation process to install the KAppTemplate package.

Enter the command **kapptemplate** to start the script. The script starts and you see the first question prompt:

```
$ kapptemplate
KAppTemplate v0.3 (C) 1999 Kurt Granroth <granroth@kde.org>

What is the application's proper name [default: KMyApp]
:
```

Enter the name of the application project that you want to start. These generally begin with a *K*, but don't have to. For example, if my project is to create a Samba server configuration tool, I might name it ksmb.

At the next prompt, enter the version number of the application (the default of 0.1 is a good place to start).

Enter the directory where the source code tree for this new application should be created.

By default this will be a subdirectory under the directory you specified in the installation of KAppTemplate. The subdirectory will be named for the application and version that you entered. For example, the default suggestion for my Samba application would be /usr/src/ksmb-0.1. If you chose to install the KAppTemplate in a location where you can create files, the default option should be fine; press Enter.

Enter your name and email address when each is requested.

A summary displays how the application will be identified and asks you to confirm that this is correct. Choose Y to continue or n to start over.

```
Here is what I have:
The app: ksmb v0.1
Installed in: /usr/src/ksmb-0.1
Author: Nicholas Wells <nwells@xmission.com>

Is this correct (Y/n)?
:
```

When you enter Y, you see a series of over 100 messages scrolling by as KAppTemplate first creates the files for your new application, and then configures, makes, and installs the application.

> If you don't have the KDE development libraries installed, KAppTemplate can't create a new application and you will see an error during the creation process. Review Hour 21 to see what additional software packages your system needs before you can compile KDE applications.

You have just created a new KDE application. To see it run, follow these steps:

1. Change to the source code directory that you specified when you ran KAppTemplate (/usr/src/ksmb-0.1 for my example).

2. The configuration and Makefiles are included in this directory.

3. Change to the subdirectory named after your application (ksmb for my example).

   This directory contains the source code for the application, plus a copy of the executable program after it is compiled (which KAppTemplate has already done for you).

4. Run the application by launching it from the command line:

   ```
   $ ksmb &
   ```

   The application appears, as shown in Figure 23.1.

23

FIGURE 23.1

KAppTemplate creates a complete KDE application that provides a simple framework that you can expand for your own projects.

Your application looks exactly like this one, except for the name in the title bar. This is a simple application template that doesn't do anything yet. But notice what it includes:

- A tear-off toolbar
- A tear-off menu bar
- Quit and Help menus, including several menu items
- About dialog boxes (which include your name and email address)
- Online help links

The online help that appears is included in the template. You can edit it in the doc/en subdirectory of your application source code tree. The .sgml file contains the help file. The en subdirectory is for English. When the documentation is translated, other language directories are added.

Although this might not seem like much, it really is a great help to get you started on a KDE development project. The source code tree is already set up. When you make changes to the source code files provided by KAppTemplate, you simply run make and start the program again to see how they worked. This way you can immediately begin to experiment and learn about KDE development.

Exploring the Source Code Tree

To begin understanding how KDE puts together an application, take a look at the source code tree generated by KAppTemplate. The listing of files for my sample Samba application is shown here:

```
[nwells@sundance ksmb]# ls /usr/src/ksmb-0.1/ksmb/
total 127
Makefile
Makefile.am
```

```
Makefile.in
doc
ksmb
ksmb.cpp
ksmb.h
ksmb.kdelnk
ksmb.moc.cpp
ksmb.moc.o
ksmb.o
ksmb.xpm
ksmbwidget.cpp
ksmbwidget.h
ksmbwidget.moc.cpp
ksmbwidget.moc.o
ksmbwidget.o
main.cpp
main.o
mini-ksmb.xpm
pics
```

23

Before you panic, you should notice right off that several of the files have similar file-names with different file extensions. The source code that you will modify is contained in the `.cpp` files (for C++). The files with the same name but different file extensions are created by the `make` program as part of the compilation process.

The `Makefiles` are part of the configuration process, which you won't have to learn right now. The `.xpm` files and the `pics` directories contain default icons used on the toolbar and to represent your application in KDE windows (such as a kfm window).

To summarize, as you look at the preceding listing, you only need to be concerned at this point with the following files:

- `ksmb.cpp`
- `ksmbwidget.cpp`
- `main.cpp`

> The files that end in `.moc.cpp` are also generated during compilation by the moc tool. The moc is the Meta Object Compiler, part of the Qt graphics toolkit. Do not try to edit the `.moc.cpp` files!

I think you can see the value of KAppTemplate. This is a much more manageable way to start learning about KDE development. In fact, the `main.cpp` and `ksmbwidget.cpp` files are very short. They initialize the application, but you won't need to edit them until you've learned more about KDE programming.

Reviewing the `main` and `widget` Files

The information in the `main.cpp` file is part of every C or C++ program. It contains the top-level starting point for the program, in which window management, command-line parameters, and exiting the application are handled. The `main.cpp` file for my sample ksmb project is shown in the following listing:

```
#include "ksmb.h"
#include <kapp.h>

int main(int argc, char *argv[])
{
        KApplication app(argc, argv, "ksmb");

        // All session management is handled in the RESTORE macro
        if (app.isRestored())
        {
                RESTORE(ksmb)
        }
        else
        {
                ksmb *widget = new ksmb;
                widget->show();
        }

        return app.exec();
}
```

While this entire listing won't make sense right now, notice the following points about it:

- The `include` statements in the first two lines tie together this `main` function with the other functions of the ksmb project. The KAppTemplate generated the `ksmb.h` file. The `kapp.h` file is provided with KDE and is part of all KDE applications.

- The `main()` line includes `argc` and `argv` as parameters. These provide access to any option information that was entered on the command line when the application was started.

- The line containing `KApplication app()` creates a new application based on the information in the `ksmb.h` file. KApplication is a class of object, and `app()` is a function or method defined for that class.

- The rest of the `main.cpp` file displays the main ksmb window and shuts it down when you close it.

If you're interested in reviewing the `kapp.h` file (which comes with KDE), you can open it in the KDE Text editor. The `kapp.h` file is located in `/opt/kde/include`. The majority of this file is comments, so it might prove instructive.

23

The widget file—`ksmbwidget.cpp` in my example—is even shorter than the `main.cpp` file. It defines the main widget for the ksmb application.

Because my application doesn't yet do anything, the widget is basically empty, as shown in this listing. As with the `main.cpp` file, the `ksmbwidget.cpp` file starts with an include file, `ksmbwidget.h`, which was created by KAppTemplate when I started this project.

```
#include "ksmbwidget.h"

ksmbWidget::ksmbWidget(QWidget *parent, const char *name)
        : QWidget(parent, name)
{
}

ksmbWidget::~ksmbWidget()
{
}
```

 You can also review the header files, such as `ksmbwidget.h` and `ksmb.h`, by loading them into the KDE Text editor.

Reviewing the `ksmb.cpp` File

The largest of the `.cpp` files in my example project is `ksmb.cpp`. This file contains 93 lines—too large to print the whole thing here. The following paragraphs describe several parts of the file, however.

The first few lines after the initial comments include header information (functions defined in other locations), which my ksmb application can use:

```
#include "ksmb.h"

#include <qkeycode.h>

#include <kfm.h>
#include <kiconloader.h>
```

Another section of the ksmb.cpp file defines the simple menu structure of this application framework. The listing that follows does the following tasks (don't worry that the exact details aren't clear yet):

```
pupMenu* p = new QPopupMenu;
        p->insertItem(i18n("&Quit"), kapp, SLOT(quit()), CTRL+Key_Q);

        // put our newly created menu into the main menu bar
        menuBar()->insertItem(i18n("&File"), p);
        menuBar()->insertSeparator();
```

- Create a new menu object of the class QPopupMenu
- Add a Quit item to the new menu just created
- Define what to do when this menu item is selected (execute the quit() method)
- Define an accelerator key for this menu item (Ctrl+Q)
- Insert the new Quit menu item on the menu bar in the File menu

A similar section adds a help menu item specific to your application (and to you). The following lines use a standard KDE function to add an About item to the help menu with the text shown here, as taken from my input when I launched KAppTemplate to create the framework for my ksmb project.

```
p = kapp->getHelpMenu(true,
                  i18n("ksmb  — -  Short Description\n\n"
                                  "(c) 1999 Nicholas Wells \n"
                                  "Long Description"));
        menuBar()->insertItem(i18n("&Help"), p);
```

Changing the Source Code

With the application framework in place as generated by KAppTemplate, you can start building your project by adding menu items, dialog boxes, and window elements. Although these tasks are left until Hour 24, you can experiment with a small change to see how the process of adding to the application works.

After you have created a project with KAppTemplate, open the main source code file in a text editor. I'm using the ksmb.cpp file.

Go to the lines described in the previous listing and change the Short Description and Long Description strings so they describe your project. I've changed the lines so that they look like this:

```
p = kapp->getHelpMenu(true,
        i18n("ksmb  — -  Samba Server Tool\n\n"
                "(c) 1999 Nicholas Wells \n"
                "Configuration Utility for the Linux SMB Samba Server"));
        menuBar()->insertItem(i18n("&Help"), p);
```

> If you want to add any comments in the `.cpp` file, start the comment lines with two slashes (`//`).

After you make changes to the source code, you can recompile the application by following these steps:

1. Save the changes that you made to the `ksmb.cpp` file (or the main file for your project).

2. Change back to the parent directory, where the configuration and `Makefiles` are located (`/usr/src/ksmb-0.3` for my project).

3. Run the `make` command (The `configure` command is only needed the first time you use the source code tree on your system or if you make changes to your development environment).

   ```
   $ make
   ```

4. Change back to the application directory.

   ```
   $ cd ksmb
   ```

5. Run the application.

   ```
   $ ksmb &
   ```

6. To see the effect of the changes that you made, choose Help, About ksmb. The dialog box is shown in Figure 23.2.

FIGURE 23.2

Any time you update the source code in your application framework, you can run make *and review the results of your changes.*

Each time you change the source code, run `make` and restart the application. The `make` utility only recompiles the parts that need to be updated.

Summary

In this hour you explored some basic concepts of object-oriented programming and learned how to use the KAppTemplate package to start a new KDE application using a simple framework. You reviewed the source code files and learned how to re-make the source files after changing it. In the next hour, you learn how to add features to your application framework and understand more about the design of KDE applications. You also learn some ways that you can assist in the development of the KDE project itself.

Questions and Answers

Q Why do I see errors when I try to install KAppTemplate?

A Most likely you don't have write permission in the directories where you are trying to install it. Enter subdirectories of your home directory rather than accepting the default directories that KAppTemplate suggests (because these require that you have write permission in areas that might be restricted to root access).

Q I see strange error messages about pre-processor directives when I run `make` after editing the source code files. What do these mean?

A You're probably using the pound sign (#) to indicate comment lines. In C++ you must start a line with two slashes (`//`) or enclose a multiline comment between `/*` and `*/` (see the top of any `.cpp` file for examples). The pound sign (or hash mark) is used to indicate a special directive such as including a header file.

Exercises

1. Review the source code for one of the KDE applications that you downloaded from the Web in Hour 21. (The structure of the source code tree is identical, so you should be able to locate the same types of files as those discussed in this hour. Compare the `main.cpp` and *appnamewidget*`.cpp` files with those generated by the KAppTemplate. Can you determine what some of the differences are for?

2. The source code shows a `quit()` command that will be executed when the File, Quit menu item is selected. In which header (`.h`) file is the `quit()` function defined? (Hint: Look in the `.h` files that are included in the `kapp.h` file.)

3. Add another menu item to the File menu and another menu to the menu bar of your application by building on the source code that is already there. (Use the `quit()` function as the action for any new menu items.)

HOUR 24

Developing for KDE

This hour builds on what you learned about KDE development in Hour 23,
"Getting Started with KDE Development." In this hour you learn more about
the outline or code structure of a simple KDE application, including how to
use simple graphical elements provided by the Qt and KDE libraries.
Starting with the ksmb project introduced in Hour 23, you add functionality
to that application framework.

In addition, you learn in this hour how to find existing KDE application projects with which you can participate, and how to introduce a KDE application that you develop to the larger KDE community.

Reviewing the Libraries

In Hour 23 you used the KAppTemplate script to create a simple application
framework that named ksmb. If you looked at the three source code (.cpp)
files that are described for that example, you can see that KDE programs can
be fairly short.

The secret to writing KDE programs is learning how to use the functions that are already provided by Qt and the KDE libraries. As you'll see in the next section of this hour, "Expanding the Sample Application," adding a menu or dialog box to an application is a trivial task, sometimes requiring only a single line of source code. This is because Qt and KDE libraries provide all the functionality to do these tasks; you define specifics such as the name of the menu item and what it should do.

Of course, it isn't *that* simple to create a KDE application. You still must write methods to complete actions specific to your application, such as loading a certain configuration file, preparing the layout of a dialog box, and so forth.

You also must know C++ programming if you want your KDE application to be more than an exercise. Only well-formed, stable programs can be released for everyone to install and use on KDE. If you don't understand some of the KDE programming tips such as those that follow, you'll need to brush up on C++ before you go much further.

- Use const when possible and avoid dynamic casts
- Declare methods overriding virtual methods as virtual
- Use incomplete declarations
- Don't reduce the visibility of overridden members

Learning about the Qt and KDE libraries will get you on the road to KDE programming fairly quickly.

The best place to start learning about the Qt and KDE libraries is at the KDE Developers' Center, located at `http://developer.kde.org/kdedev/devel/home.html`. This page includes links to the following items:

- Programming tips and guidelines related to C++ and specific to KDE projects
- Reference pages for the Qt and KDE libraries, divided into categories such as user interface, core libraries, kfm (file management), and dialog boxes
- Development tools for interface design, documentation, version portability, and so forth
- Complete documentation for the programming libraries used by KDE projects

Expanding the Sample Application

In the sample application created by KAppTemplate in Hour 23 (ksmb), the application framework consisted of nothing but an empty window, a couple of menu items, and the About dialog box.

In this section you expand that example by adding (and explaining) a few additional lines of source code. Although this is a very simple example, it should put you on the road to exploring on your own and eventually developing full-fledged KDE applications. The length of time it takes to reach that point depends on where you're starting from.

Starting with the ksmb application framework, add the following:

- Options menu to the menu bar
- Settings item on the Options menu
- Message box that appears when Options, Settings is selected

The additional menu and menu items are fairly easy. You can simply duplicate the code for the menu items already in the application framework. Adding a message box requires a little more effort (but only a little).

Throughout this section I refer to the ksmb files. If you've named your sample application something different, substitute your own filenames.

1. Change to the directory containing the source code for your sample application (`/usr/src/ksmb-0.1/ksmb`).

2. Open the `ksmb.cpp` file in a Text editor (such as KEdit).

As you begin to work with program code, it is a good idea to make a backup copy of the original file that you're editing. A single misplaced character (such as a semi-colon) can stop the program from compiling. Unless you're familiar with C++ programming, these errors can be hard to spot and correct.

3. Find the line of source code that looks like this:

```
QPopupMenu* p = new QPopupMenu;
```

With this line of code, you create a new pop-up menu named p. It is based on the class `QpopupMenu`, and is created (instantiated) using the C++ `new` keyword.

4. Now copy that line so you have two of them:

```
QPopupMenu* p = new QPopupMenu;
QPopupMenu* p = new QPopupMenu;
```

5. Change the second of these lines to say p2 instead of p:

```
QPopupMenu* p = new QPopupMenu;
QPopupMenu* p2 = new QPopupMenu;
```

With these two lines, you're creating two new pop-up menus instead of just one. They are named p and p2.

You have to create a pop-up menu before you can add it to the menu bar. The pop-up menu could actually appear in many places, such as when you right-click in your application window. But these pop-up menus will be attached to menus on the menu bar. You'll make this happen next.

1. In the ksmb.cpp file, locate this line of code (it's right after the QPopupMenu lines):

```
p->insertItem(i18n("&Quit"), kapp, SLOT(quit()), CTRL+Key_Q);
```

2. This line inserts a menu item into the pop-up menu named p. This list provides more detail on this line:

   - The insertItem() is a method for the p object (pop-up menu). The insertItem method is defined as part of the QPopupMenu class, so when you create a new object of that class (calling it p), that object has all the methods of that class.

   - The word Quit defines the text on the pop-up menu item. It is enclosed in the i18n function (short for internationalization) to make it available in a separate string file so that it can be easily translated. By enclosing all strings of text in the i18n function, your KDE application can easily be converted to multiple languages (such as French and German, not Pascal and Perl).

   - The ampersand (&) before the Q defines the keyboard shortcut to reach this menu (when the menu is visible, press Q to select this item).

   - The SLOT and quit() functions define what happens when you select the Quit menu item defined in this line. The quit() function is part of the main application definition, which you can find in a library header file if you're persistent. The quit() function gracefully exits our application.

   - Finally, the last parameter of the insertItem method is Ctrl+Key+Q. This defines an accelerator key to access this menu item when the pop-up menu is not visible. Anytime the ksmb window is active, pressing Ctrl+Q will quit the application.

     Now that it all makes a little more sense, you can add an item to the p2 pop-up menu that you created previously.

2. Copy the insertItem line so that you see this:

```
p->insertItem(i18n("&Quit"), kapp, SLOT(quit()), CTRL+Key_Q);
p->insertItem(i18n("&Quit"), kapp, SLOT(quit()), CTRL+Key_Q);
```

3. Edit the second line so that it looks like this:

```
p2->insertItem(i18n("&Settings"), kapp, SLOT(quit()), CTRL+Key_S);
```

Notice that you've changed the following:

- You're inserting an item into p2 instead of p.
- You're naming the menu item Settings instead of Quit (with S instead of Q to access the item)
- You're using Ctrl+S as an accelerator key.

If you use the code line from step 3, choosing the Settings item will still execute the quit() function, which closes the application. You'll change that later.

Now that you have your pop-up menus defined, you can add them to your menu bar. The default KDE window used by this application framework includes a standard menu bar. All you have to do is indicate the name of the menu you want included on it and which pop-up menu object to display when that menu is selected.

24

1. To add the new p2 menu to the menu bar, locate this line of code (still in the ksmb.cpp file):

```
menuBar()->insertItem(i18n("&File"), p);
```

2. Copy it so that you see this:

```
menuBar()->insertItem(i18n("&File"), p);
menuBar()->insertItem(i18n("&File"), p);
```

3. Edit the second line so that it looks like this:

```
menuBar()->insertItem(i18n("&Options"), p2);
```

On the new line of code in step 3:

- You're using the insertItem method of the menuBar object (which was pre-defined for this KDE window).
- You're using Options to name the menu, using the i18n function to allow internationalization.
- You're attaching the p2 pop-up menu object to this part of the menu bar.

Your first round of edits is complete. Follow these steps to see the results:

1. Save the ksmb.cpp file.
2. Change to the configuration directory (up one level, to /usr/src/ksmb-0.1 for ksmb).

```
$ cd ..
```

3. Run make to recompile and reassemble any files that have changed since the last time make was run (the only one changed was ksmb.cpp). Message lines indicate the progress of the make command. You can ignore the warning messages that appear.

   ```
   $ make
   ```

4. Run the application binary created by make (it's located in the source code subdirectory):

   ```
   $ ksmb/ksmb &
   ```

The resulting application, with the new Option menu opened, is shown in Figure 24.1.

FIGURE 24.1

After adding a few lines of code, the application framework includes an Options menu with a Settings menu item.

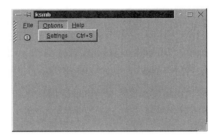

You can easily test that choosing Options, Settings closes the application.

The KDE menu bar includes a Help menu automatically, so you won't see a line to insert that menu. You still have to write the help text yourself, however!

Next you will add a dialog box, so that choosing Options, Settings displays a message to the user. You don't have to add much code to perform this function, but it does start to get more complicated to understand what's happening.

To make the message box appear when you choose Options, Settings, you must do four things:

- Create a method that displays the message box
- Add a reference to the library that handles message boxes
- Add the method to the header file so the application knows about it
- Tell the menu bar to call that method when Options, Settings is selected

First, you'll create the method to display the message box.

1. Open the `ksmb.cpp` file again and go to the end of the file.

2. Insert the following four lines at the bottom of the file:
```
void ksmb::in_progress()
{
KMsgBox::message(this,i18n("Sorry"),i18n("This function is not yet
➥operational"));
}
```

This code defines a new method within the ksmb application object. The name of the method is `in_progress`. The method only does one thing: It calls the message method from `KMsgBox`, providing it with the text to display.

> Notice that I've enclosed the strings within `i18n()` so they can be easily translated when my application goes international.

24

To make the message method of `KMsgBox` available, you must indicate where to find it. Follow these steps:

1. Go to the top of the `ksmb.cpp` file, to where you see these line:
```
#include <kfm.h>
#include <kiconloader.h>
```

2. Copy the bottom line so that you see
```
#include <kfm.h>
#include <kiconloader.h>
#include <kiconloader.h>
```

3. Edit the last line of the three to read like this:
```
#include <kmsgbox.h>
```

   Now the `ksmb` object can access the functionality of `KMsgBox`.

Next you must include your new method, `in_progress`, in the header file for ksmb itself. The header file provides preliminary information for the compiler and linker, so that all the various components can be correctly located.

1. Open the `ksmb.h` file in a Text editor.

2. Find the *public slots* section, with this line:
```
void slotDropEvent(KDNDDropZone *);
```

Slots are actions that can be called when something happens in the program. You need to add the name of your method so that it can be found when you want it to go to work.

3. Add the new `in_progress` method to the list of public slots.

4. The two public slots now look like this:

```
void slotDropEvent(KDNDDropZone *);
void in_progress();
```

5. Save and exit the `ksmb.h` file.

The last thing to do is indicate that the Options, Setting menu item should use the `in_progress` method you've defined.

1. Open the `ksmb.cpp` file again.

> These tasks can be done in any order, so long as they are all in place before using the `make` command to recompile the program. I'm following this order to better explain the reasons for each edit.

2. Go to the line that you added for the Settings menu item:

```
p2->insertItem(i18n("&Settings"), kapp, SLOT(quit()), CTRL+Key_S);
```

As you saw when you ran the edited program previously, this line made the Settings option use the `quit()` method to exit the program. Notice the `kapp` before `SLOT`. This defines where the `quit()` method is found.

To make the Settings item use a different method (do something different when selected), you must indicate a new method and where to find it (as part of which object).

You're working in the `ksmb` object (though you might not have noticed). So the new `in_progress` method that you defined is part of that object. Rather than name it, however, C++ provides a way to refer to whatever object you're working in. To do so, use the keyword `this`.

3. Edit the preceding line to look like the following line of code, changing `kpp` to `this`, and `quit()` to `in_progress()`:

```
p2->insertItem(i18n("&Settings"), this, SLOT(in_progress()),
CTRL+Key_S);
```

Now you're ready to check your work.

1. Save and exit the `ksmb.cpp` file.

2. Change back to the configuration directory.

   ```
   $ cd ..
   ```

3. Run make to recompile the changed source code.

   ```
   $ make
   ```

4. Change back to the source code directory:

   ```
   $ cd ksmb
   ```

5. Run the new version of the program:

   ```
   $ ksmb &
   ```

When you choose Options, Settings, the message box that you defined is displayed (see Figure 24.2). Choose OK to close the message box. Use File, Quit to close the program.

FIGURE 24.2

After adding the in-progress *method, the Settings item opens a message box with the text you included in your source code.*

24

The additions that you've made are simple—perhaps tedious if you already know how to program. But you should have a feeling for how easy it can be to create completed applications in KDE. With libraries to handle all the details, you can focus on the goal of your project instead of how to draw menus, load files, and so forth.

If you're curious, the final size of the ksmb program (as a single dynamically linked binary) was about 27KB. The libraries that are referenced in the source code use many times that amount when the program is executed, however.

Use the resources mentioned in the next section to continue learning about KDE development.

Learning More About KDE Programming

I hope you're now eager to go beyond these simple exercises and learn how you can develop your own KDE projects or contribute to existing projects.

Starting from the KDE Developer Web page at `http://developer.kde.org`, you can access tools and information for KDE developers.

Table 24.1 lists scripting tools available to access KDE functionality from several scripting languages (including shell scripts). The majority of these are for the Python scripting language, because KDE is based on C++, and Python is an object-oriented scripting language.

TABLE 24.1 SCRIPTING LANGUAGE SUPPORT TOOLS FOR KDE

Tool	Description	URL
Kfm client	A command-line utility to access kfm functions (for file and Web site access) from within a shell script.	`http://developer.kde.org/kfmclient.html`
PerlQt	A Perl-language interface to Qt, including creation of new Qt widgets from Perl calls.	`http://www.accessone.com/~jql/perlqt.html`
Qt/KDE Python binding	A package to allow overloading of virtual functions by Python scripts.	`http://www.river-bank.demon.co.uk/software/`
KDE Python bindings	Another package to allow binding between Python scripts and KDE libraries.	`ftp://ftp.kde.org/pub/kde/devel/kde-bindings`
Python Qt	Yet another python binding for Qt, including support for slots and signals.	`ftp://ftp.kde.org/pub/kde/devel/qt-bindings/`
KtK	A Tcl/Tk package for developing KDE-compliantapplications with newKDE-style Tk widgets.	`http://www.city.ac.uk/~sa346/Ktk.html`

Because Qt is the graphical foundation of KDE, several tools and additional widgets (graphical objects) are available to help you create your graphical interface or better utilize the existing Qt libraries. Table 24.2 shows tools available to assist in using Qt for graphical development.

TABLE 24.2 GRAPHICAL TOOLS FOR QT DEVELOPMENT

Tool	Description	URL
Xml-builder	A utility to allow Qt to be manipulated by XML (for the GUI) and Python (for the logic).	`http://www.didx.com/xml-builder.html`
QwSprite Field	A sprite library for Qt (used by KAsteroids)	`http://trolls.troll.no/warwick/QwSpriteField/`
QdbTabular widget	A powerful table widget (resizable columns, etc.) that can be used in any KDE application.	`http://www.stack.nl/~dimitri/qdbttabular/index.html`
Qt Architect	A Qt dialog box builder(with geometry management for localized applications).	`http://www.primenet.Cqtarch/`
XSpriteWorld++	A collection of Qt sprite-handling classes.	`http://home.earthlink.net/~trickys/XSW++/`
QtC	A C binding for Qt, so that C programs can use Qt (including support for slots and signals).	`ftp://ftp.kde.org/pub/kde/devel/qt-bindings/`

24

Although KDE doesn't have a true Integrated Development Environment like the Microsoft Visual development suite, it is getting more tools all the time to help you easily create a KDE project. Table 24.3 describes some of the developer tools that are available to assist in creating a KDE project.

TABLE 24.3 KDE PROJECT DEVELOPMENT TOOLS

Tool	Description	URL
KDevelop	An IDE for KDE, with a wizard-like project builder.	`http://samuel.cs.uni-potsdam.de/` `~smeier/kdevelop_new/index.html`
KBuilder	An IDE and GUI builder for KDE.	`http://www.bitgate.com/ftp/kbuilder/`
KTableView	A resizable table widget for KDE (similar in function to QdbTabular listed in Table 24.2).	`http://www.orion.co.nz/paul/`
KDE SDK	The KDE Software Development Kit (at this point, basically the current source tree of KDE with a few compilation tools, but useful to review).	`ftp://ftp.kde.org/pub/kde/unstable/` `CVS/snapshots/current/`
KDE Dialog Definition Language	An HTML-like dialog definition language for rapid dialog box development	`http://manatee.cs.man.ac.uk/~moorer/` `kde/download/kddl-0.2.tar.gz`

If you're already getting comfortable with the idea of working on a KDE project, you might be interested in some of the advanced development tools and projects described in Table 24.4. Some of these are only in the initial stages of progress (so you might be able to participate in moving them forward).

TABLE 24.4 ADVANCED PROJECTS AND TOOLS FOR KDE

Tool or Project	Description	URL
OpenParts	An object-based system for KDE, similar to OLE for MS Windows, allowinguser-created dataobjects (such as documents or spreadsheets) to be shared between KDE applications.	`http://developer.kde.org/openparts/html` `/openparts.html`

Tool or Project	Description	URL
MICO ORB	An Object Request Broker that is available under the GPL (OpenSource license) and is being considered as the KDE ORB.	`http://diamant-atm.vsb.cs.uni-frankfurt.de/~mico/`
Java-Linux porting project	A project to tie together Linux and Java.	`http://www.blackdown.org/java-linux.html`
Kaffe and KDE	Kaffe is a JIT compiler; some are considering integrating it with KDE's kfm.	`http://www.kaffe.org/`
KDE Foundation Classes and dynamic loading	A library for threading	`http://ace.ulyssis.student.kuleuven.ac.be/~bavo/kfc/`

24

Summary

In this hour you learned additional information about KDE development, including tools and learning resources that are available to help you proceed with your own development projects or assist other projects currently underway. You also learned more about the actual workings of a KDE application by expanding the sample project that was started in Hour 23.

Questions and Answers

Q I already know how to program in C. Will that be much help for KDE development?

A Yes and no. C++ includes many new concepts and some new syntax to support the implementation of those concepts. If you already know how to program, however, learning enough C++ to start understanding other KDE programs and writing your own shouldn't be hard at all, provided you can make a few conceptual leaps of faith to get you started.

Q **I'm a beginner at all this. Are there other online resources for learning step by step about KDE programming?**

A Yes. Visit the KDE developer Web site at `developer.kde.org`. A collection of tutorials is referenced on that page. Each one (provided by different individuals) walks you through a simple application to teach more about how to construct an application.

Q **Will the exercise in this hour really help me understand any real KDE applications?**

A It should. This hour only covers very few items as an introduction for non-programmers. Still, if you review the source code tree for any of the KDE applications that you download, you'll find a similar set of files that contain lines of code nearly identical to those explained here.

Exercises

1. Using the tutorials on the KDE Web site or a review of the libraries or library documentation, create a dialog box that doesn't use the KMsgBox::message method. Add a button or other widgets to the dialog box.

2. What is the difference between public and private slots in the header file? Why use one over the other?

Congratulations

Congratulations! You've learned KDE in 24 hours! You understand not only what KDE has to offer as a graphical environment and how to use its key utilities and features, but also a little about how it all works behind the scenes. You're ready to make KDE your primary Linux environment. With KDE, you might even be making Linux your primary working environment.

INDEX

Symbols

& (ampersand), 292
3D editor, 233, 312

A

Abalone game, 368
Acceleration slider, 197
accelerator keys, 303
access
applications, 15
help system, 9, 79
Panel, 76
virtual terminals, 293
accounts, *see* **user accounts**
activating
desktop borders, 121-122
windows, 82, 105
adding
address book entries, 336
bookmarks, 164

buttons to titlebar, 106
calendar appointments,
346
desktops, 98-99
icons, 61
items
to Autostart folder, 182
to main menu, 187
ksysv utility services, 210
MIME types, 398-399
non-KDE applications,
394-397, 402
text editors, 325
user accounts, 212
address book entries (kab
program), 233
adding, 336
browsing, 339
deleting, 338
editing, 338
exporting, 339
extracting, 353
fields, 336-338
KMail, 280, 339
launching, 335

printing, 339
saving, 336, 338
searching, 339
administration utilities, 14,
26, 375
advanced searches, 203-205
alarm
KOrganizer, 346-347
KNotes utility, 232
ampersand (&), 292
angles, kcalc utility, 228
applications
access, 15
automation, 245
character-based, 387
commercial, 374
copying, 377
creating, 18
Desktop, 91-92, 394
development, 374
frameworks, 9
icons, 403
integration, 10, 386-387,
402
kfm, 159-163

link files, 176, 178, 386, 388-393
Linux, 11
listing, 73-74
non-KDE, 402
  command lines, 388
  configuration, 387
  formats, 389-390
  location, 388
  logout, 42
  main menu, 395-396
  MIME types, 398-401
  Panel, 397
  Personal menu, 395-396
platforms, 377
stable, 374-377
starting, 209
unstable, 374-377
Web sites, 374
applink subdirectory (.kde directory), 59-61
applying windows configuration, 106
appointments in KOrganizer (calendar)
adding, 346
alarm, 347
editing, 347
managing, 345-348
apps subdirectory (.kde directory), 58-59
arcade games
Asteroids, 365
Smiletris, 366
Snake Race, 367
Tetris game, 366
archived files, 202
ark utility
  compression format, 221
  files, 222-226, 235
  starting, 222
command lines, 234-235
configuration, 138-139
displaying, 222-226

exiting, 222
extracting, 222-225
opening, 222
permissions, 225
source code trees, 377, 379
uncompressed, 138
untar, 138
arrow keys, 83, 318
Asteroids game, 365-366
attachments in email, 278, 280-282
audio, *see* **sound files**
authentication, kppp utility, 245
automating
source code, 378
startup applications, 245
windows, 106
Autostart folder, 75
applications
  integration, 387
  starting, 209
contents, 182
.directory file, 64
drag-and-drop option, 182
items, 182
link files, 181-183

B

backgrounds
CD Player, 362
desktops, 75, 110-113, 121
icon color, 128
manager, 14
kdm, 47, 49-50
Panel themes, 134
xdm format, 47
backups
kdisplayrc file, 149
kwmrc file, 144, 149
themes, 149

backward/forward buttons in CD Player, 363
bash shell (Bourne Again SHell), 289-290
bell sound files, 129-130
bin subdirectory (.kde directory), 29, 61
binary program
directory, 25
executing, 381-382
GNOME Project, 17
installation, 377, 381-382
KDE Project, 17
bmp graphics format, 302, 306-307
bold attribute for fonts, 127
bookmarks for Web sites, 164
boot subdirectory (.kde directory), 61
borders
active desktops, 121-122
Magic Borders, 122
themes, 134, 148
Bourne Again SHell (bash shell), 289-290
browsing
address book entries, 339
files, 15
kfm options, 170-171
BRU utility, 386
burn-in, 117
buttons
desktops, 78
help system, 80
taskbars, 72
themes, 148
title bar, 100-101, 106

C

C++ programming language, 431

cache files in kfm, 168-170
calculator (kcalc utility)
 angles, 228
 clearing, 228
 Clipboard, 228
 displaying, 227
 errors, 229
 Euler number, 228
 fonts, 229
 help, online, 228
 Hex calculations, 228
 memory, 228
 numeric base, 227
 opening, 227
 Pi, 228
 Reverse Polish Notation
  (RPN), 228
 starting, 227
Caldera OpenLinux, *see*
OpenLinux
calendar (KOrganizer)
 appointments
  adding, 346
  alarm, 346-347
  editing, 347
  managing, 345-348
 configuration, 349-350
 KNotes utility, 233
 saving, 345
 starting, 340
 To-do task list, 342-344
 view options, 341
 window, 341
canceling drag-and-drop
 operation, 183
carriage return (CR)
character, 266
cat command, 332
CD Player (kscd)
 background, 362
 backward/forward buttons,
  363
 CDDB, 357-361
 defaults, 361
 display screen, 357
 docking, 362

 ejecting, 362, 364
 email, 361-362
 help, 361
 icons, 362
 information, 363
 Loop mode, 363
 option, 172
 play/pause, 362-363
 random play, 364
 screen, 362
 sound, 370
 starting, 356-357
 ToolTips, 362
 updating, 361
 volume, 363
 Web access, 362
centered wallpaper, 51, 113
cgi-bin subdirectory, 29
cgm format, 399
character-based
 applications, 387
characters
 screen, 290, 293
 symbols, 267
chat programs (KIRC), 234
Circle drawing tool (KPaint
 utility), 309
classes, 408
clearing
 desktops, 98
 kcalc utility, 228
Clipboard
 copying, 292
 kcalc utility, 228
 KDE, 298
 KEdit files, 321
 X Window System, 298
closing
 kppp utility, 251
 windows, 81-82, 84
color
 creating, 132
 desktops, 110-113
 editing, 132
 graphics, 308-310
 icons, 128

 KEdit, 322
 KNotes utility, 233
 kvt utility, 294-295
 palettes, 313
 schemes, 115-117
 themes, 134, 144-145
 windows, 199
column headings, 211
command lines
 files, 234-235
 keyboard shortcut
  (Alt+F2), 84
 non-KDE applications,
  388
commands
 bash shell, 290
 executing, 292-293
 installation sequence, 27
 multitasking, 292
 see also specific
  commands
comments, KAppTemplate
 projects, 417
commercial applications,
 374
communication utilities, 375
Compact Disc Database
 (CDDB), 357-3
comparing GNOME with
 KDE, 17-18
compiling
 Kaffe, 431
 source code, 377-378,
  380-381
compression
 ark archival utility, 221
 email folders, 278
config subdirectory (.kde
 directory), 57-58
configuration
 CD Player
  background, 362
  backward/forward, 363
  CDDB, 360-361
  defaults, 361
  docking, 362

ejecting, 362, 364
email, 361-362
help, 361
icons, 362
Loop mode, 363
play/pause, 362-363
random play, 364
screen, 362
stopping, 362-363
ToolTips, 362
updating, 361
volume, 363
Web access, 362
desktops
background, 110-113
icons, 127-128
Disk Navigator menu, 173
drag-and-drop option, 173
DVI Viewer, 331
editing, 58
empty, 58
Ethernet, 239
files, 68
FTP servers, 171
graphical logins, 43
HTML, 171
HTTP, 171
international languages,
122-125
K-LJet utility, 262-263
kcalc utility, 229
KDE, 35, 47-48, 51, 87
KEdit
color, 322
email, 323-324
fonts, 322
indenting, 323
options, 322
page width, 323
status bar, 322
text wrap, 323
tool bar, 322
keyboard, 196-199
kfm
browser options,
170-172
cache files, 168-170

KMail, 270-274, 276
KOrganizer, 348-350
kppp utility
authentication, 245
automatic startup, 245
closing, 251
connections, 244, 248
costs, 247-248
data volume, 248
disconnecting, 251
DNS servers, 245
gateways, 245
IP address, 245
login scripts, 246
minimizing, 251
modems, 248-251
name resolution, 245
new accounts, 243
passwords, 245
phone number, 244
pppd arguments, 245
redialing, 251
kvt utility, 293
background, 296
color, 294-295
cursor key, 297
fonts, 295-296
keyboard input, 296
scrollbars, 296
sizing, 296
Linux, 44
lisa utility, 239
menus, 97, 100, 129, 296
mouse, 196-198
newsgroups, 283-284
non-KDE applications,
387
Panel, 94, 96-98, 107, 190
printers, 258
proxy servers, 171
Red Hat Linux, 239
Samba, 252
screensavers, 117-120
scripts, 380
sound files, 129-131
source code trees, 377
taskbar, 94, 96-98

themes, 134
archive files, 138-139
options, 151
updating, 141-144
title bars, 101-103
utilities, 378, 386
Web sites, 171
widgets, 128
windows, 89-90, 103
applying, 106
properties, 104
YAST utility, 239
see also Control Center
connections
Internet, 269
kppp utility, 244
PPP, 242
serial, 290
speed, 248
terminal, 290
const command, 420
Control Center, 14, 77
device types, 215
DMA Channels, 216
IO ports, 216
IRQ interrupts, 216
memory, 217
menus, 81-82
microprocessor, 218
PCI slots, 218
system information,
215-219
themes, 144-145
X servers, 219
see also configuration
converting xdm to kdm,
45-46
copying
applications, 377
KEdit text files, 321
KMail, 279
text to Clipboard, 292
core desktop, 9
costs, kppp utility, 247-248
cpp files
ksmb, 415-416
ksmbwidget, 415
main, 414-415

CR (carriage return)
  character, 266
creating
    applications, 18, 176, 178
    color schemes, 132
    email folders, 277
    graphics, 309-310
    KMail, 279-282
    KNotes utility, 231
    kppp utility, 243
    link files, 191, 403
        devices, 178-181
        files, 176, 185
        floppy drives, 179-181
    MIME types, 399-401
    non-KDE applications,
        390-393
    printcap files, 268
    themes, 135, 140, 150-151
    user accounts, 214
CRiSP, 386
cropping graphics, 303
cross-platform games, 370
csh shell, 289
cursor key, 297
cutting graphics, 311

D

daemons, 198
    pppd, 242, 245
    print jobs, 258
data volume, 248
databases
    accessories, 375
    clients, 386
date, KNotes utility, 233
Debian system, 24
declaring methods, 420
default
    KDE startup, 28-29, 36
    KEdit options, 332
    window manager, 36
    Xclients file, 28

defaults, CD Player, 361
defining
    menus, 186
    printers, 262
    Time Tracker, 350-351
deleting
    address book entries, 338
    bookmarks, 164
    desktops, 98
    files, 66, 68, 203
    icons, 189
    KEdit text files, 321
    kfm cache files, 170
    KMail, 274, 278
    KNotes utility notes, 232
    ksysv utility services, 210
    Time Tracker, 351
density
    graphics
    printing, 265
description strings,
    KAppTemplate, 416
Desktop, 74
    active borders, 121-122
    adding, 98-99
    applications, 91
        integration, 387
        positioning, 92
    Autostart folder, 64
    background, 75, 110-113,
        121
    buttons, 78
    clearing, 98
    color scheme, 115-117
    deleting, 98
    dialog, 9
    directory, 63
    displaying, 85
    drag-and-drop protocol, 9
    files, 63
    icons, 67, 75, 127-128,
        183-186
    labels, 99
    KNotes utility, 232
    Magic Borders, 122
    multiple, 85, 120

naming, 85
networks, 10
non-KDE applications,
    394
root grid spacing, 127
templates, 65-66, 75
text, 128
toggling, 84-85, 87
Trash, 66, 75
updating, 10
wallpaper, 51, 113-114,
    305
windows
    positioning, 120
    snap to grid, 122
dev subdirectory (.kde
    directory), 61
developers
    applications, 374
    KDE Project, 16
    Web sites, 409, 432
development libraries
    kdelibs-devel, 379
    kdesupport-devel, 379
    libg++-devel, 378
    qt-devel-1_4_2, 379
    XFree86-devel, 379
development tools
    KBuilder, 430
    KDE SKD, 430
    KDevelop, 430
    KTableView, 430
    MICO ORB, 431
    OpenParts, 430
    Web sites, 430
devices
    links, 178-181
    types, 215, 218
dialog boxes, 408
directories
    .kde
        applink subdirectory,
            59-61
        apps subdirectory,
            58-59
        bin subdirectory, 61

boot subdirectory, 61
config subdirectory,
57-58
dev subdirectory, 61
icons subdirectory, 61
mimelnk subdirectory,
62-63
share/subdirectory,
56-57
Desktop, 63
Disk Navigator, 155
graphic files, 158
hidden files, 167
home
displaying, 76
user accounts, 213
main menu, 187
split windows, 167
themes, 140
viewing, 153
.directory file 64
disabling pop-up hints, 96
**disconnecting kppp utility,
251**
Disk Navigator
CD-ROM option, 172-173
directories, 155
files, 154
displaying
Autostart folder contents,
182
CD Player, 357
desktops
applications, 91
multiple, 85
wallpaper, 305
device types, 215
DMA Channels, 216
files, 222-225
graphics
flipping, 304
full screen, 303, 305
multiple, 298
rotating, 304
zooming, 304
home directory, 76
IO ports, 216

IRQ interrupts, 216
kcalc utility, 227
kfm cache files, 170
memory, 217
menu items, 125
microprocessor, 218
Panel, 76
PCI slots, 218
rpm packages, 205
system information,
215-219
taskbar, 73
Trash folder, 66
user accounts, 213
windows, 104
X servers, 219
DLD-5.4, 24
DMA Channels, 216
**DNS servers, kppp utility,
245**
docking CD Player, 362
**documentation of KDE
Project, 19**
**domain name services, ping
utility, 240**
downloading
commercial applications,
374
files, 25-26, 30-31
games, 26
graphics, 26
ksysv utility, 219
kuser utility, 219
libraries, 26
Linux applications, 11
multimedia, 26
newsgroup messages, 285
software, 11
StarOffice, 374
themes, 137-138
DR DOS, 386
drag-and-drop option, 9
Autostart folder, 182
canceling, 183
configuration, 173
graphics, 302
icons, 189
kfm, 163

**drawing tools, KPaint
utility, 309-310**
DVI Viewer, 330-331
**dynamic linking/loading,
409, 420, 431**

E

editing
address book entries, 338
bookmarks, 164
color schemes, 132
configuration files, 58
email folders, 277
fonts, 48-49
General font, 126
graphics, 313
icons, 312
initialization processes,
207
keys, 332
KOrganizer appointments,
347
ksysv utility, 210
KView utility, 303
kwmrc file, 141-144
menus, 186-189
Panel, 189-191
pppd arguments, 245
source code, 416-417
themes, 151
title bars, 100-101
Trash icon, 191
user accounts, 212, 214
ejecting
CD Player, 362, 364
printing, 266
**Ellipse drawing tool
(KPaint utility), 309**
elm utility, 270
email
CD Player, 361-362
KEdit, 332
configuration, 323-324
text files, 320

KMail
    accounts, 270, 274
    Address Book, 280
    attachments, 278,
      280-282
    configuration, 270-274,
      276
    copying, 279
    creating, 279-282
    deleting, 274, 278
    filters, 278
    folders, 277
    fonts, 274-276
    forwarding, 276, 278
    headers, 280
    host server, 274
    incoming, 273
    Local Mailbox, 273
    new, 274
    passwords, 274
    PGP security, 282
    POP3, 273
    port number, 274
    printing, 279-280
    process and delivery,
      272
    reading, 270, 277-282
    replying, 270, 278
    retrieving, 276
    saving, 279
    sending, 272, 280
    signature, 271, 276
    SMTP, 272
    spam, 270
    storing, 273
    username, 274
    KNotes utility notes, 233
    undeliverable messages,
      288
emulation, terminals, 15
enabling K-LJet utility
  options, 268
End key, 318
End of Line mode, 265-266

energy-saving monitors, 117
entries in address books
    adding, 336
    browsing, 339
    deleting, 338
    editing, 338
    email, 339
    exporting, 339
    fields, 336-338
    printing, 339
    saving, 336, 338
    searching, 339
environment variables,
  functions of, 67
eps graphics format, 302
errors
    configure script, 380
    KAppTemplate, 418
    kcalc utility, 229
    pre-processor directives,
      418
    X includes, 383
Ethernet
    cards, 238
    Internet connection, 269
    kernel modules, 239
    ping utility, 239
      domain name services,
        240
      ifconfig command, 240
      route command,
        241-242
Ettrich, Matthias, 8
Euler number, 228
event sound files, 130-131
executing
    binary program, 381-382
    commands, 292-293
exiting archived files, 222
exporting address book
  entries, 339
extensions, files, 62
extracting
    address book entries, 353
    archived files, 222-225

F

fax-g3 format, 399
faxes, KFax tool, 352-353
FDDI, 238
feeding paper, 264
fields, address book entries,
  336-338
file manager utility (kfm),
  15
    applications
      defining, 159-163
      launching, 159-162
      MIME, 158, 162-163
    bookmarks, 164
    browser options, 170-172
    cache files, 168-170
    client portion, 154, 428
    directories, 153
    drag-and-drop option, 163
    files, 157-158
    icons, 157
    KNotes utility, 230-231
    location bars, 156
    objects, 165, 167-168
    opening, 156
    server portion, 154
    windows
      opening, 154, 157
      printing, 157
File menu, 85
files
    .Xsession, 45
    archiving, 202, 226
      command lines,
        234-235
      permissions, 225
    Autostart folder, 182
    browsing, 15
    compression, 58, 234-235
    deleting, 66, 68, 203
    Desktop directory, 63
    downloading, 25, 30-31
    DVI, 330-331
    editing, 58
    extensions, 62

finding, 200-205
gzipped tarball, 137
hidden, 128, 167
installation, 26
    location, 30, 67-68
    reviewing, 29
    subdirectories, 29
kfm, 157-158
links, 182, 176, 185
listing, 68
opening, 203
PostScript, 325-330
printcap, 258, 261-262, 268
printing, 258
README, 139-140
Samba, 254
selecting, 201
sharing, 252
sound, 129-131
starting, 181-183
TeX, 330
themes, 141-144
ugrading, 53
viewing, 153-154, 167, 332
filters
KMail, 278
print jobs, 258
finding, 14
files, 200-205
themes, 135-136
firewalls, 270
Fixed font, 125
flipping graphics, 304
floppy disks, 234
floppy drives, 179-181
focusing windows, 105-106
folders, KMail, 277
fonts
bold, 127
characters/symbols, 267
General, 126
italic, 127
kcalc utility, 229
KDE Base, 48-49

KEdit, 322
KMail, 274-276
KNotes utility notes, 233
kvt utility, 295-296
managing, 15
menu items, 125
non-KDE applications, 129
Panel clock, 125
printing
    End of Line mode, 265
    K-LJet utility, 266
    page description languages, 267
selecting, 267
sizing, 267
foreground color, 128
formats
faxes, 352-353
floppy disks, 234
graphics, 301-302, 307, 313
MIME types, 399
non-KDE applications, 389-390
forwarding KMail, 276, 278
fractal programs, 312
frameworks, compound, 9
Free Qt Foundation, 12
freecell game, 370
freezing terminal windows, 292
FTP site
applications
    downloading, 375
    stable/unstable, 375-377
distribution, 11
mirror sites, 23-24
servers, 171
full-screen graphics, 303, 305
function plotting, 312

G

games, 375
Abalone, 368
arcade, 365
Asteroids, 365-366
cross-platform, 370
downloading, 26
freecell, 370
KBlackBox, 368
kblackjack, 370
KDE Project, 14
kgo, 370
Konquest, 368
krossword, 370
krubik, 370
Mahjongg, 369
networked, 371
Patience, 369
Poker, 369
qchess, 370
Reversi, 369
Same Game, 370
Shisen-Sho, 370
Smiletris, 366
Snake Race, 367
Sokoban, 370
Tetris, 366
gateways, kppp utility, 245
gcc to egcs HOWTO document, 27
General font, 125-126
generic Linux, 24
gif graphics format, 302, 307, 399
GIMP (graphics program), 311, 386
GNOME (GNU Network Object Model Environment)
binary code, 17
distribution, 17
graphic user interface (GUI), 17
GTK+ toolkit, 17

KDE Project, 17-18
libraries, 18
office suites, 17
source code, 17
versions, 18
web site, 17
Window Manager, 18
working groups, 17
goals of KDE Project, 9-11
graphical libraries, *see*
libraries
graphics
accelerator keys, 303
aspect ratio, 304
bitmapped, 306-307
color, 308-310
creating, 309-310
cropping, 303
cutting, 311
desktop wallpaper, 305
directories, 158
downloading, 26
drawing tools, 309
editing, 313
faxes, 352
flipping, 304
formats, 301-302, 307,
  313
full screen, 303, 305
icons, 302
KDE Project, 14
listing, 305
loading, 307
logins, 43
MIME, 399
multiple, 298, 305, 312
naming, 308
pasting, 311
pre-alpha code, 311
printing, 266
resetting, 303
rotating, 304
screen captures, 312
shuffling, 305
sizing, 308
slideshows, 305

startup, 28-29
themes, 134, 140-141
tools, 10, 375
user interface (GUI)
  GNOME Project, 17
  KDE Project, 9, 17
  Linux, 8
  Macintosh, 9
  UNIX, 8
  Windows, 9
  viewing, 302
  zooming, 304, 308
groups, user accounts
creating, 214
displaying, 213
editing, 214
IDs (GIDs), 254
membership, 214
primary, 213
saving, 214
GTK+ Toolkit, 17
gzip command, 137

H

Harmony project, 12
headers
KMail, 280
user accounts, 211
help system
accessibility, 9
browser, 14
buttons, 80
CD Player, 361
KAppTemplate, 412
kcalc utility, 228
K-LJet utility, 266
online, 10
  access, 79
  keyboard shortcut (F1),
    83
pop-up, 79

Hewlett-Packard printers,
  K-LJet utility, 263
Hex editor utility, 228, 233
hidden files
icons, 128
listing, 68
viewing, 167
hiding
Panel, 76, 98, 191
taskbar, 74, 98
history
GNOME Project, 17
KDE Project, 8
home directories
displaying, 76
user accounts, 56, 213
Home key, 318
host server, KMail, 274
hostnames, Samba, 254
hotlist (bookmarks), 164
HTML, 171
HTTP, 171
HylaFAX package, 352

I

icons, 312
adding, 61
applications, 403
CD Player, 362
color, 128
Desktop, 67, 75, 127-128
drag-and-drop option, 189
editing, 312
graphics, 302
hidden files, 128
kfm, 163, 157
MIME types, 401
minimizing, 82
objects, 165-166
Panel, 76, 189-191
positioning, 183-186
replacing, 61
selecting, 157

standard, 62
subdirectory (.kde
    directory), 61
themes, 134
trashing, 157
ifconfig command, 240
ilbm graphics format, 302
image files, *see* **graphics**
include subdirectory, 29
incoming KMail, 273-274
indenting lines, 323
inetd configuration file, 252
information, CD Player, 363
inheritance, object-oriented
    programming, 408
initialization processes
    editing, 207
    ksysv utility, 220
        available servers, 209
        deleting services, 210
        Run level, 208, 210
        scripts, 208, 211
        services, 208, 210
        starting, 209
        Trash can, 209
    login, 207
    xdm, 43-44
initializing printers, 266
inserting KEdit text files,
    321
installation
    binary files, 377, 381-382
    command sequence, 27
    files
        directory location, 67
        downloading, 25-26
        location, 30
        reviewing, 29
        subdiretories, 29
    KAppTemplate, 409-410,
        418
    KDE, 67-68
    kdelibs-devel, 379
    kdesupport-devel, 379
    kpackage utility, 205
    libg++-devel, 378

Linux, 23, 30
non-Linux, 24
print servers, 259
qt-devel-1_4_2, 379
Red Hat 5.0, 27
root login, 27
scripts, 134-135, 148-149
source code trees, 379
StarOffice 5.0, 59
themes, 138, 151
    archive files, 138-139
    configuration files,
        141-144
    Control Center,
        144-146
    directories, 140
    graphics files, 140-141
    README file,
        139-140
    restarting, 147-148
    scripts, 148-150
    XFree86-devel, 379
    see also uninstallation
integration of applications,
    10, 386-387, 402
international languages
    configuration, 122-125
    KDE Project, 13
    keyboards, 198-199
    platforms, 10
    working groups, 17
Internet
    connections, 269
    newsgroups, 282-283
    security firewalls, 270
interrupts, 216
in_progress method (ksmb
    application), 426
IO ports, 216
IP (Internet Protocol), 238,
    245
IPX, 238
Irix, 8
IRQ interrupts, 216

ISDN connections, 252
ISPs
    connection software, 387
    newsgroups, 287
    PPP scripts, 254
italic attribute for fonts, 127
items in Autostart folder,
    182

J

Java-Linux porting project,
    431
jpeg graphics format, 302,
    307, 399

K

K menu, 78, 84
K-LJet utility
    characters/symbols, 267
    configuration, 262
    End of Line mode, 265
    fonts, 266-267
    graphics, 265
    help, 266
    options, 268
    pages
        description languages,
            267
        protection option, 266
    paper, 263-264
    Powersave mode, 266
    printers
        Hewlett-Packard, 263
        initializing, 266
        page eject, 266
        resetting, 266
        resolution, 264-265
        selecting, 265

k3de utility, 312

kab program (address book entries), 233
    adding, 336
    browsing, 339
    deleting, 338
    editing, 338
    email, 280, 339
    exporting, 339
    extracting 353
    fields, 336-338
    launching, 335
    printing, 339
    saving, 336-338
    searching, 339

Kaffe compiler, 431

KAppTemplate
    error messages, 418
    kapp.h file, 415
    installation, 409-410
    projects, 416-417
    running, 410-412
    source code
        editing, 416-417
        ksmb.cpp file, 415-416
        ksmbwidget.cpp file, 415
        main.cpp file, 414-415
        recompiling, 417
        tree, 412-413

karm (Time Tracker) utility, 234, 350-352

kaudio/kbdndwm (KDE Base), 14

KBlackBox game, 368

Kblackjack game, 370

KBuilder tool, 430

kcalc utility (calculator), 235
    angles, 228
    clearing, 228
    Clipboard, 228
    displaying, 227
    errors, 229
    Euler number, 228

    fonts, 229
    help, online, 228
    Hex calculations, 228
    memory, 228
    numeric base, 227
    opening, 227
    Pi, 228
    Reverse Polish Notation (RPN), 228
    starting, 227

kcmkpanel command, 94

KDE Base (kdm)
    background, 47, 49-50
    converting from, 45-46
    fonts, 48-49
    kcontrol, 14
    login prompt, 46-48, 51
    passwords, 46
    sessions, 52
    shutdown, 46, 52
    user accounts, 46, 51
    wallpaper, 50-51

kde command, 44

KDE Dialog Definition Language tool, 430

.kde directory/ subdirectories
    applink, 59-61
    apps, 58-59
    bin, 61
    boot, 61
    config, 57-58
    dev, 61
    icons, 61
    mimelnk, 62-63
    share/, 56-57

KDE Foundation Classes and dynamic loading, 431

KDE Project
    administration, 14
    binary code, 17
    development, 8, 16
    distribution, 17
    documentation, 19
    games, 14

    GNOME Project, 17-18
    goals, 9
    graphic user interface (GUI), 14, 17
    history, 8
    KDE Base, 14-15, 47-52
    libraries, 14, 18
    multimedia, 14
    networks, 14
    office suites, 17
    participation, 15-16
    Qt toolkit, 11-12, 17
    representatives, 8
    source code, 8, 17
    speaking, 19
    toys, 14
    translation, 19
    ugrading, 53
    utilities, 14
    versions, 18
    Window Manager, 15, 18
    working groups, 10-11, 13
    see also KDE Base, 47

KDE Python bindings, 428

kdeadmin file, 26

kdebase file, 26, 30

KDEDIR environment variable, 67

kdegames file, 26

kdegraphics file, 26

KDEicons utility, 312

kdelibs file, 26, 30, 379

kdemultimedia file, 26

kdenetwork file, 26

kdeorganizer file, 26

kdesupport file, 26, 30, 379

kdetoys file, 26

kdeutils file, 26

KDevelop tool, 430

kdisplayrc file, backups, 149

kdm (KDE Base), 14
    background, 47, 49-50
    converting from, 45-46
    fonts, 48-49
    login prompt, 46-48, 51
    passwords, 46

sessions, 52
shutdown, 46, 52
user accounts, 46, 51
wallpaper, 50-51
xdm, 45-46
KEdit
Clipboard, 321
color, 322
copying, 321
default, 332
deleting, 321
email, 320, 323-324, 332
Ethernet, 239
fonts, 322
indenting, 323
inserting, 321
keys, 318, 332
opening, 319
page width, 323
search-and-replace, 320
starting, 316-318
status bar, 322
text wrap, 323
tool bar, 322
text files
viewing, 324-325
Web sites, 318
keyboards
Asteroids game, 366
editing, 332
international, 10, 197-199
KEdit text files, 318
kvt utility, 296
less command, 324
maps, 198, 220
more command, 325
repeat option, 196
shortcuts, 10
arrow keys, 83
close window
(Alt+F4), 84
command line
(Alt+F2), 84
control menu (Alt+F3),
84

File menu (Alt+F), 85
K menu (Alt+F1), 84
online help system
(F1), 83
Print (P or arrow
keys/Ctrl+P), 85
scrolling (Tab), 83
Tetris game, 366
toggle desktops
(Ctrl+F1 to Ctrl+F4),
84
toggle windows
(Alt+Esc/Alt+Shift+
Tab/Alt+Tab), 84
KFax tool, 352
fax pages, 352-353
graphics, 352
kfind utility (KDE Base), 14
advanced searches,
203-205
finding, 200-202
**Kfloppy utility (floppy
disks), 234**
**kfm utility (file manager
utility), 15**
applications
defining, 159-163
launching, 159-162
MIME, 158, 162-163
bookmarks, 164
browser options, 170-172
cache files, 168-170
client portion, 154, 428
directories, 153
drag-and-drop option, 163
files, 157-158
icons, 157
KNotes utility, 230-231
location bars, 156
objects, 165, 167-168
opening, 156
server portion, 154
windows, 154, 157

**kfontmanager (KDE Base),
15**
kfourier utility, 312
kfract utility, 312
kgo game, 370
kiconedit utility, 312
kikbd utility, 198-199
killustrator utility, 312
Kimon utility, 252
KInetEd utility, 252
KIRC (Chat program), 234
KISDN utility, 252
KMail
accounts, 270, 274
Address Book, 280
attachments, 278, 280-282
copying, 279
creating, 279-282
deleting, 274, 278
filters, 278
folders, 277
fonts, 274-276
forwarding, 276, 278
headers, 280
host server, 274
incoming, 273
Local Mailbox, 273
new, 274
passwords, 274
PGP security, 282
POP3, 273
port number, 274
printing, 279-280
process and delivery, 272
reading, 270, 277-282
reply address, 270
replying, 278
retrieving, 276
saving, 279
sending, 280
Sendmail, 272
signature, 271, 276
SMTP, 272
spam, 270
storing, 273
username, 274

kmandel utility, 312
KmenuEdit utility (KDE Base), 15, 188
KModem utility, 252
Knetmon utility, 252
KNotes utility, 230
    3D frames, 233
    alarms, 232
    calendars, 233
    color, 233
    creating, 231
    date, 233
    deleting, 232
    email, 233
    fonts, 233
    kfm files, 230
    placing, 230
    positioning, 232
    printing, 233
    renaming, 232
    resizing, 231
    saving, 232
    selecting, 232
    sticking to Desktop, 232
KOffice suite, 10
Konquest game, 368
konsole utility, 297
KOrganizer (calendar), 26
    appointments
        adding, 346
        alarm, 346-347
        managing, 345-348
    configuration, 348-350
    Scheduling features, 353
    starting, 340
    view options, 341-345
    window, 341
kpackage utility, 30, 205
KPaint utility
    bitmapped, 306-307
    color, 308-310
    creating, 309-310
    cutting, 311
    drawing tools, 309-310

formats, 307
loading, 307
naming, 308
pasting, 311
sizing, 308
zooming, 308
kpanel application (KDE Base), 93
KPlot utility, 312
kpm utility (process management), 234
kppp utility
    accounts, 243
    authentication, 245
    automatic startup, 245
    closing, 251
    connections, 244, 248
    costs, 247-248
    data volume, 248
    disconnection, 251
    DNS servers, 245
    gateways, 245
    IP, 245
    login scripts, 246
    minimizing, 251
    modems, 248-251
    name resolution, 245
    passwords, 245
    phone number, 244
    PPP scripts, 254
    pppd arguments, 245
    redialing, 251
    starting, 242-243
kray utility, 312
krdb program, 144
krootwm (KDE Base), 15
krossword game, 370
krubik game, 370
Ksamba utility, 252
kscd (CD Player), 356-357
    background, 362
    backward/forward buttons, 363
    CDDB, 357-361
    defaults, 361

display screen, 357
docking, 362
ejecting, 362, 364
email, 361-362
help, 361
icons, 362
information, 363
Loop mode, 363
play/pause, 363
playing, 362
random play, 364
screen, 362
stopping, 362-363
ToolTips, 362
updating, 361
volume, 363
Web access, 362
ksciplot utility, 312
kscreensaver (KDE Base), 15
ksendfax utility, 352
kshow utility, 312
ksmb application, 421
    memory, 427
    menu structure, 416
    message box, 421, 424-425
    methods, 425-426
    Options menu, 421, 426
    pop-up menus, 422-423
    saving, 426-427
    Settings item, 421, 426
    viewing, 423-424
ksmbwidget.cpp file, 415
Ksnapshot utility (screen capture), 234, 312
ksysv utility
    available services, 209
    commands, 207
    downloading, 219
    initialization processes, 220
    Runlevel, 208, 210
    scripts, 211
    services, 210
    starting, 209
    Trash can, 209

KTableView tool, 430
ktalkd.wav file, 131
KtK package, 428
ktop utility (system statistics), 234
ktoys file, 26
KuickShow utility, 312
kuser utility (user accounts), 219
  addresses, 270, 274
  adding, 212
  column headings, 211
  creating, 214
  displaying, 213
  editing, 212, 214
  file definitions, 55
  home directory, 56, 213
  KDE Base, 46, 51
  KMail, 270, 274
  managing, 211
  membership, 214
  name, 270, 274
  passwords, 213
  permissions, 38
  primary, 213
  saving, 214
  sorting, 211
KView utility, 301
  accelerator keys, 303
  aspect ratio, 304
  color palettes, 313
  cropping, 303
  desktop wallpaper, 305
  editing, 303, 313
  formats, 301-302, 313
  full screen, 303, 305
  listing, 305
  multiple, 305
  resetting, 303
  rotating, 304
  shuffling, 305
  slideshows, 305
  starting, 302

  viewing, 302
  zooming, 304
kvt utility (terminal emulator windows), 290, 297
  background, 296
  color, 294-295
  commands, 292-293
  cursor key, 297
  fonts, 295-296
  keyboard input, 296
  menus, 296
  scrollbars, 296
  sizing, 296
  terminal windows, 292
  text, 292
Kwin utility, 252
kwm (window manager), 15, 90, 298
kwmcom (KDE Base), 15
kwmpager (KDE Base), 15
kwmrc file (window manager)
  backups, 144, 149
  editing, 141-144

L

labels on desktops, 99
landscape orientation, 264
languages, international, 122-125
LANs, Internet connection, 269
laptop monitors, 117
  address book, 335
  KDE on startup, 36-37
  kfm applications, 159-162
  kikbd window, 199
less command, 324
LF (line feed) character, 266
lib subdirectory, 29
libg++-devel package installation, 378

libraries, 420
  development
    kdelibs-devel, 379
    kdesupport-devel, 379
    libg++-devel, 378
    qt-devel-1_4_2, 379
    XFree86-devel, 379
  dialog boxes, 408
  downloading, 26
  GNOME Project, 18
  KAppTemplate, 411
  KDE Project, 14, 18
  programming functions, 408
  Qt graphical functions, 408
  X Window System, 408
Line drawing tool (KPaint utility), 309
line feed (LF) character, 266
lines per page, printing, 264
link files
  applications, 176, 178
  Autostart folder, 182
  creating, 176, 191, 403
  data files, 185
  devices, 178-181
  dynamic, 409
  floppy drives, 179-181
  MIME types, 398
  non-KDE applications, 386, 390-393
  source code trees, 377-378
  static, 409
Linux
  applications, 11
  Debian system, 24
  GNOME, 18
  graphic user interface (GUI), 8
  installation from CD, 23
  KDE, 18, 30
  kdm, 46
  Open Source software, 8
  Panedistributions, 76
  popularity, 8

rpm subdirectories, 24
run level, 43-44
shutdown, 44
Web sites, 17
xdm, 46
lisa utility (Caldera OpenLinux), 239, 260
List view option (KOrganizer), 341
listing
applications, 73-74
Desktop directory
files, 63
wallpapers, 114
files, 68
graphics, 305
MIME types, 398
print jobs, 259-260
windows, 76
loading graphics, 307
Local Mailbox, 273
location
bars, 156
KAppTemplate, 410
non-KDE applications, 388
locking screens, 77
login
graphical, 43
initialization processes, 207
KDE Base, 46, 48, 51
kdm, 47
KMail, 274
kppp utility, 246
root
access, 195
installation, 27
serial connections, 290
system, 14
xdm, 47
logout, 77
command, 147
non-KDE applications, 42
running, 40-41
X window System, emergency, 42

Loop mode, CD Player, 363
lpd utility
print jobs, 258
starting, 259
lpq utility
installation, 259
print jobs, 259-260
print queues, 258
lpr utility
installation, 259
parameters, 259
print jobs, 258
lprm utility, 258-259
ls command, 63
lsm file, 376

M

Macintosh, graphic user interface (GUI), 9
Magic Borders desktops, 122
magic number passwords, 34
Mahjongg game, 369
mail, *see* **email**
main menu, 97
defining, 186
directories, 187
editing, 186-189
items, 187
networking utilities, 255
non-KDE applications
adding, 395
saving, 396
Personal menu, 188
submenus, 187
main.cpp file, 414-415
make command
error messages, 418
source code, recompiling, 427

make utility
configure script, 380
source code
automating, 378
compiling, 380-381
managing
KOrganizer
alarm, 346
appointments, 345-348
print jobs, 258
themes, 134
user accounts, 211
maps for keyboards, 198
maximizing windows, 81-82, 104
Media Player, 364
membership, user account groups, 214
memory
displaying, 217
kcalc utility, 228
ksmb application, 427
virtual, 217
menus, 10, 100
editing, 15
fonts, 125
keyboard shortcuts (arrow keys), 83
kvt utility, 296
main, 97
adding items, 187
defining, 186
directories, 187
editing, 186-189
Personal menu, 188
submenus, 187
main K, 78
menubars, 129
pop-up, 157
messages
ksmb application , 421, 424-425
newsgroups
downloading, 285
Netiquette, 286
reading, 285-287

retrieving, 286
saving, 286
sending, 287
methods
declaring, 420
ksmb application ,
425-426
object-oriented
programming, 408
overriding, 420
**mgetty/sendfax package,
352**
MICO ORB tool, 431
MIDI Player, 364
**MIME (Multiformat
Internet Mail Exchange),
62**
kfm applications, 158,
162-163
non-KDE applications
adding, 398-399
creating, 399-401
icons, 401
image formats, 399
link files, 398
listing, 398
**mimelnk directories, 62-63,
400**
minimizing
kppp utility, 251
windows, 81-82
mirrored wallpaper, 113
mirroring
faxes, 352
ftp sites, 23-24
modems
kppp utility, 248
ports, 248
status, 252
timeout, 249, 251
modifying, *see* **editing**
monitoring
ISDN connection, 252
KDE startup, 39

monitors
burn-in, 117
energy-saving, 117
laptops, 117
Samba, 253
group IDs (GIDs), 254
hostnames, 254
open files, 254
process IDs (PIDs),
254
services, 253
status, 253
users IDs (UIDs), 254
**Month view option
(KOrganizer), 341**
more command
keystrokes, 325
text files, 324
**mounting Windows file
systems, 252**
mouse
Acceleration slider, 197
buttons, 197
configuration, 196-198
scrolling wheels, 219
Threshold slider, 197
moving
email folders, 278
windows, 104
**Multiformat Internet Mail
Exchange,** *see* **MIME**
multilevel bookmarks, 164
multimedia
applications, 375
downloading, 26
KDE Project, 14
Media Player, 364
MIDI Player, 364
Sound Mixer Panel, 364
video players, 364
see also sound files
multitasking
commands, 292
printing, 257
screensavers, 118
windows, 90

N

naming
desktops, 85
graphics, 308
kppp utility, 245
Netiquette, 286
**Netscape Communicator,
270, 386**
**NetWare administration
tools, 387**
networks, 237
application-level
tranpsarency, 10
Ethernet, 238-239
games, 371
FDDI, 238
HTTP, 238
ifconfig command, 240
IP, 238
IPX, 238
KDE Project, 14
Kimon utility, 252
KInetEd utility, 252
KISDN utility, 252
KModem utility, 252
Knetmon utility, 252
Ksamba utility, 252
Kwin utility, 252
ping utility, 239-240
printing, 268
route command, 241-242
TCP/IP, 238
Token Ring, 238
utilities, 255, 375
newsgroups, 282-283, 287
messages
downloading, 285
Netiquette, 286
reading, 285-287
retrieving, 286
saving, 286
sending, 287
news client, 283-284
news reader replies, 287

non-KDE applications
adding
Desktop, 394
main menu, 395
Panel, 397
Personal menu,
395-396
command lines, 388
configuration, 387
fonts, 129
formats, 389-390, 339
link files, 386, 390-393,
398
location, 388
logout, 42
MIME types, 398
creating, 399-401
icons, 401
listing, 398
saving, 396
**numeric base (kcalc utility),
227**

O

**Object Request Broker
(ORB), 18**
**object-oriented
programming, 408**
**objects, viewing, 165,
167-168**
office suites
GNOME Project, 17
KDE Project, 17
utilities, 375
online help system, 10
access, 79
KAppTemplate, 412
keyboard shortcut (F1), 83
Opaque windows, 104
**Open Source graphical
libraries,** *see* **libraries**
opening
files, 203
archived, 222
Samba, 254

kcalc utility, 227
KEdit text files, 319
kfm, windows, 154,
156-157
PS Viewer, 327
terminals, 290-292
OpenLinux, 24, 85
BRU, 386
CRiSP, 386
desktops, 85
DR DOS, 386
KDE, 33-36
kpackage utility, 205
lisa utility, 239, 260
Netscape Communicator,
386
startup, 35
user accounts, 56
OpenParts tool, 430
/opt/kde directories, 29, 67
options
KEdit
configuration, 322
default, 332
ksmb application, 426
themes, configuration, 151
Options menu
**ORB (Object Request
Broker), 18**
**orientation (portrait/
landscape), 264**
overriding methods, 420

P

package storage, 30
**page description languages,
267, 325-330**
Page Down/Up key, 318
Page Protection option, 266
**page width, KEdit
configuration, 323**
palettes, color, 313
Panel, 93
access, 76

application integration,
387
Autostart folder, 75
background, 134
clock, 125
configuration, 94, 96-98,
107, 190
Control Center, 77
desktops, 78
displaying, 76
editing, 191
fonts, 125
hiding, 74, 76, 98, 191
home directory, 76
icons, 76
deleting, 189
editing, 189-191
positioning, 189
K icon, 76
logout, 77
non-KDE applications,
397
pop-up hints, 96
positioning, 94
screens, 77
sizing, 95, 191
submenus, 190
swallowing, 177
taskbar, 94
versions, 76
windows, 76
paper
feeding, 264
lines per page, 264
number of copies, 264
orientation, 264
size, 263
**participation in KDE
Project, 13, 15-16**
passwords
kdm, 46
KMail, 274
kppp utility, 245
magic number, 34
screensavers, 132
startup, 39
user accounts, 213

pasting graphics, 311
PATH command, 29
Patience game, 369
PCI slots, 218
PCL page description
  language, 267
pcx graphics format, 302
PDF files, 330
Pen drawing tool (KPaint
  utility), 309
PerlQt, 428
permissions for user
  accounts, 38
personal manager, 26
Personal menu
  main menu, 188
  non-KDE applications,
    395-396
PGP security, 282
Pi, 228
ping utility
  Internet connections, 270
  networking
    ifconfig command, 240
    route command,
      241-242
    testing, 239-240
pixmaps, title bars, 101-102
placing KNotes utility notes,
  230
platforms, applications, 377
play/pause, CD Player,
  362-363
png format, 399
pnm graphics format, 302,
  307
Point to Point Protocol, *see*
  PPP, 242
Poker game, 369
pop-up help, 79
  kfm, 157
  ksmb application ,
    422-423
POP3, KMail, 273
popularity of Linux, 8
port number, 274

portrait orientation, 264
positioning
  desktop
    applications, 92
    icons, 138-186
    multiple, 85
  KNotes utility notes, 232
  Panel, 94, 189
  taskbar, 94
  windows, 82, 87, 104, 120
PostScript files, 267,
  325-330
Powersave mode, 266
ppm graphics formats, 313
PPP (Point to Point
  Protocol)
  connections, 242
  daemons, 245
  kppp utility, 242-243
    authentication, 245
    automatic startup, 245
    closing, 251
    configuration, 243,
      245, 247
    connection speed, 248
    connections, 244
    costs, 247-248
    data volume, 248
    disconnecting, 251
    DNS servers, 245
    gateways, 245
    IP address, 245
    login scripts, 246
    minimizing, 251
    modem ports, 248
    modem timeout, 249,
      251
    name resolution, 245
    new accounts, 243
    passwords, 245
    phone number, 244
    pppd arguments, 245
    redialing, 251
  pppd daemon, 242
  script, 254

pre-alpha code, 311
pre-processor directive
  error messages, 418
primary groups, user
  accounts, 213
print jobs
  address book entries, 339
  characters/symbols, 267
  daemons, 258
  dialog box, 85
  End of Line mode, 265
  faxes, 352
  files, 258
  filter script, 258
  fonts, 266
  graphics, 265
  initializing, 266
  keyboard shortcut (P or
    arrow keys), 85
  kfm windows, 157
  KMail, 279-280
  KNotes utility, 233
  managing, 258
  multitasking, 257
  networks, 268
  pages
    descriptions languages,
      267
    protection option, 266
  paper
    lines per page, 264
    number of copies, 264
    orientation, 264
    size, 263
  Powersave mode, 266
  PS Viewer, 328
  quality, 264
  queues, 258-260
  removing from print
    queues, 258
  resolution, 264-265
  servers, 259
  sharing, 252
  spools, 258
  submitting, 258

printcap file, 258, 261-262, 268

printers

configuration, 258

default, 260

Hewlett-Packard, 263

options, 266

page eject, 266

PostScript, 325-330

selecting, 265

private reply (news reader), 287

processes

IDs (PIDs), 254

initialization

editing, 207

ksysv utility, 220

login, 207

management, 234

terminal windows, 292

process and delivery, 272

programming functions, 408

programs, 176

link files, 403

see also applications

projects, KAppTemplate

comments, 417

description strings, 416

editing, 416

properties, windows configuration, 104

protocols

drag-and-drop, 9, 238

see *also* networks

proxy servers, 171

ps command

applications, 73-74

terminal windows, 292

PS Viewer

opening, 327

printing, 328

public reply (news reader), 287

Python Qt, 428

Q

qchess game, 370

QdbTabular widget, 429

Qt Architect, 429

Qt development

Free Qt Foundation, 12

Harmony project, 12

KDE Project, 11-12, 17

QdbTabular widget, 429

Qt Architect, 429

QtC, 429

QwSpriteField, 429

source code, 12

Xml-builder, 429

XSpriteWorld++, 429

Qt graphical library, 408

compiling, 378

themes, 135

versions, 382

qt-1.42 file, 26, 30

qt-devel-1.42 file, 26

qt-devel-1_4_2 package, 379

Qt/KDE Python binding client, 428

quality of printing, 264

queues, 258, 260

QwSpriteField, 429

R

raising windows, 91, 105-106

random play, CD Player, 364

ray tracing, 312

reading

KMail, 270, 277-282

newsgroup messages, 285-287

README file

source code trees, 379

themes, 134, 139-140

receiving faxes, 352

recompiling KAppTemplate source code, 417

Rectangle drawing tool (KPaint utility), 309

Red Hat Linux

configuration tools, 239

installation, 27

submenus, 385

versions, 24-25

X Window System, 37-38

redialing kppp utility, 251

redistributing themes, 151

reloading

kfm cache files, 170

ksysv utility scripts, 211

Web sites, 170

removing print jobs from queues, 260

renaming KNotes utility notes, 232

repeat option, keyboard, 196

replacing

icons, 61

themes, 134

replying, KMail, 270, 278

representatives, KDE Project, 8

resetting

graphics, 303

printer options, 266

resizing, see sizing

resolution, printing, 264-265

restarting KDE, 147-148

restoring

themes, 149

windows, 82

retrieving

KMail, 276

newsgroup messages, 286

Reversi game, 369

reverting

Character-mode screen, 293

virtual terminals, 293

reviewing
  kfm configuration files,
    172
  installation files, 29
root access
  grid spacing, 127
  installation, 27
  login, 195
rotating
  faxes, 352
  graphics, 304
**Round Angle drawing tool
  (KPaint utility), 309**
**route command, networking
  configuration, 241-242**
rpm command
  displaying, 205
  installation sequence, 27
  uninstallation, 207
rpm subdirectory, 24
Runlevel
  ksysv utility, 208, 210
  Linux configuration, 43-44
**running KAppTemplate,
  410**
  libraries, 411
  online help, 412
Russell, George, 136

S

Samba
  configuration, 252
  file sharing, 252
  monitors, 253
    group IDs (GIDs), 254
    hostnames, 254
    open files, 254
    process IDs (PIDs),
      254
    services, 253
    status, 253
    user Ids (UIDs), 254

  print sharing, 252
  servers, 252
  web site, 254
Same Game, 370
saving
  address book entries, 336,
    338
  kfm cache files, 170
  KMail, 279
  KNotes utility notes, 232
  KOrganizer, 344-345
  ksmb application,
    426-427
  newsgroup messages, 286
  non-KDE applications,
    396
  user account groups, 214
scaled wallpaper, 51, 113
Scheduling features, 353
screens
  captures, 234, 312
  CD Player, 362
  Character-mode, 290
  locking, 77
  screensavers, 15
    configuration, 117-120
    multitasking, 118
    passwords, 132
  sizing, 191
  startup, 72
scripts
  At/KDE Python binding,
    428
  configure, 380
  filter, 258
  Kfm client, 428
  ksysv utility, 208
  KtK, 428
  login, 246
  PerlQt , 428
  PPP, 254
  Python Qt, 428
  startup, 38-39
  themes, 148-149
  xdm, 43-44

scrolling
  keyboard shortcut (Tab),
    83
  kvt utility, 296
  mouse, 219
  title bars, 103
SDK (developer kit), 10, 430
searching, 203-205
  address book entries, 339
  search-and-replace, 320
  see also finding
security
  Internet, 270
  screensavers, 132
  shutdown, 52
selecting
  area, 309
  files, 157, 201
  fonts, 267
  icons, 157
  KNotes utility notes, 232
  printers, 265
sending
  email, 272, 320, 339
  faxes, 352
  KMail, 272, 280, 320
  newsgroup messages, 287
serial connections, 290
**Server Message Block
  (SMB) protocol,** *see*
  Samba
services, ksysv utility, 208
sessions, KDE Base, 52
setserial command, 216
**Settings item, ksmb
  application, 426**
sh shell, 289
**share subdirectory (.kde
  directory), 29, 56-57**
shells, 289
Shift key, 318
Shisen-Sho game, 370
shuffling graphics, 305
shutdown
  KDE Base, 52
  kdm, 46

Linux, 44
security, 52
signature, KMail, 271, 276
Simple Mail Transport
   Protocol (SMTP), 272
sizing
   fonts, 267
   graphics, 308
   KNotes utility, 231
   kvt utility, 296
   Panel, 95, 191
   paper for printing, 263
   screens, 191
   terminal emulator
      windows, 291
   windows, 82, 104
slideshows, 305
SMB (Server Message
   Block) protocol, *see*
   Samba
Smiletris game, 366
SMTP (Simple Mail
   Transport Protocol), 272
Snake Race game, 367
snap to grid option, 122
Sokoban game, 370
Solaris, 8
sorting user accounts, 211
sound files, 14
   bell, 129-130
   CD Player, 370
   configuration, 129-131
   events, 130-131
   Media Player, 364
   MIDI Player, 364
   Sound Mixer Panel, 364
   storing, 132
   themes, 134
   see also multimedia
source code
   archives, 377
   compiling, 377-378,
      380-381
   configuration, 377
   development, 8
   editing, 416-417

GNOME Project, 17
INSTALL file, 379
KAppTemplate
   ksmb.cpp file, 415-416
   ksmbwidget.cpp file,
      415
   main.cpp file, 414-415
   recompiling, 417
   tree, 412-413
KDE Project, 17
linking, 377-378
README file, 379
Qt toolkit, 12
recompiling, 427
unpacking, 379
spam, 270
speaking, KDE Project, 19
speed, kppp utility,
   connection, 248
split windows, 167
Spray can drawing tool
   (KPaint utility), 309
spreadsheet application, 10
stable applications, 374-377
standard icons, 62
StarOffice 5.0, 62
   installation, 59
   Scheduling features, 353
starting
   applications
      automatically, 209
      from icons, 403
   ark archival utility, 222
   bash shell, 290
   CD Player, 356-357
   DVI Viewer, 330
   files, 181-183
   kcalc utility, 227-228
   KEdit, 316-318
   KOrganizer, 340
   kpackage utility, 205
   kppp utility, 242-243
   ksysv utility, 209
   KView utility, 302
   lpd utility, 259

Reverse Polish Notation
   (RPN), 228
slideshows, 305
terminal windows, 292
Time Tracker utility, 350
startup
   configuration, 35
   default, 36
   graphical system, 28-29
   kppp utility, 245
   launching, 36-37
   monitoring, 39
   OpenLinux, 33-36
   passwords, 39
   PATH command, 29
   screens, 72
   scripts, 38-39
   Suse Linux, 36-37
   troubleshooting, 39-40
   window managers, 35
   X Window System, 22,
      37-38
   xdm, 45
startx command, 36-37, 39,
   44
static linking, 409
status bar, 322
Stickpin button, 81-82
stopping CD Player, 362-363
storing KMail, 273
   sound files, 132
   themes, 140-141
style options
   menubars, 129
   widgets, 128
su command, 44
subdirectories
   files, 29
   rpm, 24
submenus
   main menu, 187
   Panel, 190
submitting print jobs, 258
SuSE Linux, 24
   startup, 36-37
   YAST utility, 239

Swallowing on Panel option,
177
swap space (virtual
memory), 217
switching, *see* **toggling**
symbols (characters), 267
symmetrical wallpaper, 113
system
device types, 215
DMA Channels, 216
information, 215-219
IO ports, 216
IRQ interrupts, 216
memory, 217
microprocessor, 218
PCI slots, 218
statistics (ktop utility), 234
X servers, 219
SysV Init Editor, *see*
initialization processes

T

tar command, 137, 379
.tar.gz format, 377
task manager (Karm
utility), 234
taskbar, 93
buttons, 72
configuration, 94, 96-98
displaying, 73
editing, 15
hiding, 98
Panel, 74
windows 73
tasks
defining Time Tracker,
350-351
timing, 350-352
TCP/IP protocol stacks, 238
templates
desktops, 75
folder, 65-66

terminals
active windows, 292
background, 296
connections, 290
cursor key, 297
emulator windows, 15
opening, 290-292
sizing, 291
fonts, 295
freezing, 292
keyboard input, 296
menus, 296
processes, 292
starting, 292
virtual, 293
windows, 73
testing xdm, 43
Tetris game, 366
TeX files, 330
text
copying, 292
editors, 316, 325
KEdit
Clipboard, 321
copying, 321
deleting, 321
email, 320
inserting, 321
keystrokes, 318
opening, 319
search-and-replace,
320
sendmail, 320
uploading to Web sites,
318
viewing, 324-325
less command, 324
more command, 324
objects, 165
wrapping, 323
tga graphics format, 302
.tgz file format, 222, 377
themes, 375
archive files, 138-139

backups, 149
borders, 134, 148
buttons, 134, 148
color schemes, 134,
144-145
configuration files, 134
options, 151
updating, 141-144
creating, 135, 150-151
directories, 140
downloading, 137-138
editing, 151
finding, 135-136
future releases, 135
graphics files
motifs, 133
storing, 140-141
icons, 134
installation scripts,
134-135, 151
KDE, 147-148
managers, 134
Panel background, 134
Qt libraries, 135
README files, 134,
139-140
redistributing, 151
replacement files, 134
restoring, 149
script installation, 148-149
sound files, 134
title bars, 134, 148
uninstallation, 149-150
wallpaper, 134, 144-145,
148
Threshold slider, 197
tiff format, 399
tiling
wallpaper, 50, 113
windows, 91, 105
Time Tracker (karm) utility,
234, 350-352

title bars, 81
buttons
adding, 106
editing, 100-101
configuration, 101-103
pixmaps, 101-102
scrolling, 103
themes, 134, 148
To Desktop menu (KView utility), 305
To-do task list (KOrganizer), 341
creating, 342-344
saving, 344-345
toggling
desktops, 84-85, 87
windows, 83-84, 90
Token Ring, 238
tools
KEdit, 322
KPaint, 309-310
tips, 362
toys, KDE Project, 14
tracking time, *see* **Time Tracker utility**
Transform menu (KView utility), 304
translation, KDE Project, 19
transparency
networks, 10
text on desktops, 128
windows, 104
Trash folder, 75
displaying, 66
editing, 191
files, 66, 68
icons, 157
ksysv utility, 209
troubleshooting, 53
CD Player sound, 370
Internet connections, 269
KDE startup, 39-40
xdm, 53
tsh shell, 289
tutorials, 27

U

uncompress, themes, 138
undeliverable email messages, 288
uninstallation
rpm, 207
themes, 149-150
UNIX
graphic user interface (GUI), 8
non-Linux installation, 24
Solaris, 8
see also Linux
unpacking source code tree archives, 377-379
unstable applications, 374-377
untar, themes, 138
updating
CD Player, 361
desktop, 10
ksysv utility scripts, 211
theme configuration files, 141-144
upgrading KDE files, 30, 53
uploading text files to Web sites, 318
URLs, *see* **Web sites**
user accounts (kuser)
addresses, 270, 274
adding, 212
column headings, 211
editing, 212
file definitions, 55
groups
creating, 214
displaying, 213
editing, 214
membership, 214
primary, 213
saving, 214
home directory, 56, 213
IDs, 254
KDE Base, 51

kdm, 46
KMail, 270, 274
managing, 211
name, 270, 274
passwords, 213
permissions, 38
sorting, 211
utilities
access, 15
KDE Project, 14
main menu, 255
screensaver, 15

V

versions
GNOME Project, 18
KDE Project, 18
Qt graphical library, 382
rpm subdirectories, 24
video players, 364
viewing
directories, 153, 158
DVI, 330-331
files, 153-154, 332
graphics, 302
hidden files, 167
KEdit text files, 324-325
KOrganizer, 341-345
ksmb application, 423-424
objects, 165, 167-168
PostScript files, 325-330
split windows, 167
TeX files, 330
X Window System, 22-23
see also displaying
virtual memory (swap space), 217
virtual terminals, 293
volume CD Player, 363

W

wallpaper
  centered, 113
  desktop, 114, 305
  KDE Base, 50-51
  mirrored, 113
  scaled, 113
  symmetrical, 113
  themes, 134, 144-145, 148
  tiled, 113
WAV files, *see* **sound files**
Web sites
  advanced projects,
    430-431
  applications, 374
  bookmarks, 164
  CD Player, 362
  configuration, 171
  developers, 409, 432
  development tools, 430
  FTP distribution, 11
  GNOME Project, 17
  KDE Project, 8, 15
  KEdit, 318
  Linux, 17
  reloading, 170
  Samba, 254
  Show History listing, 169
  themes, 135-136
Week and Work Week view
  options (KOrganizer), 341
widgets
  color schemes, 116
  configuration, 128
window managers utility
  (kwmrc), 141
  backups, 144, 149
  default, 36
  editing, 141-144
  GNOME Project, 18
  KDE Project, 15, 18
  OpenLinux, 35
windows
  activating, 82
  closing, 81-82, 84

  color, 199
  configuration, 89-90, 103
    applying, 106
    properties, 104
  Control menu, 81-84
  displaying while moving,
    104
  file systems, 252
  focusing, 105-106
  fonts, 125, 295
  kfm
    background, 134
    opening, 154
    printing, 157
  KOrganizer, 341
  listing, 76
  maximizing, 81-82, 104
  minimizing, 81-82
  multitasking, 90
  opening from other
    terminals, 291-292
  positioning, 82, 87, 104
  raising, 91, 105-106
  resizing display, 104
  restoring, 82
  sizing, 82
  snap to grid, 122
  split, 167
  Stickpin button, 81-82
  switching, 84
  taskbar, 73
  terminals, 73
    active, 292
    background, 296
    cursor key, 297
    emulators, 290-291
    freezing, 292
    keyboard input, 296
    menus, 296
    starting, 292
  tiling, 91, 105
  title bars, 81
    configuration, 101-103
    pixmaps, 101-102
    scrolling, 103

  toggling, 83, 90
  widgets, color schemes,
    116
word processor application,
  10
WordPerfect for Linux, 386
working groups, 10
  GNOME Project, 17
  goals, 10-11
  international, 17
  KDE Project, 13
wrapping text, 323

X

X Window System
  Clipboard, 298
  graphic user interface
    (GUI), 9
  includes, 383
  keyboards, 196
  libraries, 408
  logout, 42
  mouse, 196
  multiple, 298
  Red Hat Linux, 37-38
  servers, 219
  terminal emulator
    windows, 290, 292
  viewing, 22-23
  xterm utility, 290, 292
xbm graphics format, 302,
  307, 399
xcalc calculator, 235
Xclients file, 23, 28
xdm graphics format, 53
  background, 47
  converting from, 45-46
  initialization scripts, 43-44
  kdm, 45-46
  Linux, 44
  login screen, 47
  startup, 45
  testing, 43
  troubleshooting, 53

XFree86-devel package, 379
xinit program, 22, 38
Xml-builder, 429
xpm graphics format, 302,
   307, 313, 399
.Xsession file, 45
XSpriteWorld++, 429
xterm utility (terminal
   emulator window),
   290, 292
xv drawing program, 311

Y

YAST configuration utility,
   239
yellow pop-up hints, 96

Z

zooming
   faxes, 352
   graphics, 304, 308

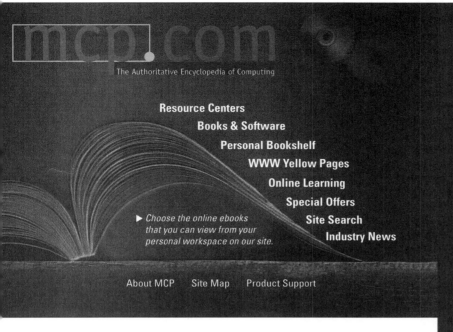

Other Related Titles

STY KDE 1.1 in 24 Hours

What's On the Disc

The companion CD-ROM contains all the tools needed to start using the KDE 1.1 and creating your own themes within the K desktop environment.

CD Root Directories

Theme Gallery from `themes.org` `<index.html>`

- Install scripts
- Theme Manager (contains source and binary)
- Install scripts for KDE themes
- GZIP (binary and source)
- Over 70 tarballs

Snapshot of the stable subtree of KDE 1.1 (as of 3-26-99)

- Applications (contains KDE administration, communications, games, graphics, multimedia, networking, scientific, themes, and utilities)
- Generic source code you can compile yourself
- Compiled binaries and source for many distributions, including:

  Solaris, SuSE, Red Hat, Caldera OpenLinux, Slackware version 3.5 and others.

UNIX Install

As each flavor of UNIX has its own method of mounting a CD-ROM, we will only outline the most common method of mounting a CD-ROM on a UNIX workstation. If you need additional instructions, please consult the main pages for mounting a CD-ROM, a UNIX book, or your system administrator.

1. Insert the CD-ROM into your CD-ROM drive.

2. Issue the appropriate mount instruction to mount the CD-ROM, such as

   ```
   mount [options] [device] [mountpoint]
   ```

   where [options] are the parameters for mounting the CD-ROM, [device] is the device associated with your CD-ROM, and [mountpoint] is where the CD-ROM will be mounted in the file system. The mountpoint must exist before you issue the mount command. For example, a typical mount command for a Red Hat® Linux workstation would be

   ```
   mount -t iso9660 /dev/cdrom /mnt/cdrom
   ```

3. Navigate to your mountpoint and explore.

Macmillan Computer Publishing User Services Information—Contacting Us For Support

We cannot help you with computer problems, UNIX-based system problems, or third-party application problems, but we can assist you with a problem you have with the book or CD-ROM.

Note: Problems with other companies' programs on the disc must be resolved with the company that produced the program or demo.

If you need assistance with the information provided in this product, please feel free to access our Web site at http://www.mcp.com/info. Here you can enter the book's ISBN number and view a product information page that will include any available downloads or updates. Our User Services department can also be reached at http://www.mcp.com/support.

Thanks

Macmillan Publishing would like to thank Themes.org (www.themes.org) for their contributions to the companion CD-ROM.